This ambitious and comprehensive handbook not only goes beyond money-metric poverty measurement to multidimensional approaches but also tackles problems of intrahousehold allocation, multigenerational poverty, and inequality. The persistence of poverty and rising inequality are challenges that demand appropriate policies and partnerships among various segments of society. Unlike treatises that stick only to academic exercises in poverty measurement, this book dares to tread on the riskier ground of anti-poverty programs and policies, and how they can be informed by data and measurement. Researchers, policymakers, and practitioners will benefit from reading this accessible guide to the most recent literature, with examples from policies and interventions in low- and middle-income countries.

—Agnes R. Quisumbing
Senior Research Fellow, International Food Policy Research Institute

How do we examine poverty in today's world? The *Handbook on Poverty Measurement and Policy* goes far beyond monetary deprivation, uncovering the many faces of socioeconomic disadvantage—from health and education to living standards and social inclusion. With vivid real-world examples, clear explanations, and hands-on tools, this handbook empowers readers to understand, measure, and respond to poverty's complex development challenges. Whether you're an academic, development practitioner, or policymaker, you'll find practical strategies and fresh insights to help you design effective poverty-reduction initiatives.

—Arturo Martinez, Jr.
Senior Statistician, Statistics and Data Innovation Unit, Economic Research and Development Impact Department, Asian Development Bank (ADB)

Rich with country case studies, practical tools, and clear nontechnical explanations, this poverty measurement handbook equips students, researchers, and policymakers with the analytical foundations needed to diagnose and reduce poverty in all its complexity.

—Aziz Atamanov
Senior Economist, Poverty Global Practice Group, World Bank

The *Handbook on Poverty Measurement and Policy* by poverty guru Dr. Albert is a comprehensive guide for researchers, policymakers, and development practitioners seeking to understand and address poverty in all its complexity. Moving beyond traditional income-based measures, it explores multidimensional frameworks that capture overlapping deprivations in health, education, and living standards. The book covers monetary and nonmonetary approaches, poverty dynamics, inequality, and intrahousehold disparities, and offers practical tools, case studies, and policy insights from global and national contexts. With its blend of theory, methodology, and actionable strategies, this handbook serves as an essential resource for designing evidence-based interventions to eradicate poverty and promote inclusive development.

—Afsaneh Yazdani
Statistician, Statistics Division, Population and Social Statistics Section
United Nations Economic and Social Commission for Asia and the Pacific (UNESCAP)

The *Handbook on Poverty Measurement and Policy* provides state-of-the-art guidance on the full spectrum of poverty analysis: from measuring monetary and multidimensional poverty and inequality, to understanding poverty across different contexts to assess its determinants, to designing appropriate policy responses. This handbook is essential for development practitioners and policymakers alike to capture deprivations in income, health, education, housing, and more—while delivering actionable, evidence-based policy strategies proven to drive real change—and turn data into impact.

—Mia Hyun
Gender and Inclusive Development Advisor; Former Senior Regional Gender and Inclusive Development Advisor for USAID's Asia Regional Office

I have read this handbook with much interest and found it to be an extremely valuable and timely resource. In this handbook, Dr. Albert provides clear conceptual and methodological guidance that is highly relevant for measuring poverty and multidimensional poverty in Mongolia. The handbook will be particularly useful for statisticians, policymakers, and researchers working on poverty analysis and evidence-based policy design.

—Davaajargal Davaatseren
Director, Social Statistics Division, National Statistics Office (NSO), Mongolia

Jose Ramon Albert's *Handbook on Poverty Measurement and Policy* offers a definitive, comprehensive guide for understanding and tackling poverty in its multifaceted complexity. Bridging theory and practice with exceptional depth, it equips researchers with cutting-edge methodologies—from traditional monetary metrics and multidimensional indices to innovative household models that examine intrahousehold resource allocation and collective decision-making processes. The handbook provides policymakers with evidence-based insights on effective interventions like social safety nets, conditional cash transfers, graduation programs, and integrated social protection systems, complete with implementation challenges and success factors. Practitioners will find actionable frameworks for designing inclusive policies and fostering cross-sector partnerships that address both immediate needs and structural causes of poverty.

With comprehensive case studies from diverse global contexts, including Mexico, Rwanda, Bangladesh, and the Philippines, and a nuanced focus on both chronic and transient poverty dynamics, this handbook is an indispensable resource for translating sophisticated measurement approaches into meaningful action toward sustainable poverty reduction. Its technical annexes with mathematical foundations of multidimensional poverty measurement and practical exercises using Stata and R further enhance its utility for applied research and policy implementation. This publication represents an essential contribution to the field, offering both theoretical rigor and practical guidance for the global fight against poverty in all its dimensions.

—Dr. Try Sothearith
Director of the National School of Planning and Statistics, Cambodia

The *Handbook on Poverty Measurement and Policy* challenges the old way of simply "counting the poor." It discusses traditional methods and also introduces multidimensional approaches that reveal poverty in health, education, and living standards, exposing hidden inequalities within households. More than a guide to measurement, it is a blueprint for smarter, fairer policies that truly reach the vulnerable. This book transforms data into action—reshaping how societies fight poverty in the modern world.

—Cheku Dorji
Founder and Lead Consultant Statistician
Kuenden Statistical Services, Bhutan

Dr. Albert was my teacher in poverty analysis. I learned about concepts in poverty measurement in a two-week-long training course more than two decades ago. I am glad he has put his thoughts including discussions on new emerging practices in this handbook. The book challenges us to go from insights to action. A must read!

—Mme. Phetsamone Sone
Head, Lao Statistics Bureau

Handbook on Poverty Measurement and Policy

From Counting the Poor to Multidimensional Approaches

Handbook on Poverty Measurement and Policy

From Counting the Poor to Multidimensional Approaches

Jose Ramon G Albert

Philippine Institute for Development Studies, Philippines

World Scientific

NEW JERSEY • LONDON • SINGAPORE • BEIJING • SHANGHAI • HONG KONG • TAIPEI • CHENNAI • TOKYO

Published by

World Scientific Publishing Co. Pte. Ltd.
5 Toh Tuck Link, Singapore 596224
USA office: 27 Warren Street, Suite 401-402, Hackensack, NJ 07601
UK office: 57 Shelton Street, Covent Garden, London WC2H 9HE

Library of Congress Control Number: 2026000427

British Library Cataloguing-in-Publication Data
A catalogue record for this book is available from the British Library.

HANDBOOK ON POVERTY MEASUREMENT AND POLICY
From Counting the Poor to Multidimensional Approaches

ISBN 978-981-98-2303-1 (hardcover)
ISBN 978-981-98-2304-8 (ebook for institutions)
ISBN 978-981-98-2305-5 (ebook for individuals)

For any available supplementary material, please visit
https://www.worldscientific.com/worldscibooks/10.1142/14579#t=suppl

Desk Editor: Geysilla Jean Ortiz
Cover design: Lionel Seow

Project managed and typeset by Manila Typesetting Company (MTC)

Foreword: Handbook on Poverty Measurement and Policy

Defining, identifying and measuring are the first steps in better understanding poverty and then designing improved policies and programs to reduce poverty. This book, "Counting and Helping the Poor: Handbook on Poverty Measurements and Policy," serves as a manual for poverty measurement and as a guide to understanding poverty in all its complexity. In it, the author explores how to measure poverty, what it means for society, and what policies can help reduce it. The first part of the book looks at different ways to define and understand poverty. While people often think of poverty as just not having enough money, defining poverty is more complex than this. Being poor might mean not getting a good education, not having access to healthcare, or being stuck in low-quality jobs - not just having too little money.

In addition to providing a broad discussion of the various attributes of what it means to be poor, the Handbook explores the many challenges of poverty measurement. One often overlooked measurement challenge is that poverty is typically reported for people but income and consumption are often measured at the level of the household. Most all poverty estimates simply allocate household income evenly across all individual members, failing to see any inequities within the household. The Handbook shines light on this blind spot and explores nuanced approaches to measuring poverty that look at the behavior of individuals within households. Instead of assuming everyone in a family is equally poor or well-off, these methods examine how resources are shared between family members. This Handbook explains many different measurement concerns such as this in detail because measuring things well is crucial for governments and civil society to create better programs and policies to fight poverty.

The Handbook also looks at how poverty and inequality change over time, using information collected from the same families over many years. This helps us understand the difference between transient poverty (when people are poor for a short time) and chronic poverty (when people stay poor for years). The book include real examples from different countries to show what causes poverty and how this knowledge can help create better anti-poverty programs. It examines different strategies for fighting poverty and argues that everyone - governments, businesses, charities, and communities - need to work together to address the complex problem of poverty. The book looks at three main types of anti-poverty policies:

- Quick-help (alleviative) policies that address immediate needs (like food aid)
- Deep-change (transformative) policies that address the root causes of poverty (like improving education systems)
- Support policies that create better conditions for people to escape poverty (like making it easier to start small businesses)

It also provides practical guidance on how countries can combine these different types of policies in ways that fit their specific situations.

The Handbook guides the reader to a better understanding of what keeps people trapped in poverty across generations. It looks at how various systems in society - like schools, healthcare, and job markets - can either help people escape poverty or regrettably, keep them trapped in it. The final chapters focus on what works in fighting poverty. We see real examples from around the world, including:

- Programs that provide basic support when people need it
- Small loan programs that help people start businesses
- Improvements in education systems
- Programs that give money directly to poor families

The Handbook examines several different approaches and discusses which ones are the effective in reducing poverty, and offers explanations for their success or, in some cases, failure.

Because poverty is such a complex problem, this Handbook delivers an extensive examination of several aspects of poverty, including how we define it, measure it, what causes it, how it changes over time, and what we can do about it. After reading this Handbook, you will not only understand poverty better but also feel inspired to help fight it. This isn't just a textbook – it is a call to action. It challenges everyone - government officials, business leaders, academics, researchers, and ordinary citizens - to look at poverty in this complete way and work together to create a world where everyone has a fair chance to succeed. Whether you're studying poverty for the first time, working on policy, or simply care about making the world better, this book will give you the understanding and tools you need to help make a real difference.

Dean Jolliffe
World Bank, Research Manager
Poverty, Inequality & Human Development

Preface

My journey in understanding poverty began over two decades ago, amid the lingering shadows of the Asian Financial Crisis. As a young researcher, I was fortunate to be among a select group of statisticians and economists selected by the World Bank Institute for an intensive two-week long training course on poverty measurement using panel data from Vietnam. The focus was urgent and practical: to dissect the crisis's profound impacts on households, revealing not just snapshots of deprivation but the churning dynamics of vulnerability and resilience. This training ignited a lifelong passion for turning raw data into actionable stories about human lives.

Building on that foundation, I crafted a country paper for the Philippines with another statistician, delving into the nuances of household surveys and econometric tools to map poverty's contours amid the crisis. What followed was a whirlwind of global engagement—I traveled to countries across Asia, the Pacific and sub-Saharan Africa, training economists, statisticians, and development practitioners in the intricate arts and sciences of poverty measurement and analysis. From constructing poverty lines to dissecting inequality with decomposition techniques, these workshops were more than technical exchanges; they were bridges between evidence and empathy, equipping practitioners to confront poverty's complexities head-on.

Over the years, the field of poverty diagnostics evolved dramatically. What started as primarily monetary assessments—counting the poor through income thresholds—matured into multidimensional frameworks that capture deprivations in health, education, housing, and beyond. Multidimension poverty indices became cornerstones, reminding us that poverty is not a single thread but a tangled web of intersecting hardships. My own work mirrored this shift, as I adapted tools for dynamic panel analyses and explored chronic versus transient poverty, always with an eye toward policy relevance.

As a policy researcher and statistician at the Philippine Institute for Development Studies (PIDS)—the Philippine government's premier think tank—I have witnessed firsthand the chasm that often separates data from effective programs. In the Philippines, where poverty persists amid rapid growth in recent years, I saw how siloed statistics fail to inform inclusive policies. This book emerges from that conviction: the urgent need for synergies between data and decision-making. It bridges the gap, offering a handbook that evolves from basic counting to sophisticated multidimensional approaches, while grounding theory in real-world applications—from regression diagnostics to policy simulations.

In today's data-rich era, with the rise of data science, machine learning, and big data analytics, the imperative has only intensified. We must not merely amass data but transform it into information, then insight, and ultimately, impact. This volume is my contribution to that mission—a toolkit for analysts, policymakers, and practitioners to measure poverty holistically, understand its drivers, and design interventions that uplift. May it inspire both the current a new generations to see beyond numbers, toward ensuring the dignity of every life.

Jose Ramon G. Albert
Philippine Institute for Development Studies
January 2026

About the Author

Dr. Jose Ramon G. Albert is a distinguished statistician and policy researcher with over two decades of experience in development economics and public policy. As a Senior Research Fellow at the Philippine Institute for Development Studies (PIDS), a premier think tank affiliated with the Philippines' Department for Economy, Planning and Development, he brings extensive expertise to policy research and statistical analysis across critical development issues.

Dr. Albert holds the Ph.D. and M.S. degrees in Statistics from the State University of New York at Stony Brook, earned in 1993 and 1989, respectively, and a Bachelor's degree in Applied Mathematics (Summa Cum Laude) from De La Salle University in 1985. He has made significant contributions to poverty measurement, education policy, social protection, gender and social inclusion, climate change, and data analytics.

His professional career reached a notable milestone when he served as Secretary General (Undersecretary rank) of the National Statistical Coordination Board from 2012 to 2014. Throughout his career, Dr. Albert has established himself as a sought-after consultant, collaborating with international organizations such as the World Bank Group, various United Nations agencies, the Asian Development Bank, and the UK Department for International Development. His expertise has taken him to work in over 30 countries across Asia, Africa, Europe, and the Americas.

Dr. Albert's research portfolio spans critical development issues, with recent notable publications examining poverty among the elderly in Asia and the Pacific, returns to education in the Philippines, sustainable development goals, and energy-saving behaviors of middle-class households. His work consistently bridges the gap between rigorous statistical analysis and practical policy applications.

He currently serves as a Professorial Lecturer at De La Salle University, teaching Multivariate Statistics for doctoral programs and Bayesian Statistics and Probability in the Data Science program. He has previously held teaching positions at the Asian Institute of Management, University of the Philippines, and other leading academic institutions. His commitment to education is reflected in his extensive training programs across multiple countries.

Dr. Albert holds significant leadership positions in key professional organizations, having served as Past President of the Philippine Statistical Association, Inc. He is an elected member of the International Statistical Institute and the National Research Council of the Philippines, and serves as a Fellow of the Social Weather Stations. His editorial contributions include serving as Editor-in-chief of The Philippine Statistician.

Currently, Dr. Albert serves on several international advisory bodies, including the UN Global Pulse Data Privacy Advisory Group. His expertise in statistical software includes proficiency in Stata, R, SPSS, SAS, and other analytical tools.

With over 100 published papers, policy notes, and discussion papers to his credit, Dr. Albert has established himself as a thought leader in development statistics and poverty analysis. His unique combination of theoretical expertise, practical experience, and policy insight makes him particularly qualified to guide researchers, practitioners, and students through the complexities of poverty measurement and statistical analysis in developing country contexts.

Contents

CHAPTER 1
Defining Poverty

"The greatest of evils and the worst of crimes is poverty."
—GEORGE BERNARD SHAW

SUMMARY

This first chapter of the handbook explores how our understanding of poverty has changed over time, moving beyond simply looking at how much money people have or whether they have enough food to eat. It shows that poverty is far more complex than just lacking money. Being poor can mean not getting proper healthcare, missing out on education, living in poor housing conditions, and feeling excluded from society.

The chapter looks at poverty in four main ways: through money (economic), through access to basic services and social inclusion (social), through how it affects people's dignity and mental well-being (psychological) and through multiple dimensions (economic, health, education and labor outcomes). It shows that different groups—whether women, ethnic minorities, or people living in rural areas—experience poverty differently. While measuring income and spending helps us understand who is poor, these numbers do not tell the whole story of how people actually experience poverty in their daily lives.

The chapter also emphasizes that we need to include poor people's own views and experiences when measuring and understanding poverty. It concludes that poverty is not just about individual hardship but shows how society is failing to take care of everyone. To fight poverty effectively, we need to change both the systems that keep people poor and the attitudes that exclude certain groups from opportunities.

1.1. Introduction

Imagine trying to live on less than $2.15 per day. For nearly 700 million people worldwide, this is not just an exercise—it is their daily reality (World Bank, 2022). This is why in 2015, world leaders gathered at the United Nations and made ending extreme poverty their first of 17 goals in the Sustainable Development Goals (SDGs) (United Nations, 2015). But before we can eradicate poverty, we need to answer the question "what exactly is poverty?". The answer is not as simple as you might think. While many people think of poverty as just not having enough money, researchers and policymakers have found that it is much more complex than that.

Think of poverty like a puzzle with many pieces. Some pieces represent not having enough money for food or rent. Other pieces might show someone unable to go to school, get medical care when sick, or find a decent job. When we put all these pieces together, we start to see the full picture of what poverty really means in people's lives.

When we study poverty, we need to look at many different aspects of people's lives. A person experiencing poverty might not only struggle to buy food and pay rent but also face challenges in getting healthcare, education, and respect from others in society. They might feel powerless to change their situation or participate in community decisions. These economic, social, and psychological challenges are all part of what makes poverty such a complex problem.

Over time, our understanding of poverty has grown. In the early days, researchers mainly focused on whether people had enough calories to eat or money to spend. Now we understand that poverty means lacking many different kinds of opportunities and capabilities that people need to live fulfilling lives. This broader view helps us better understand how poverty affects people's overall well-being, their ability to achieve their goals, and their sense of having control over their lives (World Bank, 2018; Kakwani, 2024; Burchi et al., 2022; Alkire et al., 2015; Sen, 1999).

In this chapter, we will explore the different ways to understand poverty. We will look at

- How much money people need to survive (economic perspective)
- How poverty affects people's relationships and place in society (social perspective)
- How being poor impacts people's mental health and dignity (psychological perspective)
- How all these different aspects of poverty connect (multidimensional perspective)

We will also see how poverty can mean different things in different places. What counts as poverty in a rich country might be considered comfortable living in a poor country. And we will learn how being poor affects how people think about themselves and their place in society (Townsend, 1979; Walker, 2014).

Throughout this book, we will get insights that poverty affects different people in different ways. A woman raising children alone faces different challenges than an elderly man living with a disability. Someone living in a remote rural village might experience poverty differently than a person living in an urban slum. These varying experiences of poverty make it crucial to understand the specific challenges that different groups face when trying to design effective solutions (Narayan et al., 2000).

While we can measure poverty by looking at how much money people have or spend, these numbers only tell part of the story. We also need to understand how people experience poverty in their daily lives—their struggles, their strategies for coping, and their hopes for the future. This combination of measuring both the numbers and the human experience gives us a fuller picture of what poverty really means (Ravallion, 2016).

Nobel Prize winner Amartya Sen changed how we think about poverty. Instead of just asking whether people have enough money to survive, he suggested we should ask whether they have the freedom and ability to live the kind of life they value. Having enough money for food, for instance, is important, but so is having the opportunity to get an education, stay healthy, and participate in community life (Sen, 1999).

This way of thinking shows that giving people money alone is not enough. They also need access to good schools, healthcare, and fair treatment in society. These opportunities help people build capabilities and thus better lives for themselves. Researchers have thus created new ways to measure poverty that look at many aspects of well-being at once—like health, education, and living conditions (Alkire and Foster, 2011; Burchi and Malerba, 2023; Kakwani, 2024). These measurements, called multidimensional indices, give us a more complete picture of poverty. However, they need to be adapted for different places because what matters for well-being in one country might be different in another. For instance, having a winter coat might be essential in Norway but not in Tanzania.

Measuring income is, however, still important because it tells us whether people can afford basic necessities. Money might not be everything, but it is still crucial for survival and daily life.Today, we understand poverty better by looking at three things together: how much money people have, how they compare to others in their society, and what they say about their own experiences of being poor.

1.2. Economic Definitions

Let us start with the most basic way of measuring poverty: looking at whether people have enough money or resources to meet their basic needs. The World Bank currently uses $2.15 per day in purchasing power parity (PPP)[1] as the international poverty line for measuring poverty especially in very poor countries. This means anyone living on less than this amount is considered to be in extreme poverty. They might struggle to afford even basic food and shelter (Ferreira et al., 2016; World Bank, 2015, 2022). Higher international poverty thresholds are used in lower middle income countries ($3.65 per day PPP) and in upper middle income countries ($6.85 per day PPP).

Several researchers, however, argue that using the same dollar amount for all countries does not make sense—one size fits all just does not work. What $2.15 can buy varies greatly between countries and even between cities and rural areas in the same country (Reddy and Pogge, 2010). Another way to think about poverty is by comparing people's living standards to what is normal in their society. For instance, a family might have enough money for food and basic shelter, but if they cannot afford things that most people in their society consider necessary—like a phone or proper winter clothing—they might still be considered poor (Townsend, 1979). This relative approach to poverty has its own challenges, though. In countries where most people have similar incomes, it might make even small income differences look like significant poverty. Despite these complications, looking at people's income and spending remains important. After all, in today's world, people need money to buy food, pay for housing, and maintain a decent standard of living.

1.2.1. *Absolute (monetary) poverty*

Absolute poverty refers to using a fixed standard for measuring poverty: do people have enough money to meet their most basic needs for

[1] PPP is a way to compare money's real value across different countries. For example, while $1 might buy one loaf of bread in the United States, that same $1 converted to local currency might buy three loaves in India — PPP adjustments help us account for these differences when measuring poverty globally.

survival? This is different from relative poverty, which we will discuss later.

The most common way to measure absolute poverty is to set a minimum amount of money people need for basic survival. The World Bank uses $2.15 per day as the international poverty line. Different countries also set their own national poverty lines based on local costs. For instance, India has its own poverty line that considers how much it costs to buy basic necessities in rural India: 27 rupees per day (Government of India, 2009; World Bank, 2022).

Some researchers measure poverty by looking directly at whether people get enough food to eat. They might check if people consume enough calories each day (such as 2100 Calories) or ask people if they often go hungry (Abad Santos et al., 2008). This helps us understand poverty in a very basic way—can people meet their most fundamental need for food? (FAO, 2018).

Income-based metrics

When we measure poverty through income, we look at how much money people earn and whether it is enough to buy basic necessities. But comparing incomes across countries can be tricky because the same amount of money buys different amounts in different places. That is why economists adjust these numbers to reflect local purchasing power called PPP (Ferreira et al., 2016; World Bank, 2015, 2022). While income is important—after all, people need money to buy food and other necessities—it is not always the best way to measure poverty. Many poor people work in informal jobs where their income changes a lot from day to day or season to season. A farmer, for instance, might earn most of their money during harvest time but very little during other months (Chen and Ravallion, 2010).

Consumption-based metrics

Because of problems with measuring income (described earlier), many researchers prefer to look at how much people spend rather than how much they earn. Spending tends to be more stable than income because people find ways to maintain their basic consumption even when their income goes up and down. They might borrow money or use savings during tough times (Deaton and Zaidi, 2002; Mancini and Vecchi, 2022). However, measuring consumption is not perfect either. It is expensive and time-consuming to collect this information through surveys. It is also complicated to figure out how to count things like the value of living in a house you own or using appliances that last many years. Despite these challenges, looking at what people consume usually gives us a better picture of their standard of living than just looking at their income.

Caloric intake measures

Some researchers try to measure poverty in an even more direct way—by looking at whether people get enough calories to eat each day. The idea is simple: if someone cannot get enough food to meet their basic energy needs, they are living in poverty (FAO, 2018). However, measuring calories is not as simple as it sounds. People's needs for calories differ based on their age, job, and lifestyle. Plus, getting enough calories does not tell us about other important needs like housing, clothing, or healthcare.

Still, looking at hunger and nutrition gives us valuable information about poverty, especially when we combine it with other measures like income. If we find an area where people have low incomes and high rates of malnutrition, we can be more confident that we are identifying real poverty (Klasen, 2000).

Critiques of absolute measures

Several experts criticize the way we set absolute poverty lines. They argue that choosing any single dollar amount as a poverty line—whether it is $2.15 or any other number—is somewhat arbitrary. Here is an interesting bit of history: when the World Bank first created the dollar-a-day poverty line in 1991, they only looked at poverty lines from eight poor countries (Ravallion et al., 1991). Critics say this was too small a sample to represent poverty worldwide. When the poverty line was updated to $1.90 in 2011 (and later to $2.15 in 2017), some researchers argued that it still did not capture the true extent of global poverty. They say this amount is too low to meet the basic needs in many places (Reddy and Lahoti, 2016).

What people need to live varies greatly from place to place. Someone living in a cold climate needs warm clothing and heating, while these are not necessary in tropical areas. Healthcare costs vary enormously between countries. Even basic needs like food differ based on local customs and what is available. Families of different sizes and types need different amounts of money to avoid poverty. A single parent with three children needs more resources than a single adult. This makes it hard to use one poverty line for everyone, though having a standard measure helps us track global progress (Klasen et al., 2016).

Another limitation of absolute poverty lines is that they do not consider how standards of living change as societies get richer. What was considered adequate 50 years ago might certainly be considered poverty today. Despite all these criticisms, absolute poverty lines are still useful, especially when they are adjusted for local conditions. They help us identify the most severe poverty—situations where people struggle to meet even their most basic needs. They also help governments and international organizations make decisions about where to focus their anti-poverty efforts.

1.2.2. Relative poverty

Relative poverty looks at whether people can afford what is considered normal in their society. Someone might have enough money for basic food and shelter but still be considered poor if they cannot afford things that most people in their society take for granted—like a smartphone, Internet access, or occasional meals out with friends (Townsend, 1979). Most high-income countries measure relative poverty by looking at how much money people have compared to the "middle" income in their country. In European countries, for instance, households earning less than 60 percent of the median income are considered relatively poor (Haughton and Khandker, 2009).

In rich countries, very few people might live in absolute poverty (lacking basic necessities), but many more might experience relative poverty. Think of a family that can afford food and basic housing but cannot afford to send their children on school field trips or buy them a computer for homework—things that most other families in their society can afford.

Relative poverty defines economic hardship by comparison against contemporary societal standards of prosperity signifying exclusion from ordinary living patterns (Townsend, 1979). Incomes below a percentage threshold of median or mean household earnings often denote relative poverty, viz. below 50 or 60 percent (Haughton and Khandker, 2009). Relative poverty can exceed absolute poverty in prosperous societies having met basic needs but permitting significant hardship and exclusion for those left behind. However, it poorly captures gradation at lower income levels and potential overestimation in more egalitarian societies.

The relative conception of poverty accords primacy to the relational aspects of economic deprivation in terms of alienation from customary modes of existence in each socioeconomic order. Social exclusion from ordinary activities and relationships contributes to adverse psychological impact and reinforcement of marginalization (Walker et al., 2013). Relative poverty lines must thus respond to rising general prosperity rather than indicating merely basic needs deficiency in absolute terms.

Relative poverty measures have now been adopted for monitoring the SDGs with

> SDG Indicator 10.2.1: Proportion of people living below 50 percent of median income, by sex, age, and persons with disabilities
> Metadata: https://unstats.un.org/sdgs/metadata/files/Metadata-10-02-01.pdf

Using relative poverty measures has some problems, though. Just looking at income differences does not tell us about other important aspects of poverty, like access to good schools or healthcare. Also, this way of measuring poverty might make rich countries look like they have more poverty than they really do.

Relative deprivation theory

When people feel poor compared to others around them, it can cause stress and unhappiness, even if they have enough money for basic needs. This feeling of being worse off than others is called relative deprivation (Smith et al., 2012). But just because statistics say someone is relatively poor does not always mean they feel poor. Some people might be content with having less than others, while some might feel poor even when statistics say they are not. Research shows that how poor people feel does not always match up with how poor they are according to relative income measures (Nolan and Whelan, 2010).

When thinking about relative poverty, we need to consider how being unable to live up to society's standards makes people feel insecure and left out. When researchers actually talk to people living in poverty, they often find that feeling excluded from society hurts more than not being able to buy things. Not being able to attend a friend's wedding or buy children new school clothes can be deeply painful experiences (Walker, 2014).

Let us look at how this works in practice. In Europe, the statistical agency Eurostat considers someone poor if their income is less than 60 percent of their country's median income. They chose this number because they believe anyone living below this level might struggle to participate in normal social activities (Atkinson et al., 2002). This is not just a random number—it is chosen based on what experts think people need to live a normal life in European society. It looks at whether people can afford to do the things most people in their society do, not just how their income compares to others. This way of measuring poverty makes more sense to people in high-income countries than absolute poverty measures. After all, in rich countries, what matters is not just having enough to survive but having enough to participate fully in society.

Issues in setting (relative) poverty thresholds

There is no consensus about where to draw the line for relative poverty. Is it 50 percent of median income? 60 percent? Any number we choose is somewhat arbitrary (although the SDG indicator 10.2.1 uses 50 percent and asks for breakdowns of national data by sex and by disability status). Using the 60 percent threshold, a country like Norway, where even the poor have good housing and healthcare, might show the same poverty rate as a much poorer country where people struggle to meet basic needs.

Another problem is that these measures usually look at entire households rather than individuals. They assume everyone in a household shares money equally, which often is not true.

In reality, women, children, elderly people, or people with disabilities within the same household might experience very different levels of poverty. In some families, men might control most of the money while women and children have very limited access to resources (Chant, 2008).

Nevertheless, the relative poverty concept enriches measurement by emphasizing comparative disadvantage, precariousness, and social exclusion amidst rising general prosperity. Several middle- and high-income countries monitor relative poverty along with multidimensional indices to identify populations left behind despite meeting basic needs in absolute terms.

1.3. Social Dimensions of Poverty

Poverty is not just about not having enough money. It is also about not being able to access important services that everyone should have for a decent life. Everyone should have certain basic rights—like being able to see a doctor when sick, get an education, and live in decent housing. But poor people often cannot access these essential services, even in countries where they are supposed to be available to everyone (United Nations, 2021). When poor people have to pay for healthcare out of their own pockets, it can push them even deeper into poverty. The World Bank found that medical expenses push about 60 million people into poverty each year globally (World Bank, 2018).

In India, the government spends very little on public healthcare—only about 1 percent of the country's GDP. This means poor people often have to pay for healthcare themselves or go without it (Balarajan et al., 2011). When poor people have to pay for healthcare out of their own pockets, it can push them even deeper into poverty.

1.3.1. Lack of access to healthcare

In many developing countries, people must pay for most of their healthcare themselves. When someone gets seriously ill, the medical bills can be so high that a family that was not poor before might become poor. Very few people in developing countries have health insurance. In India, for example, only about 18 percent of people in urban areas and 14 percent in rural areas had any kind of health insurance in 2017 (Singh, 2016). This means most people have no protection against high medical costs. Consequently, most healthcare spending even for serious ailments is borne out-of-pocket pushing millions into poverty.

Getting sick can make people poor in two ways. First, they have to pay for treatment, medicine, and hospital stays. Second, they often cannot work while they are sick, so they lose income just when they need it most (Garg and Karan, 2008). When governments spend money on public healthcare, it helps reduce poverty much more effectively than when people's private spending increases. A study focusing on low- and middle-income nations found a substantial positive relationship between increased public health expenditure and poverty reduction, both in the short and long term (Idris, Seraj, and Ozdeser, 2024). This suggests that government investments in healthcare services can effectively diminish poverty levels by enhancing health outcomes and economic productivity.

So when we think about poverty, we need to consider not just whether people have enough money but also whether they can get healthcare when they need it. This is especially important in developing countries where public healthcare systems are often weak or missing.

1.3.2. Limited access to education

More children are going to school in developing countries than ever before, but there are still big problems with education. Many schools are of poor quality, and some families still cannot afford to send their children to school. This keeps poverty passing from parents to children. Take India as an example. In rural areas, most children go to government schools that do not have enough teachers, proper buildings, or basic facilities like libraries and computers (Drèze and Sen, 2013). Because of these problems, by the time children reach middle school, 90 percent of them struggle with basic reading and understanding. This makes it very hard for them to learn more advanced things or get better jobs when they grow up (ASER, 2018).

International organizations have proposed various measures to quantify "education poverty" beyond mere enrollment statistics. UNESCO reports that someone is "education poor" if they have less than four years of schooling. They chose four years because that is the minimum time they think people need to learn basic reading, writing, and math (UNESCO, 2010). Using this definition, they found that in the poorest countries, almost half the people (44 percent) are education poor. Separately, UNICEF measures the proportion of children unable to read and understand a simple text by age 10 (UNICEF, 2022). The numbers are shocking: as of 2019, more than half of all 10-year-olds in poor and middle-income countries cannot read and understand a simple story. In parts of Africa and South Asia, it is even worse—80 to 90 percent of children struggle with basic reading. Learning deficits are likely to have even worsened given school closures during the pandemic. Such widespread learning deficits severely constrain children's future educational progress and economic prospects, underscoring the urgent need to focus on education quality, equity, and efficiency beyond access alone.

The problem gets even worse when we look at college and university education. Children from wealthy families have many more opportunities to get higher education than children from poor families. Because poor children often cannot get higher education, they have trouble getting good jobs or passing competitive exams for government positions. This means poverty keeps passing from one generation to the next (Tilak, 2013). So it is not just about not having enough money for school—the whole education system makes it harder for poor people to escape poverty. When we think about what poverty really means, we must consider whether people can get good quality education at all levels—from primary school through university.

1.3.3. Poor quality housing conditions

Good housing is not just about having a roof over your head. It means having clean water coming from taps, having reliable electricity, having proper toilets, and being close enough to important services like schools and hospitals. The numbers are staggering: about 1.6 billion people worldwide do not have proper housing. They are missing at least one basic thing that makes a house truly livable (United Nations, 2021). Consider India as an illustration: 95 million households do not have electricity, 80 million do not have running water, and 75 million do not have sanitary toilets. That is more than the entire population of most countries (Census, 2011).

This shows us that when we think about poverty, especially in cities, we cannot just look at how much money people have. We also need to look at whether they have decent housing with basic facilities. People living in slums might earn more money than rural poor people, but they often live in terrible conditions. Bad housing leads to health problems and fewer opportunities in life, keeping families trapped in poverty for generations (Marx et al., 2013). Our ways of measuring and defining poverty need to do a better job of counting people who live without basic services like electricity, water, and sanitation. These people often live right next to wealthy neighborhoods in cities, but official statistics sometimes miss them entirely.

1.3.4. Food insecurity

Obviously, people with very little money often go hungry. But looking at income alone does not tell us the whole story about who is struggling to get enough food. Even people who are not normally considered poor might struggle to get enough food at certain times—like farmers between harvests, workers who lose their jobs, or families facing unexpected expenses (Swindale and Bilinsky, 2006). In many societies, women eat last after serving the men, meaning they often get less food or lower-quality food. Children and elderly people are also more likely to suffer from poor nutrition (Haddad et al., 1996).

These problems can happen even in farming families that grow their own food. To really understand food insecurity, researchers need to spend time with families and observe how they manage their food throughout the year. When researchers look closely at how families live, they find that going hungry for even part of the year causes great hardship, even if yearly income figures suggest people should have enough to eat. This means we need carefully designed policies to help people during these difficult periods (Tsiboe et al., 2016). What counts as necessary food varies between cultures. We cannot use the same standards everywhere to judge whether people have enough to eat (Coates et al., 2006).

1.3.5. Social exclusion

Poverty is not just about not having things or services—it is also about being left out of normal social and economic activities that most people take for granted. People might be excluded from society because of their caste, religion, gender, race, or the language they speak. This discrimination means they are not treated as equal citizens, making it harder to escape poverty (Das et al., 2013). Being treated as a second-class citizen hurts people's dignity and sense of belonging, even if they have enough money to meet their basic needs.

Take India again as an example. Over the past few decades, many people from the lowest castes and tribes (about 160 million people) have seen their incomes increase. But these groups still struggle to move up in society because they face discrimination and do not have the social connections needed to deal with powerful institutions, whether in villages or cities (Thorat and Neuman, 2012). One of the biggest challenges is overcoming the shame and stigma attached to certain jobs or social positions. This means that just giving people money is not enough—we need to change how society treats different groups of people if we want to make real progress against poverty. But that is easier said than done in a world where discrimination thrives.

Psychological dimensions of poverty

When people are excluded from society because of discrimination, it does not just affect their opportunities—it also affects how they think and feel about themselves and change the structural conditions that create such mindsets. When people constantly worry about not having enough money and feel cut off from society, they often develop what researchers call a "scarcity mindset". This means they stop believing they can achieve better things in life, and they lose confidence in themselves (Mullainathan and Shafir, 2013). People might give up trying to improve their situation, lose motivation, and avoid taking risks that could help them escape poverty. This happens even when they have opportunities to get ahead (Appadurai, 2004).

Studies show that growing up in poverty can make people feel like they have no control over their lives. They come to expect little from life because they are so used to uncertainty and hardship. When people feel this way, they often do not make full use of their skills and resources, making it even harder to escape poverty (Narayan et al., 2009). This means that anti-poverty programs need to do more than just provide material help. They also need to change the social and cultural attitudes that keep people trapped in poverty.

Hopelessness and learned helplessness

When people face constant discrimination because of their race, caste, religion, sex, gender identity, or disability status, they can often become hopeless and pessimistic about their future. People start to believe that their circumstances can never change, that it is their "destiny" to be poor. This belief makes them less likely to try to improve their situation. When people face daily discrimination and feel hopeless about their future, they often do not use their full potential. Even when help is available, this psychological trap can keep families poor for generations (Duflo, 2012).

Research in psychology has found that when groups of people face exploitation for many generations, they start to believe they have no control over their lives (Maier and Seligman, 2016). This means poverty creates more than just material hardship—it makes people feel that no matter what they do, nothing will get better. When people feel this way, they often mentally "check out" and do not take advantage of opportunities that could help them, which keeps them trapped in poverty. People learn to be passive and avoid taking risks, which keeps them disadvantaged. This is why we need programs that change how people think about themselves, not just programs that provide material help (Bertrand et al., 2004).

Loss of dignity

When people live in poverty, they often lose their sense of dignity. It is not just about not having money or access to services—it is about feeling helpless, depending on others for survival, and facing daily humiliation (Narayan et al., 2000). Having a good, meaningful job is crucial for people to regain their self-respect. However, many poor people can only find insecure, informal jobs because of discrimination, even when they have skills for better work. In India, for instance, people from certain castes are often stuck in low-status jobs their whole lives, regardless of their abilities (Thorat and Neuman, 2012).

To help people regain their dignity, it is not enough just to teach them new job skills. We need policies that help them access better jobs that were previously off-limits because of social hierarchies. However, even when people get better economic opportunities, they might still face discrimination that hurts their dignity. This means we need programs that work to change society's attitudes and prejudices (Ray and Esteban, 2017). People need to feel they belong in their community and are recognized as equal members—this is as important for self-respect as having money. That is why empowering people socially is just as important as helping them economically when fighting poverty.

1.4. Multidimensional Poverty

The interconnected facets of income poverty, capability deprivations, and psychological distress together constitute multidimensional poverty, which recognizes that being poor is not just about lacking money. Poverty is about facing multiple challenges that are all connected: not having enough income, lacking opportunities to develop skills and abilities, and suffering psychological stress. To better understand poverty, researchers created tools called "composite indices" that measure multiple problems at once—like lack of education, poor health, bad housing, and no electricity. The most famous of these is the Global Multidimensional Poverty Index (MPI), which was developed based on Nobel Prize winner Amartya Sen's ideas. The Global MPI is now used alongside traditional income measures to give a fuller picture of poverty (Alkire et al., 2015), especially in Human Development publications of the UN Development Programme (UNDP). Some alternatives to the Global MPI include the World Bank's Multidimensional Poverty Measure, which considers monetary poverty as one of its components.

Experts have started thinking differently about development with multidimensional poverty. Instead of just focusing on giving people more things to buy, they began thinking about how to fairly distribute basic rights that help people live well, like education and healthcare (Sen, 1999). This means poverty is not just about slow economic growth or low private incomes—it is also about governments failing to provide healthcare, education, and other opportunities. To fight poverty effectively, we need to understand how economic, social, and political exclusion are all connected. We must address the barriers that different groups face because of their class, caste, gender, or other identities (Stewart, 2005).

The Global MPI and other similar indices look at whether people have access to basic necessities like food, clean water, toilets, decent housing, and education. They also consider things like whether children and mothers are surviving and staying healthy (Alkire and Santos, 2014). These measurements show how poor public services—like bad healthcare, low-quality schools, and inadequate housing—make life even harder for people who already do not have enough money. This is especially true when people also face discrimination and negative stereotypes.

1.4.1. *Intersection of economic and social facets of deprivation*

When people are poor, different problems combine to make their lives harder. They might not have money, cannot get healthcare or education, live in bad housing, and face discrimination because of their caste, race, gender, or disability. All these problems together create what we call "lived poverty"—the real experience of being poor. When people constantly worry about survival and making enough money to live, it takes up so much mental energy that they struggle to think about or plan for anything else. Scientists call this the "mental bandwidth" problem (Mani et al., 2013). This constant stress makes it harder for people to take steps to improve their lives, even when they have the ability to do so.

When people cannot get basic services, it makes their poverty worse and helps pass it on to their children. For instance, when rural women cannot get proper healthcare during pregnancy, and families have no safety net when they lose income, it keeps them trapped in disadvantage (Drèze and Sen, 2013). People who do not have much money but can access good public services (like healthcare and education) often cope better with hardship than those who have more money but cannot access these services.

This means governments need to change how they think about development and how they formulate development policies. Instead of just trying to focus on growing the economy, governments need to refocus on fairly providing basic rights like healthcare, education, housing, and support when people lose their jobs (Mkandawire, 2005). This also means fighting discrimination that keeps certain groups excluded. A case in point: people from lower castes and religious minorities in India often have to live in separate areas where they cannot get proper housing or sanitation (Thorat et al., 2017). Therefore, helping people escape poverty requires more than just creating economic growth and jobs. We need to break down the barriers that keep people excluded because of their class, gender, age, race, or disabilities.

1.4.2. Evolving multidimensional indices

Because poverty involves many connected problems—lack of money, poor healthcare, limited education, not enough food, and no basic utilities—researchers developed new ways to measure it that look at all these factors together. These new measurements, especially the Global MPI, came from Nobel Prize winner Amartya Sen's ideas. The Global MPI looks at 10 different statistical indicators (or signals) of poverty across health, education, and living conditions (Alkire and Foster, 2011).

Many countries now use these more comprehensive ways to measure poverty. Mexico looks at whether people can get education, healthcare, social security, and decent living conditions. Colombia revised the MPI to check also if families have access to childcare, good nutrition, and basic utilities. India and Pakistan combine traditional income measures with various aspects of the Global MPI (CONEVAL, 2010; Angulo et al., 2016; Alkire and Seth, 2015; GoP, 2016). The Kingdom of Bhutan took an interesting approach—they created a "Happiness Index" that measures not just money but also people's mental well-being, health, education, cultural life, community connections, and environmental quality (Ura et al., 2012).

The Global MPI works by checking three main areas of life:

- Education: How many years did people study? Are children in school?
- Health: Are people well-nourished? Do children survive?
- Living standards: Do people have clean cooking fuel, toilets, clean water, electricity, and decent housing?

If a household lacks one-third or more of these basic needs, they are considered "MPI poor". Researchers then calculate how many people are poor (in relation to the entire population), the so-called poverty headcount ratio, and how many different hardships they face on average, referred to as the average intensity of deprivation (Alkire et al., 2015).

When we measure poverty this new way, we sometimes get very different results than when we just look at income. Take India as an illustration: between 2005 and 2015, multidimensional poverty was cut almost in half (from 55 to 28 percent) because people got better access to healthcare, toilets, and electricity, along with earning more money (Alkire et al., 2021). However, when counted this way, there were 292 million more poor people in India than when counting by income alone. This is because the MPI sets higher standards and looks at more aspects of poverty.

The Global MPI was not the first attempt to measure poverty in a more comprehensive way. Earlier, researchers like Filmer and Pritchett (2001) developed methods to measure asset poverty in India by looking at what assets households owned—things like TVs, refrigerators, or vehicles—and using a statistical method called principal components analysis for creating an asset-based wealth index to understand the long-term economic situations of households in India. They believed looking at what people owned gave a better picture of their true economic status than just looking at what they spent, and it was easier to measure. Other researchers built on this idea and improved it for different countries and situations (Vyas and Kumaranayake, 2006; Howe et al., 2008).

The World Bank developed its own way of measuring multidimensional poverty that looks at both what people can buy and what services they can access. They check not only if people have enough money to meet basic needs but also if they can get education, basic services like water, toilets, and electricity (World Bank, 2018). In the World Bank's method, all these different aspects of poverty are considered equally important. If a household lacks a third or more of these basic needs, they are considered poor. When they used this method in 119 developing countries, they found that 50 percent more people were poor than when they just looked at money alone.

1.4.3. Measuring intensities of deprivations

These new ways of measuring poverty also show us how severely different people experience poverty—in other words, how many different hardships they face at once. For example, we have learned that while more people in cities are becoming poor, rural poor people tend to face more hardships at the same time. Religious minorities and people from lower castes tend to face more types of hardship at once. While differences between men and women have gotten smaller, minorities still face deeper poverty. City residents usually have better housing and basic services but often struggle more with healthcare and education (Alkire et al., 2021).

Looking at India, we see big differences between states. Assam and Bihar have the most multidimensional poverty, while Kerala and Goa have the least. Interestingly, some states like Andhra, West Bengal, and Odisha managed to reduce poverty even while inequality was increasing, showing that their public services were working well. Even in states where inequality grew by 25 percent, multidimensional poverty still went down considerably. This shows that government programs aimed at helping the poor were effective (Alkire et al., 2021).

This tells us that to reduce poverty, we need both economic growth AND better public services—healthcare, education, sanitation, housing, and social security. Governments need to pass laws that guarantee these as rights, raise and spend money fairly, and make sure services actually reach people at the local level (Mkandawire, 2005). Even when they have similar incomes, women and minority groups often face more poverty. This means we need special programs to fight discrimination and make sure these groups can access public services. Changing people's prejudiced attitudes is just as important as improving government services.

While these new ways of measuring poverty are better than just looking at income, they still have problems. Researchers have to make assumptions about what counts as basic needs and what level of deprivation makes someone poor. Often, they make these decisions without asking poor people themselves what they think matters most (Alkire et al., 2021). What is considered necessary for a decent life varies between places and cultures. Different religious and cultural groups have their own ideas about what people need to live well and what counts as an acceptable standard of living. For instance, India's traditional households may value drinking water accessibility over indoor plumbing.

This means we need to include more input from poor people themselves when deciding how to measure poverty. We need to use research methods that capture people's actual experiences and what they consider important. When measuring poverty through income, we need to consider many factors: how many people live in each household, how prices change over time, benefits people get that are not money (like growing their own food), and how costs differ between places (Deaton and Zaidi, 2002; Mancini and Vecchi, 2022). While these measurements help policymakers see the big picture, they can miss how poverty is actually experienced differently by different people. That is why we need to combine these broad measurements with detailed understanding of how poverty affects specific communities.

1.5. Subjectivity of Poverty

While measuring multiple aspects of poverty gives us a better understanding than just looking at money, these measurements still have limitations. Researchers have to make judgment calls about what to measure and what level counts as poverty, and these decisions might not make sense for all places. Moreover, these measurements often miss how different cultures view what is necessary for a decent life, what gives people dignity, and what it really means to be poor. To make better policies, we need to include poor people's own views and experiences.

1.5.1. Perceived relative poverty

When people compare themselves to others around them, feeling poorer than their neighbors can hurt them psychologically more than actually having less money. This is what we call relative poverty (Townsend, 1979). Research on happiness shows that people often feel frustrated not based on what they have but on how they compare to others they look up to (Clark et al., 2008). As societies get richer, what people consider necessary for a decent life changes. So even people who have enough money for basic needs might feel poor if they cannot afford what is normal in their society.

While extreme poverty has significantly decreased in India, perceptions of poverty remain high among the population (Patnaik, 2023).

This phenomenon is influenced by factors such as financial insecurity, lack of safety nets, and income inequality, leading individuals to feel impoverished despite economic progress. Such subjective feelings of poverty can contribute to social tensions comparable to those arising from actual material deprivation.

1.5.2. *Heterogeneity in poverty experiences*

Poor people are not all poor in the same way or for the same reasons. Research shows that poverty looks very different depending on whether you are studying different social groups, different types of jobs, different places, or different cultures. In India, people from different castes see their chances of escaping poverty very differently, even when they have similar incomes. Your caste can affect whether you believe you or your children can have a better life (Kapur et al., 2010).

When minority groups face discrimination for generations, they might start believing they cannot succeed, which makes it even harder to escape poverty. We can see this in how food is distributed within families—even when there is enough food overall, women and girls might go hungry because of traditional practices that favor men and boys. Similarly, when communities do not have ways to discuss and ensure everyone, especially the elderly and persons with disability, gets healthcare, health problems among poor people continue. This is why anti-poverty programs need to be carefully designed for different groups' specific situations. To understand these differences, researchers need to have detailed conversations (say using semi-structured in-depth interviews) with poor people and not just look at their income levels (Narayan et al., 2000).

1.5.3. *Importance of subjective metrics*

Because many people criticize how we set poverty lines (whether using money or multiple factors), there is growing support for including poor people's own views about what poverty means. Current measurements do not capture how poverty feels—the worry about the future, the anxiety, and the frustration of having less than others, even when people have enough to meet basic needs. By asking people about their own experiences of poverty and happiness, we can better understand whether economic growth is actually improving everyone's lives or just helping some people (Ravallion and Lokshin, 2002).

Looking at how satisfied people are with their lives helps us compare different countries and see which societies are better at turning economic growth into better lives for their citizens. When we ask people about their own experiences, we often discover that even when a country is getting richer overall, certain groups—based on class, caste, ethnicity, or region—are being left behind. This helps governments know where they need to focus their efforts.

Amartya Sen suggested we need open discussions involving everyone to agree on what counts as an adequate standard of living. He built this idea from earlier work by Adam Smith on the concept of the "impartial spectator" test, showing that these conversations have been important for centuries (Sen, 2000). When we include poor people's own experiences in research, it helps create better policies that actually matter to communities. This can also help change how society thinks about poverty.

By listening to poor people themselves, instead of just relying on experts, we can avoid creating programs that do not really understand or meet people's needs. The real experiences of poor people dealing with failed public services often get ignored when experts make plans that treat everyone the same way. When researchers spend time living in communities and listening to people's stories, they can better understand how poverty affects different groups differently. These ethnographic studies reveal how issues of dignity, discrimination, and power relationships are often more important than just differences in income. Anti-poverty programs need to address these deeper problems.

1.6. Conclusion

Poverty is complex and has many faces—it involves not having enough money, but also social exclusion, lack of political voice, and psychological suffering. While many people in developing countries still struggle with extreme poverty—not having enough food or a place to live—even in rich countries, people can feel poor because of high inequality. Women, racial minorities, and lower caste groups often face worse poverty, even when they have similar incomes to others. This happens because poverty is not just about money—it is also about not having access to healthcare, education, decent housing, and good jobs. The way poverty affects people psychologically is also crucial—when people face constant discrimination, they might lose their sense of dignity and hope for the future. How poor people feel compared to others around them can be just as important as their actual income when we are trying to understand if policies are working.

When we measure poverty, we need to recognize that it looks different in different places, with different social rules and different access to services. While our current measurements are good at identifying extreme poverty, they often miss people who are moderately poor, especially in middle-income countries. Also, experts often decide how to measure poverty without asking poor people what they think matters. We need to include poor people's own views and experiences to better understand what keeps them from accessing services and opportunities for a better life.

Poverty is not just about falling below certain measurements—it is about people being unable to develop their abilities, achieve their goals, and live with dignity, especially when they start from a disadvantaged position. When we define poverty, we need to focus on how governments can help people help themselves and make sure institutions serve everyone fairly through proper laws. Poverty is not just about individual problems—it shows how society and government policies are failing. To eliminate poverty, we need to address the deep causes that keep certain groups from accessing basic needs, opportunities, and dignity, as well as the causes why some nonpoor groups fall into poverty. This means changing discriminatory attitudes and beliefs that create hierarchies in society. We need to combine our broad measurements of poverty with understanding of how different groups struggle for power, identity, and respect, so we can create policies that help build a more equal society.

References

Abad-Santos, C. O., Edillon, R. G., Piza, S. F. A., delos Reyes, V., & Diokno, M. S. I. (2008). *Right to food assessment: Philippines.* Food and Agriculture Organization of the United Nations. https://www.fao.org/4/ap598e/ap598e.pdf

Alkire, S., & Foster, J. (2011). Counting and multidimensional poverty measurement. *Journal of Public Economics, 95*(7–8), 476–487. https://www.sciencedirect.com/science/article/abs/pii/S0047272710001660

Alkire, S., Foster, J., Seth, S., Santos, M. E., Roche, J. M., & Ballon, P. (2015). *Multidimensional poverty measurement and analysis.* Oxford University Press. https://academic.oup.com/book/11882

Alkire, S., Oldiges, C., & Kanagaratnam, U. (2021). Examining multidimensional poverty reduction in India 2005/6–2015/16: Insights and oversights of the headcount ratio. *World Development, 142*, 105454. https://www.sciencedirect.com/science/article/pii/S0305750X21000668

Alkire, S., & Santos, M. E. (2014). Measuring acute poverty in the developing world: Robustness and scope of the multidimensional poverty index. *World Development, 59*, 251–274. https://www.sciencedirect.com/science/article/abs/pii/S0305750X14000278

Alkire, S., & Seth, S. (2015). Multidimensional poverty reduction in India between 1999 and 2006: Where and how? *World Development, 72*, 93–108. https://www.sciencedirect.com/science/article/abs/pii/S0305750X1500042X

Angulo, R., Díaz, Y., & Pardo, R. (2016). The Colombian multidimensional poverty index: Measuring poverty in a public policy context. *Social Indicators Research, 127*(1), 1–38. https://link.springer.com/article/10.1007/s11205-015-0964-z

Appadurai, A. (2004). The capacity to aspire: Culture and the terms of recognition. In V. Rao & M. Walton (Eds.), *Culture and public action* (pp. 59,

62–63). Stanford University Press. https://gsdrc.org/document-library/the-capacity-to-aspire-culture-and-the-terms-of-recognition/

ASER. (2018). *Annual status of education report (Rural) 2018*. New Delhi: ASER Centre. https://img.asercentre.org/docs/ASER%202018/Release%20Material/aserreport2018.pdf

Atkinson, A. B., Cantillon, B., Marlier, E., & Nolan, B. (2002). *Social indicators: The EU and social inclusion*. Oxford University Press. https://academic.oup.com/book/4330

Balarajan, Y., Selvaraj, S., & Subramanian, S. V. (2011). Health care and equity in India. *The Lancet, 377*(9764), 505–515. https://pubmed.ncbi.nlm.nih.gov/21227492/

Bertrand, M., Mullainathan, S., & Shafir, E. (2004). A behavioral-economics view of poverty. *American Economic Review, 94*(2), 419–423. https://www.aeaweb.org/articles?id=10.1257/0002828041302019

Burchi, F., Malerba, D., Montenegro, C. E., & Rippin, N. (2022). Assessing trends in multidimensional poverty during the MDGs. *Review of Income and Wealth, 68*(S2), S317–S346. https://doi.org/10.1111/roiw.12578

Burchi, F., & Malerba, D. (2023). Are women poorer? A cross-country analysis of gender differentials in multidimensional poverty. In U. R. Wagle (Ed.), *Research handbook on poverty and inequality* (pp. 103–117). Edward Elgar Publishing. https://doi.org/10.4337/9781800882300.00014

Census of India. (2011). *Houselisting and housing census data highlights*. New Delhi: Office of the Registrar General and Census Commissioner, India.

Chant, S. (2008). The "feminisation of poverty" and the "feminisation" of anti-poverty programmes: Room for revision? *The Journal of Development Studies, 44*(2), 165–197. https://www.tandfonline.com/doi/abs/10.1080/00220380701789810

Chen, S., & Ravallion, M. (2010). The developing world is poorer than we thought, but no less successful in the fight against poverty. *The Quarterly Journal of Economics, 125*(4), 1577–1625. https://academic.oup.com/qje/article-abstract/125/4/1577/1916270?redirectedFrom=fulltext

Clark, A. E., Frijters, P., & Shields, M. A. (2008). Relative income, happiness, and utility: An explanation for the Easterlin paradox and other puzzles. *Journal of Economic Literature, 46*(1), 95–144. https://www.aeaweb.org/articles?id=10.1257/jel.46.1.95

Coates, J., Frongillo, E. A., Rogers, B. L., Webb, P., Wilde, P. E., & Houser, R. (2006). Commonalities in the experience of household food insecurity across cultures: What are measures missing? *The Journal of Nutrition,*

136(5), 1438S–1448S. https://www.sciencedirect.com/science/article/pii/S0022316622082670

CONEVAL. (2010). *Methodology for multidimensional poverty measurement in Mexico*. Mexico City: National Council for the Evaluation of Social Development Policy. https://www.coneval.org.mx/rw/resource/coneval/med_pobreza/MPMMPshortversion100903.pdf

Das, M. B., Fisiy, C. F., & Kyte, R. (2013). *Inclusion matters: The foundation for shared prosperity*. New frontiers of social policy Washington DC; World Bank. http://documents.worldbank.org/curated/en/114561468154469371

Deaton, A., & Zaidi, S. (2002). *Guidelines for constructing consumption aggregates for welfare analysis* (Vol. 135). World Bank Publications. https://openknowledge.worldbank.org/entities/publication/05705853-f9bc-5bbb-9658-c254a2eae048

Drèze, J., & Sen, A. (2013). *An uncertain glory: India and its contradictions*. Princeton University Press. https://press.princeton.edu/books/hardcover/9780691160795/an-uncertain-glory

Duflo, E. (2012). Human values and the design of the fight against poverty. In G. B. Peterson (Ed.), *The Tanner lectures on human values* (Vol. 29, pp. 119–164). Massachusetts Institute of Technology. Retrieved from https://www.povertyactionlab.org/sites/default/files/documents/TannerLectures_EstherDuflo_draft.pdf

Food and Agriculture Organization (FAO). (2018). *The state of food security and nutrition in the world 2018: Building climate resilience for food security and nutrition*. Food and Agriculture Organization of the United Nations. https://openknowledge.fao.org/server/api/core/bitstreams/f5019ab4-0f6a-47e8-85b9-15473c012d6a/content

Ferreira, F. H. G., Chen, S., Dabalen, A., Dikhanov, Y., Hamadeh, N., Jolliffe, D., Narayan, A., Prydz, E. B., Revenga, A., Sangraula, P., Serajuddin, U., & Yoshida, N. (2016). A global count of the extreme poor in 2012: Data issues, methodology and initial results. *The Journal of Economic Inequality, 14*(2), 141–172. https://link.springer.com/article/10.1007/s10888-016-9326-6

Filmer, D., & Pritchett, L. H. (2001). Estimating wealth effects without expenditure data—or tears: An application to educational enrollments in states of India. *Demography, 38*(1), 115–132. https://citeseerx.ist.psu.edu/document?repid=rep1&type=pdf&doi=26807cf0409821bedc6e259c74ca68710a8f063c

Garg, C. C., & Karan, A. K. (2008). Reducing out-of-pocket expenditures to reduce poverty: A disaggregated analysis at rural-urban and state level in

India. *Health Policy and Planning, 24*(2), 116–128. https://academic.oup.com/heapol/article/24/2/116/590631

Government of India. (2009). *Report of the expert group to review the methodology for measurement of poverty*. New Delhi: Planning Commission. http://www.indiaenvironmentportal.org.in/files/rep_pov.pdf

Government of Pakistan [GoP]. (2016). *Multidimensional poverty in Pakistan*. Islamabad: Ministry of Planning, Development and Special Initiatives. https://pc.gov.pk/uploads/report/Multidimensional-Poverty-in-Pakistan.pdf

Haddad, L., Peña, C., Nishida, C., Quisumbing, A., & Slack, A. (1996). *Food security and nutrition implications of intrahousehold bias* (No. 19). International Food Policy Research Institute (IFPRI). https://hdl.handle.net/10568/157092

Haughton, J., & Khandker, S. R. (2009). *Handbook on poverty and inequality*. World Bank Publications. https://documents1.worldbank.org/curated/en/488081468157174849/pdf/483380PUB0Pove101OFFICIAL0USE0ONLY1.pdf

Howe, L. D., Hargreaves, J. R., & Huttly, S. R. (2008). Issues in the construction of wealth indices for the measurement of socio-economic position in low-income countries. *Emerging Themes in Epidemiology, 5*(1), 1-14. https://link.springer.com/article/10.1186/1742-7622-5-3

Idris, F. M., Seraj, M., & Ozdeser, H. (2024). Impact of health expenditure on poverty in low- and middle-income countries: An autoregressive distributed lag bounds approach. *Global Health Economics and Sustainability, 2*(1), Article 2383. https://doi.org/10.36922/ghes.2383

Kakwani, N. (2024). *Multidimensional poverty: A new thinking on measurement* (Gulati Institute of Finance and Taxation Discussion Paper No. 21). https://www.gift.res.in/wp-content/uploads/2024/08/DP-21-Multi-dimensional-Poverty-Nanak-Kakwani.pdf

Kapur, D., Prasad, C. B., Pritchett, L., & Babu, D. S. (2010). Rethinking inequality: Dalits in Uttar Pradesh in the market reform era. *Economic and Political Weekly*, 45(35), 39–49. https://www.epw.in/journal/2010/35/special-articles/rethinking-inequality-dalits-uttar-pradesh-market-reform-era.html

Klasen, S. (2000). Measuring poverty and deprivation in South Africa. *Review of Income and Wealth, 46*(1), 33–58. https://onlinelibrary.wiley.com/doi/abs/10.1111/j.1475-4991.2000.tb00390.x

Klasen, S., Krivobokova, T., Greb, F., Lahoti, R., Pasaribu, S. H., & Wiesenfarth, M. (2016). International income poverty measurement: Which way now? *The Journal of Economic Inequality, 14*(2), 199–225. https://link.springer.com/article/10.1007/s10888-016-9324-8

Maier, S. F., & Seligman, M. E. (2016). Learned helplessness at fifty: Insights from neuroscience. *Psychological Review, 123*(4), 349. https://doi.org/10.1037/rev0000033

Mancini, G., & Vecchi, G. (2022). *On the construction of a consumption aggregate for inequality and poverty analysis (English).* Washington, D.C.: World Bank Group.

Mani, A., Mullainathan, S., Shafir, E., & Zhao, J. (2013). Poverty impedes cognitive function. *Science, 341*(6149), 976–980. https://www.science.org/doi/10.1126/science.1238041

Marx, B., Stoker, T., & Suri, T. (2013). The economics of slums in the developing world. *Journal of Economic Perspectives, 27*(4), 187–210. https://pubs.aeaweb.org/doi/pdfplus/10.1257/jep.27.4.187

Mkandawire, T. (2005). *Targeting and universalism in poverty reduction.* United Nations Research Institute for Social Development. https://www.files.ethz.ch/isn/102839/23.pdf

Mullainathan, S., & Shafir, E. (2013). *Scarcity: Why having too little means so much.* Macmillan. https://us.macmillan.com/books/9781250056115/scarcity/

Narayan, D., Chambers, R., Shah, M. K., & Petesch, P. (2000). *Voices of the poor: Crying out for change.* New York: Oxford University Press for the World Bank. https://openknowledge.worldbank.org/entities/publication/39bf2bb1-e06d-5044-91f2-2451c7339384

Narayan, D., Pritchett, L., & Kapoor, S. (2009). *Moving out of poverty: Success from the bottom up* (Vol. 2). World Bank Publications. https://openknowledge.worldbank.org/entities/publication/8ccfe651-e7ff-556b-a503-fa0b941b1b4d

Nolan, B., & Whelan, C. T. (2010). Using non-monetary deprivation indicators to analyze poverty and social exclusion: Lessons from Europe? *Journal of Policy Analysis and Management, 29*(2), 305–325. https://onlinelibrary.wiley.com/doi/abs/10.1002/pam.20493

Patnaik, P. (2023, March 29). The government's claims on poverty reduction are false. Here's why. *The Wire.* Retrieved from https://m.thewire.in/article/government/the-governments-claims-of-poverty-reduction-are-false-heres-why

Ravallion, M. (2016). *The economics of poverty: History, measurement, and policy.* Oxford University Press. https://academic.oup.com/book/10927

Ravallion, M., Datt, G., & Van de Walle, D. (1991). Quantifying absolute poverty in the developing world. *Review of Income and Wealth, 37*(4), 345–361. https://onlinelibrary.wiley.com/doi/abs/10.1111/j.1475-4991.1991.tb00378.x

Ravallion, M., & Lokshin, M. (2002). Self-rated economic welfare in Russia. *European Economic Review, 46*(8), 1453–1473. https://www.sciencedirect.com/science/article/abs/pii/S0014292101001519

Ray, D., & Esteban, J. (2017). Conflict and development. *Annual Review of Economics, 9*, 263–293. https://www.annualreviews.org/content/journals/10.1146/annurev-economics-061109-080205

Reddy, S. G., & Lahoti, R. (2016). $1.90 a day: What does it say? *New Left Review, 97*, 106–127. https://newleftreview.org/issues/ii97/articles/sanjay-reddy-rahul-lahoti-1-90-a-day-what-does-it-say

Reddy, S. G., & Pogge, T. (2010). How not to count the poor. In S. Anand, P. Segal, & J. Stiglitz (Eds.), *Debates on the measurement of global poverty* (pp. 42–51). Oxford University Press. https://academic.oup.com/book/36418/chapter-abstract/320148073?redirectedFrom=fulltext

Sen, A. (1999). *Commodities and capabilities.* Oxford University Press. https://global.oup.com/academic/product/commodities-and-capabilities-9780195650389

Sen, A. (2000). *Social exclusion: Concept, application and scrutiny.* Asian Development Bank, Office of Environment and Social Development. https://www.adb.org/sites/default/files/publication/29778/social-exclusion.pdf

Singh, A. (2016). Current situation of health care coverage in India. *News Across Asia, 5*(1), 10. International Society for Pharmacoeconomics and Outcomes Research (ISPOR).

Smith, H. J., Pettigrew, T. F., Pippin, G. M., & Bialosiewicz, S. (2012). Relative deprivation: A theoretical and meta-analytic review. *Personality and Social Psychology Review, 16*(3), 203–232. https://doi.org/10.1177/1088868311430825

Stewart, F. (2005). Groups and capabilities. *Journal of Human Development, 6*(2), 185–204. https://www.tandfonline.com/doi/full/10.1080/14649880500120517

Swindale, A., & Bilinsky, P. (2006). *Household dietary diversity score (HDDS) for measurement of household food access: Indicator guide* (Version 2). Washington DC: Food and Nutrition Technical Assistance Project, Academy for Educational Development, 11. https://www.fantaproject.org/sites/default/files/resources/HDDS_v2_Sep06_0.pdf

Thorat, A., Vanneman, R., Desai, S., & Dubey, A. (2017). Escaping and falling into poverty in India today. *World Development, 93*, 413–426. https://www.sciencedirect.com/science/article/abs/pii/S0305750X17300062

Thorat, S., & Neuman, K. S. (Eds.). (2012). *Blocked by caste: Economic discrimination in modern India*. Oxford University Press. https://global.oup.com/academic/product/blocked-by-caste-9780198081692?cc=ph&lang=en&

Tilak, J. B. (2013). *Higher education in India: In search of equality, quality and quantity*. Orient Blackswan. https://www.orientblackswan.com/details?id=9788125051312

Townsend, P. (1979). *Poverty in the United Kingdom: A survey of household resources and standards of living*. University of California Press. https://www.degruyterbrill.com/document/doi/10.1525/9780520325760/html?lang=en&srsltid=AfmBOopJsQIZeEzX9THK4xzrCJJcL4I76v2XjuB3MUDfPQOFJVeZICzT

Tsiboe, F., Zereyesus, Y. A., & Osei, E. (2016). Non-farm work, food poverty, and nutrient availability in northern Ghana. *Journal of Rural Studies, 47*, 97–107. https://doi.org/10.1016/j.jrurstud.2016.07.024

United Nations. (2015). *Transforming our world: The 2030 agenda for sustainable development*. General Assembly 70 session. https://docs.un.org/en/A/RES/70/1

United Nations. (2021). *The Sustainable Development Goals report 2021*. United Nations. https://unstats.un.org/sdgs/report/2021/

United Nations Educational, Scientific and Cultural Organization [UNESCO]. (2010). *Reaching the marginalized: EFA Global Monitoring Report 2010*. Paris: UNESCO. Retrieved from https://unesdoc.unesco.org/ark:/48223/pf0000186606

United Nations International Children's Emergency Fund [UNICEF]. (2022). *The state of learning poverty: 2022 update*. United Nations Children's Fund. New York: UNICEF. https://www.unicef.org/media/122921/file/StateofLearningPoverty2022.pdf

Ura, K., Alkire, S., Zangmo, T., & Wangdi, K. (2012). *An extensive analysis of GNH index*. Centre for Bhutan Studies. https://assets.publishing.service.gov.uk/media/57a08a8be5274a27b2000651/60954_Extensive_Analysis.pdf

Vyas, S., & Kumaranayake, L. (2006). Constructing socio-economic status indices: How to use principal components analysis. *Health Policy and Planning, 21*(6), 459–468. https://academic.oup.com/heapol/article/21/6/459/612115

Walker, R. (2014). *The shame of poverty*. Oxford University Press. https://global.oup.com/academic/product/the-shame-of-poverty-9780199684823?cc=ph&lang=en&

Walker, R., Kyomuhendo, G. B., Chase, E., Choudhry, S., Gubrium, E. K., Nicola, J. Y., Lødemel, I., Mathew, L., Mwiine, A., Pellissery, S., & Ming, Y. (2013). Poverty in global perspective: Is shame a common denominator? *Journal of Social Policy, 42*(2), 215–233. https://doi.org/10.1017/S0047279412000979

World Bank. (2015). *FAQs: Global poverty line update*. Washington, DC: World Bank. https://www.worldbank.org/en/topic/poverty/brief/global-poverty-line-faq

World Bank. (2018). *Poverty and shared prosperity 2018: Piecing together the poverty puzzle*. Washington, DC: World Bank. https://www.worldbank.org/en/publication/poverty-and-shared-prosperity-2018

World Bank. (2022). *Poverty and shared prosperity 2022: Correcting Course*. Washington, DC: World Bank. https://www.worldbank.org/en/publication/poverty-and-shared-prosperity

CHAPTER 2

Monetary Approach of Measuring Poverty

"Poverty is like punishment for a crime you didn't commit."
—ELI KHAMAROV

SUMMARY

Have you ever wondered how we can tell if someone is poor or not? This chapter will show you how researchers and governments typically measure poverty, i.e., by looking at people's money—both what they earn (their income) and what they spend (their consumption). We will explore three main steps that help us understand and measure poverty in a practical way.

1. Deciding what to measure—should we look at how much money people earn or how much they spend? We will look at the advantages and disadvantages of measuring both income and spending, and discuss why it is sometimes tricky to get accurate measurements. We will explore why it can be challenging to measure poverty accurately, especially in developing countries where people might get their money

from many different sources—like farming their own food, running small businesses, or working occasional jobs.

2. Setting a poverty line—how much money does someone need to not be considered poor? One of the most important things we will learn is how to set a "poverty line"—that is the amount of money that separates people who are considered poor from those who are not. The main way we do this is by figuring out how much money someone needs to buy enough food and other basic necessities: this is called "cost-of-basic-needs" method. We will see why prices need to be adjusted for different areas—after all, living in a city usually costs more than living in a rural area.
3. Summarizing poverty data—how do we turn data into useful summaries that describe poverty? We will also learn about three common ways to count and understand poverty in a population, viz.: (a) the poverty rate (or headcount index)—what percentage of people are poor?; (b) the poverty gap—how far below the poverty line are poor people?; (c) the squared poverty gap—are there many people who are very poor, or are most people just slightly poor.

Throughout the chapter, we will use real examples from developing countries like Lao PDR and the Philippines to understand these concepts better. Throughout the chapter, we will also address important practical challenges, such as how to account for different family sizes (since a family of five naturally has different needs and spending from a single person for maintaining the same standard of living). Another challenge is understanding how resources are shared within families. Just knowing a family's total income or spending does not tell us whether everyone in the family benefits equally. In many households, for instance, men might get more resources than women and children, creating hidden poverty that basic measurements might miss.

We will also learn how to compare poverty between different countries—which is not as simple as it sounds because $100 can buy different amounts in different places. We will look at how to create "poverty profiles"—detailed pictures of who is poor, where they live, and what makes them poor. Calculations for many examples in this chapter are shown with statistical software such as R and Stata in the Annex.

2.1. Introduction

Think about what it means to be poor. For most people, the first thing that comes to mind is not having enough money—not having enough to buy food, pay rent, or cover basic needs. This simple but powerful idea is why the most common way to measure poverty is by looking at how much money people have (their income) or spend (their consumption). We say someone is poor when they fall below what we call the "poverty line"—a minimum amount of money needed to meet basic needs. This way of measuring poverty is used by governments and organizations worldwide because it is relatively straightforward and allows us to compare poverty across different places and times (World Bank, 2015).

When we measure poverty using money, we need to follow three key steps:

(1) First, we need to **choose what to measure**. For example, in a farming community, looking at what families spend might tell us more than looking at what they earn, since they might grow much of their own food.
(2) Second, we need to **set a poverty line**. This is not just picking a random number—we need to calculate how much money someone needs for basic food, shelter, and other necessities in their specific area.
(3) Finally, we need to **turn our data into useful summary poverty measures** that describe the overall poverty conditions.

Let us look at a simple example (which we will use throughout this chapter) to understand how measuring poverty works in real life. Imagine a small community with just five households. Their monthly incomes are \$700, \$300, \$400, \$200, and \$800. Now, let us say we have decided that any household with monthly income below \$500 is poor. Using this definition, we can easily spot which households are poor (the ones earning \$300, \$400, and \$200), and we can also figure out how poor they are by seeing how far they fall below our \$500 line. This simple calculation only scratches the surface of poverty measurement. Each step requires careful consideration of various methodological choices and assumptions, which can significantly impact the resulting poverty estimates. This chapter will explore these steps in detail, examining the advantages and limitations of different approaches and providing practical examples and exercises using R and Stata (in the Annex) and data from household surveys in developing countries.

Let us see how this works in developing countries. National statistics offices (NSOs) often pay special attention to what families actually consume—both what they buy and what they produce themselves (rather than what families earn). Why? Because many people in these countries work informal jobs or grow their own food, making it hard to measure their income accurately. A farmer's income might look low on paper, but if they grow most of their own food, they might be living better than their income suggests.

2.2. Choosing a Monetary Welfare Indicator

The first big question we need to answer when measuring poverty is: should we look at how much money people earn, or how much they spend? This might seem like a simple choice, but it makes a big difference in how we understand poverty.

Think about two different families. The first family has regular jobs with steady paychecks, making it easy to measure their income. The second family runs a small farm, sometimes selling crops at the market, sometimes eating what they grow—how do we measure their "income"? This is why the choice between measuring income or consumption (spending) is so important.

While our opening example used income in measuring poverty among five households for simplicity, there are several options available as a welfare indicator, each with its own strengths and limitations. The two most common indicators of welfare are based on income and consumption. Beyond these monetary measures, non-monetary indicators like educational attainment, housing conditions, or access to basic services can also be used. In this chapter, we examine each approach in detail.

2.2.1. *Using income to measure poverty*

When we use income to measure poverty, we are asking a basic but important question: "Does this person or family earn enough money to meet their basic needs?" But measuring income is not as simple as it might sound. Think about all the different ways a family might get money throughout the year. This might include income from regular jobs (like a monthly salary), small businesses or farming, renting out property, remittances sent by family members working abroad (or in other areas within the country), government support payments, and interest from savings (Haughton and Khandker, 2009; UNSD, 2005). Let us look at an example in Box 2.1, which shows something important: most families often get money from many different places. To understand if they are poor, we need to add up all these sources of income. But there is another challenge: we also need to think about how many people this money needs to support. After all, 19,500 Philippine pesos might be enough for a family of three but not for a family of ten.

Suppose that the data in Box 2.1 are just one of several data compiled in a comma separated value file called "ph_fies_sample.csv". Regardless of the statistical software application used (say, R or Stata), we can examine such data:

Box 2.1. Sources of Income in a Filipino Family

Imagine a family participating in a household survey in the Philippines (and that income data are collected in this survey), and suppose that here is how they get their money throughout the year:

- Salary from formal job: 120,000 pesos/year
- Income from small *sari-sari* store: 36,000 pesos/year
- Remittances from a daughter working abroad: 60,000 pesos/year
- Government conditional cash transfer: 18,000 pesos/year

Total income: 234,000 pesos/year

- With R

```
library(dplyr)
# Load Philippines FIES sample data
phfies <- read.csv("ph_fies_sample.csv")

# Calculate total household income
phfies <- phfies %>%
  mutate(total_income = salary + business_income +
  remittances + govt_transfers,
       income_per_capita = total_income /
       household_size)

# Basic income statistics
summary_stats <- phfies %>%
  summarize(
    mean_income = mean(income_per_capita),
    median_income = median(income_per_capita),
    sd_income = sd(income_per_capita)
)
```

- With Stata

```
* Stata code example
use "ph_fies_sample.dta", clear

* Calculate total household income
egen total_income = rowtotal(salary business income
remittances govt_transfers)
gen income_per_capita = total_income /
household_size
```

When we measure poverty using income, we are asking a seemingly simple question: does a person or family earn enough money to meet their basic needs? To figure this out, the typical data source for income data is household surveys where families are asked about all the money they receive—from jobs, businesses, rent from properties, money sent by relatives (remittances), and government aid. Then we compare this total income to a "poverty line"—the amount of money needed to afford basic necessities.

Often, rather than using total household income, the welfare indicator used is per capita income, i.e., total income divided by the household size, although to communicate poverty lines, NSOs represent poverty lines for a family of five and in monthly terms. Returning to our example of five households with monthly incomes of $700, $300, $400, $200, and $800, we can see how income provides a straightforward way to assess poverty. Income represents the resources available to a household and directly determines their purchasing power.

While there are several ways a family might get money in a year, measuring income is not as straightforward as it might seem. Let us look at the advantages and disadvantages of using income to measure poverty (Table 2.1).

Using a poverty line of $500 per month, we might conclude that two households in the example we considered (i.e., those earning $300 and $400) are poor. However, this simple comparison of total household income can be misleading because it does not account for

Table 2.1. Advantages and disadvantages of income-based measures

Advantages	Limitations
✓ **Fairly easy to collect**—Just need to ask about main sources of income. ✓ **Helps understand impact of government policies**—Shows how taxes and benefits affect different families (Atkinson, 1987).	✗ **Can be hard to get accurate numbers**—Especially in rural areas where many people farm or have irregular jobs (Deaton, 1997). ✗ **Income goes up and down**—A farmer might earn most money during harvest but very little the rest of the year (Morduch, 1994). ✗ **Misses other resources**—Does not capture how families use savings or borrow money when income is low, called consumption smoothing (Deaton, 1997). ✗ **Might miss informal earnings**—Hard to track income from casual work or small trading.

household size. Suppose that we also know this information for each household:

- Household earning $700/month: 2 people
- Household earning $300/month: 6 people
- Household earning $400/month: 5 people
- Household earning $200/month: 1 person
- Household earning $800/month: 3 people

Now, let us calculate how much money each person has by dividing the household's total income by the number of people (we call this "per capita income"):

- First household: $700 ÷ 2 = $350 per person
- Second household: $300 ÷ 6 = $50 per person
- Third household: $400 ÷ 5 = $80 per person

- Fourth household: \$200 ÷ 1 = \$200 per person
- Fifth household: \$800 ÷ 3 = \$267 per person

This changes our understanding completely! If we set our poverty line at \$100 per person per month, we get a very different picture of who is poor. The household earning \$200 total, which seemed poor before, actually has enough money per person (\$200). Meanwhile, the household earning \$300, which did not seem as bad, is actually quite poor when we consider they only have \$50 per person.

Let us look at how different countries handle this challenge in poverty measurement:

<u>Example 1</u>: In the United States, they take an interesting three-step approach to measuring poverty. The Census Bureau starts by calculating the cost of a basic food diet. Then they multiply this by three, assuming families typically spend about one-third of their money on food. Finally—and this is important—they adjust this amount based on how many people are in the family and how old they are (Dalaker, 2022). This helps account for the fact that a teenage athlete might need more food than a toddler. ∇

<u>Example 2</u>: Asian countries often take different approaches that fit their local situations better. China, Malaysia, and the Philippines use income to measure poverty, but they do it differently. In Malaysia, they have a sophisticated calculator that sets different (income) poverty lines for different types of families. China adjusts poverty lines between urban and rural areas to account for different living costs. The Philippines look at how much income a family needs across urban and rural areas in about 80 different provinces, recognizing that living costs can be very different between big cities and rural areas. ∇

These different approaches in Examples 1 and 2 show us something important: there is no one "right way" to measure poverty. Each country needs to consider its own unique situation, like how people earn money and how living costs vary across different areas.

To understand why income can be tricky to measure, let us note how farmers' income changes dramatically throughout the year, making it hard to determine if they're really poor based on income alone. That's why many poverty measurements, including those done by governments in developing countries, specifically NSOs, involve what families spend rather than what they earn, which we'll discuss next. But before we discuss this, we also point out that the welfare indicator used is often per capita income and not total household income.

If we were to visit these five households (with monthly incomes of $700, $300, $400, $200, and $800) the following year, we might find significantly different income levels. The household earning $700 might face temporary unemployment and earn only $400, while the household previously earning $300 might find better employment and earn $600. This illustrates one of the key limitations of income-based measures: income can fluctuate significantly over short periods, making it an unstable indicator of long-term economic well-being. Furthermore, in developing countries with large informal sectors, income is often irregular and undocumented, making it difficult to measure accurately.

2.2.2. Looking at what people spend: Consumption-based measures

Let us think about measuring poverty in a different way. Instead of asking "How much money do you earn?," we could ask "How much do you spend?" This simple change can tell us a lot more about how people actually live.

Here is why this matters. Imagine two families who both earn $300 per month:

- The first family might actually spend $400 by using savings or getting help from relatives.
- The second family might only spend $200 and save the rest.

Which family is better off? Looking only at income ($300) would not tell us the whole story.

In many developing countries, NSOs focus particularly on what families actually consume—including both what they buy and what they produce themselves—to get an accurate picture of poverty (Deaton and Zaidi, 2002; Mancini and Vecchi, 2022) rather than what they earn. Why? Because measuring consumption often works better than measuring income in these countries, where many people farm their own food or work informal jobs. This is why understanding both the theory and practical challenges of poverty measurement is so important.

When measuring consumption, NSOs typically track several categories of spending:

- Food (both bought and home-grown)
- Housing (rent or estimated value if they own their home)
- Basic utilities (electricity, water, fuel)
- Healthcare and education costs
- Transportation
- Other essential needs

To gather these data, NSOs visit families and ask them detailed questions about everything they buy and use, including food they grow themselves for personal use (and here, assigning market-equivalent values to these items). Let us look at the advantages and challenges of measuring consumption (Table 2.2).

When collecting data on consumption in rural areas, NSOs need to be especially careful. Here is why: many rural families do not buy all their food—they might grow vegetables in their garden, raise chickens for eggs, or gather food from nearby forests. If NSOs only collected data on what families bought with money, we might think that these families were much poorer than they really are.

Let us imagine two families with the same monthly income of $400:

- Family A lives in the city:
  - Buys all their food from markets
  - Pays rent for their apartment
  - Has to pay for transportation to work

- Family B lives in a rural area:
  - Grows half of their food
  - Owns their small house
  - Walks to most places

Even though both families have the same income, Family B might be living better because they spend less on food and housing. This shows why looking at consumption patterns, not just income, gives us a more complete picture of poverty.

To get accurate data about household consumption in a sample survey, NSOs typically visit families multiple times. They also ask detailed questions about what they buy and grow, keep track of seasonal changes in food production, and consider how long different items last (like refrigerators versus food).

Table 2.2. Advantages and disadvantages of consumption-based measures

Advantages	Limitations
✓ **More stable**—Does not change as much month to month as income does and is less prone to underreporting than income (Ravallion, 1998).	✗ **Takes longer to collect data**—Need to ask about many different types of spending (Deaton and Grosh, 2000).
✓ **Shows real living standards**—Captures how families actually live, including using savings or help from others (Deaton, 1997; Deaton and Zaidi, 2002; Mancini and Vecchi, 2022).	✗ **People might forget**—Hard to remember everything bought in past months (Beegle et al., 2012).
✓ **Includes home-produced food**—Counts food families grow themselves.	✗ **Some items last long**—Hard to value things like houses or cars that are used for many years.
✓ **More accurate in rural areas**—Better at capturing farmer and informal worker welfare.	✗ **Costs more**—Surveys take longer and need more trained staff.
	✗ **Survey questions can change poverty estimates**—The way we ask questions in household surveys, including the choice of recall period and the level of aggregation of consumption items, can significantly change our poverty estimates (Deaton and Kozel, 2005).

Example 3: The World Bank helps us understand global poverty by setting what they call an "international poverty line" (see Ferreira et al., 2016). Think of this as a worldwide standard for measuring extreme poverty. Currently, this line is set at $3.00 per person per day in 2021 purchasing power parity (PPP)[1] prices. But how did they come up with this threshold?

Here is how the World Bank did it:

- First, they looked at how the world's poorest countries measure poverty.
- They noticed that most of these countries look at consumption rather than income.
- They converted all these local poverty lines into US dollars.
- They chose $3.00 (originally $1 in 1991 PPP prices) because that is about what the poorest countries considered the minimum needed to not be poor.

The World Bank also uses other poverty lines:

- $4.20 per day (in 2021 PPP prices) for lower-middle-income countries
- $8.30 per day (in 2021 PPP prices) for upper-middle-income countries

These different lines help us understand poverty in countries at different stages of development. After all, what counts as "poor" in a very

[1] Purchasing power parity (PPP) adjusts the nominal exchange rate (e.g., the market rate) between two currencies to account for differences in price levels of tradeable goods between countries. Unlike the nominal exchange rate, which reflects prices of both tradeable (e.g., electronics) and non-tradeable goods (e.g., haircuts), PPP focuses solely on tradeable goods. This ensures that a given amount of one currency, such as Philippine pesos, can buy the same basket of tradeable goods either directly or when converted to another currency, like US dollars, using the PPP-adjusted exchange rate.

low-income country might be different from what counts as "poor" in a high-income country. ∇

2.2.3. Non-monetary welfare indicators

Money is not everything when it comes to measuring poverty. Sometimes we need to look at other important aspects of people's lives. Let us see what this means:

Think about two families:

- Family A has a decent income but their children cannot go to school.
- Family B has a lower income but all their children are in school and they have good housing.

Which family is better off? Looking only at money alone would not tell us the whole story.

Education poverty is particularly important. International organizations have developed specific thresholds to measure this form of poverty. UNESCO (2010) and ADB (2014)

- Look at people aged 15 and over
- Consider someone "education poor" if they have less than four years of schooling
- Call it "extreme education poverty" if someone has less than two years of schooling

Why these numbers? Because four years is usually the minimum needed to learn basic reading and math skills. Many countries now look at multiple aspects of poverty, including education levels of household members, health status of members, housing quality, access to clean water and electricity, and food security. For example, Indonesia's NSO, BPS Statistics Indonesia, has developed special scores that combine all these factors. This helps BPS Statistics Indonesia identify poor households that might need government help, even if their income is not too low. This multidimensional approach recognizes that poverty manifests in various ways beyond just limited income or consumption. For example, a household might have adequate income but lack access to education or healthcare, significantly impacting their overall well-being.

2.2.4. Which works better: Income or consumption or non-monetary indicators?

So which way of measuring poverty is best? The answer is: it depends on what we are trying to understand and where we are measuring poverty. The choice between income, consumption, and non-monetary welfare indicators depends on several factors, including data availability, measurement accuracy, and policy objectives. In our example of five households, using per capita income identified two households as poor (those with monthly per capita incomes of $50 and $80, falling below the $100 poverty line). However, examining their consumption patterns might reveal a different picture—the household with six members and $50 per capita income might actually consume $75 worth of goods per person by drawing on savings or receiving assistance from relatives. Similarly, looking at education levels might show that all household members in the poorest household have completed secondary education, suggesting better long-term prospects than their current income indicates.

A global survey conducted by the United Nations Statistical Division in 2004–2005 revealed diverse practices in welfare measurement across countries (UNSD, 2005). Of 84 responding countries, about half look at consumption/spending (including Cambodia, Laos, Thailand, and Vietnam), about 30 percent look at income (including China, Malaysia, and the Philippines), and about 12 percent use both methods. Why such different choices? Each country has its reasons. Countries with lots of farmers often choose consumption measures. Countries with more formal jobs might use income measures. Some richer countries look at both to get a complete picture.

Here is why these choices matter for policy: when governments want to help poor people, they often need to decide how much money to give them. For instance, if governments plan to give $30 per person to poor families,

- They need to know exactly who is poor.
- They need to know how many people are in each poor family.
- They need to calculate how much money this will cost in total.

While other measures of poverty (like education or health) are important, having monetary poverty measures helps governments plan these kinds of direct assistance programs.

When we measure poverty, especially monetary poverty, in developing countries, we can look at either income or consumption (spending). While both approaches can work, most poverty analysts prefer looking at consumption, especially in poorer countries (Box 2.2). The first reason is that what people spend tends to stay more stable than what they earn (Deaton, 1997). Think about a farmer's family—they might earn most of their money during harvest season, but they find ways to spread this money throughout the year by saving, borrowing, or getting help from relatives. By looking at their spending instead of income, we get a better picture of how they actually live throughout the year. Let us demonstrate this with data:

Another important reason is that consumption measures capture many things that income measures miss (Haughton and Khandker, 2009). In developing countries, many people work in informal jobs, grow their own food, or receive help from family and friends in the form of food or other goods. Income measures often miss these important parts of how people live, but consumption measures capture all of these. For example, if a family grows rice for their own use, this will not show up as income, but we can count it when measuring their consumption.

A third advantage is that consumption measures give us more reliable poverty estimates (Ravallion, 1998). When we use income, small

Box 2.2. Why Consumption Is Often Better Than Income for Measuring Poverty in Developing Countries

Consumption data are often preferred over income for measuring poverty in developing countries due to several practical and conceptual reasons. Firstly, income goes up and down—a farmer might earn most of their yearly income during one harvest season, but they need to eat all year round. Secondly, in developing countries, many people work informal jobs—it is hard to track income when people work occasional jobs or run small businesses with no records (Haughton and Khandker, 2009; UNSD, 2005).

On the other hand, people tend to remember better what they buy—families can usually remember their recent purchases better than their various sources of income (Deaton, 1997). Furthermore, consumption tells us more—looking at spending shows us how families manage through both good and bad times, using savings or help from others when needed. This makes it a better proxy for long-term well-being, particularly in contexts where income fluctuates widely.

By focusing on consumption rather than income, researchers and policymakers can gain a more accurate understanding of poverty dynamics, which is essential for designing effective poverty alleviation programs and policies.

Sources:

Deaton, A. (1997). *The Analysis of Household Surveys: A Microeconometric Approach to Development Policy.* World Bank Publications.

Haughton, J., and Khandker, S. R. (2009). *Handbook on Poverty and Inequality.* World Bank Publications.

United Nations Statistics Division (UNSD). 2005. Handbook on Poverty Statistics: Concepts, Methods, and Policy Use. United Nations Statistics Division.

changes in where we set the poverty line can lead to big changes in who we count as poor. But with consumption, these estimates are more stable. This is especially important when governments are deciding who should receive help from poverty programs. Let us see this with real numbers:

Even though consumption usually works better, sometimes looking at income makes more sense. Income measures are particularly useful when we want to understand how government policies affect different groups of people. For example, if we want to know whether poor families benefit from tax changes or government aid programs, we need to look at their income (rather than their spending). Income measures can also help us understand how families move in and out of poverty over time.

The decision to use income or consumption (or both) really depends on what we are trying to understand and what data we can actually collect. In high-income countries with formal economies, income often works well. But in developing countries where many people farm or work informal jobs, consumption usually gives us a better picture. The best approach is often to collect both types of data when possible. This gives us a more complete understanding of poverty and helps us check our findings. As Nobel laureate Angus Deaton put it, "Using both income and consumption is like looking at poverty through two different lenses—each shows us something important that the other might miss" (Deaton, 1997).

Finally, we need to keep working on better ways to collect both income and consumption data, especially in developing countries. Current methods are not perfect—people might forget some expenses, be reluctant to share income information, or have trouble estimating irregular earnings. Some countries collect consumption data through both recall and diary methods. When diary and recall methods show similar results, we can be more confident in our poverty measurements.

2.3. How Much Money Does Someone Need to Not Be Poor?

Once we have decided whether to measure income or spending, we face another big question: how much money does someone need to not be considered poor? This amount is called the poverty line.

As Ravallion (1998) explains, there are two main ways to set this line:

- **Absolute poverty lines**: based on the cost of basic needs—like food, housing, and clothing
- **Relative poverty lines**: based on how much money other people in the society have

Each approach tells us something different about poverty.

Let us use our five households to understand this better. Remember their monthly per person incomes:

- First household: $350
- Second household: $50
- Third household: $80
- Fourth household: $200
- Fifth household: $267

If we set our poverty line at $100 per person per month, we need to ask

- How did we choose this number?
- Should it be the same everywhere in the country?
- How often should we change it?

These questions show why setting poverty lines is not as simple as picking a number.

2.3.1. Setting fixed poverty lines: The absolute approach

When we set absolute poverty lines, we are asking a practical question: "How much money does someone need to afford the basics of life?" The most common way to answer this is called the cost-of-basic-needs (CBN) method. Here is how this method works:

Let us say we want to set a poverty line of $100 per person per month. We might break it down like this:

- $70 for enough food to provide 2,100 calories per day
- $30 for other basic needs (housing, clothing, etc.)

But here is where it gets interesting: what if someone lives in a city where food costs 20 percent more? Their poverty line would need to be different:

- Food cost: $70 × 1.20 = $84
- Other needs: $30
- Total poverty line: $114

While absolute poverty lines are meant to be fixed in real terms (to be able to see if "reductions" are made in poverty conditions with a fixed metric), requiring only regular price adjustments to maintain their purchasing power, many developing countries review their poverty measurement methods every 10 years or so. Why? Because what counts as "basic needs" changes over time. Think about mobile phones—20 years ago, they were luxury items, but today, they might be essential for finding work or accessing services.

Cost-of-basic-needs (CBN) method

As was mentioned earlier, the CBN method is the most common way of determining the poverty line; it starts by considering food needs. Let us see how countries, particularly NSOs, actually figure out their poverty lines in practice. They usually start with food, following these steps:

1) Work with nutrition experts to determine daily calorie needs—most countries use 2,100 calories as the standard amount needed per person each day.
2) Create a food basket that matches local eating habits—different countries use different approaches:
   - Philippines: uses a one-day food menu[2] (rather than a food basket) created and developed by the Food and Nutrition Research Institute (FNRI), featuring lots of rice
   - African countries: might focus more on maize or cassava
   - Mountain countries (like Nepal, Bhutan, and Afghanistan): might increase calories because people need more energy in cold climates

Once we know how much the basic food basket costs, we need to add non-food necessities. Ravallion (1998) explains that people need more than just food to live—they need shelter, clothing, and basic healthcare. There are two main ways to figure out how much to add for these non-food needs. The first way is to look at how much poor people typically spend on non-food items when they can just barely afford their basic food needs. The second way is to directly calculate the cost of essential non-food items. In practice, most countries use the first approach because it is simpler and reflects local spending patterns.

Regional differences in prices make this calculation more complex. Something that costs 100,000 kip in Vientiane Capital might cost only 80,000 kip in a rural area in Lao PDR.

The way we set poverty lines can have big effects on who gets counted as poor and who does not. For instance, in China, we can see how sensitive these calculations are to different assumptions about what counts as "basic needs". Different provinces might have different needs—people in cooler areas might need to spend more on warm clothing and heating, while those in urban areas might need to spend more on transportation.

[2] The food menus in the Philippines are set to be satisfying roughly 2,000 calories of energy per day, aside from various recommended energy nutrient intake (RENI).

To make these ideas more concrete, let us look at how an actual poverty line is calculated in practice. The first step focuses on food needs. While we know people need about 2,100 calories per day (based on World Health Organization recommendations), we cannot just use any combination of foods that provides these calories. Instead, we look at what poor people in each area actually eat and create a food basket based on these local preferences. For example, in the Philippines, the food basket includes more rice and fish, while in India, it might include more lentils and wheat (Haughton and Khandker, 2009).

As Ravallion and Bidani (1994) explain, researchers typically look at a reference population, say what the poorest 20 percent of people eat when creating this food basket. This makes sense because these families have to be very careful with their money, so they tend to choose the most economical foods that fit their tastes and traditions.

In the next example, we work through details of how a food poverty line is calculated.

Example 4: In computing the food component of a poverty line, first, we observe typical daily consumption patterns of households in a reference population, say those in the bottom 30 percent of the population from food consumption expenditures data:

(1) Rice: 300 grams = 1,050 calories
(2) Vegetables: 100 grams = 35 calories
(3) Fish: 100 grams = 100 calories
(4) Meat: 50 grams = 150 calories
(5) Fruits: 50 grams = 25 calories
Total: 1,360 calories

Since this only provides 1,360 calories, and we need 2,100, we multiply everything by 1.54 (2,100 ÷ 1,360). Then we calculate the cost:

- Rice: 462 grams × \$0.50/kg = \$0.23
- Vegetables: 154 grams × \$1/kg = \$0.15

- Fish: 154 grams × \$3/kg = \$0.46
- Meat: 77 grams × \$4/kg = \$0.31
- Fruits: 77 grams × \$2/kg = \$0.15

The total comes to \$1.30 per day or approximately \$40 per month for the food poverty line. This represents the minimum cost to achieve the required caloric intake while respecting local dietary preferences. ∇

After figuring out the food part of poverty lines, we need to add non-food basics. There are two main ways to do this:

1. **The direct method:** Make a list of essential non-food items. Find out how much they cost. Add up all these costs. For example, given the following: basic housing, \$15 per month; utilities (water, electricity), \$5 per month; clothing, \$3 per month; transportation, \$5 per month; healthcare, \$5 per month; total non-food needs, \$33 per month.
2. **The indirect method:** Look at families who spend about \$40 (our food poverty line) on food. See what percentage of their total spending goes to food, referred to as Engle's coefficient. If these families typically spend 60 percent of their money on food, we can calculate the following: Total poverty line = Food poverty line ÷ 0.60 \$40 ÷ 0.60 = \$66.67 total poverty line. This means they spend about \$26.67 on non-food items.

Example 5: In Lao PDR, the official poverty lines are first calculated using the CBN method to determine how much it costs to get 2,100 calories per day using the average food consumption patterns of a reference group, i.e., the 20th to 50th percentiles (see Box 2.3). The non-food component was estimated using the indirect method by dividing the food poverty line by the food share of total expenditure for the reference group, resulting in a total poverty line of 280,000 kip per person per month in 2018/2019 (Lao Statistics Bureau and World Bank, Poverty Profile in Lao PDR 2020; Pimhidzai et al., 2014). ∇

Box 2.3. How Lao PDR Sets Its Poverty Line

Lao PDR's approach to setting its national poverty line offers a step-by-step methodology that balances technical rigor with contextual relevance. The process begins with calculating the cost of meeting basic food needs, typically defined as 2,100 calories per person per day. This food basket reflects the dietary patterns of the local population, ensuring that the calculation is grounded in actual consumption habits. For example, rice, a staple in Lao PDR, forms a significant part of this basket, alongside vegetables, fish, and other locally consumed items.

Once the food poverty line is established, an allowance is made for non-food essentials such as housing, clothing, and healthcare. Lao PDR employs an indirect approach to estimate this component by observing the spending patterns of households near the food poverty line. This ensures that the non-food allowance reflects actual behavior and local conditions.

Regional price differences pose another challenge in setting a poverty line. Lao PDR addresses this by using spatial price indices, which adjust the poverty line to account for variations in the cost of living across different provinces. For instance, the cost of food and other essentials might be higher in urban centers like Vientiane Capital compared to rural areas. By incorporating these adjustments, the poverty line maintains its relevance and comparability across diverse geographic regions.

This systematic methodology, detailed in the Lao PDR Poverty Profile Report, highlights the importance of tailoring poverty measurement tools to the specific socioeconomic and geographic context of a country. It also underscores the need for regular updates to poverty lines to reflect changes in prices, consumption patterns, and living standards over time.

Sources:

Pimhidzai, O., Fenton, N. C., Souksavath, P., and Sisoulath, V. (2014). Poverty Profile in Lao PDR: Poverty Report for the Lao Consumption and Expenditure Survey, 2012–2013. World Bank.

World Bank (2022). Poverty and Equity Briefs for Lao PDR.

Most countries prefer the indirect method because it is simpler to calculate. Furthermore, it reflects what poor families actually spend. It automatically adjusts to local conditions. But both direct and indirect methods have their limitations.

Setting poverty lines is not perfect—there are several challenges faced with the CBN method:

- **The food (and non-food) basket challenge**. Different experts might choose different foods (and non-foods) for the basic basket, and the basket may not accurately reflect the actual consumption patterns of the poor (Ravallion and Bidani, 1994). For example, should we include more expensive proteins like meat? Should we stick to cheaper options like beans? What if people's food preferences vary by region? If we had used the bottom 20 percent instead of the bottom 30 percent of households to observe typical food consumption patterns, we might have gotten different results because these groups might have different dietary preferences.
- **The calorie problem**. Not everyone needs the same amount of calories (Haughton and Khandker, 2009). A teenage athlete needs more food than a toddler. Pregnant women have different nutritional needs. People doing heavy physical work need more calories. In Chapter 4, we discuss a way to address these inequalities of needs of household members by way of the notion of assignable goods.
- **The family size issue**. Bigger families might need less money per person for some things. Think about housing: a family of two needs one kitchen, but a family of six also needs just one kitchen. So the cost per person is lower in the larger family. This is referred to as economies of scale.
- **Regional differences**. Prices and lifestyles can be very different in different places. Rice might cost $0.50/kg in rural areas but $0.75/kg in cities. City dwellers might need to pay for transportation. Rural families might need different tools or equipment. These price variations, combined with different consumption patterns

across regions, make it challenging to maintain consistency in poverty measurement while reflecting local conditions.

- **Issues on indirect method.** The indirect method of estimating the non-food component assumes that the food share of total expenditure is a good proxy for the share of basic non-food needs, which may not always be the case (Ravallion, 1998). In our example, we assumed that households spending $40 on food typically spend 40 percent of their budget on non-food items. However, this proportion might vary significantly based on household composition, location, and other factors. Urban households might spend more on transportation while rural households walk more, suggesting the non-food component should differ between urban and rural areas.

To address some of these limitations, many countries now use multiple poverty lines that vary by region and household type. They might also conduct periodic reviews of their poverty measurement methodology to ensure it remains relevant as consumption patterns change with economic development. Furthermore, as will be discussed in Chapter 4, we can also develop individual poverty lines using the household model and the notion of assignable goods. Despite its limitations, the CBN method remains the most widely used approach for setting absolute (national) poverty lines in developing countries because it provides a clear and intuitive link between poverty measurement and the actual cost of meeting basic needs.

Food-energy-intake (FEI) method

There is another way to set absolute poverty lines called the food-energy-intake method. Instead of pricing a food basket, this method asks: "How much money do people typically need to get enough calories?"

According to Ravallion (1998), this method identifies the income or expenditure level at which the expected caloric intake is just sufficient to meet a predetermined food energy requirement. In other words, here is how it works:

(1) Collect data about
- How much money different families have
- How many calories they typically consume

(2) Look for patterns, like
- Do families with more money eat more calories?
- How much money do families need to get 2,100 calories?

Example 6: Let us understand the FEI method using data from our example households:

- Household 1 (per capita values): income, \$350/month; caloric intake, 2,400 calories/day
- Household 2 (per capita values): income, \$50/month; caloric intake, 1,600 calories/day
- Household 3 (per capita values): income, \$80/month; caloric intake, 1,800 calories/day
- Household 4 (per capita values): income, \$267/month; caloric intake, 2,200 calories/day
- Household 5 (per capita values): income, \$200/month; caloric intake, 2,300 calories/day

Using regression analysis, we can estimate the relationship between income and caloric intake. If we find that each additional \$100 of monthly income is associated with an increase of 300 calories in daily intake, we can solve for the income level that would yield our target of 2,100 calories. This becomes our poverty line. ∇

The FEI method thus involves three key steps:

1. **Data collection and analysis**: First, we gather data on both income/expenditure and caloric intake for a sample of households. In our example, we might survey more households in the community to get a larger sample, asking about their food consumption and converting this into calories using food composition tables.
2. **Statistical estimation**: We then estimate the relationship between income and caloric intake (with regression analysis). If we find

the relationship is Calories = 1,500 + 3(Income), then to achieve 2,100 calories, we would need: 2,100 = 1,500 + 3(Income). Solving this equation gives us a poverty line of $200 per month.

3. **Setting the poverty line**: The income level that corresponds to the minimum caloric requirement (typically 2,100 calories per day) becomes the poverty line.

However, the FEI method has several significant limitations. First, it does not explicitly account for non-food needs, which may lead to an underestimation of the poverty line (Ravallion and Bidani, 1994). For instance, in our example, a household might achieve 2,100 calories at $200 per month but have nothing left for housing, clothing, or other essential needs. By focusing solely on the relationship between caloric intake and income or consumption, the FEI method overlooks the importance of other essential needs, such as shelter, clothing, healthcare, and education. Consequently, poverty lines derived using this method may not reflect the true cost of achieving a minimum standard of living, particularly in contexts where non-food costs are a significant proportion of total household expenditure.

Second, the relationship between caloric intake and income can be influenced by factors other than poverty, such as tastes, preferences, and cultural norms (Deaton and Grosh, 2000). For instance, urban households in our sample might choose more expensive but less calorie-dense foods as their income increases, while rural households might maintain traditional, more calorie-dense diets even at higher income levels. These factors can introduce noise into the estimation of the poverty line, making it less accurate in capturing the true level of deprivation.

Third, the method is sensitive to the choice of functional form in the regression analysis and the treatment of outliers (Ravallion, 1998). The functional form, such as linear, quadratic, or logarithmic, can significantly impact the estimated relationship between caloric intake and income or consumption. If we had used a logarithmic relationship instead of a linear one in our example, we might have gotten a different poverty line: Calories = 1,200 + 300*log(Income) This would yield a different solution and thus a different poverty line. Different functional forms may lead to different poverty line estimates, even when using the same data. Similarly, the presence of outliers, such as households with unusually high or low caloric intakes relative to their income or consumption, can distort the regression results and affect the derived poverty line.

These limitations have led most countries to prefer the CBN method despite its own challenges. To mitigate the limitations of the FEI method, researchers have proposed various modifications and extensions. For example, some studies have included non-food components in the estimation by using a broader definition of basic needs or by applying a fixed ratio of non-food to food expenditure (Wodon, 1997). Others have used more flexible functional forms, such as non-parametric regression techniques, to better capture the relationship between caloric intake and income or consumption (Ravallion and Bidani, 1994).

Despite these efforts, the limitations of the FEI method underscore the importance of using multiple approaches and considering context-specific factors when setting poverty lines. Combining insights from different methods, such as the FEI and the CBN approaches, can help to provide a more comprehensive and robust assessment of poverty. Additionally, sensitivity analyses should be conducted to examine the impact of different methodological choices on poverty estimates and to ensure that the derived poverty lines are consistent with other indicators of well-being.

In conclusion, while the FEI method offers a unique perspective on poverty measurement, its limitations should be carefully considered when applying this approach. Researchers and policymakers should be aware of the potential biases and uncertainties associated with the FEI method and interpret the resulting poverty estimates with caution. By understanding and addressing these limitations, analysts can make more informed decisions when using the FEI method and contribute to a more nuanced understanding of poverty and its determinants.

2.3.2. Relative poverty lines

While absolute poverty lines focus on basic needs, relative poverty lines work differently—they look at how much money people have compared to others in their society. Think about it this way: being "poor" in a rich country might mean something different than being "poor" in a developing country. Relative poverty lines try to capture this difference.

Relative poverty lines are based on the overall distribution of income or consumption in a society. Here is how they usually work:

- Find the middle income in a country (called the median).
- Set the poverty line as a percentage of this middle income.
- Usually, it is around 50 or 60 percent of the median.

Relative poverty lines are useful for assessing inequality and social exclusion, as they capture the extent to which individuals or households are able to participate in the normal activities of their society (Atkinson, 1987).

Example 7: In the European Union, they say you are "at-risk-of poverty" if you earn less than 60 percent of what the typical person in your country earns. That is, the relative poverty line is 60 percent of the national median equivalized disposable income (Eurostat, 2021). This relative poverty line is used to monitor poverty and social exclusion across EU member states.

Let us see how this works with our five families:

- Their incomes per person: \$350, \$50, \$80, \$267, and \$200.
- The middle income (median) is \$200.
- If we set the poverty line at 60 percent of this (\$120).
- Now, three families are considered poor (those earning \$50, \$80, and \$200).

This relative approach shows us something different from our absolute poverty line of $100. It helps us understand who might be struggling to maintain a normal lifestyle in their society, even if they can afford basic necessities.∇

Advantages of using relative poverty lines for middle and high-income countries

The relative poverty line works especially well in richer countries because it adjusts automatically as countries get richer, reflecting the reality that what constitutes poverty changes with rising living standards. What counted as "normal" 20 years ago might be considered poor today. For example, having Internet access was once a luxury; now, it is often necessary for work and school. Furthermore, it helps identify social exclusion. While a household earning $120 per month might have enough for food and basic shelter, they might not have enough to participate in normal social activities, such as using mobile phones or having Internet access. As Sen (1983) argues, the ability to participate in community life without shame is an important aspect of welfare that relative poverty lines help capture.

Limitations of relative poverty lines

One significant limitation of relative poverty lines is that they do not reflect the absolute standard of living and may not capture the extent of deprivation in poor countries, and thus comparison of relative poverty rates across time is not useful (Ravallion, 1998). In low-income countries, the bigger concern is often: "Do people have enough for basic needs?" or "Can they afford food and shelter?" In these countries where a large proportion of the population may live below an absolute poverty line, relative poverty lines can fail to identify the true magnitude of poverty. For example, if a country has a very low median income, even those identified as non-poor by a relative poverty line may still experience significant deprivation in terms of their ability to meet basic needs. In such cases, relative poverty lines may not provide an accurate picture of the actual living conditions of the poor and may underestimate the urgency of poverty alleviation efforts.

Moreover, something strange can happen when a country grows rapidly: everyone might be getting richer, but if some people's incomes grow faster than others, the relative poverty line might actually increase and a larger proportion of the population may fall below it (Sen, 1983). This can occur even if the absolute living standards of the poor have improved. If all incomes in our example doubled, the relative poverty line would also double to $240, and the same three households would still be considered poor despite their absolute living standards having improved substantially. Conversely, think about what happens during an economic crisis: if everyone's income falls, the poverty line also falls. People might be worse off than before, but relative poverty might not show this. Consequently, relative poverty measures may not always accurately reflect changes in the actual well-being of the poor over time. This paradoxical situations arise because relative poverty lines are tied to the income or consumption distribution rather than an absolute standard.

Another limitation of relative poverty lines is that they can be influenced by social and cultural norms, which may vary across countries and over time. The perception of what constitutes an acceptable standard of living can differ significantly between societies, depending on factors such as economic development, social expectations, and cultural values. This can make comparisons of relative poverty rates across countries or time periods challenging, as the underlying benchmarks may not be consistent.

Another challenge comes from applying relative poverty lines in highly unequal societies or during periods of significant economic transition. If our example community included several very high-income households earning thousands of dollars per month, the median income would rise substantially, potentially classifying as poor households that can meet their basic needs adequately. This sensitivity to income distribution makes relative poverty lines less suitable for developing countries where meeting basic needs remains a primary concern.

Despite these limitations, relative poverty lines remain a valuable tool for understanding poverty and inequality within a society. They provide insights into the extent of relative deprivation and social exclusion, which can have significant impacts on individual well-being and social cohesion. Relative poverty measures can also be useful for guiding policies aimed at reducing inequality and promoting inclusive growth.

To mitigate the limitations of relative poverty lines, researchers and policymakers should use them in combination with other poverty measures, such as absolute poverty lines and multidimensional poverty indicators. This approach can provide a more comprehensive understanding of poverty and its various dimensions. Additionally, when using relative poverty lines, it is important to consider the specific context and interpret the results in light of other relevant economic and social indicators.

In conclusion, while relative poverty lines have their limitations, they remain an important component of poverty analysis. By understanding and acknowledging these limitations, researchers and policymakers can use relative poverty measures more effectively, in conjunction with other approaches, to gain a deeper understanding of poverty and inequality. This understanding can inform the design and implementation of policies and programs aimed at reducing poverty and promoting inclusive development. The choice between absolute and relative poverty lines often reflects different conceptions of poverty and different stages of economic development. Many countries, particularly middle-income ones, now use both types of lines to capture different aspects of poverty. They might maintain an absolute poverty line to track progress in meeting basic needs while also monitoring relative poverty to understand social inclusion and inequality. The World Bank's adoption of different international poverty lines for countries at different income levels ($3.00, $4.20, and $8.30 per day) represents a hybrid approach that acknowledges how poverty standards evolve with development.

2.3.3. Adjusting poverty lines for differences in needs and prices

One size does not fit all when it comes to poverty lines. Different families have different needs, and prices vary from place to place. These differences matter tremendously when we are trying to understand who is truly poor.

Adjusting for household size and composition

Until now, we have discussed poverty measurement in simple terms, dividing a family's total income by the number of people. However, real life is more complex. Consider two families who each have $1,000 per month—one with two adults and another with two adults and two children. At first glance, we might say the first family has $500 per person while the second has $250 per person. But this simple calculation overlooks some important realities about how families live.

First, many household expenses do not double or triple with more family members. A family of four does not need four kitchens or four living rooms. They can share one Internet connection and one television. Economists call these "economies of scale" in household consumption (Deaton and Zaidi, 2002; Mancini and Vecchi, 2022). Second, different family members have different needs. Young children typically need less food than adults, while teenagers might need more. Elderly family members might have special healthcare needs that increase household expenses.

<u>Example 8</u>: The "OECD-modified scale" assigns a weight of 1 to the first adult in a household, 0.5 to each additional adult, and 0.3 to each child (under 14 years of age) (OECD, 2011). A household with two adults and two children would have an equivalence scale of 2.1 (1 + 0.5 + 0.3 + 0.3). ∇

Applying this OECD scale to our example households dramatically changes their effective per capita incomes:

Household 1: Monthly income $700 (2 adults)

- Equivalence scale = 1.5 (1.0 + 0.5)
- Adjusted per capita income = $467 (up from $350)

Household 2: Monthly income $300 (2 adults, 4 children)

- Equivalence scale = 2.7 (1.0 + 0.5 + 4×0.3)
- Adjusted per capita income = $111 (up from $50)

Household 3: Monthly income $400 (2 adults, 3 children)

- Equivalence scale = 2.4 (1.0 + 0.5 + 3×0.3)
- Adjusted per capita income = $167 (up from $80)

Household 4: Monthly income $800 (1 adult, 2 children)

- Equivalence scale = 1.6 (1.0 + 2×0.3)
- Adjusted per capita income = $500 (up from $267)

Household 5: Monthly income $600 (2 adults, 1 elderly)

- Equivalence scale = 2.0 (1.0 + 2×0.5)
- Adjusted per capita income = $300 (up from $200)

These adjustments highlight the limitations of simple per capita measures. While our original per capita calculations suggested Household 2 was the poorest by far, the equivalence scale adjustment shows them closer to Household 3 in terms of living standards. Similarly, Household 4, which appeared moderately well off in per capita terms, looks considerably better-off after accounting for household composition.

Different countries adapt these scales to their local contexts. Some might give more weight to elderly family members or adjust for other factors like disability status. For example, Indonesia's poverty measurement system uses different caloric requirements for different age and gender groups, effectively creating an implicit equivalence scale through their poverty line calculations. The key idea is to recognize that family needs do not increase in direct proportion to family size, and different family members have different needs.

The choice of equivalence scale can significantly affect poverty measurements and the targeting of social programs. Using our example, if we set the poverty line at $150 in equivalence-adjusted terms, Households 2 and 3 would be considered poor, while using unadjusted per capita income with a $100 poverty line would also classify these households as poor but suggest much deeper poverty. These differences can have important implications for policy design and the allocation of social assistance.

Adjusting for regional price differences

Another crucial factor in setting poverty lines is recognizing that the same amount of money buys different amounts in different places. Living costs can vary dramatically between cities and rural areas, or even between different regions of the same country. This means we need to adjust our poverty lines (using "spatial price indices") to reflect these price differences (Deaton and Zaidi, 2002; Mancini and Vecchi, 2022).

Consider what happens in most countries: city dwellers typically face higher prices for housing and food than people living in rural areas. A family earning $500 per month in a rural area might live quite comfortably, while the same amount in a big city might barely cover basic needs. This is not just about housing—everything from food to transportation often costs more in urban areas.

<u>Example 9:</u> Lao PDR provides a good illustration of how countries handle these regional differences. Their NSO, the Lao Statistics Bureau, adjusts poverty lines for different parts of the country using what

economists call regional price indices based on the Laspeyres formula (Pimhidzai et al., 2014). They look at the cost of a typical basket of goods and services in each region, then adjust the poverty line accordingly. So if food and housing cost 20 percent more in the capital city compared to rural areas, the urban poverty line would be set 20 percent higher. ∇

This adjustment process requires careful attention to local conditions. Researchers must consider not just price differences but also variations in consumption patterns. Urban families might need to spend money on transportation to work, while rural families might walk or ride a bicycle. Rural families might grow some of their own food, while urban families buy everything from markets. Some goods available in cities might not even exist in rural areas, making direct price comparisons impossible.

The differences can be substantial. In many developing countries, urban poverty lines might be 20–30 percent higher than rural ones. This does not mean urban families are given an advantage; rather, it recognizes that they need more money to maintain the same standard of living. Without these adjustments, we might either overestimate poverty in rural areas or underestimate it in urban areas.

Beyond simple urban–rural differences, many countries also consider regional variations. For instance, mountainous areas might need higher poverty lines because transportation costs make everything more expensive, while coastal areas might have different costs for food due to easy access to fish but higher prices for other goods. Some countries even adjust poverty lines for each state or province, recognizing that living costs can vary significantly across their territory.

2.3.4. Poverty measurement over time

When we track poverty over time, we need to consider two important things: how prices change and how people's needs change. Let us follow our five households over a five-year period to understand these challenges. Suppose we start with their initial monthly equivalence-adjusted incomes from our previous discussion: $467, $111, $167, $500, and $300, and track how their economic situations and the poverty line change over time.

Inflation presents the first major challenge in comparing poverty over time. If prices rise by 5 percent each year, our initial poverty line of $150 would need to increase to about $191 after five years just to maintain the same purchasing power. NSOs use Consumer Price Index (CPI) data to make these adjustments. However, this apparently straightforward adjustment faces several complications.

Poor households often experience inflation differently from the general population. Why? Because they spend their money differently. If food prices rise faster than general inflation, poor families suffer more because they typically spend a larger share of their money on food.

Beyond simple price adjustments, we need to consider how consumption patterns change over time. What counts as a "basic need" is not fixed. Twenty years ago, having a mobile phone was a luxury. Today, it might be essential for finding work or accessing services. This suggests that poverty lines might need periodic revisions beyond simple inflation adjustments.

Household composition also changes over time, affecting our measurements. In our example, the children in Households 2, 3, and 4 are five years older. Teenagers typically need more food than young children, effectively increasing these families' needs. Similarly, the elderly member in Household 5 might require more healthcare as they age, changing their family's necessary expenses.

Changes in relative prices between regions can further complicate temporal poverty measurement. If urban housing costs rise faster than rural prices, the spatial price adjustments discussed earlier might need regular updates. For instance, if Household 1 in the urban capital city faces rapidly rising housing costs while Household 2 in the rural area experiences more stable prices, maintaining comparability across both space and time becomes increasingly challenging.

2.4. Summarizing Poverty Data

After establishing our welfare indicators and poverty lines, we need ways to summarize how many people are poor and how severe their poverty is. Different measures tell us different things about poverty, and each has its strengths and limitations. Let us use our five households one more time to understand these measures, using their Year 5 monthly incomes after adjusting for family size: \$600, \$150, \$220, \$580, and \$400, with our poverty line at \$191.

2.4.1. *Headcount index (poverty incidence)*

The simplest and most widely used measure is the poverty headcount ratio, often called the poverty rate or poverty incidence (P_0). This measure simply calculates what percentage of people live below the poverty line. It is popular because it is easy to understand and explain. The headcount index can be readily calculated using data from household surveys or censuses, and it provides a clear and straightforward assessment of the extent of poverty in a given population. It is calculated as follows:

$$P_0 = N_p / N$$

where N_p is the number of poor individuals or households, and N is the total population.

In our example of five households, Household 2 (\$150) falls below the poverty line of \$191, while Household 3 (\$220) has recently escaped poverty. This means our headcount ratio is 1/5 or 20 percent—one out of five households is poor.

In both the Sustainable Development Goals (SDGs) and its predecessor Global Goals Agenda, the Millennium Development Goals, the first indicator monitored is the poverty headcount index (using the international poverty line for measuring extreme poverty). For the SDGs, poverty rates using national poverty lines are also monitored.

Table 2.3 provides a comparative analysis of national poverty thresholds and corresponding poverty headcount ratios for selected Asian countries.

Table 2.3. Comparison of poverty lines and rates across selected Asian countries (2018–2023)

Country	National Poverty Line (Local Currency per Day)	Poverty Headcount Ratio (%)	Survey Year
Bangladesh	114.00 BDT (Constant 2016 terms)	20.5	2019
Bangladesh	114.00 BDT (Constant 2016 terms)	18.7	2022
China	8.8 CNY (Constant 2010 terms)	0.0	2020
India	32.00 INR (Rural), 47.00 INR (Urban) (Constant 2011 terms)	21.9	2019
Indonesia	11,000.00 IDR (Constant 2012 terms)	9.4	2019
Indonesia	11,000.00 IDR (Constant 2012 terms)	9.8	2020
Indonesia	11,000.00 IDR (Constant 2012 terms)	10.1	2021
Indonesia	11,000.00 IDR (Constant 2012 terms)	9.5	2022
Indonesia	11,000.00 IDR (Constant 2012 terms)	9.4	2023
Philippines	71.50 PHP (Constant 2012 terms)	16.7	2018
Philippines	71.50 PHP (Constant 2012 terms)	18.1	2021
Philippines	71.50 PHP (Constant 2012 terms)	15.5	2023
Viet Nam	4,800 VND (Constant 2010 terms)	5.7	2019
Viet Nam	4,800 VND (Constant 2010 terms)	4.8	2020
Viet Nam	4,800 VND (Constant 2010 terms)	4.4	2021
Viet Nam	4,800 VND (Constant 2010 terms)	4.3	2022

Sources: (i) World Bank Poverty and Equity Briefs (2018–2023). Available at: World Bank Poverty Data. (ii) United Nations Sustainable Development Goals (SDG) Database (2018–2023). Available at: UN SDG Database. (iii) National Statistical Offices (NSOs) of Bangladesh, China, India, Indonesia, the Philippines, and Viet Nam.

The table outlines poverty lines expressed in local currencies per day, adjusted to constant terms with specified base years to ensure comparability across time. Additionally, it includes poverty headcount ratios, reflecting the proportion of the population living below the defined poverty thresholds during the surveyed years. The table spans data from 2018 to 2023, offering insights into poverty trends and reductions over the period (and thus suggests how the COVID-19 pandemic affected poverty trends, mostly reversing the gains in poverty reduction prior to the onset of the virus). In Bangladesh, the poverty rate dropped from 20.5 percent in 2019 to 18.7 percent in 2022, meaning fewer people were living below their national poverty line. Meanwhile, Indonesia maintained relatively stable poverty rates of around 9–10 percent during 2019–2023, showing how some countries manage to keep poverty levels steady even during difficult times. By highlighting the variation in national poverty lines and rates, the table underscores the diversity in methodologies used across countries, influenced by factors such as local prices, consumption patterns, and purchasing power. It serves as a valuable resource for understanding how different countries define and measure poverty, illustrating the challenges of cross-country comparisons and the importance of using context-sensitive metrics.

Despite its widespread use and acceptance, the headcount index has an important limitation: it treats all poor people the same regardless of how far they fall below the poverty line. For instance, our household earning $150 is counted the same way as if they earned only $50, even though the second situation would clearly be much worse. Thus, it fails to capture the depth or severity of poverty among those living below the poverty line (Sen, 1976). This is why we need additional ways to measure poverty.

This limitation can lead to an incomplete or even misleading picture of poverty, as it does not distinguish between those who are barely poor and those who are severely deprived. For example, consider two hypothetical countries with the same headcount poverty rate of 30 percent. In country A, most of the poor are clustered just below the poverty line, while in country B, a significant proportion of the poor are far below the poverty line. The headcount index would treat these two countries as having the same level of poverty, even though the poor in country B are experiencing much more severe deprivation.

Furthermore, the headcount index is insensitive to changes in the distribution of income or consumption among the poor (Sen, 1976). This means that if a poor household becomes even poorer, or if income or consumption is redistributed from a poorer household to a less poor household, the headcount index will not reflect these changes. This can be problematic when assessing the effectiveness of poverty reduction policies or programs, as improvements in the living conditions of the poorest of the poor may not be captured by the headcount index.

To illustrate this point, consider a scenario where a poverty reduction program targets the poorest households and succeeds in raising their income or consumption levels, but not enough to lift them above the poverty line. The headcount index would not register any improvement, even though the program has made a meaningful difference in the lives of the poorest. Conversely, if a program were to focus on those closest to the poverty line and manage to lift them just above it, the headcount index would show a reduction in poverty, even though the conditions of the poorest households may not have changed.

Given these limitations, it is important to use the headcount index in conjunction with other poverty measures that capture the depth and severity of poverty, such as the poverty gap index and the squared poverty gap index. These measures take into account the distance between the income or consumption levels of the poor and the poverty line, providing a more nuanced understanding of the poverty situation.

Moreover, it is crucial to complement the headcount index with other indicators of well-being, such as measures of access to education, health, and basic services. This can help policymakers and researchers gain a more comprehensive understanding of the multidimensional nature of poverty and inform the design of more effective and targeted interventions.

In conclusion, while the headcount index is a simple and widely used measure of poverty, its limitations should be carefully considered when interpreting its results. By using the headcount index in combination with other poverty measures and indicators of well-being, policymakers and researchers can gain a more accurate and comprehensive understanding of poverty, enabling them to design and implement more effective policies and programs to support those in need.

Example 10: Data from the Lao Expenditure and Consumption Survey (LECS) show a significant decline in poverty in Lao PDR, with the poverty headcount rate dropping from 24.6 percent in 2012/2013 to 18.3 percent in 2018/2019. The reduction was more pronounced in rural areas, where poverty decreased by 7.6 percentage points compared to a mere 0.9 percentage point reduction in urban areas.

Disparities remain, however: 9 in 10 persons continue to reside in rural areas, though rural poverty has reduced much more than in urban areas. Furthermore, regions like the North and South are experiencing more rapid poverty reduction than the Central region. The

Table 2.4. Trends in poverty in Lao PDR (2013–2019)

Region	Poverty Headcount Rate (%)		Change (Percentage Points)	Distribution of Poor (%)		Distribution of Population (%)	
	2013	2019		2013	2019	2013	2019
Lao PDR	24.6	18.3	−6.3	100.0	100.0	100.0	100.0
Urban	7.9	7.0	−0.9	9.2	12.4	28.8	32.5
Rural	31.4	23.8	−7.6	90.8	87.6	71.2	67.5
North	31.0	20.7	−10.3	38.6	35.5	30.6	31.4
Central	23.5	21.5	−2.0	34.0	41.9	35.8	35.7
South	29.9	17.7	−12.2	26.2	19.0	21.6	21.6

Source: Lao Statistics Bureau and World Bank, Poverty Profile in Lao PDR 2020.

findings underscore the challenges of addressing geographic and socioeconomic inequalities in poverty reduction efforts (Source: Lao Statistics Bureau and World Bank, Poverty Profile Report 2020). ∇

2.4.2. Poverty gap index (depth of poverty)

The poverty gap index (P_1) goes beyond simply counting who is poor—it measures how poor people are. Think of it as measuring the distance between poor people's income and the poverty line. The formula works like this:

$$P_1 = (1/N)\sum_{i=1}^{N_p}\left(\frac{z - y_i}{z}\right)$$

where z is the poverty line, y_i is the income (or consumption) of the i-th poor individual or household, and N_p and N are defined as before.

Let us see how this works with our example. Looking at Household 2, which earns \$150 with a poverty line of \$191:

- The gap is \$191 – \$150 = \$41.
- As a percentage of the poverty line: \$41/\$191 = 0.214 or 21.4 percent.
- Since only one of our five households is poor, we divide this by 5.
- Our poverty gap index is 0.214/5 = 0.043 or 4.3 percent.

This 4.3 percent tells us something important—it shows not just that we have poverty but also how deep that poverty is. If we had multiple poor households with different incomes, the poverty gap would tell us whether poverty was shallow (many households just below the line) or deep (many households far below the line).

Example 11: In Lao PDR, we can see how this works in practice. Their poverty gap index fell from 5.5 percent in 2012/2013 to 3.9 percent in 2018/2019. This tells us not only that fewer people were poor but also that those who remained poor were, on average, closer to escaping poverty. ∇

The poverty gap measure is particularly useful for policymakers because it helps them understand how much money might be needed to eliminate poverty through direct assistance. For instance, if we wanted to bring Household 2 up to the poverty line through direct aid, we would know that they need $41 per month. This kind of calculation helps governments plan their poverty reduction programs.

One of the main strengths of the poverty gap index is its ability to capture the extent to which the poor fall below the poverty line. Unlike the headcount index, which simply counts the number of people below the poverty line, the poverty gap index measures the average shortfall of the poor from the poverty line, expressed as a percentage of the poverty line (Ravallion, 1998). This means that the poverty gap index is sensitive to changes in the income or consumption levels of the poor, even if these changes do not necessarily lift them above the poverty line.

This feature of the poverty gap index makes it particularly useful for estimating the minimum cost of eliminating poverty through targeted transfers (Ravallion, 1998). By calculating the average poverty gap, policymakers can determine the amount of resources needed to raise the income or consumption levels of the poor to the poverty line. This information can be valuable in designing and implementing poverty reduction programs, as it helps to ensure that resources are allocated efficiently and effectively to those who need them most.

Consider a country with a poverty line of $2 per day and an average poverty gap of 20 percent. This means that, on average, the poor have an income or consumption level that is 20 percent below the poverty line, or $1.60 per day. To eliminate poverty in this country, policymakers would need to transfer an average of $0.40 per day to each poor person, bringing their income or consumption level up to the poverty line. By using the poverty gap index to estimate the minimum cost of poverty elimination, policymakers can better plan and allocate resources for poverty reduction efforts.

However, while the poverty gap index offers several advantages over the headcount index, it also has some limitations. One notable limitation is that it does not capture the severity or depth of poverty, as it gives equal weight to all income or consumption shortfalls, regardless of their size (Sen, 1976). This means that the poverty gap index does not distinguish between a situation where many individuals are marginally below the poverty line and one where a smaller number of individuals are far below the poverty line.

To illustrate this point, consider two countries with the same poverty gap index of 20 percent. In country A, most of the poor are clustered just below the poverty line, with an average shortfall of 10 percent. In country B, a significant proportion of the poor are far below the poverty line, with an average shortfall of 30 percent. Although both countries have the same poverty gap index, the severity of poverty is clearly higher in country B. However, the poverty gap index does not reflect this difference, as it gives equal weight to all poverty gaps, regardless of their size.

To address this limitation, researchers have proposed the use of the squared poverty gap index, which gives greater weight to larger poverty gaps, thereby capturing the severity of poverty (Foster, Greer, and Thorbecke, 1984). The squared poverty gap index is calculated by taking the square of each individual poverty gap before averaging them, thus placing a higher emphasis on the poorest of the poor.

In conclusion, the poverty gap index is a valuable tool for measuring the depth of poverty and estimating the minimum cost of poverty elimination through targeted transfers. However, its limitations in capturing the severity of poverty should be considered when interpreting its results. By using the poverty gap index in conjunction with other poverty measures, such as the squared poverty gap index and the headcount index, policymakers and researchers can gain a more comprehensive understanding of the poverty situation and design more effective interventions to support those in need.

2.4.3. *Squared poverty gap index (severity of poverty)*

The squared poverty gap index (P_2), also called the poverty severity index, takes our measurement one step further. While the poverty gap tells us how far people are from the poverty line, the squared poverty gap gives extra weight to those who are furthest below the line. The formula is similar to the poverty gap, but we square the differences:

$$P_2 = (1/N)\sum_{i=1}^{N_p}\left(\frac{z - y_i}{z}\right)^2$$

where the terms are defined as before, i.e., z is the poverty line, y_i is each poor person's income, and N is the total population.

The squared poverty gap index is an extension of the poverty gap index. It takes the concept of the poverty gap index further by giving more weight to those furthest below the poverty line. It squares each poverty gap before averaging, making larger gaps count more heavily. For our example household, the squared gap would be $(0.214)^2 = 0.046$, and the average for all five households would be 0.046/5 = 0.009 or 0.9 percent.

This number might seem less intuitive than our previous measures, but it tells us something important. By squaring the gaps, we are saying that being very poor is more than twice as bad as being just a little poor. This matches how most people think about poverty—falling $10 below the poverty line is not twice as bad as falling $5 below; it might be four times as bad.

Example 12: Looking at Lao PDR again, the LSB and the World Bank have reported that the squared poverty gap index fell from 1.9 percent in 2012/2013 to 1.3 percent in 2018/2019. This smaller number compared to the regular poverty gap (which was 3.9 percent) is normal—we are looking at squared percentages. The decline tells us that not only did overall poverty decrease but also the situation of the very poorest people improved (Source: Lao Statistics Bureau and World Bank, Poverty Profile Report 2020). ∇

This measure is particularly useful when policymakers want to focus on helping the poorest of the poor. While the headcount tells us who is poor and the poverty gap tells us how poor they are on average, the squared poverty gap draws special attention to those in the most severe poverty.

One of the main advantages of the squared poverty gap index is its ability to capture the severity of poverty by giving greater weight to larger poverty gaps. This is achieved by squaring the poverty gaps before averaging them, which places a higher emphasis on the poorest of the poor. By doing so, the squared poverty gap index is sensitive to changes in the distribution of income or consumption among the poor (Foster, Greer, and Thorbecke, 1984). This means that if income or consumption is redistributed from a poorer household to a less poor household, the squared poverty gap index will reflect this change, even if the overall poverty gap remains the same.

Consider two countries with the same poverty gap index of 20 percent. In country A, most of the poor are clustered just below the poverty line, with an average shortfall of 10 percent. In country B, a significant proportion of the poor are far below the poverty line, with an average shortfall of 30 percent. While the poverty gap index would treat these two countries as having the same level of poverty, the squared poverty gap index would show a higher value for country B, reflecting the greater severity of poverty in that country.

The sensitivity of the squared poverty gap index to changes in the distribution of income or consumption among the poor makes it a valuable tool for evaluating the effectiveness of poverty reduction policies and programs. By monitoring changes in the squared poverty gap index over time, policymakers can assess whether their interventions are not only reducing the overall level of poverty but also improving the conditions of the poorest of the poor.

However, despite its advantages, the squared poverty gap index has some limitations that should be considered. One notable limitation is that it is less intuitive and harder to interpret than the headcount index or the poverty gap index (Haughton and Khandker, 2009). The squared poverty gap index is expressed as a percentage of the poverty line squared, which can be difficult to communicate to non-technical audiences. This complexity can limit its use in policy discussions and public debates, where simpler measures like the headcount index are often preferred.

Another limitation of the squared poverty gap index is that it is rarely used in policy discussions due to its complexity (Haughton and Khandker, 2009). While the index provides valuable insights into the severity of poverty, its technical nature can make it less accessible to policymakers and the general public. This can lead to a situation where the insights provided by the squared poverty gap index are overlooked in favor of simpler, more widely understood measures.

To address these limitations, it is important to use the squared poverty gap index in conjunction with other poverty measures, such as the headcount index and the poverty gap index, when analyzing poverty and communicating the results to policymakers and the public. By presenting a range of poverty measures, researchers can provide a more comprehensive picture of the poverty situation and ensure that the insights provided by the squared poverty gap index are not lost in the complexity of the measure.

In conclusion, the squared poverty gap index is a valuable tool for capturing the severity of poverty and monitoring changes in the distribution of income or consumption among the poor. However, its complexity and limited use in policy discussions should be considered when using the index for poverty analysis. By using the squared poverty gap index in combination with other poverty measures and presenting the results in an accessible manner, researchers can ensure that the valuable insights provided by this measure are effectively communicated to policymakers and the public, ultimately contributing to the design and implementation of more effective poverty reduction policies and programs.

2.4.4. Foster–Greer–Thorbecke (FGT) class of poverty measures

All three poverty summary measures we have discussed thus far—the headcount index, the poverty gap index, and the squared poverty gap index—are actually part of a single family of measures called the Foster–Greer–Thorbecke (FGT) measures (Foster, Greer, and Thorbecke, 1984). Think of them as different members of the same family, each telling us something slightly different about poverty.

The general formula for all FGT measures is

$$P_\alpha = (1/N)\sum_{i=1}^{N_p}\left(\frac{z-y_i}{z}\right)^\alpha$$

where α is a non-negative parameter that determines the sensitivity of the measure to the distribution of income or consumption among the poor.

The value of α determines which measure we get:

- When $\alpha = 0$, we get the headcount index (P_0).
- When $\alpha = 1$, we get the poverty gap index (P_1).
- When $\alpha = 2$, we get the squared poverty gap index (P_2).

Let us see how this works with our Household 2 (the only poor household in our example). Its gap from the poverty line is (191 – 150)/191 = 0.214 (proportional shortfall). Averaging over all five households gives us our three poverty measures:

- Headcount ratio (P_0) = 1/5 = 0.200 or 20 percent
- Poverty gap index (P_1) = 0.214/5 = 0.043 or 4.3 percent
- Squared poverty gap index (P_2) = $(0.214)^2/5$ = 0.009 or 0.9 percent

As α increases, the measure becomes more sensitive to larger poverty gaps. This means that the FGT measures give us increasingly detailed views of poverty—from simply counting the poor to measuring how poor they are and to emphasizing the situation of the very poorest.

This family of measures has become popular among researchers and policymakers because it provides a complete toolkit for understanding poverty. Each measure helps answer a different question about poverty in a society, from "How many poor people are there?" to "How severe is their poverty?"

2.4.5. *Properties of poverty measures*[3]

Good poverty measures should satisfy certain basic properties that align with our common-sense understanding of poverty. Let us explore these properties using our five households (with Year 5 monthly incomes of \$600, \$150, \$220, \$580, and \$400, and poverty line of \$191) to understand why these properties matter.

The focus axiom

This property says that poverty measures should only care about poor people's incomes, not what happens to people above the poverty line. For example, if Household 1's income increased from \$600 to \$800, or if Household 4's income decreased from \$580 to \$400 (but stayed above the poverty line), our poverty measures should not change. This makes sense—if we are measuring poverty rather than general inequality, we should not care about changes among non-poor people as long as they stay non-poor.

The monotonicity axiom

This property requires that poverty measures should show higher poverty when a poor person's income falls. Imagine if Household 2's income dropped from \$150 to \$120:

[3] This subsection is advanced material; novices to poverty diagnostics may want to initially skip reading this.

- The headcount ratio would stay at 0.2 (violating this property).
- The poverty gap would increase from 0.043 to 0.075.
- The squared poverty gap would increase from 0.009 to 0.028.

This shows why we need measures beyond the simple headcount—they help us recognize when poor people become poorer, not just how many poor people there are.

The transfer axiom

Also called the Pigou–Dalton principle, this property says that transferring money from a poorer to a richer person should increase measured poverty. Suppose Household 2 (our only poor household) gave $30 to Household 3. Their incomes would become $120 and $250, respectively:

- The headcount ratio would stay at 0.2.
- The poverty gap would show the same total shortfall.
- But the squared poverty gap would increase.

This reflects the principle that a given shortfall matters more for those with lower incomes.

Decomposability

This useful property allows us to break down poverty measures by groups while maintaining consistency between subgroup and overall poverty levels. If we divide our five households into urban (Households 1, 4, and 5) and rural (Households 2 and 3), we can calculate poverty measures separately for each region:

- Urban (3 households):
  - Headcount ratio = 0
  - Poverty gap = 0
  - Squared gap = 0
- Rural (2 households):
  - Headcount ratio = 0.5

- Poverty gap = 0.107
- Squared gap = 0.023

The overall measures are weighted averages of these subgroup measures:

- Overall headcount = (3×0 + 2×0.5)/5 = 0.2
- Overall poverty gap = (3×0 + 2×0.107)/5 = 0.043
- Overall squared gap = (3×0 + 2×0.023)/5 = 0.009

This decomposability property is particularly valuable for policy purposes, allowing us to identify where poverty is concentrated and target interventions accordingly. In our example, we can clearly see that poverty is entirely concentrated in the rural region, suggesting where resources might be most needed.

2.4.6. Policy applications of and insights from poverty measures

Different poverty measures suggest different approaches to fighting poverty. Let us examine how our various measures might guide policy decisions using our five households to understand the practical implications of different measurement approaches.

Consider three potential poverty reduction programs, each costing the same amount but structured differently: Program A provides $41 to the poorest household (Household 2); Program B provides $20 each to Households 2 and 3; and Program C provides $10 each to Households 2, 3, 4, and 5.

The headcount ratio would favor Program A because it lifts Household 2 above the poverty line (reducing the ratio from 0.2 to 0), while Programs B and C leave the headcount unchanged at 0.2. However, if we could not afford such a large transfer, Program B might be preferable according to the poverty gap measure because it reduces the depth of poverty more effectively than spreading smaller amounts more widely under Program C.

The squared poverty gap measure provides additional insights for targeting decisions. Because it gives more weight to those furthest below the poverty line, it would strongly favor directing resources to Household 2 rather than households closer to the poverty line. If we had multiple poor households with different income levels, the squared poverty gap measure would suggest concentrating resources on the poorest first, while the simple poverty gap measure would be indifferent between equal transfers to any poor household.

These measures also help evaluate the impact of economic growth and redistribution on poverty. Suppose our community experiences economic growth that increases all incomes by 10 percent. The new incomes would be $660, $165, $242, $638, and $440. The headcount ratio would still show Household 2 as poor, but the poverty gap and squared poverty gap measures would show improvement in their situation. Alternatively, consider a redistributive policy that taxes the richest household 5 percent of their income ($30) and transfers it to the poorest. This would have a larger impact on all poverty measures than the 10 percent growth scenario.

Poverty measures also inform geographic targeting of anti-poverty programs. Our earlier decomposition showed poverty concentrated in the rural region (Households 2 and 3). However, if we further decompose by household type, we might find that single-parent households (like Household 4) or those with elderly members (like Household 5) face different risks of falling into poverty. Such decompositions help policymakers decide whether to target by geography or household composition or both.

The different FGT measures also help monitor poverty dynamics over time. If Household 2's income gradually increased from $150 to $180 over several years, the headcount ratio would not reflect this improvement until they crossed the $191 threshold. However, the poverty gap and squared poverty gap measures would show steady progress, providing a more nuanced view of poverty reduction efforts. This illustrates why many countries now report multiple poverty measures rather than relying solely on the headcount ratio.

2.5. Poverty Profiles, Decompositions, and Analysis

Poverty profiles and decomposition help us understand who is poor and how poverty varies across different groups. These tools break down poverty measures by regions, urban/rural areas, ethnicity, and other characteristics to identify which groups are most affected by poverty.

2.5.1. *Poverty profiles*

A poverty profile, typically illustrated with a table or graph, provides a detailed picture of how poverty varies across different population groups and helps identify what characteristics are associated with poverty. Using our five households, we can demonstrate how to construct and interpret poverty profiles, though real-world applications would use much larger samples.

It can be used to compare poverty levels across regions, urban and rural areas, or other relevant categories. Poverty profiles can also include information on the characteristics of the poor, such as their demographic composition, education levels, or employment status (Haughton and Khandker, 2009). Using our five households, we can illustrate how to construct and interpret poverty profiles, keeping in mind that real-world applications would use much larger samples to ensure statistical reliability.

Let us expand our understanding of these households by adding more characteristics. Household 1 ($600) represents urban professionals with college education, Household 2 ($150) consists of rural agricultural workers with primary education, Household 3 ($220) includes rural workers with some secondary education, Household 4 ($580) is an urban single-parent household with secondary education, and Household 5 ($400) represents suburban service workers with secondary education.

A basic poverty profile by education level reveals clear patterns in our sample. Among households with only primary education, the poverty rate is 100 percent (one out of one household) compared to

0 percent for those with college education (zero out of one) and 0 percent for those with secondary education (zero out of three). While our sample is too small for reliable conclusions, this pattern often appears in larger datasets, suggesting education's crucial role in poverty reduction.

Geographic analysis of our sample shows significant urban–rural differences. The poverty rate in rural areas (one out of two households) is higher than in urban areas (zero out of two) or suburban areas (zero out of one). Moreover, even the non-poor rural household (Household 3 at $220) lives closer to the poverty line than most urban households, suggesting greater economic vulnerability in rural areas. This type of analysis often informs decisions about geographic targeting of poverty reduction programs.

Occupational patterns also emerge from our sample. Agricultural workers (represented by Households 2 and 3) show higher poverty rates and greater vulnerability than professional workers (Household 1) or service workers (Household 5). The single-parent service worker (Household 4) maintains a relatively high income, though their situation might be more precarious due to depending on a single earner. These occupational patterns help policymakers understand how labor market factors influence poverty.

Household composition adds another crucial dimension to poverty profiles. Households with more children (like Households 2 and 3) tend to show higher poverty rates in our sample, even after applying equivalence scales. This pattern, often confirmed in larger datasets, suggests the importance of family-oriented poverty reduction strategies. The presence of elderly members (as in Household 5) or single parenthood (Household 4) might also affect vulnerability to poverty through their impact on earning capacity and care responsibilities.

Dynamic analysis adds depth to poverty profiles by examining how circumstances change over time. If we followed these households over several years, we might find that Household 3's slightly above poverty-line position represents recent escape from poverty through education, while Household 5's elderly care responsibilities might increase their risk of falling into poverty. Understanding these dynamics helps design policies that not only reduce current poverty but also prevent future poverty.

Example 13: Consider the poverty profile for Lao PDR in 2018/2019. The headcount index varies significantly:

- **by region:** Vientiane Capital (3.6 percent), North (20.7 percent), Central (21.5 percent), South (17.7 percent)
- **by urban/rural areas:** Urban (7.0 percent), Rural (23.8 percent)
- **by ethnicity of household head:** Lao-Tai (12.8 percent), Mon-Khmer (38.0 percent), Hmong-Mien (32.9 percent), Chinese-Tibetan (14.5 percent)

This profile, compared to 2012 data, shows progress in reducing poverty across all groups, though significant disparities remain. Rural areas and ethnic minorities, particularly the Mon-Khmer and Hmong-Mien groups, continue to experience higher poverty rates than urban areas and the majority Lao-Tai ethnic group (Source: Lao Statistics Bureau and World Bank, Poverty Profile Report 2020).∇

Example 14: The distribution of poverty across Philippine provinces reveals an important distinction between poverty incidence rates and the actual share of poor Filipinos (Figure 2.1). While provinces with severe poverty rates of 50 percent or higher (including Lanao del Sur, Basilan, Sulu, and the highly urbanized Isabela City) as of 2018 appear to be the most impoverished areas, they actually only account for 10.4 percent of the country's total poor population. Even when combined with provinces having moderately high poverty rates of between 30 and 50 percent, these areas represent only about a third (31.6 percent) of all poor Filipinos.

In contrast, looking at the absolute numbers tells a different story—provinces with more than 500,000 poor people (such as Camarines Sur, Leyte, Negros Occidental, Maguindanao, Sulu, Cebu,

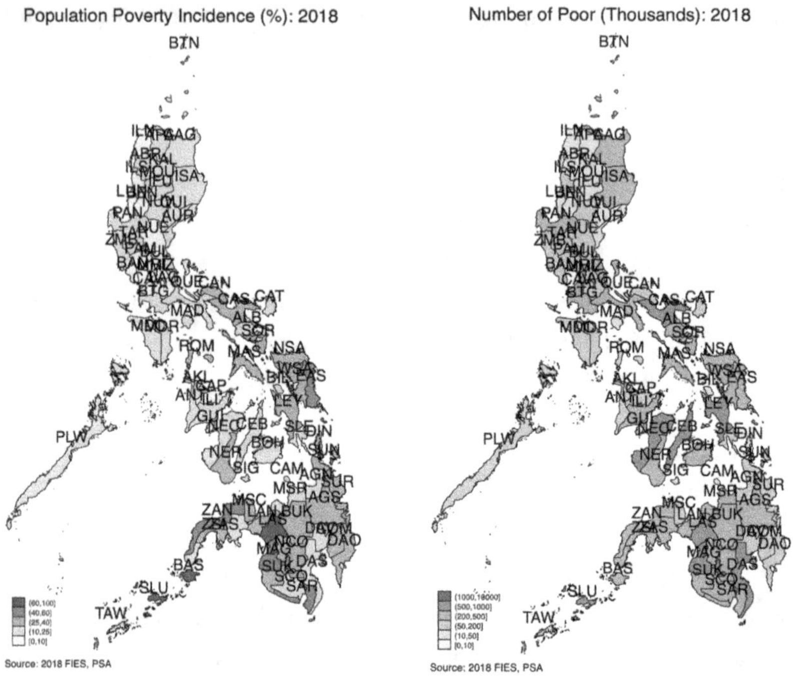

Figure 2.1. Poverty across provinces in 2018 in terms of poverty incidence (in %) and number of poor Filipinos (in thousands).

and Lanao del Sur) account for nearly a fifth (17.9 percent) of the country's poor. When these are combined with provinces having 250,000 to 500,000 poor people, they collectively represent more than half (55.3 percent) of all poor Filipinos. This stark contrast is evident in the geographic distribution—while areas like Pampanga, Laguna, Rizal, La Union, Ilocos Norte, and the National Capital Region show poverty rates below 5 percent, some of them may still have significant numbers of poor people due to their large populations. Conversely, smaller provinces like Batanes, Siquijor, Guimaras, and Camiguin have fewer than 50,000 poor people despite potentially higher poverty rates. Thus, it is important to consider both metrics when developing poverty-reduction strategies, as focusing solely on poverty incidence rates by provinces might overlook populous areas with lower rates but significant numbers of poor residents requiring assistance. ∇

As shown by Examples 13 and 14, poverty profiles can help policymakers identify the groups most in need of assistance and, consequently, design targeted interventions for these vulnerable groups to reduce poverty. This is why disaggregated data are extremely important, as they provide inputs to policy design and implementation, as well as monitoring and evaluation.

2.5.2. Poverty decomposition

Poverty decomposition involves breaking down a poverty measure into its contributing factors, such as within-group and between-group components. This can help identify the sources of poverty and how they change over time or across subgroups (Ravallion and Huppi, 1991). By breaking down poverty changes into different components, we can better identify effective poverty reduction strategies. Let us examine our five households over a longer period with data from Years 1, 5, and 10 (all adjusted for inflation to Year 1 prices):

- Year 1: Household 1 (urban professionals), $600; Household 2 (rural agricultural), $150; Household 3 (rural workers), $220; Household 4 (urban single-parent), $580; Household 5 (suburban service), $400; poverty line: $191
- Year 5: Household 1, $650 (education-driven growth); Household 2, $175 (agricultural modernization); Household 3, $280 (skills training impact); Household 4, $540 (job market challenges); Household 5, $420 (steady service sector); poverty line, $191 (real terms)
- Year 10: Household 1, $800 (career advancement); Household 2, $195 (gradual improvement); Household 3, $350 (education benefits); Household 4, $600 (recovery); Household 5, $450 (modest growth); poverty line, $191 (real terms)

This temporal comparison reveals several important patterns. First, we observe different growth trajectories across households. Household 1's income shows strong growth due to career advancement in the professional sector, while Household 2's improvement is more modest despite agricultural modernization efforts. These differential growth rates suggest that economic growth alone might not reduce poverty uniformly.

One common method of poverty decomposition, called the Datt–Ravallion decomposition (Datt and Ravallion 1992), is to separate the change in poverty over time into three components:

(1) Growth component: The change in poverty due to economic growth, holding the distribution of income or consumption constant
(2) Redistribution component: The change in poverty due to changes in the distribution of income or consumption, holding the mean income or consumption constant
(3) Residual component: The change in poverty due to the interaction between growth and redistribution

Example 15: A growth-inequality poverty decomposition for Lao PDR between 2012/2013 and 2018/2019 reveals the following:

- **Total change in headcount index:** –6.3 percentage points
- **Growth component:** –4.8 percentage points
- **Redistribution component:** –1.2 percentage points
- **Residual component:** –0.3 percentage points

This decomposition shows that economic growth was the main driver of poverty reduction in Lao PDR, though improvements in income distribution also helped reduce poverty. The small residual component suggests the decomposition captures most factors affecting poverty change (Source: Lao Statistics Bureau and World Bank, Poverty Profile Report 2020).∇

The Datt–Ravallion decomposition helps us understand how much poverty reduction comes from overall economic growth versus redistribution. In our example, between Years 1 and 10, average income grew by 33 percent for Household 1 but only 30 percent for Household 2. The poverty gap measure would show improvement primarily through growth effects (as the poorest household's income rose) rather than redistribution (as relative positions remained similar).

Spatial comparisons add another layer of complexity. If our five households lived in different regions with different price levels, we would need spatial price indices for meaningful comparison. For example, if Household 1's urban area had prices 20 percent above the national average while Household 2's rural area had prices 20 percent below, their real income gap would be even larger than nominal figures suggest. Regional poverty lines might need to reflect these price differences while maintaining equivalent living standards.

Changes in household composition over time further complicate poverty comparisons. Children in Households 2, 3, and 4 age over the decade, changing the household's needs and equivalence scales. Household 5's elderly member might require increasing healthcare expenditure, effectively reducing their disposable income despite nominal income growth. These demographic changes mean that even real income comparisons might not fully capture changes in living standards.

The choice of poverty measure affects our interpretation of these changes. The headcount ratio shows Household 2 remaining poor throughout the period, missing their gradual improvement. The poverty gap measure better captures their progress but might understate the importance of Household 3's escape from near-poverty through education. The squared poverty gap measure would show the most improvement, as Household 2's situation, though still poor, becomes less severe.

2.5.3. Policy implications of poverty profiles and diagnostics

How we measure poverty fundamentally shapes how we respond to it. Using our examination of five households over time, we can see how different measurement approaches suggest different intervention strategies.

Targeting of poverty interventions requires careful consideration of measurement methods. Using our example households, a policy based purely on the headcount ratio might focus all resources on Household 2 ($195 in Year 10), trying to push them above the poverty line of $191. However, a policy informed by the poverty gap measure might also consider preventive support for Household 3 ($350), which remains vulnerable to falling into poverty despite having escaped it. The squared poverty gap measure would prioritize more generous support for Household 2, recognizing that their deep poverty requires more substantial intervention.

The choice between absolute and relative poverty measures also has significant policy implications. Our absolute poverty line of $191 suggests focusing on Household 2, but a relative measure set at 50 percent of median income would identify additional households as needing support. If the Year 10 median income is $450, a relative poverty line of $225 would classify both Households 2 and 3 as poor, suggesting a broader scope for intervention.

Geographic considerations in poverty measurement influence regional development policies. In our example, the stark urban–rural divide between Households 1 and 4 versus 2 and 3 might suggest targeting rural infrastructure and services. However, spatial price adjustments might reveal that urban poverty, though less prevalent, requires larger transfers to achieve the same improvement in living standards due to higher urban prices.

Equivalence scales and household composition affect the design of social protection programs. The varying needs of children in

Households 2, 3, and 4 and the elderly member in Household 5 suggest that one-size-fits-all poverty thresholds or transfer amounts may be inadequate. Programs might need to adjust benefit levels based on household composition while considering economies of scale in consumption.

Temporal patterns in poverty measurement inform the balance between immediate relief and long-term poverty reduction strategies. The gradual improvement in Household 2's situation and the more substantial progress of Household 3 through education suggest complementary policy approaches: direct support for immediate needs combined with investments in human capital.

2.6. International Poverty Comparisons

Comparing poverty levels across countries helps us understand global progress in fighting poverty and identify which regions need more attention and resources. However, making these comparisons is not simple.

2.6.1. International poverty lines

While national poverty lines are important for each country's policies, comparing them directly across countries is challenging. Imagine if our five example households lived in different countries—the household earning \$200 per month might be above the poverty line in a low-income country but below it in a middle-income country. Moreover, \$200 might buy different amounts of food and other necessities in different places.

To address this challenge, the World Bank has developed international poverty lines based on the national poverty lines of the world's poorest countries. Currently, they use \$3.00 per person per day (in 2021 PPP terms) as the international poverty line for measuring extreme poverty (Foster et al., 2025).

Example 16: To understand what international poverty lines mean, let us convert our households' monthly incomes to daily PPP dollars:

- Household 1: \$350/month = \$11.67/day
- Household 2: \$50/month = \$1.67/day
- Household 3: \$80/month = \$2.67/day
- Household 4: \$267/month = \$8.90/day
- Household 5: \$200/month = \$6.67/day

Using the \$3.00 PPP poverty line, both Household 2 (\$1.67/day) and Household 3 (\$2.67/day) would be considered extremely poor globally, as both fall below the \$3.00 threshold. ∇

The international poverty line for global monitoring of extreme poverty has evolved over time to reflect changing understanding of poverty:

- 1990: \$1 per day (in 1991 PPP prices)
- 2008: Updated to \$1.25 (in 2005 PPP prices)
- 2015: Became \$1.90 (in 2011 PPP prices)
- 2022: Further updated to \$2.15 (in 2017 PPP prices)
- 2025: Now \$3.00 (in 2021 PPP prices)

The \$1 per day in 1991 PPP prices was derived from the national poverty lines of six of the poorest countries in the world at that time: Bangladesh, Indonesia, Kenya, Morocco, Nepal, and Tanzania (Ravallion, Chen, and Sangraula, 2009). The idea behind using this approach was to anchor the international poverty line to the poverty lines of the poorest countries, ensuring that it reflected the minimum standard of living necessary to meet basic needs in these contexts. Over time, the international poverty line has been updated to account for changes in the cost of living and to incorporate new data from a larger set of countries. In 2008, the international poverty line was updated to \$1.25 per day in 2005 PPP prices, based on the average poverty lines of the 15 poorest countries (Ravallion, Chen, and Sangraula, 2009).

This update allowed for a more representative poverty line that better reflected the living conditions in the poorest countries.

In 2015, the international poverty line was further updated to $1.90 per day in 2011 PPP prices using the same approach of averaging the poverty lines of the 15 poorest countries (Ferreira et al., 2016). This update not only accounted for changes in the cost of living but also incorporated new PPP data from the 2011 International Comparison Program (ICP).

Most recently, in 2025, the World Bank updated the international poverty line to $3.00 per day in 2021 PPP prices (Foster et al., 2025). This update was based on the average poverty lines of the same 15 poorest countries using the latest available PPP data from the 2021 ICP. Thus, each update maintains the same purchasing power while accounting for changes in prices around the world.

Purchasing power parity (PPP)

Purchasing power parity (PPP) helps us compare how much money is worth in different countries by looking at what it can actually buy. PPP exchange rates compare prices of goods and services across countries, expressed in a common currency (usually US dollars) (Haughton and Khandker, 2009). The key difference between PPP and regular market exchange rates is that PPP looks at both tradable and non-tradable goods. Here is what this means:

Consider the price of a haircut in two countries: the United States and India. In the United States, a haircut might cost $20, while in India, the same haircut might cost 100 Indian Rupees (INR). If we use the market exchange rate of 1 USD = 75 INR, the haircut in India would be equivalent to $1.33 (100 INR / 75). However, this comparison does not accurately reflect the purchasing power of the two currencies in their respective countries, as it does not account for the differences in the cost of living.

In contrast, PPP exchange rates take into account the prices of a broader range of goods and services, excluding non-tradables like prices of haircuts. Tradeable goods such as cost of computers are relatively the same across countries with some variations from the addition of transportation costs to these items. By using PPP exchange rates, we can better compare the real purchasing power of different currencies and more accurately assess the living standards across countries.

A popular way to understand PPP is through the "Big Mac Index", created by *The Economist* magazine. This index compares the price of a McDonald's Big Mac across different countries. Why a Big Mac? Because it is made the same way everywhere, using similar ingredients, making it a good standard for comparison. Here is how it works:

Imagine that a Big Mac costs

- $5.00 in the United States
- 150 pesos in Mexico
- 3.50 euros in France
- 21 yuan in China

Using market exchange rates might not tell us the true story about purchasing power in each country. But by comparing Big Mac prices, we can see if a currency might be overvalued or undervalued. For example, if the market exchange rate is 20 pesos = 1 USD, then the Mexican Big Mac costs $7.50 USD (150/20). This might suggest that the peso is overvalued compared to what it can actually buy locally.

While the Big Mac Index is a simplified and even somewhat humorous way to understand PPP, it helps illustrate why we need PPP calculations for poverty measurement. Just as a Big Mac's price tells us something about local costs and purchasing power, comprehensive PPP calculations look at thousands of goods and services to give us a more accurate picture of what money can buy in different countries.

When measuring poverty across countries, PPP rates play a crucial role in ensuring fair comparisons. These rates help us compare living standards meaningfully across different countries by accounting for varying price levels in different places. Importantly, PPP rates consider both tradable goods, such as computers that tend to cost similar amounts worldwide, and non-tradable goods like haircuts, whose prices can vary significantly between countries.

Multiple international poverty lines

The World Bank has developed a sophisticated system of international poverty lines to reflect the different contexts of countries at various stages of development. At the most basic level, they use $3.00 per person per day to measure extreme poverty globally. For lower-middle-income countries, such as India, Nigeria, and Pakistan, they set the line at $4.20 per day, while upper-middle-income countries use $8.30 per day as their threshold (Foster et al., 2025). The latter poverty line is based on the median poverty line of countries among the upper-middle-income group and represents a higher standard of living compared to the lower-middle-income poverty line. The $8.30 per day poverty line is used to assess poverty in countries such as Brazil, China, and South Africa, which have higher income levels but still face challenges in reducing poverty and inequality.

For high-income countries, the World Bank does not have a specific international poverty line, as poverty in these countries is often measured using relative poverty thresholds or national poverty lines. Relative poverty thresholds are typically set at a percentage of the median income in a country, such as 50 or 60 percent of the median income (Haughton and Khandker, 2009). These thresholds are used to identify individuals or households whose income falls significantly below the median income in their country, indicating a higher risk of social exclusion and reduced access to opportunities.

In addition to relative poverty thresholds, many high-income countries also use national poverty lines that are based on the cost of a basket of goods and services deemed necessary for a minimum standard of living in that specific country. These national poverty lines take into account the higher costs of living in high-income countries and are used to guide national poverty reduction policies and programs.

This tiered approach acknowledges several important realities about how poverty manifests differently across countries. As countries develop, the cost of meeting basic needs typically increases. Moreover, living costs can vary dramatically between countries at different income levels. Perhaps most importantly, what constitutes poverty itself often changes as countries become more prosperous. High-income countries generally take a different approach altogether, preferring to use their own relative poverty measures rather than these international lines. They typically set their poverty thresholds as a percentage of their country's median income, reflecting the higher living standards and expectations in more advanced economies.

By using these different poverty lines, policymakers and researchers can better assess the nature and extent of poverty in countries with different income levels and develop targeted interventions to address the specific challenges faced by the poor in each context. This approach also allows for a more comprehensive analysis of global poverty trends and the identification of areas where progress is lagging or where new challenges are emerging.

The evolution of international poverty lines reflects changing understanding of poverty measurement. The original dollar-a-day line introduced in 1990 was based on the national poverty lines of some of the poorest countries. For example, if the low-income countries in our dataset had national poverty lines around \$30–40 per month in 1990 prices, this would have informed the setting of the international line. Over time, as prices and standards of living changed, the line was updated to \$1.25 (2005 PPP), then \$1.90 (2011 PPP), then \$2.15 (2017 PPP), and now \$3.00 (2021 PPP).

However, international poverty lines face several challenges:

1. **Price differences**: Even with PPP adjustments, the same amount of money might buy different quantities of goods in different places. In our example, if Household 2's \$50 per month buys more food in a rural area than in an urban area, the international poverty line might not reflect these local differences.

2. **Quality differences**: The same goods might have different qualities across countries. A basic food basket in one country might be considered inadequate in another.
3. **Consumption patterns**: What constitutes basic needs varies across countries. While our example households might consider rice a staple food, households in other regions might rely on different staples with different costs.

2.6.2. Regional price adjustments and implementation challenges

Converting international poverty lines into meaningful national thresholds requires careful attention to both regional price differences and local consumption patterns. The process becomes particularly complex when we consider how prices and living costs vary within countries. For instance, while the national equivalent of the $3.00 PPP international poverty line might be $65 per month in a given country, this amount needs different adjustments for different areas—perhaps $78 in the capital city where costs are typically 20 percent above the national average, $71.50 in secondary cities where prices run 10 percent higher, $65 in suburban areas at the national average, $58.50 in rural towns where costs are 10 percent lower, and $52 in remote rural areas where prices might be 20 percent below average.

Let us extend our example to understand how this works. Suppose our five households live in different areas:

- Household 1 ($350/month): Urban capital city
- Household 2 ($50/month): Remote rural area
- Household 3 ($80/month): Rural town
- Household 4 ($267/month): Secondary city
- Household 5 ($200/month): Suburban area

Price variations across regions can be substantial and systematic. These challenges become evident in our example. Household 2's

$50 monthly income might buy more in their remote rural area than Household 5's $200 in the suburban area, but exactly how much more requires careful price data collection and analysis. Some goods might not even be available in the remote area, making price comparisons impossible.

In many countries, NSOs construct spatial price indices to capture these differences. A typical pattern might show the capital city's prices running 20 percent above the national average, secondary cities 10 percent above, suburban areas at the national average, rural towns 10 percent below, and remote rural areas 20 percent below. These variations mean that the $3.00 PPP international poverty line needs different local currency equivalents in each area. If we assume that the national equivalent is $65 per month, this would translate to $78 in the capital city, $71.50 in secondary cities, $65 in suburban areas, $58.50 in rural towns, and $52 in remote rural areas.

The construction of spatial price indices, as outlined by Deaton and Dupriez (2011), presents several significant challenges that NSOs must navigate carefully. They must account for quality differences in similar goods across regions—the rice available in capital cities, for example, might be of different quality than that found in rural areas, making direct price comparisons problematic. Similarly, seasonal vegetables might be available year-round in urban markets but only during specific seasons in rural areas, complicating price comparisons further. These variations in availability and quality make it difficult to maintain consistent standards for price comparison across regions.

Administrative considerations add another layer of complexity to regional price adjustments as Ravallion (2018) discusses. NSOs must make crucial decisions about whether to use political or economic boundaries for defining regions, how to handle border areas where prices might gradually transition between regions, and how to account for people who shop across regional boundaries. Consider suburban residents who might work in the city and make purchases in both urban and suburban areas, or rural residents who travel to larger towns for certain goods. These patterns of movement and purchase make it challenging to assign households to a single regional price level.

The implementation of regional price adjustments requires substantial resources and careful planning. NSOs typically conduct regular market surveys in representative locations, often leveraging their existing CPI data collection infrastructure. They supplement this with community price surveys in rural areas to capture local market conditions. Understanding consumption patterns requires household expenditure surveys by region, often complemented by focus group discussions to understand local preferences and expert consultations on regional differences.

Regular updates are essential to maintain the relevance of regional price adjustments, but this requirement demands significant institutional capacity and resources. Most countries annually adjust their poverty lines using CPI data and conduct more comprehensive revisions every 5 to 10 years. Some implement special surveys during periods of rapid price changes. This dynamic approach helps ensure that poverty measurements remain meaningful across both space and time, though it requires substantial ongoing commitment from statistical offices and policymakers.

2.6.3. Differences in monetary welfare indicators

International comparisons face multiple challenges in reconciling different approaches to measuring poverty across countries. The fundamental difference often lies in whether countries choose to measure income or consumption as their primary welfare indicator. This choice, which might seem technical at first, has profound implications for how we understand and compare poverty across nations (Ravallion, 2016; World Bank, 2015).

The variation in measurement approaches often reflects different economic structures and statistical capacities. High-income countries typically rely on income measures because their economies are highly monetized, with most people receiving regular salaries and maintaining detailed financial records (Atkinson et al., 2010). For example, European Union countries primarily use income data for their poverty statistics, as most of their citizens have formal employment and documented income sources (Eurostat, 2021).

In contrast, many developing countries prefer consumption-based measures for several compelling reasons. In rural areas where farming and informal work predominate, consumption patterns often provide a more reliable picture of living standards than reported income (Deaton and Zaidi, 2002; Mancini and Vecchi, 2022). Consider a farmer in rural Thailand who grows rice for both sale and personal consumption—their actual living standard might be better reflected by what they consume rather than their cash income alone (Deaton, 1997).

These different approaches can lead to significantly different poverty estimates even within the same country. For instance, in countries where both measures are available, income-based poverty rates often show more volatility than consumption-based rates, particularly in agricultural economies where income fluctuates seasonally while consumption remains relatively stable (Meyer and Sullivan, 2012). This difference becomes especially important when making international comparisons.

The World Bank has developed several strategies to address these comparability challenges. Their preferred approach is to use consumption data whenever available, particularly for developing countries (Ferreira et al., 2016). When only income data are available, they make adjustments based on typical relationships between income and consumption observed in countries where both measures exist. These adjustments consider factors such as savings rates, self-consumption of agricultural products, and informal sector activity (Jolliffe and Prydz, 2015).

Additionally, the timing of data collection can affect comparability. Income might be reported annually, while consumption data are often collected with shorter recall periods (Beegle et al., 2012). The World Bank and other international organizations work to standardize these temporal aspects of data collection and make appropriate adjustments when standardization is not possible. They also provide technical assistance to national statistical offices to help improve the consistency of poverty measurement approaches across countries (World Bank, 2018).

2.6.4. *Differences in data quality and availability*

The quality and availability of poverty data vary substantially across countries, creating significant challenges for international comparisons. Some countries conduct regular, high-quality household surveys that provide reliable poverty estimates. Others might have irregular surveys or gaps in their data, or face technical challenges in data collection that affect the reliability of their poverty measurements.

To address these challenges, international organizations have developed several important initiatives. The World Bank's Living Standards Measurement Study (LSMS) provides technical assistance and sets standards for household surveys in developing countries, while the International Comparison Program (ICP) works to collect reliable price data and calculate PPP rates (World Bank, 2015). These programs help improve the quality and comparability of poverty data worldwide.

<u>Example 17</u>: The World Bank's global poverty estimates for June 2025 illustrate both the power and limitations of international poverty measurement. Their data showed that 10.5 percent of the world's population (corresponding to around 838 million people) lived below the $3.00 per day poverty line, but this global figure masked significant regional variations. While poverty affected 45.5 percent of people in Sub-Saharan Africa (equivalent to 558.8 million people), it touched only 1.1 percent in Europe and Central Asia (equivalent to 5.3 million people). Perhaps most striking was the overall trend: the number of people living in extreme poverty fell from 2.3 billion in 1990 to 838 million in June 2025. This dramatic decline demonstrates real progress in fighting global poverty, while the persistent regional disparities highlight the ongoing challenges. ∇

The variation in poverty rates across regions reflects not only real differences in living standards but also differences in measurement approaches and data quality. Some regions have more robust statistical systems and more frequent surveys, while others face significant challenges in data collection and analysis. These differences in statistical capacity can affect our understanding of global poverty patterns and trends.

Beyond technical challenges, political and institutional factors can also affect poverty measurement. Some countries may lack the resources or capacity to conduct regular surveys. Others might face challenges in reaching certain populations or areas within their territory. These practical limitations remind us that while international poverty comparisons provide valuable insights, they should be interpreted with an understanding of their limitations and the contexts in which the data were collected.

2.7. Concluding Remarks

The measurement of monetary poverty, while technically complex, remains fundamental to understanding and addressing deprivation in society. This chapter has shown how different measurement choices can lead to different understandings of who is poor and what should be done about it.

Our exploration of welfare indicators has revealed important tradeoffs. While income measures might work well in high-income economies with formal employment, consumption measures often provide a better picture in developing countries where informal work and subsistence farming are common. The choice between these measures is not just technical—it fundamentally affects how we understand poverty and how we design policies to address it.

Setting appropriate poverty lines requires balancing absolute and relative concepts of poverty. The cost-of-basic-needs method provides a foundation for absolute poverty lines, focusing on the minimum resources needed for survival and basic dignity. Meanwhile, relative measures help us understand poverty as social exclusion, recognizing that poverty means different things in different societies. These different approaches serve different purposes, and many countries now use both to get a more complete picture of poverty.

Various summary measures capture different aspects of poverty. While the headcount ratio tells us how many people are poor, the poverty gap and squared poverty gap measures reveal the depth and severity of poverty. Each measure suggests different policy approaches—from focusing on those closest to the poverty line to prioritizing help for the very poorest.

Comparisons across time and space require careful attention to price differences and changing needs. Our households' experiences over 10 years showed how economic growth affected different groups differently, while spatial variations in prices and needs complicated comparisons between urban and rural households. The use of appropriate price indices and equivalence scales helps ensure meaningful comparisons, though perfect comparability remains elusive.

The evolution of poverty measurement methods reflects growing recognition of poverty's complexity. From simple headcounts to sophisticated multidimensional measures (Alkire and Foster, 2011), from national poverty lines to international standards, the field continues to develop. Yet our five households remind us that behind the technical complexity lie real families whose experiences of poverty and prosperity shape their opportunities and challenges.

Figure 2.2 collectively illustrate how different ways of measuring poverty can tell vastly different stories, both in terms of levels and trends. Consumption-based poverty rates in Bangladesh are consistently lower than income-based rates due to the volatility of income in a predominantly agrarian economy. However, both measures show a downward trend between 2016 and 2018, suggesting that households are improving their ability to manage income fluctuations, potentially through better access to credit or savings. Varying thresholds also have an impact in the data stories: India's national poverty line consistently reporting higher poverty rates than the international poverty line

($1.90/day). While both measures indicate a decline in poverty from 2019 to 2021, the magnitude of reduction is modest, reflecting persistent challenges in addressing structural inequalities. Finally, stark disparities between urban and rural poverty in Nigeria can be noticed: rural poverty rates are significantly higher due to limited access to infrastructure and services. Although both urban and rural poverty rates declined slightly from 2018 to 2020, the slower pace of reduction in rural areas underscores the need for targeted development interventions. Together, these figures underscore the importance of understanding the methodological nuances in poverty measurement, as different approaches can shape narratives and policy priorities in distinct ways.

The chapter has also highlighted crucial challenges in poverty measurement. Accounting for different family sizes and needs, adjusting for regional price differences, and ensuring comparability across time and space all require careful attention. These technical challenges remind us that poverty measurement is not just about counting the poor—it is about understanding the complex reality of poverty in all its dimensions.

Looking ahead, several challenges remain. We need better ways to account for how resources are shared within households, to incorporate non-market dimensions of welfare, and to improve the quality of data collected in developing countries. New technologies and data collection methods offer opportunities to address some of these challenges, though others will require continued theoretical and methodological innovation.

Ultimately, good poverty measurement serves a practical purpose—it helps design and evaluate policies that affect millions of lives. Whether targeting social assistance and protection such as conditional cash transfers, planning regional development, or assessing program effectiveness, reliable poverty measures provide the foundation for effective poverty reduction efforts. Understanding both the power and limitations of these poverty measures helps ensure they are used appropriately in the ongoing fight to eradicate poverty.

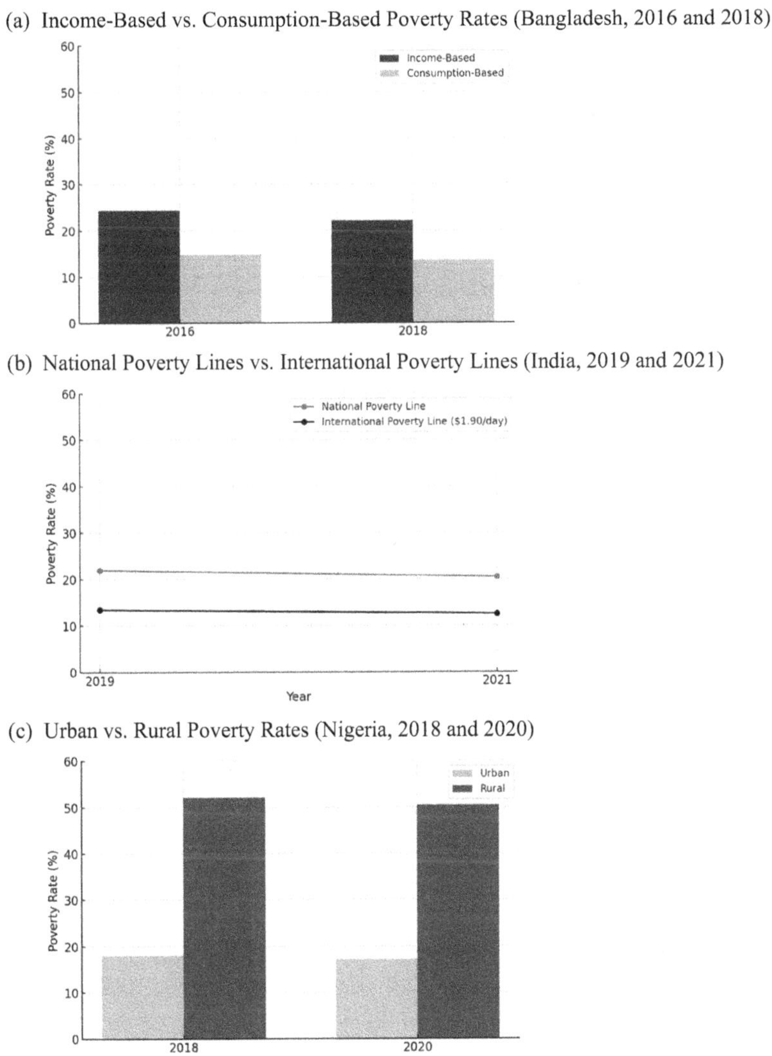

Figure 2.2. How different ways of measuring poverty tell different stories.
Sources: (i) World Bank Poverty and Equity Briefs (2016–2021): Data on income-based and consumption-based poverty rates for Bangladesh, and poverty rates for India and Nigeria. Accessible at World Bank Poverty and Inequality Platform (PIP). (ii) National Statistical Offices (NSOs): Bangladesh Bureau of Statistics for income and consumption data. India's Ministry of Statistics and Programme Implementation (MOSPI) for national poverty line estimates. Nigeria's National Bureau of Statistics for urban and rural poverty rates. (iii) World Development Indicators (WDI) Database: Provides complementary data on poverty trends and methodologies. Accessible at World Development Indicators.

References

Alkire, S., & Foster, J. (2011). Counting and multidimensional poverty measurement. *Journal of Public Economics, 95*(7–8), 476–487. https://www.sciencedirect.com/science/article/pii/S0047272710001660

Atkinson, A. B. (1987). On the measurement of poverty. *Econometrica, 55*(4), 749–764. https://www.jstor.org/stable/1911028

Atkinson, A. B., Marlier, E., & Wolff, P. (2010). Beyond GDP, measuring well-being and EU-SILC. In *Income and living conditions in Europe* (pp. 1–24). https://liser.elsevierpure.com/en/publications/beyond-gdp-measuring-well-being-and-eu-silc

Asian Development Bank (ADB). (2014). *Key indicators for Asia and the Pacific 2014: Poverty in Asia—A deeper look.* Manila: ADB. https://www.adb.org/publications/key-indicators-asia-and-pacific-2014

Beegle, K., De Weerdt, J., Friedman, J., & Gibson, J. (2012). Methods of household consumption measurement through surveys: Experimental results from Tanzania. *Journal of Development Economics, 98*(1), 3–18. https://www.sciencedirect.com/science/article/pii/S0304387811001039

Dalaker, J. (2022, July 19). *The supplemental poverty measure: Its core concepts, development, and use* (CRS Report No. R45031). Congressional Research Service. https://crsreports.congress.gov/product/pdf/R/R45031

Datt, G., & Ravallion, M. (1992). Growth and redistribution components of changes in poverty measures: A decomposition with applications to Brazil and India in the 1980s. *Journal of Development Economics, 38*(2), 275–295. https://www.sciencedirect.com/science/article/pii/030438789290001P

Deaton, A. (1997). *The analysis of household surveys: A microeconometric approach to development policy.* World Bank Publications. https://documents.worldbank.org/en/publication/documents-reports/documentdetail/593871468777303124/the-analysis-of-household-surveys-a-microeconometric-approach-to-development-policy

Deaton, A., & Grosh, M. (2000). Consumption. In M. Grosh & P. Glewwe (Eds.), *Designing household survey questionnaires for developing countries: Lessons from 15 years of the Living Standards Measurement Study* (Vol. 1, pp. 91–133). World Bank Publications. https://openknowledge.worldbank.org/entities/publication/a57f3993-e976-580c-96a8-4ba7dbda53c1

Deaton, A., & Kozel, V. (2005). Data and dogma: The great Indian poverty debate. *The World Bank Research Observer, 20*(2), 177–199. https://academic.oup.com/wbro/article-abstract/20/2/177/1623486

Deaton, A., & Dupriez, O. (2011). *Spatial price differences within large countries* [Working paper]. Princeton University & World Bank. https://www.princeton.edu/~deaton/downloads/spatial_price_differences_in_large_countries%20_10%20jul_2011_complete.pdf

Deaton, A., & Zaidi, S. (2002). *Guidelines for constructing consumption aggregates for welfare analysis* (Vol. 135). World Bank Publications. https://openknowledge.worldbank.org/entities/publication/05705853-f9bc-5bbb-9658-c254a2eae048

Eurostat. (2021). *Glossary: At-risk-of-poverty rate*. Retrieved from https://ec.europa.eu/eurostat/statistics-explained/index.php?title=Glossary:At-risk-of-poverty_rate

Ferreira, F. H., Chen, S., Dabalen, A., Dikhanov, Y., Hamadeh, N., Jolliffe, D., Narayan, A., Prydz, E. B., Revenga, A., Sangraula, P., Serajuddin, U., & Yoshida, N. (2016). A global count of the extreme poor in 2012: Data issues, methodology and initial results. *The Journal of Economic Inequality, 14*(2), 141–172. https://link.springer.com/article/10.1007/s10888-016-9326-6

Foster, J., Greer, J., & Thorbecke, E. (1984). A class of decomposable poverty measures. *Econometrica, 52*(3), 761–766. https://www.jstor.org/stable/1913475

Foster, E., Jolliffe, D., Lara Ibarra, G., Lakner, C., & Tetteh-Baah, S. (2023). *Global poverty revisited using 2021 PPPs and new data on consumption* (Policy Research Working Paper No. 11137). World Bank. https://documents1.worldbank.org/curated/en/099503206032533226/pdf/IDU-e2e09dcf-0af2-481a-a60a-64adf28171d0.pdf

Haughton, J., & Khandker, S. R. (2009). *Handbook on poverty and inequality*. World Bank Publications. https://documents1.worldbank.org/curated/en/488081468157174849/pdf/483380PUB0Pove101OFFICIAL0USE0ONLY1.pdf

Lao Statistics Bureau, & World Bank. (2020). *Poverty profile in Lao PDR*. Vientiane: Lao Statistics Bureau. https://documents.worldbank.org/en/publication/documents-reports/documentdetail/685131623647655386

Mancini, G., & Vecchi, G. (2022). *On the construction of a consumption aggregate for inequality and poverty analysis (English)*. Washington, D.C.: World Bank Group.

Meyer, B. D., & Sullivan, J. X. (2012). Identifying the disadvantaged: Official poverty, consumption poverty, and the new supplemental poverty measure. *Journal of Economic Perspectives, 26*(3), 111–136. https://www.aeaweb.org/articles?id=10.1257/jep.26.3.111

Morduch, J. (1994). Poverty and vulnerability. *The American Economic Review, 84*(2), 221–225. https://www.jstor.org/stable/2117833

Organization of Economic Cooperation and Development (OECD). (2011). *What are equivalence scales?* OECD Project on Income Distribution and Poverty. Retrieved from http://www.oecd.org/els/soc/OECD-Note-EquivalenceScales.pdf

Pimhidzai, O., Fenton, N. C., Souksavath, P., & Sisoulath, V. (2014). *Poverty profile in Lao PDR: Poverty report for the Lao Consumption and Expenditure Survey, 2012–2013.* World Bank. https://documents.worldbank.org/en/publication/documents-reports/documentdetail/868521467998508506/poverty-profile-in-lao-pdr-poverty-report-for-the-lao-consumption-and-expenditure-survey-2012-2013

Prydz, E. B., & Jolliffe, D. (2015). *Global poverty goals and prices: How purchasing power parity matters* (Policy Research Working Paper No. 7256). Washington, D.C.: World Bank. https://openknowledge.worldbank.org/entities/publication/d788eac5-3839-56bd-83bb-44f34111fe7c

Ravallion, M. (1998). *Poverty lines in theory and practice.* World Bank. https://documents1.worldbank.org/curated/en/916871468766156239/pdf/multi-page.pdf

Ravallion, M. (2016). *The economics of poverty: History, measurement, and policy.* Oxford University Press. https://academic.oup.com/book/10927

Ravallion, M. (2018). *Poverty comparisons.* London: Routledge. https://www.routledge.com/Poverty-Comparisons/Ravallion/p/book/9780415866217?srsltid=AfmBOoo329KhsQhyanNg2x62h4BJkFROUxrnDbEnKlHN9Gxl-lc7j9Gu

Ravallion, M., & Bidani, B. (1994). How robust is a poverty profile? *The World Bank Economic Review, 8*(1), 75–102. https://documents1.worldbank.org/curated/en/991591468764687666/pdf/multi-page.pdf

Ravallion, M., & Huppi, M. (1991). Measuring changes in poverty: A methodological case study of Indonesia during an adjustment period. *The World Bank Economic Review, 5*(1), 57–82. https://documents1.worldbank.org/curated/en/431901468771657263/pdf/multi-page.pdf

Sen, A. (1976). Poverty: An ordinal approach to measurement. *Econometrica, 44*(2), 219–231. https://www.jstor.org/stable/1912718

Sen, A. (1983). Poor, relatively speaking. *Oxford Economic Papers, 35*(2), 153–169. https://academic.oup.com/oep/article-abstract/35/2/153/2360982

United Nations. (2021). *The Sustainable Development Goals report 2021.* New York: United Nations. https://unstats.un.org/sdgs/report/2021/

United Nations Statistics Division (UNSD). (2005). *Handbook on poverty statistics: Concepts, methods, and policy use*. United Nations Statistics Division. https://unstats.un.org/unsd/methods/poverty/pdf/un_book%20 final%2030%20dec%2005.pdf

United Nations Educational, Scientific and Cultural Organization (UNESCO). (2010). *Education counts: Towards the Millennium Development Goals*. Paris: UNESCO. https://unesdoc.unesco.org/ark:/48223/pf0000190214

Wodon, Q. T. (1997). Food energy intake and cost of basic needs: Measuring poverty in Bangladesh. *The Journal of Development Studies, 34*(2), 66–101. https://econpapers.repec.org/article/tafjdevst/v_3a34_3ay_3a1997_3ai_3a2_3ap_3a66-101.htm

World Bank. (2015). *A measured approach to ending poverty and boosting shared prosperity: Concepts, data, and the twin goals*. The World Bank. https://www.worldbank.org/en/research/publication/a-measured-approach-to-ending-poverty-and-boosting-shared-prosperity

World Bank. (2018). *Poverty and shared prosperity 2018: Piecing together the poverty puzzle*. Washington, DC: World Bank. https://www.worldbank.org/en/publication/poverty-and-shared-prosperity-2018

World Bank. (2022). *Poverty and shared prosperity 2022: Correcting course*. Washington, DC: World Bank. https://openknowledge.worldbank.org/entities/publication/a33782e6-415e-5699-a9a8-4a50dc4ae3bc

CHAPTER 3

Multidimensional Poverty Indices

"Poverty is multidimensional. It extends beyond money incomes to education, health care, political participation and advancement of one's own culture and social organisation."

—Atal Bihari Vajpayee

SUMMARY

This chapter examines poverty measurement by evaluating multiple aspects of people's lives simultaneously—not just income but also access to education, healthcare, housing, and other essential needs. Combining these dimensions whether through a data dashboard, a composite index, or an examination of the joint distribution offers a more complete understanding of poverty than income alone. The measurement of multidimensional poverty represents a fundamental shift in how we understand and address deprivation in society. Traditional income-based measures, while important, often miss crucial aspects of how people experience poverty in their daily lives. This chapter examines how newer measurement approaches capture multiple, overlapping disadvantages that characterize poverty across different contexts and populations.

An examination of multidimensional poverty begins with the theoretical foundations, including Amartya Sen's capabilities approach and developments in welfare economics. The chapter reviews methodological frameworks for integrating different deprivation dimensions, focusing on the Global Multidimensional Poverty Index (MPI) developed by the Oxford Poverty and Human Development Initiative (OPHI) and the United Nations Development Programme (UNDP). Through country case studies, it demonstrates how nations adapt multidimensional frameworks to their specific contexts while maintaining methodological rigor. The chapter provides detailed country case studies demonstrating how different nations have adapted multidimensional frameworks to their specific contexts while maintaining methodological rigor. Cases from diverse settings—from Colombia's pioneering national MPI to Vietnam's adaptation for tracking ethnic minority poverty—illustrate both the flexibility and challenges of implementing these measurement systems. The chapter pays particular attention to how measurement choices affect policy design and implementation, examining how different approaches to weighting and aggregation influence poverty reduction strategies.

The chapter demonstrates the importance of considering multiple dimensions of living conditions through both theoretical frameworks and practical examples. It explains various approaches to combining these dimensions into comprehensive measures called "multidimensional poverty indices", with particular focus on how different countries have adapted and implemented these frameworks to match their specific needs and policy priorities. Technical considerations receive careful attention, but the discussion maintains focus on practical applications, examining how technical choices affect measurement outcomes and policy decisions. The chapter concludes by exploring emerging challenges and opportunities while considering how measurement systems might evolve to capture new forms of deprivation.

Finally, the chapter explores emerging challenges and opportunities, including big data applications and environmental poverty dimensions, and how measurement systems may evolve to capture new forms of deprivation. Overall, it showcases methodological innovations in multidimensional poverty measurement with a focus on practical policy applications, using country examples and technical discussions to highlight the strengths and limitations of different approaches in capturing poverty's complexity.

3.1. Introduction

The conceptualization and measurement of poverty have undergone a fundamental transformation over the recent decades. The recognition that poverty extends beyond just lacking money has fundamentally changed how we measure and understand poverty in recent decades (Sen, 1999; World Bank, 2018). When poverty researchers actually talk to poor people about their experiences, they consistently describe multiple, overlapping hardships—not just insufficient income but also poor health, limited education, inadequate housing, and social exclusion (Narayan et al., 2000). These insights from participatory poverty assessments have pushed poverty measurement beyond purely monetary approaches toward methods that capture poverty's multiple dimensions.

The evolution toward multidimensional measurement emerged from both theoretical advances and practical necessities in development research. Early researchers working with Demographic and Health Survey data faced a practical challenge of having detailed health information but no income or consumption data. To address this, researchers like Filmer and Pritchett (2001) developed wealth indices that combined information about household assets and housing characteristics into single measures ranking households from poorest to richest. While simpler than modern multidimensional measures, these early composite indices demonstrated both the possibility and value of measuring welfare through multiple indicators.

Understanding poverty requires recognizing its multiple dimensions. Consider five families living in the same community, each facing different combinations of disadvantage:

- The Gomez family appears well-off if we only look at their monthly income of $400, which puts them above the typical poverty line. However, they face significant hardships—their children cannot attend school because they cannot afford the associated costs like uniforms and supplies, and they live in a house without basic sanitation facilities. Their situation shows how having enough money does not always translate into meeting all basic needs.
- In contrast, the Martinez household might be considered poor based solely on their $150 monthly income, but their situation is more complex. They have managed to achieve several important aspects of wellbeing—their children attend school through a government support program, they have access to basic healthcare, and they supplement their low income by growing their own food. Their case demonstrates how looking only at money might make a family appear poorer than they really are.
- The Rodriguez family presents yet another pattern of deprivation. With a monthly income of $300, they prioritize education and manage to keep their children in school, but this comes at the cost of living in substandard housing without access to clean water.
- Meanwhile, the Perez family earns what might seem like a comfortable $500 per month, but caring for a disabled family member who lacks access to proper healthcare creates significant hardship.
- Finally, the Santos family, earning $350 monthly, has access to basic services but faces constant uncertainty due to irregular employment, leading to periods of food insecurity.

These situations reflect what Amartya Sen calls the "coupling of disadvantages"—how different aspects of poverty often reinforce each other (Sen, 1999, 2000). The Rodriguez family's need to choose between education and adequate housing, the Perez family's struggles with disability and healthcare access, and the Santos family's combination of irregular employment and food insecurity all demonstrate how various deprivations interact and compound each other (Drèze and Sen, 2013).

The recognition that poverty comprises multiple, overlapping disadvantages has led to increasingly sophisticated approaches for measuring poverty across multiple dimensions (Alkire and Santos, 2014). From early wealth indices using PCA, the field has evolved to include the Global Multidimensional Poverty Index (MPI) developed by the United Nations Development Programme (UNDP) and Oxford Poverty and Human Development Initiative (OPHI), various national multidimensional poverty measures adapted to country contexts, and other frameworks like the World Bank's Multidimensional Poverty Measure (MPM) and the European Union's material deprivation measures (Alkire and Santos, 2014; World Bank, 2018; UNDP and OPHI, 2019). These diverse approaches reflect both methodological advances and growing recognition that effective poverty measurement must capture the multiple dimensions that shape people's experiences of deprivation.

Traditional poverty measures focusing solely on income or consumption miss these important variations in how families experience hardship (Alkire and Foster, 2011; Ravallion, 2016). Researchers began developing alternative approaches as early as the 1970s, including basic needs measures and relative deprivation indices (Townsend, 1979). By the 1990s, asset indices using principal components analysis offered new ways to measure household wealth, particularly where income was difficult to measure accurately (Filmer and Pritchett, 2001).

The field of multidimensional poverty measurement has evolved significantly in recent decades. The evolution toward truly multidimensional poverty measurement accelerated in the 2000s, driven by both theoretical advances and practical needs (Kakwani and Silber, 2013). The development of the Global Multidimensional Poverty Index by UNDP and OPHI researchers marked a significant milestone, providing a systematic way to measure overlapping deprivations across health, education, and living standards (Alkire and Santos, 2014). This approach has since inspired many countries to develop their own national multidimensional poverty measures, adapted to their specific contexts and policy needs (UNDP and OPHI, 2019).

Multiple methodological frameworks have emerged for capturing poverty's various dimensions. Various approaches can be used for estimating multidimensional poverty, ranging from simpler "marginal" methods that use a data dashboard (providing separate indicators without a single aggregated number) to more integrated methods that produce a composite index, summing across deprivations. Additionally, some approaches examine the joint distribution of deprivations—identifying whether the same people suffer from multiple deprivations simultaneously.

The Sustainable Development Goals (SDGs) have popularized an alternative measurement approach through data dashboards (Figure 3.1). Rather than combining multiple dimensions into a single index, dashboards present separate indicators for each dimension (UNSD, 2025). The SDGs track 232 indicators across 17 goals, providing a comprehensive picture of global development progress without forcing aggregation. This dashboard approach offers several advantages: it maintains the distinct nature of different dimensions, avoiding contentious decisions about weights and aggregation methods, and allows for tracking progress in specific areas without having indicators' movements cancel each other out. The global SDG indicator framework demonstrates how dashboards can effectively monitor multiple dimensions of poverty and development simultaneously.

However, dashboards also face important limitations. Without aggregation, they cannot provide a single headline number for poverty, making it harder to compare overall progress across countries or time. They may overwhelm users with too much information, making it difficult to identify priority areas for intervention. These tradeoffs between dashboards and composite indices reflect a fundamental

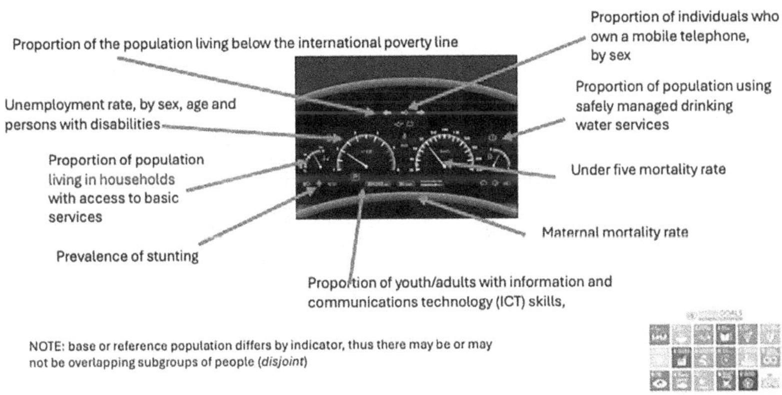

Figure 3.1. SDG data dashboard.
Note: SDG Global Indicator Data can be sourced from the UNSD's Global SDG Indicators Database https://unstats.un.org/sdgs/dataportal. Visualizations on SDG indicators and other key indicators for ADB member economies are available at ADB's Key Indicators Database https://kidb.adb.org/

tension in poverty measurement between maintaining dimensional clarity and providing summary measures for policy use.

This chapter examines the evolution of multidimensional poverty measurement but focusing on composite indices and their applications. We begin by exploring what makes a good composite index and common approaches to combining multiple dimensions of poverty. We then examine in detail the Global MPI—the most widely used framework—before considering how different countries have adapted and implemented their own national measures. The chapter also reviews other important multidimensional frameworks, including the World Bank's MPM approach and the European Union's material deprivation measures. We pay particular attention to technical considerations in measurement design and implementation, including the crucial choices of dimensions, indicators, weights, and cutoffs. Finally, we explore how these measures are being used in practice to inform policy, from targeting social programs to monitoring progress in poverty reduction. Throughout, we highlight both the significant advances in measuring poverty's multiple dimensions and the ongoing challenges in capturing this complex phenomenon.

3.2. Understanding Composite Indices

Effective composite indices require careful consideration of both theoretical foundations and practical measurement challenges. These single summary measures combine different types of information in ways that should provide meaningful insights while remaining technically sound and practically useful.

Using our five families example—with their varying income, education access, housing conditions, healthcare access, and employment stability—the challenge lies in combining all this information to determine who experiences multidimensional poverty. This challenge lies at the heart of multidimensional measurement (Nardo et al., 2008).

Early composite measures focused on material living standards. Researchers working with Demographic and Health Surveys (DHS) in developing countries developed asset-based indices when surveys collected detailed health information but no income data. Researchers like Filmer and Pritchett (2001) created indices based on household assets and housing characteristics using principal components analysis (PCA) to combine this information into single measures ranking households from poorest to richest.

PCA identifies assets that most effectively distinguish between households of different economic status. Rather than simply counting assets, it creates a weighted index where the most discriminating assets receive greater weight in determining household rankings. This approach creates objective measures based on actual patterns in the data rather than predetermined assumptions about what constitutes wealth.

This asset-based approach proved remarkably useful. When researchers compared these asset indices to traditional consumption-based poverty measures in countries where both were available, they found that the asset index did a good job identifying who was poor (Vyas and Kumaranayake, 2006). The index also had practical advantages—asking about asset ownership was simpler and more reliable than collecting detailed income or consumption data. Soon, many researchers were using asset indices to study how poverty related to health, education, and other outcomes (Howe et al., 2012).

However, asset indices still focused mainly on material living standards. They did not capture other important aspects of poverty that our five families face—like the Perez family's lack of healthcare access or the Gomez children's inability to attend school. The need to capture these non-monetary dimensions led researchers to develop more sophisticated composite indices that explicitly include multiple dimensions of wellbeing (Kakwani and Silber, 2013).

The construction of multidimensional indices requires several fundamental methodological decisions.

- First, researchers must choose which dimensions to include. The Global MPI, for instance, focuses on three broad dimensions—health, education, and living standards (used also for the Human Development Index)—based on what poor people themselves say matters most and what data are widely available (Alkire and Santos, 2014). Other indices might include additional dimensions like employment, security, or social participation, depending on their purpose and context (UNDP and OPHI, 2019).
- Second, poverty researchers must decide how to measure each dimension. For education, should we look at years of schooling, literacy, or school attendance? For health, should we consider nutrition, access to healthcare, or specific health outcomes? These choices often depend on both conceptual arguments about what matters most and practical considerations about what data are available (Alkire et al., 2015).
- Third, and perhaps most challengingly, poverty analysts must decide how to combine different dimensions into a single index. This involves both technical questions (like what mathematical formula to use) and value judgments (like how much weight to

give each dimension). If we think education is twice as important as housing quality in determining poverty, we might give it twice the weight in our index. But such judgments are inherently debatable—who decides what matters most? Different approaches to these questions have led to different types of multidimensional poverty measures, each with its own strengths and limitations (Atkinson, 2003).

The choice of measurement approach reflects fundamental conceptual and methodological priorities in poverty analysis (Ravallion, 2011; Alkire and Foster, 2011). Different approaches to multidimensional measurement reflect varying conceptual understandings of poverty and different measurement priorities. While the Global MPI emphasizes basic capabilities following Sen's framework (Alkire and Santos, 2014), alternative approaches like the World Bank's Multidimensional Poverty Measure (MPM) explicitly incorporate monetary dimensions, recognizing income's fundamental role in avoiding deprivation (World Bank, 2018). Similarly, relative approaches like the EU's material deprivation measures focus on social inclusion through access to goods and activities considered normal in more high-income societies (Whelan and Maître, 2012).

3.2.1. Properties of good composite indices

The construction of effective composite indices requires careful attention to several fundamental characteristics. What makes a good composite index for measuring poverty? A good composite index must balance several key requirements:

(1) Validity: The index should actually measure what it claims to measure. For poverty measurement, this means capturing meaningful deprivations that reflect people's lived experiences of poverty.
(2) Reliability: Results should be stable and reproducible, not highly sensitive to minor methodological choices or data issues.

(3) Transparency: The construction of the index should be clear and understandable, with explicit documentation of assumptions and choices made.
(4) Policy relevance: The measure should provide insights that can inform practical interventions to reduce poverty.

Recent methodological innovations have helped refine our understanding of essential properties for meaningful poverty measurement (Alkire et al., 2020; Permanyer and Hussain, 2018). Effective multidimensional poverty measures must satisfy several key properties that ensure they accurately reflect the reality of poverty while remaining useful for policy purposes (Alkire et al., 2021; Dotter and Klasen, 2014). The "focus axiom" requires that changes in circumstances of non-poor families should not affect poverty measures, ensuring that attention remains concentrated on those actually experiencing deprivation. The "monotonicity axiom" demands that poverty measures increase when poor people become worse off, capturing deteriorating conditions among those already struggling. "Decomposability" enables breaking down poverty measures by different groups or regions, facilitating targeted policy interventions by revealing where poverty concentrates most severely.

These properties work together to create poverty measures that respond appropriately to real changes in welfare while providing clear guidance for policy interventions. Detailed mathematical formulations of these axioms and their implications are provided in the Chapter Technical Annex for readers interested in technical specifications.

Beyond these technical properties, good composite indices should also satisfy practical requirements (Nardo et al., 2008). They must be

- Transparent: Allowing anyone to understand how the index is calculated and what assumptions it makes.
- Robust: Ensuring small changes in measurement components do not lead to large changes in conclusions about who is poor.
- Policy-relevant: Helping to understand not just who is poor but also what kinds of interventions might help reduce poverty.

3.2.2. Approaches to aggregation

The process of combining multiple indicators into a unified poverty measure requires careful methodological consideration. Recent methodological innovations have expanded the toolkit for aggregating multiple dimensions of poverty. The simplest approach involves counting the number or proportion of deprivations a household faces, providing transparency but treating all deprivations as equally important. More sophisticated methods have emerged to address this limitation. Weighted averaging introduces different weights for different dimensions while raising important questions about how to determine these weights. Statistical techniques like PCA offer data-driven approaches to weighting, though these can be more difficult to interpret and explain to policymakers and the public.

3.2.3. The challenge of weighting

Perhaps the most fundamental challenge in constructing composite indices is determining how much importance to give different components. This involves complex judgments such as: Is lacking access to education more or less serious than lacking access to healthcare? Should poor housing conditions count as much as unemployment? These questions involve both empirical and normative considerations about what matters most for wellbeing.

Different approaches to weighting include

- **Equal weighting**, which assigns the same importance to all dimensions or indicators providing transparency and ease of understanding but may not reflect real differences in importance.
- **Normative weighting**, which sets weights based on expert judgment or public consultation about the relative importance of different dimensions, reflecting social priorities but incorporating subjective judgments.
- **Data-driven weighting**, which derives weights from the data using methods like PCA. While this seems more objective, the

resulting weights may not align with policy priorities or public understanding.

- **Hybrid approaches**, which combine different weighting methods, for example using equal weights across dimensions but allowing statistical methods to weight indicators within dimensions.

The development of the Global MPI illustrates how these methodological challenges can be addressed in practice. The development of the Global MPI and similar national measures represents a careful attempt to balance these various requirements (Alkire and Santos, 2014). For instance, the Global MPI uses a "dual cutoff" approach—first setting thresholds for deprivation in each dimension (like minimum years of schooling), then requiring multiple deprivations for someone to be considered poor. This approach helps ensure the measure identifies people facing genuine multiple disadvantages rather than just single deprivations.

However, even well-designed composite indices face inherent challenges. One fundamental issue is the question of weights—how much importance should we give to each dimension? The Global MPI gives equal weight to health, education, and living standards, but this is a normative choice that reasonable people might disagree with (Ravallion, 2011). Some might argue that health should receive more weight because it is fundamental to everything else, while others might prioritize education as key to breaking intergenerational poverty.

3.3. The Global Multidimensional Poverty Index

The Global Multidimensional Poverty Index (MPI) represents the most comprehensive and widely adopted framework for measuring poverty's multiple dimensions (Alkire and Santos, 2014). First introduced in the 2010 Human Development Report, it now covers over 100 countries and has inspired many national adaptations (UNDP, 2010; UNDP and OPHI, 2019). The Global MPI directly measures deprivations that matter in people's lives; captures how these deprivations overlap at the household level; and can be broken down by region, ethnicity, or other subgroups to show how poverty varies across different populations.

The framework examines poverty through 10 indicators grouped into 3 core dimensions—health, education, and living standards. Each dimension receives equal weight (one-third), reflecting their fundamental importance to human development, while the indicators within each dimension also receive equal weights. A family is considered multidimensionally poor if they are deprived in enough indicators to sum to one-third or more of the total weighted indicators (Alkire et al., 2015).

In the health dimension, the Global MPI measures nutrition and child mortality. A household is deprived in nutrition if any adult under 70 years or any child is undernourished, and in child mortality if any child has died in the family in the five years preceding the survey. To illustrate with our example households, the Martinez family, despite their low income, might not be considered deprived in health if all family members are well nourished, and they have not experienced child mortality. The Perez family, however, would likely show deprivation in health due to their disabled member's lack of proper healthcare.

The education dimension considers both educational attainment and current school attendance. For education, the measure considers years of schooling and school attendance. A household is deprived if no adult has completed six years of schooling or if any school-age child is not attending school up to the age at which they would complete class 8. The Gomez family, unable to send their children to school, would be considered deprived in education despite their above-poverty-line income. In contrast, the Rodriguez family, managing to keep their children in school despite housing difficulties, avoids this particular deprivation.

The living standards dimension encompasses six indicators: electricity, drinking water, sanitation, housing, cooking fuel, and assets. Being deprived in any single indicator constitutes a living standards deprivation. The Santos family, while having access to basic services, might still be considered deprived in living standards if their housing conditions are inadequate or they lack basic assets. Conversely, the

Martinez family, despite their low income, might fare better in this dimension if they have access to basic infrastructure.

A distinctive feature of the Global MPI is its approach to identifying poverty through a "dual cutoff" method instead of just counting individual deprivations (Alkire and Foster, 2011). First, it determines whether a household is deprived in each indicator using specific thresholds. Then, it adds up the weighted deprivations to see if they exceed the poverty cutoff of one-third. This means a family must face multiple significant deprivations to be considered multidimensionally poor (see Chapter Technical Annex for Details).

3.3.1. Understanding the Global MPI framework

The Global MPI employs a systematic three-step process to transform household-level data into meaningful poverty measurements. First, it identifies whether households are deprived in each of the 10 specific indicators across health, education, and living standards dimensions. Second, it uses a "dual cutoff" approach where households must face deprivations totaling at least one-third of weighted indicators to be classified as multidimensionally poor. Finally, it generates summary statistics including the headcount ratio (percentage of people who are poor), intensity of poverty (average share of deprivations among the poor), and the MPI itself (headcount times intensity). The detailed mathematical formulations and worked examples of these calculations are provided in the Chapter Technical Annex for readers seeking technical precision.

This systematic approach captures both who is poor and how deeply they experience poverty across multiple dimensions simultaneously. Unlike simple headcount measures, the Global MPI's intensity component reveals whether poor households face just a few deprivations near the threshold or experience severe deprivation across most indicators. This nuanced measurement proves particularly valuable for policy design, as it helps distinguish between households needing targeted support in specific areas versus those requiring comprehensive, integrated interventions.

3.3.2. Policy applications of the Global MPI and adjusted FGT measures

The Global MPI framework provides powerful insights for policymaking. Consider how multidimensional measurement can inform different aspects of poverty reduction strategy (Alkire et al., 2015).

First, the stark urban–rural divide in our example—with an MPI of 0.833 in rural areas compared to 0.000 in urban areas—suggests that geographic targeting of anti-poverty programs would be highly effective. The rural households (2 and 4) face multiple, overlapping deprivations across all dimensions, while urban households experience either no deprivations (Household 3) or deprivations that do not reach the poverty threshold (Household 1). This pattern, common in many developing countries, often reflects systematic differences in access to infrastructure and services between urban and rural areas (Ravallion, 2016).

Second, the high intensity of poverty (A = 0.833) among those identified as poor reveals that poor households face deprivations in most indicators. Both poor households in our example are deprived in nearly all indicators except child mortality. This suggests that single-dimension interventions—like just providing electricity or improving water access—might not be sufficient. Instead, the data point toward the need for coordinated interventions that address multiple deprivations simultaneously (UNDP and OPHI, 2019).

Third, the dimensional breakdown reveals that while all three dimensions contribute to poverty, education and living standards deprivations are particularly severe. All poor households in our example are deprived in both education indicators (years of schooling and school attendance) and all six living standards indicators. This suggests that improving access to education and basic infrastructure should be policy priorities.

The Global MPI can support policymaking in several specific ways:

(1) **Targeting**: The measure helps identify who is poor and how they are poor. In our example, rural households clearly need the most

assistance, but the detailed deprivation profiles show exactly which interventions each household needs. Household 1, while not identified as multidimensionally poor, still needs support for school attendance and sanitation.

(2) **Program design**: The intensity measure (A) and dimensional breakdown help design comprehensive poverty reduction programs. The high intensity score in our example (0.833) suggests that poor households need support across multiple dimensions simultaneously, pointing toward integrated anti-poverty programs rather than single-sector interventions.

(3) **Monitoring**: Changes in the MPI and its components over time can track progress in reducing poverty. If our community implemented an education program, we could monitor not just whether it reduced education deprivations but also whether it affected other dimensions of poverty.

(4) **Budget allocation**: The measure can guide resource allocation across regions and sectors. In our example, the concentration of poverty in rural areas and the prominence of education and living standards deprivations suggest where resources might be most effectively deployed.

The Global MPI's design offers several important strengths. Its standardized methodology allows for meaningful international comparisons, while its ability to be decomposed by subgroups helps identify which populations face the greatest disadvantages (Alkire and Foster, 2011; UNDP and OPHI, 2020). The measure directly captures actual deprivations rather than relying on indirect proxies, and its specific, actionable indicators provide clear guidance for policy interventions (Alkire et al., 2015).

However, the Global MPI also faces important limitations. Available survey data often constrain which indicators can be included, potentially missing important aspects of poverty (Ravallion, 2011). The equal weighting across dimensions, while transparent, may not reflect local priorities or circumstances. The use of binary cutoffs for each indicator might miss important gradations in deprivation severity (Dotter and Klasen, 2014). Perhaps most importantly, measuring at the household level may mask significant inequalities between household members, particularly along gender lines (Bessell, 2015; Espinoza-Delgado and Klasen, 2018).

As regards the adjusted poverty gap (M_1) and squared gap (M_2) measures, these provide policymakers with crucial insights beyond what the basic adjusted headcount ratio (M_0) can reveal. Consider Mexico's Prospera program, which used M_1 to identify not just which households were multidimensionally poor but also how far they fell below deprivation thresholds in each dimension. This information helped program administrators vary benefit levels—households with deeper educational deprivations received larger educational subsidies, while those facing severe health deprivations qualified for enhanced medical support. Similarly, Chile's social programs used M_2's sensitivity to severe deprivations to identify households requiring the most intensive interventions. When M_2 revealed particularly deep poverty in certain rural regions, with households falling far below thresholds in multiple dimensions simultaneously, the government responded by bundling multiple interventions—combining housing improvements with educational support and healthcare access—rather than addressing each dimension separately. These examples demonstrate how M_1 and M_2 can help policymakers not just identify who is poor but also design interventions that match the depth and pattern of deprivations households face.

The Global MPI's widespread adoption reflects its balance between methodological rigor and practical applicability. While technical details of its calculation may seem complex, the underlying logic remains straightforward: identify meaningful deprivations, determine who faces multiple disadvantages, and measure both the extent and intensity of multidimensional poverty. This framework has inspired numerous national adaptations while maintaining sufficient standardization for international comparisons. Readers interested in the mathematical foundations and detailed calculation procedures can find comprehensive explanations and worked examples in the Chapter Technical Annex.

3.4. National MPIs

While the Global MPI provides a standardized framework for international comparisons, many countries have found compelling reasons to develop their own national multidimensional poverty measures. These national adaptations reflect the understanding that poverty's manifestations and priorities vary significantly across contexts (UNDP and OPHI, 2019). For instance, what constitutes basic housing standards in Finland differs markedly from what might be appropriate in Ghana, while access to air conditioning might be considered a basic need in Qatar but not in Mongolia.

National MPIs typically emerge from extensive consultation processes involving government agencies, researchers, civil society organizations, and affected communities. This participatory approach helps ensure that measures reflect local understandings of poverty while maintaining technical rigor (Zavaleta et al., 2017). Mexico's experience with CONEVAL (2019) demonstrates how institutional frameworks can support sustained measurement efforts despite political changes.

Countries typically develop national MPIs for several key reasons. First, they can incorporate dimensions and indicators that are particularly relevant to their context. Colombia's inclusion of formal employment as a dimension reflects the country's specific concern with labor market formalization, while Bhutan's incorporation of cultural participation indicators aligns with its emphasis on preserving traditional values. Second, national MPIs can use existing data collection systems and align with national statistical capacities. Mexico designed its MPI around indicators available in its regular household surveys, ensuring sustainable measurement over time. Third, national measures can directly connect to existing policy frameworks and institutional structures. Chile's MPI dimensions correspond to specific ministry responsibilities, facilitating clear lines of accountability for poverty reduction.

The contrast between national MPIs and the Global MPI reveals interesting patterns. Consider Mexico's experience. While the Global MPI shows Mexico having relatively low multidimensional poverty compared to other middle-income countries, Mexico's national measure reveals higher poverty rates because it includes dimensions like social security coverage and food security that reflect national standards of wellbeing. Similar patterns emerge in Chile, where the national MPI uses higher thresholds for education and housing quality than the Global MPI, reflecting the country's higher overall development level.

National MPIs often exhibit several key differences from the Global MPI:

- Dimensions: While most retain the core dimensions of health, education, and living standards, many add dimensions like employment, social security, or environmental quality. Panama's MPI includes vulnerability to natural disasters, reflecting its specific geographic risks.
- Indicators: Countries frequently use more sophisticated indicators than the Global MPI's basic measures. Colombia's education dimension includes quality measures beyond simple enrollment, while Vietnam's health indicators incorporate access to health insurance.
- Thresholds: National measures typically set higher deprivation cutoffs than the Global MPI, reflecting higher local standards. Costa Rica's housing quality indicators, for instance, use stricter criteria than the Global MPI's basic standards.
- Weights: Some countries modify the equal weighting scheme based on local priorities or statistical analysis. Ecuador assigns higher weights to dimensions identified as priorities through public consultation.

The policy applications of national MPIs demonstrate their practical value. Mexico's CONEVAL (2019) uses its MPI to coordinate actions across government agencies, with each ministry responsible for specific dimensions. When the MPI revealed high deprivation in both education and nutrition in certain regions, it led to coordinated interventions combining school feeding programs with educational support. Colombia uses its MPI to allocate resources across regions and target social programs, with households' specific deprivation profiles determining which combination of interventions they receive.

Chile's experience particularly illustrates how national MPIs can evolve with a country's development. Initially focused on basic needs, Chile's measure now incorporates indicators of social inclusion and quality of life, such as Internet access and local environment quality. This evolution helps maintain the measure's relevance as absolute poverty declines and relative deprivation becomes more salient.

However, national MPIs also face important challenges. The proliferation of country-specific measures makes international comparisons difficult. Technical capacity constraints can limit some countries' ability to implement sophisticated measurements. Perhaps the most challenging is maintaining measurement consistency while allowing the measure to evolve with changing standards of living and social priorities.

Despite these challenges, the trend toward national MPIs continues to grow, with over 100 countries now having official multidimensional poverty measures (UNDP and OPHI, 2023). This growth reflects both the limitations of international standardized measures and the value of poverty measurements that reflect local contexts and priorities. The experience of these pioneer countries provides valuable lessons for others considering developing their own national measures. Let us examine several key examples of how countries have adapted and implemented national MPIs, each highlighting different aspects of measurement design and policy application.

Example 1: India's experience demonstrates the power of national MPIs in a large, diverse federal system. Between 2005/2006 and 2015/2016, India's Global MPI score fell dramatically from 0.283 to 0.123, representing one of the largest reductions in multidimensional poverty ever recorded. During this period, 271 million people escaped multidimensional poverty across the country (Alkire et al., 2020). However, this national success masked important regional variations that proved crucial for policy design.

Progress varied dramatically by region—while Kerala's MPI was only 0.015 in 2015/2016, Bihar's was 0.248, more than 16 times higher. These geographic disparities helped policymakers identify priority areas for intervention. Some states, like Jharkhand, showed rapid improvement, reducing their MPI by more than half over 10 years, while others like Uttar Pradesh made slower progress despite significant investment. Dimensional breakdowns revealed different patterns of deprivation—Kerala's remaining poverty centered on living standards, particularly housing quality and sanitation, while Bihar's stemmed more from educational deprivations. These insights helped state governments tailor interventions to local needs (Seth and Alkire, 2014). Furthermore, when India's Global MPI calculations showed that 21 percent of poor people lacked access to clean cooking fuel, contributing significantly to health deprivations, the government launched the Pradhan Mantri Ujjwala Yojana program. This initiative provided free LPG connections to poor households, targeting areas where the MPI showed the highest concentration of cooking fuel deprivation.

The intensity measure (A) proved particularly valuable for policy design. In Madhya Pradesh, for instance, the average poor person was deprived in 47 percent of weighted indicators in 2015/2016. This high-intensity score suggested that poor households faced multiple, overlapping disadvantages. In response, the state government designed integrated poverty reduction programs that addressed several deprivations simultaneously rather than taking a sector-by-sector approach.

India also used MPI data to improve targeting of existing programs. The Public Distribution System, which provides subsidized food to poor households, began using MPI data alongside income measures to identify beneficiaries. This helped ensure that households facing multiple deprivations were not excluded just because their income was slightly above the poverty line.

The decomposability of the MPI proved especially useful for monitoring progress. When Jharkhand showed rapid improvement between 2005/2006 and 2015/2016, researchers could break down the change to understand what worked. They found that improvements in electricity access and housing conditions drove much of the reduction in multidimensional poverty, while education deprivations remained stubbornly high. This analysis helped the state government adjust its poverty reduction strategy, leading to increased investment in education programs.

While India's experience demonstrates how a large federal country can use the MPI, other countries have adapted multidimensional poverty measurement to quite different contexts. Let us examine three contrasting cases: Colombia's early adoption of a national MPI, Mexico's institutional framework for coordinating multi-sectoral policy responses, and Vietnam's application of the MPI to rapid economic transformation. ∇

Example 2: Colombia's experience shows how national MPIs can be designed explicitly for policy application. Rather than adopting the Global MPI framework directly, Colombia developed its own measure with 15 indicators across five dimensions: education, childhood and youth conditions, health, employment, and housing and public services (Angulo et al., 2016). This adaptation reflected specific national priorities—for instance, including long-term unemployment and informal employment as indicators because Colombia identified labor market conditions as crucial to understanding poverty.

Colombia's MPI calculations revealed an important mismatch between monetary and multidimensional poverty. While monetary poverty concentrated in rural areas, significant pockets of multidimensional poverty existed in urban areas, particularly informal settlements. In Bogotá, for example, while only 12.8 percent of the population was monetarily poor in 2014, the city's MPI identified 24.3 percent as multidimensionally poor, mainly due to employment informality and low educational achievement (Zavaleta et al., 2017). This finding led to targeted urban interventions complementing rural poverty programs. The Red Unidos program, for instance, assigns social workers to help poor families develop personalized strategies to overcome specific deprivations identified through MPI analysis. By 2018, Colombia's national MPI had fallen from 30.4 to 19.6 percent, with particularly strong improvements in education and health dimensions. ∇

Example 3: Mexico provides a compelling demonstration of how national MPIs can guide coordinated government responses to overlapping deprivations. Mexico's CONEVAL (National Council for the Evaluation of Social Development Policy) developed a sophisticated MPI framework with dimensions spanning income, education, health, social security, housing quality, and basic services. When CONEVAL's MPI analysis identified regions where educational and nutritional deprivations coincided, it exposed a critical policy challenge requiring coordinated action across multiple government ministries. Traditional sector-by-sector approaches would have addressed education and nutrition separately, potentially missing the synergies between these dimensions (CONEVAL, 2019).

Mexico's institutional framework—with CONEVAL coordinating across agencies and each ministry responsible for specific dimensions—enabled integrated interventions combining school feeding initiatives with educational support. By 2018, regions receiving these coordinated programs showed improvements in both nutrition and educational attendance that exceeded what separate programs had achieved. The MPI's decomposability allowed tracking progress across different dimensions and regions, revealing varied patterns of improvement across states. Mexico's experience demonstrates how embedding MPI use within permanent institutional structures like CONEVAL helps maintain consistent poverty measurement and policy coordination across political cycles (CONEVAL, 2019). ∇

Example 4: Vietnam's adaptation of multidimensional poverty measurement demonstrates how these tools can support rapid economic transformation. As Vietnam's economy grew rapidly in the 2000s, traditional income poverty measures showed dramatic improvement. However, the country's MPI calculations revealed persistent deprivations in education and health among certain groups, particularly ethnic minorities in mountainous regions (Tran et al., 2015).

While Vietnam's national monetary poverty rate fell to 9.8 percent by 2016, the MPI showed that 21.2 percent of households remained multidimensionally poor. The intensity measure (A) revealed that poor ethnic minority households typically faced deprivations in 45–50 percent of weighted indicators, compared to 35–40 percent for poor majority Kinh households. This led Vietnam to develop targeted programs for ethnic minority areas combining infrastructure development with education and health interventions (UNDP, 2018). ∇

Example 5: Mexico has recently pioneered the integration of subjective wellbeing into multidimensional poverty measurement. Beyond traditional deprivation indicators, they now collect data on self-reported satisfaction with living standards, perceived social inclusion/exclusion, sense of agency and empowerment, and access to social support networks. Initial results showed interesting disparities—some households classified as non-poor by traditional indicators reported high levels of subjective deprivation, particularly regarding social inclusion and agency. This led to new social programs focusing on community building and empowerment alongside material assistance (CONEVAL, ca. 2009). ∇

These country experiences in Examples 2 to 6 reveal both the power and limitations of multidimensional poverty measurement. While each country adapted the approach to its specific context, several common lessons emerge about how these measures work in practice and what they suggest for future development of poverty measurement (Alkire et al., 2021). These varied experiences demonstrate both the flexibility of the MPI framework and the importance of adapting it to local contexts. They also highlight common implementation challenges, from data quality and availability to balancing technical rigor with practical utility. Perhaps most importantly, they show how multidimensional poverty measurement can inform and improve policy responses across widely varying contexts while maintaining methodological consistency.

However, these experiences also highlight several challenges in implementing multidimensional poverty measures. One persistent issue involves data quality and availability. While the Global MPI framework specifies ideal indicators, countries often must modify these based on what data they can reliably collect. Colombia's decision to include employment informality as an indicator, while theoretically sound, required significant investment in data collection systems.

Another challenge involves the political economy of poverty measurement. When Vietnam's MPI revealed persistent deprivations among ethnic minorities despite rapid national economic growth, it created pressure for targeted interventions that some saw as politically sensitive. Similar tensions arose in India when state-level MPI comparisons highlighted regional inequalities. These experiences suggest that while multidimensional measures can provide valuable policy insights, implementing their findings often requires careful political navigation.

Technical challenges also persist, particularly around setting weights and cutoffs. While the Global MPI uses equal weights for simplicity and transparency, many researchers argue that this approach might not reflect the relative importance of different dimensions. Colombia's national MPI tried to address this by using participatory methods to set weights, but this process proved time-consuming and sometimes contentious. Similarly, the choice of deprivation cutoffs—like how many years of education constitutes a deprivation—often involves difficult value judgments.

These limitations have spurred interest in alternative approaches to measuring multidimensional poverty. The World Bank, for instance, has developed its own multidimensional poverty measure that explicitly includes monetary poverty as one dimension alongside education and basic infrastructure access. The European Union uses a different approach entirely, focusing on material deprivation and social exclusion rather than the three dimensions emphasized by the Global MPI. Understanding these alternatives helps clarify both the strengths and limitations of different approaches to capturing poverty's multiple dimensions.

3.5. Other Multidimensional Indices

Beyond the Global MPI and national measures, several other frameworks for measuring multidimensional poverty have emerged. These alternatives often emphasize different aspects of poverty or serve specific policy needs. The World Bank's MPM, introduced in 2018, takes an innovative approach by explicitly including monetary poverty alongside non-monetary dimensions (World Bank, 2018). The European Union's material deprivation measures focus on social inclusion through access to goods and activities considered normal in European society (Eurostat, 2021).

The Arab MPI, developed by the UN Economic and Social Commission for Western Asia, provides another example of regional adaptation. This measure includes indicators related to food security and exposure to conflict-related vulnerabilities, reflecting specific challenges in the Arab region. It has proved particularly valuable for understanding poverty in conflict-affected countries where traditional data collection is difficult (UN-ESCWA, 2017).

These different approaches reflect varying conceptual understandings of poverty and different measurement priorities. While the Global MPI emphasizes basic capabilities following Sen's framework (Alkire and Santos, 2014), the World Bank's approach recognizes monetary resources as fundamentally important for avoiding deprivation. The EU's focus on relative deprivation and social exclusion reflects higher overall living standards in European countries (Whelan and Maître, 2012). Consider how they evaluate the same population:

Using data from Vietnam, the World Bank's MPM identified 12.8 percent of the population as poor in 2018 compared to 5.9 percent using only the international poverty line. The EU's material deprivation measure, if applied, would likely show even higher rates given its relative standard. Meanwhile, the Global MPI identified 4.9 percent as multidimensionally poor. These varying results do not reflect measurement error but rather different conceptual approaches to understanding poverty.

Each approach offers distinct advantages. The World Bank's MPM provides continuity with traditional monetary measures while capturing non-monetary deprivations. The EU's approach better reflects evolving social standards in more high-income economies. Regional measures can capture context-specific aspects of poverty while maintaining cross-country comparability within regions. Together, they demonstrate both the complexity of measuring multidimensional poverty and the value of having multiple complementary approaches.

3.5.1. Multidimensional poverty measure (MPM)

The World Bank's MPM, introduced in 2018, represents an innovative approach to poverty measurement by explicitly including monetary poverty alongside non-monetary dimensions. Unlike the Global MPI, which focuses entirely on non-monetary indicators, the World Bank measure recognizes that inadequate consumption remains a fundamental aspect of poverty even while acknowledging that poverty extends beyond monetary deprivation (World Bank, 2018).

The MPM framework examines poverty across three key dimensions:

- Monetary poverty using the international poverty line
- Education, focusing on both access and completion
- Basic infrastructure, including electricity, water, and sanitation

A distinctive feature of the MPM is its identification approach. A household can be classified as poor through two routes: either by falling below the monetary poverty line ($2.15/day in 2017 PPP) or by being deprived in multiple non-monetary dimensions. This "union" approach differs fundamentally from the Global MPI's dual cutoff method, reflecting the World Bank's view that severe deprivation in either monetary or non-monetary dimensions constitutes poverty.

The power of this approach became evident in the World Bank's study of 119 developing countries, which found that the MPM identified 50 percent more people as poor than monetary measures alone. These "additional" poor often had consumption levels above the monetary poverty line but faced significant deprivations in education or basic services. Mexico's experience illustrates this well—while monetary poverty affected 23 percent of the population in 2018, the MPM identified 34 percent as poor, primarily due to deprivations in education and basic services despite adequate income (World Bank, 2018).

3.5.2. EU's material deprivation approach

The European Union takes a markedly different approach through its material deprivation measures, reflecting the different nature of poverty in high-income economies. Rather than setting fixed dimensions or combining monetary and non-monetary indicators, the EU focuses on whether households can afford items and activities considered normal in European society (Eurostat, 2021).

The EU measure considers nine specific items:

(1) Ability to face unexpected expenses
(2) Ability to afford one week's annual holiday
(3) Ability to pay for arrears (mortgage, rent, utility bills)
(4) Ability to afford a meal with meat, chicken, or fish every second day
(5) Ability to keep home adequately warm
(6) Having a washing machine
(7) Having a color TV
(8) Having a telephone
(9) Having a car

A household is considered "severely materially deprived" if they cannot afford four or more of these items. This approach reflects a fundamentally different conception of poverty—one focused on relative deprivation and social exclusion rather than absolute deprivation in basic needs dimensions.

The EU's approach proves particularly valuable in high-income countries where absolute poverty is rare, but relative deprivation remains a significant social issue. For example, in 2019, while less than 1 percent of EU households lived below the World Bank's international poverty line, about 5.6 percent were severely materially deprived according to the EU measure. This disparity highlights how poverty manifests differently in more affluent societies.

The measure has also helped identify hidden pockets of deprivation. In several Eastern European countries, material deprivation rates increased during their economic transitions even as monetary incomes rose, revealing how market reforms affected households' ability to maintain customary living standards (Whelan and Maître, 2012).

The differences between measurement approaches become clear when comparing how the World Bank's MPM and EU's material deprivation measures evaluate the same households. While the Global MPI focuses entirely on basic capabilities, the World Bank's MPM includes monetary poverty as a direct criterion alongside education and infrastructure access. The EU's approach emphasizes social inclusion through access to goods and activities considered normal in European society. When applied to the same set of households, these different frameworks can yield varying conclusions about who experiences poverty, reflecting their distinct conceptual foundations and priorities. Detailed comparative calculations demonstrating these differences are provided in the Chapter Technical Annex.

3.5.3. Regional adaptations

Regional adaptations of multidimensional poverty measurement have also emerged, often reflecting shared challenges or priorities across neighboring countries. In Latin America and the Caribbean (LAC), a regional Multidimensional Poverty Index (MPI) has been proposed (CEPAL, 2025; Santos and Villatoro, 2018), incorporating dimensions pertinent to middle-income countries, such as employment quality and social protection. Similarly, the Arab MPI includes indicators related to food security and conflict-related vulnerabilities, reflecting the unique challenges in that region (UN-ESCWA, 2017).

These different measurement approaches can yield varying insights when applied to the same population. Consider Vietnam's experience: the World Bank's MPM identified 12.8 percent of the population as poor in 2018, while the Global MPI showed 4.9 percent as multidimensionally poor. If the EU's material deprivation measure were applied, it would likely show even higher rates given its relative standard. These varying results do not reflect measurement error but rather different conceptual approaches to understanding poverty.

3.5.4. Policy implications of different measurement approaches

These different approaches to measuring multidimensional poverty lead to distinctly different policy prescriptions. The World Bank's MPM, by including monetary poverty as a direct criterion, naturally emphasizes income-generating programs and economic growth as poverty reduction strategies. For instance, in our sample, Household 4 is classified as poor primarily because of its low income, even though it faces fewer non-monetary deprivations than some other households. This approach would support traditional poverty reduction strategies like cash transfers or employment programs (World Bank, 2018).

Consider how different countries have implemented policies based on these varying measurement approaches. Mexico, which developed its own multidimensional poverty measure similar to the World Bank's MPM, uses a two-track approach to poverty reduction. The Prospera program provides cash transfers to address monetary poverty while simultaneously requiring participation in education and health services to address non-monetary deprivations. This dual focus reflects the MPM's recognition of both monetary and non-monetary aspects of poverty (CONEVAL, 2019).

The EU's material deprivation approach leads to quite different policy priorities. By focusing on access to items and activities considered normal in society, this measure emphasizes social inclusion over absolute deprivation. For example, the EU's inclusion of "ability to afford one week's annual holiday" as an indicator has led to programs like Spain's social tourism initiative, which subsidizes vacations for low-income families. Such programs might seem luxurious in developing country contexts but reflect the EU's understanding of poverty as relative deprivation and social exclusion (Eurostat, 2021).

Regional variations in measurement approaches also reflect different understandings of poverty. Latin American countries often include employment formality in their national multidimensional poverty measures, reflecting the region's particular concerns about labor market conditions. Colombia's MPI, for instance, considers long-term unemployment and informal employment as direct indicators of poverty, leading to policy emphasis on labor market formalization (Angulo et al., 2016).

The choice of measurement approach can significantly affect how we understand poverty dynamics. Using the World Bank's MPM, economic growth that raises incomes above the international poverty line directly reduces poverty, even if non-monetary deprivations persist. In contrast, under the Global MPI, similar income growth would not affect poverty measurements unless it led to improvements in health, education, or living standards indicators. This difference can lead to varying assessments of policy success.

Consider Vietnam's experience during rapid economic growth in the 2000s. Using the World Bank's MPM, Vietnam showed dramatic poverty reduction as household incomes rose above the international poverty line. However, the Global MPI revealed persistent deprivations in education and basic services, particularly among ethnic minorities. These different measurements led to heated policy debates about whether Vietnam's growth-focused development strategy was truly succeeding in reducing poverty (Tran et al., 2015).

Similarly, the EU's material deprivation measure can show increasing poverty during economic growth if inequality rises and more households cannot afford socially normal items. This happened in several Eastern European countries during their economic transitions—while average incomes rose, material deprivation increased as previously universal public services became market-based and some households could not afford them (Whelan and Maître, 2012).

3.5.5. *Methodological innovations in multidimensional poverty measurement*

Several important methodological innovations are reshaping how we measure multidimensional poverty. One significant development involves the treatment of continuous variables. Traditional approaches typically convert continuous measures (like years of education or income) into binary indicators of deprivation using cutoffs. However, new methods allow for more nuanced treatment of continuous variables, recognizing that poverty often exists on a spectrum rather than as a simple yes/no condition.

For example, consider educational attainment. The Global MPI uses a binary cutoff—typically six years of schooling—to determine whether someone is education-deprived. But newer approaches, like those developed by Permanyer and Hussain (2018), allow for graduated achievement scores. Under these methods, someone with five years of schooling would be considered less deprived than someone with no education, rather than both being simply classified as "deprived". This approach better captures the reality that each additional year of schooling typically brings some benefit.

Time dynamics represent another area of methodological innovation. Traditional poverty measures provide snapshots of deprivation at specific points in time, but new approaches attempt to capture how poverty evolves. Alkire et al. (2020) have developed methods for measuring chronic multidimensional poverty—identifying households that remain poor over extended periods. These methods help distinguish between transient poverty, which might result from temporary setbacks, and persistent deprivation requiring different policy responses.

Consider a practical application from Ethiopia, where researchers tracked households over five years. Using traditional measures, they found that 45 percent of households were multidimensionally poor at any given time. However, when applying new dynamic measurement techniques, they discovered that 65 percent of households experienced multidimensional poverty at some point during the five years, with 30 percent remaining consistently poor throughout the period. This distinction helped target different interventions for chronically versus temporarily poor households.

A recent contribution by Kakwani (2024) proposes modifying the multidimensional poverty framework to more explicitly incorporate the role of resources or "means" in determining multidimensional poverty. He argues that capability deprivation should only count toward poverty if it results from insufficient resources rather than other factors. For instance, under this approach, poor health would only contribute to measured poverty if it resulted from inability to afford healthcare rather than genetic factors or lifestyle choices. While theoretically appealing, implementing this distinction poses significant practical challenges.

Spatial analysis methods are becoming increasingly sophisticated. While traditional measures typically provide poverty estimates at national or regional levels, new techniques allow for much finer geographic resolution. Researchers at the World Bank have developed methods combining survey data with satellite imagery and other geographic information to create detailed poverty maps. These methods can identify pockets of poverty within cities or regions, allowing for more targeted interventions (World Bank, 2021).

The treatment of missing data has also seen important advances. Traditional approaches often exclude households with missing data on any indicator, potentially biasing results. New methods developed by Alkire et al. (2021) allow for the estimation of multidimensional poverty even with partially missing data using techniques like multiple imputation while explicitly accounting for uncertainty introduced by missing values.

Another significant innovation involves measuring the depth of deprivation within dimensions. Rather than simply counting dimensions in which people are deprived, newer methods attempt to measure how severely deprived they are in each dimension. For instance, in measuring health deprivation, these approaches distinguish between households with one undernourished member versus those where all members are severely undernourished.

Mexico's National Council for the Evaluation of Social Development Policy (CONEVAL) has enhanced the statistical rigor of its multidimensional poverty measurements by incorporating standard errors and confidence intervals. This advancement acknowledges the inherent sampling variability in poverty estimates and provides a clearer understanding of their precision. By routinely publishing these statistical measures, CONEVAL (2010) offers policymakers and researchers more reliable data for informed decision-making.

3.6. Technical Considerations

The construction of multidimensional poverty indices requires careful consideration of both technical rigor and practical applicability (Alkire et al., 2015; Permanyer and Hussain, 2018; UNDP and OPHI, 2019; Alkire and Santos, 2014). While detailed mathematical formulations are provided in the Chapter Technical Annex, understanding the key decision points remains essential for anyone working with these measures. The primary challenges involve selecting appropriate dimensions and indicators, determining weights and cutoffs, choosing aggregation methods, and ensuring robustness across different contexts and time periods.

3.6.1. Choice of dimensions and indicators

The selection of dimensions and indicators represents perhaps the most fundamental technical decision in multidimensional poverty measurement. While theoretical frameworks suggest considering all aspects of deprivation that matter for wellbeing, practical constraints around data availability and measurement feasibility often limit what can be included. Alkire (2013) suggests several key criteria for selecting dimensions:

- First, the chosen dimensions should reflect capabilities that people have reason to value. Education, for instance, appears in nearly all multidimensional poverty measures because it represents a widely valued capability. However, the specific aspects of education that matter most may vary by context—years of schooling might be most relevant in developing countries, while quality measures become more important in advanced economies.
- Second, dimensions should be responsive to policy interventions. Vietnam's experience illustrates this principle—when their MPI revealed persistent educational deprivations among ethnic minorities, the government could respond with targeted educational programs. In contrast, dimensions that policy cannot readily influence may be less useful for poverty measurement.
- Third, dimensions should maintain relevance across the population being measured. Mexico modified its education indicators for different age groups, recognizing that appropriate educational standards vary across generations. This approach helps ensure that the measure remains meaningful for all population subgroups.

The selection of specific indicators within dimensions requires additional technical considerations. Indicators should be

- Valid: Actually measuring what they claim to measure
- Reliable: Providing consistent results when repeated
- Comparable: Meaningful across different contexts
- Available: Regularly collected in existing data systems

Recent methodological innovations have introduced new considerations for dimension selection (Alkire et al., 2021). The increasing availability of high-frequency data sources has made it possible to include dimensions that can be measured more regularly, allowing for more dynamic poverty tracking (World Bank, 2021). Additionally, emerging concerns about environmental vulnerability and digital inclusion have prompted the consideration of new dimensions that may not have been feasible or relevant in earlier poverty measures (UNDP, 2020; Zavaleta et al., 2017).

The treatment of continuous variables represents another area of innovation in indicator selection (Permanyer and Hussain, 2018). While traditional approaches typically use binary indicators based on fixed cutoffs, newer methods allow for graduated achievement scores that better capture the spectrum of deprivation. For example, in measuring educational deprivation, newer approaches might consider not just whether someone completed six years of schooling but also how far they progressed and the quality of that education (Alkire et al., 2020).

3.6.2. *Weights and cutoffs*

The assignment of weights to different dimensions and indicators involves both technical and normative considerations. The Global MPI uses equal weights across dimensions for transparency and simplicity, but alternative approaches include the following:

Statistical weights: Using techniques like PCA to let the data determine weights. Colombia experimented with this approach but found the resulting weights difficult to explain to policymakers.

Participatory weights: Based on public consultation about the relative importance of different dimensions. Mexico used this approach to refine its weighting scheme, though reaching consensus proved challenging.

Hybrid approaches: Combining different methods, such as equal weights across dimensions but data-driven weights within dimensions.

Setting cutoffs—both for individual indicators and across dimensions—requires similar careful consideration. Individual indicator cutoffs should reflect meaningful deprivation thresholds while remaining feasible to measure. The choice of cross-dimensional cutoff (k in the Alkire–Foster method) significantly affects who is identified as poor. Chile found that varying k from 20 to 40 percent changed their poverty headcount by almost 15 percentage points, leading them to conduct extensive sensitivity analysis before selecting their final cutoff.

Recent methodological innovations have expanded our understanding of weighting approaches (Dotter and Klasen, 2014; Kakwani and Silber, 2013). While maintaining the importance of transparency advocated by early researchers (Atkinson, 2003), newer methods offer more sophisticated options for weight determination that better reflect local contexts and priorities (Alkire et al., 2015).

These innovations include regression-based weights that account for the empirical relationships between different dimensions of poverty (Ravallion, 2016), adaptive weights that change based on a country's development level (UNDP and OPHI, 2019), and fuzzy set approaches that avoid sharp distinctions between poor and non-poor states (Kakwani, 2024). These advances help address longstanding concerns about weight selection while maintaining interpretability for policy use.

3.6.3. Aggregation methods

The choice of aggregation method determines how individual deprivations combine into an overall poverty measure. The Alkire–Foster method, used in the Global MPI and many national measures, offers several advantages:

- Decomposability: The measure can be broken down by subgroup and dimension.
- Dimensional monotonicity: Reflects when poor people become deprived in additional dimensions.

- Ordinal data handling: Works with both cardinal and ordinal indicators.

However, alternative aggregation approaches exist. The World Bank's MPM uses a union approach to combine monetary and non-monetary dimensions. Some researchers advocate fuzzy set methods that avoid sharp cutoffs between poor and non-poor states.

Recent innovations in aggregation methods have significantly expanded available approaches (Alkire et al., 2021). While the Alkire–Foster method remains widely used for its clarity and decomposability (UNDP and OPHI, 2019), newer techniques offer additional insights. Fuzzy set methods, gaining prominence through work by researchers like Kakwani (2024), offer ways to handle gradual transitions between poor and non-poor states.

Machine-learning techniques are beginning to influence aggregation methods, though their application remains experimental (World Bank, 2021). These approaches offer potential for identifying complex patterns in how different dimensions of poverty interact, while raising important questions about transparency and interpretability (World Bank, 2021).

3.6.4. Robustness and sensitivity

Given the many technical choices involved, assessing robustness becomes crucial. Key aspects to examine include

- Sensitivity to weights: How much do poverty rankings change with different weighting schemes?
- Cutoff stability: Do conclusions hold across different dimensional cutoffs?
- Indicator robustness: How much do results depend on specific indicator choices?

Mexico's CONEVAL provides an exemplary approach to robustness testing. They regularly publish sensitivity analyses showing how their poverty estimates vary with different technical choices. This transparency helps build credibility while acknowledging inevitable measurement uncertainty.

Beyond statistical robustness, measures should also demonstrate conceptual robustness—maintaining relevance as societies develop and poverty patterns change. Vietnam's MPI, for instance, has evolved to include new indicators of social exclusion and quality of life while maintaining its core structure.

Methodological advances have introduced more sophisticated approaches to robustness testing (Alkire et al., 2015). Bootstrap methods allow for better analysis of sampling variability (Alkire and Santos, 2014), while new sensitivity analysis techniques help understand how results might change under different assumptions (Permanyer and Hussain, 2018).

The increasing availability of high-frequency data has enabled new forms of validation (World Bank, 2021). Countries like Mexico now routinely cross-validate their multidimensional poverty measures against other welfare indicators (CONEVAL, 2019), while statistical agencies increasingly publish confidence intervals alongside point estimates (OPHI, 2018).

Technical considerations ultimately must balance rigor with practicality. While sophisticated techniques exist for many aspects of measurement, the most successful applications often combine technical soundness with transparency and ease of communication. Mexico's experience shows how rigorous measurement can support effective policy when technical choices are clearly explained and justified.

3.7. Policy Applications

Multidimensional poverty measures serve several distinct policy functions that extend beyond simple poverty counting. The ability to identify patterns of overlapping deprivations helps policymakers design more effective interventions, while decomposability by population subgroups and dimensions supports targeted programming (UNDP and OPHI, 2019). Experience from countries implementing MPIs demonstrates both the potential and challenges of translating measurement into action.

In the realm of targeting, MPIs provide crucial information about not just who is poor but how they are poor. Mexico's experience with its Prospera program illustrates this advantage—rather than providing uniform benefits, the program varies support based on households' specific deprivation patterns (CONEVAL, 2019). For instance, households showing deep educational deprivations receive enhanced educational subsidies, while those facing severe health deprivations qualify for additional medical support. This nuanced approach helps ensure interventions match households' actual needs.

The monitoring function of MPIs offers insights that complement traditional poverty measures. Colombia uses its MPI to track progress across different dimensions and regions, helping identify both successes and areas needing additional attention.

For policy design and evaluation, MPIs help governments understand how different interventions affect various aspects of poverty. Chile's experience proves instructive—when their MPI revealed that some households escaped income poverty while remaining deprived in education and health, they redesigned social programs to ensure more comprehensive support. This led to the creation of integrated family support programs that address multiple deprivations simultaneously.

The ability to decompose MPI results by dimension and subgroup particularly aids policy design. When Vietnam's MPI showed that ethnic minority households faced especially severe educational deprivations, this led to targeted programs combining infrastructure development with educational support. The dimensional analysis helped policymakers understand not just where to intervene but also what kind of intervention might prove most effective.

Implementation challenges often arise from institutional arrangements rather than technical limitations. Coordinating responses across multiple government agencies requires new administrative processes and incentive structures. Mexico addressed this through its CONEVAL framework, which assigns specific dimensional responsibilities to different ministries while maintaining central coordination of poverty reduction efforts.

Another implementation challenge involves data collection and analysis capacity. Many countries find their statistical systems strained by the demands of regular multidimensional poverty measurement. Rwanda approached this challenge incrementally, starting with readily available indicators while gradually building capacity for more sophisticated measurement. This allowed them to begin using their MPI for policy while developing more comprehensive data collection over time.

Perhaps most challenging is communicating complex multidimensional metrics to policymakers and the public while maintaining technical rigor. Colombia developed a tiered communication strategy—detailed technical documentation for specialists, simplified explanations for policymakers, and concrete examples for the general public. This layered approach helped maintain methodological sophistication while ensuring that the measure remained useful for policy discussions.

Budget constraints often affect how countries implement MPI-based policies. Rather than trying to address all deprivations simultaneously, many countries use their MPIs to sequence interventions. Panama, for instance, used its MPI to identify the most severe deprivations and areas of greatest need, then phased in interventions as resources became available. This strategic approach helped maximize the impact of limited poverty reduction budgets.

The temporal dimension of policy implementation deserves particular attention. While MPIs can identify current deprivations, effective policy must consider how interventions play out over time. Chile's approach to educational deprivation illustrates this—rather than focusing solely on current school attendance, their programs address factors like early childhood development and parent education that influence long-term educational outcomes.

Geographic targeting based on MPI results has proven particularly effective. Colombia uses detailed MPI maps to identify poverty pockets within cities, leading to highly targeted urban renewal programs. These spatial analyses help ensure that resources reach areas of greatest need while accounting for local context in program design.

Experience suggests several key lessons for effective policy application of MPIs:

- First, institutional frameworks matter tremendously. Countries that establish clear lines of responsibility for different dimensions while maintaining overall coordination tend to implement more effective policies. Mexico's success stems partly from having CONEVAL as a dedicated institution for poverty measurement and policy coordination.
- Second, flexibility in implementation proves crucial. While MPIs provide detailed poverty diagnostics, effective policy responses must adapt to local conditions and capabilities. Vietnam's ethnic minority programs succeeded partly because they allowed local authorities to adjust intervention designs while maintaining overall poverty reduction goals.
- Finally, sustained political commitment makes a crucial difference. Countries that maintain consistent poverty measurement and policy focus across political cycles show better long-term results. Colombia's institutional framework has helped maintain poverty reduction efforts despite changes in government, demonstrating the value of embedding MPI use in permanent state institutions.

3.7.1. Applications of recent innovations

Methodological innovations have enabled new types of policy applications (Alkire et al., 2021). High-resolution poverty mapping, combining traditional survey data with satellite imagery and other geographic data, allows for more precise targeting of interventions (World Bank, 2021). Some countries now use machine-learning techniques to predict areas at risk of falling into multidimensional poverty (UNDP, 2018).

Innovations in measuring deprivation depth have influenced program design (Alkire and Foster, 2011). Mexico's Prospera program uses information about deprivation severity to calibrate benefits (CONEVAL, 2019), while Chile's social programs use measures of overlapping deprivations to identify households needing intensive support (Ministerio de Desarrollo Social, 2020).

3.8. Conclusion

The evolution of multidimensional poverty measurement reflects broader changes in how we understand and address poverty. From early composite indices using principal components analysis to sophisticated measures capturing multiple dimensions of deprivation, the field has made significant technical advances while maintaining focus on practical policy applications. This evolution demonstrates both the value of systematic approaches to measuring poverty's multiple dimensions and the ongoing challenges in capturing this complex phenomenon.

Looking ahead, several key trends shaped by recent methodological innovations will likely influence future developments. Big data analytics and artificial intelligence may enable more frequent and detailed poverty measurement (World Bank, 2021), though raising important questions about privacy and representation. Climate change creates new forms of vulnerability requiring innovative measurement approaches, as seen in efforts to develop "climate-adjusted" poverty measures (Schleicher et al., 2025; UNDP, 2020). Growing interest in subjective wellbeing and relational aspects of poverty may expand measurement beyond material deprivations (Zavaleta et al., 2017).

Key ongoing debates in multidimensional poverty measurement have evolved with recent methodological innovations (Alkire et al.,

2021; Ravallion, 2011). The question of balancing standardization for international comparison with flexibility for local contexts has gained new dimensions as countries develop sophisticated national measures (UNDP and OPHI, 2019). The role of monetary measures alongside multidimensional indices continues to generate discussion, with new approaches like the World Bank's MPM attempting to bridge this divide (World Bank, 2018). Environmental sustainability, digital inclusion, and other emerging dimensions pose fresh challenges for measurement frameworks (UNDP, 2020).

Technical challenges persist even as methodological innovations offer new solutions (Alkire et al., 2015). The increasing availability of big data and machine-learning techniques presents opportunities for poverty measurement but raises questions about data quality and representativeness (World Bank, 2021). Traditional survey methods remain crucial but must evolve to complement newer data sources (Alkire and Santos, 2014).

Implementation challenges often prove as significant as technical ones (UNDP and OPHI, 2019). Countries struggle to coordinate poverty reduction efforts across agencies, maintain measurement quality with limited resources, and communicate complex metrics to diverse audiences. The experience of pioneer countries offers valuable lessons, but each context requires careful adaptation of these lessons (Zavaleta et al., 2017).

Looking forward, several priorities emerge for advancing multidimensional poverty measurement (Alkire et al., 2021). First, measurement systems must become more responsive to emerging forms of deprivation—from digital exclusion to environmental vulnerability (UNDP, 2020). Second, greater attention to intra-household differences in poverty experience is needed, particularly regarding gender and disability status (Bessell, 2015; Espinoza-Delgado and Klasen, 2018). Third, the dynamic aspects of poverty require better incorporation into measurement frameworks, including understanding how households move into and out of multidimensional poverty (Alkire et al., 2020).

Success in multidimensional poverty measurement ultimately requires balancing multiple demands: combining rigorous methodology with clear communication, maintaining international comparability while ensuring local relevance, and providing comprehensive assessment while generating actionable insights (Alkire and Foster, 2011; UNDP and OPHI, 2019). As countries gain experience with these measures and methodological innovations continue to emerge, focus may shift from technical refinement toward strengthening implementation capacity and policy applications.

References

Alkire, S. (2013). Choosing dimensions: The capability approach and multidimensional poverty. In N. Kakwani & J. Silber (Eds.), *The many dimensions of poverty*. London: Palgrave Macmillan. https://doi.org/10.1057/9780230592407_6

Alkire, S., & Foster, J. (2011). Counting and multidimensional poverty measurement. *Journal of Public Economics, 95*(7–8), 476–487. https://www.sciencedirect.com/science/article/abs/pii/S0047272710001660

Alkire, S., & Santos, M. E. (2014). Measuring acute poverty in the developing world: Robustness and scope of the multidimensional poverty index. *World Development, 59*, 251–274. https://www.sciencedirect.com/science/article/abs/pii/S0305750X14000278

Alkire, S., Foster, J., Seth, S., Santos, M. E., Roche, J. M., & Ballón, P. (2015). *Multidimensional poverty measurement and analysis*. Oxford University Press. https://global.oup.com/academic/product/multidimensional-poverty-measurement-and-analysis-9780199689491?cc=ph&lang=en&

Alkire, S., Dirksen, J., Nogales, R., & Oldiges, C. (2020). *Multidimensional poverty and vulnerability to COVID-19: A rapid overview of disaggregated and interlinked vulnerabilities in Sub-Saharan Africa* (OPHI Briefing No. 54a). Oxford Poverty and Human Development Initiative (OPHI), University of Oxford. Retrieved from https://ophi.org.uk/sites/default/files/2024-03/OPHI_Briefing_54a_2020_%28online%29.pdf

Alkire, S., Kanagaratnam, U., & Suppa, N. (2021). *The global multidimensional poverty index (MPI) 2021* (OPHI MPI Methodological Note No. 51). Oxford Poverty and Human Development Initiative. https://ophi.org.uk/sites/default/files/2024-03/OPHI_MPI_MN_51_2021_4_%282022%29.pdf

Angulo, R., Díaz, Y., & Pardo, R. (2016). The Colombian multidimensional poverty index: Measuring poverty in a public policy context. *Social Indicators Research, 127*(1), 1–38. https://link.springer.com/article/10.1007/s11205-015-0964-z

Atkinson, A. B. (2003). Multidimensional deprivation: Contrasting social welfare and counting approaches. *Journal of Economic Inequality, 1*(1), 51–65. https://link.springer.com/article/10.1023/A:1023903525276

Bessell, S. (2015). The individual deprivation measure: Measuring poverty as if gender and inequality matter. *Gender and Development, 23*(2), 223–240. https://doi.org/10.1080/13552074.2015.1053213

Comisión Económica para América Latina y el Caribe (CEPAL). (2025). *Índice de pobreza multidimensional para América Latina*. CEPAL. Recuperado de https://www.cepal.org/es/publicaciones/81425-indice-pobreza-multidimensional-america-latina

Consejo Nacional de Evaluación de la Política de Desarrollo Social (National Council for the Evaluation of Social Development Policy or CONEVAL). (ca. 2009). *Multidimensional measurement of poverty in Mexico*. CONEVAL. https://www.coneval.org.mx/Informes/Coordinacion/Publicaciones%20oficiales/BROCHURE_MULTIDIMENSIONAL_POVERTY_MEASUREMENT_IN_MEXICO.pdf

CONEVAL. (2010). *Multidimensional measurement of poverty in Mexico: An economic wellbeing and social rights approach*. CONEVAL. https://www.coneval.org.mx/informesPublicaciones/FolletosInstitucionales/Documents/Multidimensional-Measurement-of-poverty-in-Mexico.pdf

CONEVAL. (2019). *Metodología para la medición multidimensional de la pobreza en México*. Consejo Nacional de Evaluación de la Política de Desarrollo Social. https://www.coneval.org.mx/Medicion/MP/Paginas/Metodologia.aspx

Dotter, C., & Klasen, S. (2014). The multidimensional poverty index: Achievements, conceptual, and empirical issues. In *Monitoring global poverty* (pp. 140–198). UNDP. https://hdr.undp.org/system/files/documents/mpidotterandklasen.pdf

Drèze, J., & Sen, A. (2013). *An uncertain glory: India and its contradictions*. Princeton University Press. https://press.princeton.edu/books/hardcover/9780691160795/an-uncertain-glory

Espinoza-Delgado, J., & Klasen, S. (2018). Gender and multidimensional poverty in Nicaragua: An individual based approach. *World Development, 110*, 466–491. https://www.sciencedirect.com/science/article/abs/pii/S0305750X18302079

Eurostat. (2021). *Material deprivation statistics – early results*. European Commission. https://ec.europa.eu/eurostat/statistics-explained/index.php?title=Material_deprivation_statistics_-_early_results

Filmer, D., & Pritchett, L. H. (2001). Estimating wealth effects without expenditure data—or tears: An application to educational enrollments in states of India. *Demography*, *38*(1), 115–132. https://citeseerx.ist.psu.edu/document?repid=rep1&type=pdf&doi=26807cf0409821bedc6e259c74ca68710a8f063c

Howe, L. D., Galobardes, B., Matijasevich, A., Gordon, D., Johnston, D., Onwujekwe, O., Patel, R., Webb, E. A., Lawlor, D. A., & Hargreaves, J. R. (2012). Measuring socio-economic position for epidemiological studies in low- and middle-income countries: A methods of measurement in epidemiology paper. *International Journal of Epidemiology, 41*(3), 871–886. https://academic.oup.com/ije/article/41/3/871/833303

Kakwani, N. (2024). *Multidimensional poverty: A new thinking on measurement* (Gulati Institute of Finance and Taxation Discussion Paper No. 21). https://www.gift.res.in/wp-content/uploads/2024/08/DP-21-Multi-dimensional-Poverty-Nanak-Kakwani.pdf

Kakwani, N., & Silber, J. (2013). *The many dimensions of poverty*. Palgrave Macmillan. https://link.springer.com/book/10.1057/9780230592407

Ministerio de Desarrollo Social. (2020). *Informe de desarrollo social 2020*. Gobierno de Chile. https://www.desarrollosocialyfamilia.gob.cl/storage/docs/Informe_de_Desarrollo_Social_2020.pdf

Narayan, D., Patel, R., Schafft, K., Rademacher, A., & Koch-Schulte, S. (2000). *Voices of the poor: Can anyone hear us?* Oxford University Press for the World Bank. https://documents.worldbank.org/en/publication/documents-reports/documentdetail/131441468779067441/voices-of-the-poor-can-anyone-hear-us

Nardo, M., Saisana, M., Saltelli, A., Tarantola, S., Hoffman, A., & Giovannini, E. (2008). *Handbook on constructing composite indicators: Methodology and user guide*. OECD Publishing. https://doi.org/10.1787/9789264043466-en

Oxford Poverty and Human Development Initiative (OPHI). (2018). *Global Multidimensional Poverty Index 2018: The most detailed picture to date of the world's poorest people* [Report]. OPHI, University of Oxford. ISBN 978-1-912291-12-0.

Permanyer, I., & Hussain, M. A. (2018). First order dominance techniques and multidimensional poverty indices: An empirical comparison of different approaches. *Social Indicators Research, 137*(3), 867–893.

https://forskning.ruc.dk/en/publications/first-order-dominance-techniques-and-multidimensional-poverty-ind

Ravallion, M. (2011). On multidimensional indices of poverty. *Journal of Economic Inequality, 9*(2), 235–248. https://link.springer.com/article/10.1007/s10888-011-9173-4

Ravallion, M. (2016). *The economics of poverty: History, measurement, and policy*. Oxford University Press. https://academic.oup.com/book/10927

Santos, M. E., & Villatoro, P. (2018). A multidimensional poverty index for Latin America. *Review of Income and Wealth, 64*(1), 52–82. https://doi.org/10.1111/roiw.12275

Schleicher, J., van Soesbergen, A., Schaafsma, M., Dyngeland, C., Oldekop, J. A., Maioli, V., … Vira, B. (2025). Where nature and poverty meet: Developing a multidimensional environment-poverty measure. *The Journal of Development Studies, 61*(6), 869–889. https://doi.org/10.1080/00220388.2024.2434248

Sen, A. (1976). Poverty: An ordinal approach to measurement. *Econometrica, 44*(2), 219–231. https://doi.org/10.2307/1912718

Sen, A. (1999). *Development as freedom*. Oxford University Press. http://www.c3l.uni-oldenburg.de/cde/OMDE625/Sen/Sen-intro.pdf

Seth, S., & Alkire, S. (2014). *Did poverty reduction reach the poorest of the poor? Assessment methods in the counting approach* (OPHI Working Paper No. 77). Oxford Poverty & Human Development Initiative, University of Oxford. https://ophi.org.uk/publication/WP-77

Townsend, P. (1979). *Poverty in the United Kingdom: A survey of household resources and standards of living*. University of California Press. https://www.degruyterbrill.com/document/doi/10.1525/9780520325760/html

Tran, V. Q., Alkire, S., & Klasen, S. (2015). Static and dynamic disparities between monetary and multidimensional poverty measurement: Evidence from Vietnam. In *Measurement of poverty, deprivation, and economic mobility* (pp. 249–281). Emerald Group Publishing Limited. https://www.emerald.com/insight/content/doi/10.1108/S1049-258520150000023008/full/html

United Nations Economic and Social Commission for Western Asia (UN-ESCWA). (2017). *Arab multidimensional poverty report*. UN-ESCWA. https://archive.unescwa.org/publications/multidimensional-arab-poverty-report

United Nations Development Programme (UNDP). (2010). *Human Development Report 2010: The real wealth of nations—Pathways to human development*. UNDP. https://hdr.undp.org/content/human-development-report-2010

UNDP. (2018). *Multidimensional poverty in Viet Nam: Reducing poverty in all its dimensions to ensure a good quality life for all*. UNDP Viet Nam. https://www.undp.org/sites/g/files/zskgke326/files/migration/vn/MDP-full-E.pdf

UNDP. (2020). *Human Development Report 2020: The next frontier—Human development and the Anthropocene*. UNDP. https://hdr.undp.org/sites/default/files/hdr2020.pdf

UNDP & OPHI. (2019). *How to build a national multidimensional poverty index (MPI): Using the MPI to inform the SDGs*. UNDP and OPHI. https://www.undp.org/publications/how-build-national-multidimensional-poverty-index

UNDP & OPHI. (2020). *Global Multidimensional Poverty Index 2020: Charting pathways out of multidimensional poverty—Achieving the SDGs*. UNDP and OPHI. https://ophi.org.uk/Publications/GMPI11-2020

UNDP & OPHI. (2023). *Global Multidimensional Poverty Index 2023*. New York: UNDP. https://hdr.undp.org/content/2023-global-multidimensional-poverty-index-mpi

United Nations Statistics Division (UNSD). (2025). *Global indicator framework for the Sustainable Development Goals*. New York: UNSD. https://unstats.un.org/sdgs/indicators/indicators-list/

Vyas, S., & Kumaranayake, L. (2006). Constructing socio-economic status indices: How to use principal components analysis. *Health Policy and Planning, 21*(6), 459–468. https://academic.oup.com/heapol/article/21/6/459/612115

Whelan, C. T., & Maître, B. (2012). Understanding material deprivation: A comparative European analysis. *Research in Social Stratification and Mobility, 30*(4), 489–503. https://www.esri.ie/system/files/media/file-uploads/2015-07/OPEA85.pdf

World Bank. (2018). *Poverty and Shared Prosperity 2018: Piecing together the poverty puzzle*. Washington, DC: World Bank. https://www.worldbank.org/en/publication/poverty-and-shared-prosperity-2018

World Bank. (2021). *Poverty and Shared Prosperity 2020: Reversals of Fortune*. Washington, DC: World Bank. https://www.worldbank.org/en/publication/poverty-and-shared-prosperity-2020

Zavaleta, D., Samuel, K., & Mills, C. (2017). Measures of social isolation for improved understanding of poverty. *Social Indicators Research, 131*(1), 367–391. https://openaccess.city.ac.uk/id/eprint/21610/3/Zavaleta%2C%20Samuel%20and%20Mills%20-%20Measures%20of%20Social%20Isolation.pdf

CHAPTER 3

Technical Annex: Mathematical Foundations of Multidimensional Poverty Measurement

3A.1. Principal Components Analysis

The first principal component is essentially a mathematical way of combining assets into a single score that best captures underlying economic differences. For PCA, the approach creates a wealth "fingerprint" for each household where the most distinctive assets receive the most weight in the final measure.

Mathematical Formulation

The PCA approach involves calculating eigenvalues and eigenvectors of the correlation or covariance matrix of asset variables. For household assets $x_1, x_2, \ldots, x_k$, the first principal component is

$$PC_1 = a_{11}x_1 + a_{12}x_2 + \ldots + a_{1k}x_k$$

where the weights (a_{1j}) are chosen to maximize $\mathrm{Var}(PC_1)$ subject to the constraint that

$$\sum_{i=1}^{n} a_{11}^2 = 1$$

Since the first principal component maximizes the variance explained by a linear combination of the original variables, this means that it captures the maximum amount of information about differences between households using a single index.

Asset Weight Interpretation

Assets that vary most systematically with overall wealth receive higher weights in the principal component. For example, if refrigerator ownership strongly distinguishes between rich and poor households while radio ownership does not, refrigerators will receive a higher weight in the final wealth index.

Practical Implementation

In practice, researchers standardize asset variables before applying PCA to ensure that all assets contribute meaningfully to the analysis regardless of their original measurement scales. The resulting wealth index provides a continuous measure of household economic status that can be used for ranking households or creating wealth quintiles.

This technical framework underlies the wealth indices developed by Filmer and Pritchett (2001) and subsequent researchers. While the full mathematical derivation of eigenvalues and eigenvectors extends beyond this discussion, this formulation provides the essential mathematical foundation for understanding how PCA creates meaningful wealth measures from multiple asset indicators.

3A.2. Global MPI Calculation Steps

The Global MPI follows a precise methodology for transforming household-level data into meaningful poverty measurements. This process involves three key steps (Alkire et al., 2015):

(1) identifying who is deprived in each indicator,
(2) determining who is multidimensionally poor (using some cut-offs), and
(3) calculating summary statistics that describe both the extent and intensity of poverty.

For each indicator, the Global MPI uses carefully defined cutoffs to determine whether a household is deprived. These thresholds reflect severe deprivations that would be widely recognized as aspects of poverty. For instance, in education, a household is considered deprived if no adult member has completed six years of schooling—a threshold that represents a fundamental level of educational attainment needed for basic literacy and numeracy (Alkire and Santos, 2014).

The measure employs a nested weighting structure to create deprivation scores. After identifying deprivations in each indicator, the measure assigns weights to create a deprivation score for each household. The Global MPI uses a nested weight structure: Each of the three dimensions (health, education, and living standards) receives equal weight of 1/3, and this weight is divided equally among the indicators within each dimension. Thus, each of the two education indicators gets a weight of 1/6, each health indicator gets 1/6, and each of the six living standards indicators gets a weight of 1/18 (UNDP and OPHI, 2019).

The Global MPI uses an innovative "dual cutoff" approach to identify who is poor. First, for each indicator, a deprivation cutoff determines whether a household is deprived—for example, whether any school-age child is not attending school. Then, a poverty cutoff determines whether a household faces enough deprivations to be considered multidimensionally poor. Under the Global MPI, a household must be deprived in at least one-third of weighted indicators to be identified as poor. This approach ensures that poverty identification reflects multiple disadvantages simultaneously rather than just a single deprivation (Alkire and Foster, 2011).

Once the poor are identified, three main statistics summarize poverty levels. The headcount ratio (H) shows what percentage of people are multidimensionally poor. The intensity of poverty (A) reveals the average share of weighted deprivations experienced by poor people. Multiplying the headcount ratio and the intensity (H × A) together gives the MPI itself, which captures both how many people are poor and how poor they are.

Example A-1: To demonstrate how the Global Multidimensional Poverty Index (MPI) functions in practice, we examine four households representing diverse living conditions. This case study is smaller than what would be used in real-world applications, but it effectively illustrates how the key concepts and computational steps are involved in transforming household-level data into meaningful insights about multidimensional poverty. The MPI analysis begins with a comprehensive snapshot of each household's circumstances, examining factors like family size, location, income, education, health, and access to basic services (Table 1).

Each household in this example represents a unique story of deprivation and resilience.

- The first household, an urban family of four, demonstrates moderate challenges despite their $400 monthly income. While the household head has completed basic education, they face specific deprivations—one child cannot attend school, and they share sanitation facilities.
- In contrast, the second household exemplifies severe rural poverty, with six members surviving on $150 monthly, minimal education, undernourishment, and lacking basic infrastructure.
- The third household provides an important reference point for non-poor conditions. This urban family of three earns $600 monthly, has completed secondary education, and owns substantial assets including a car and modern appliances.
- At the other extreme, the fourth household embodies entrenched rural poverty—five members with $200 monthly income, minimal education, undernourished members, and multiple children out of school.

Table 1. Household information

Variable	Household			
	1	**2**	**3**	**4**
Household size	4	6	3	5
Location	Urban	Rural	Urban	Rural
Monthly income	$400	$150	$600	$200
Highest schooling (Head)	6 years	3 years	10 years (secondary)	1 year
Number of school-aged children not attending	1	1	0	2
Undernourished member?	No	Yes	No	Yes
Child death in past 5 years?	No	No	No	No
Has electricity?	Yes	No	Yes	No
Drinking water	Piped in dwelling	40 min walk	Piped in dwelling	Fetch from river (35 min)
Sanitation	Shared latrine	Open defecation	Private improved latrine	Shared pit latrine
Housing	Solid floor/ walls	Mud walls/ thatch roof	Brick walls; good quality	Partial wood walls/thatch roof
Cooking fuel	LPG (gas)	Wood/ charcoal	LPG (gas)	Wood/ charcoal
Assets owned	TV + fridge	1 small radio only	Car, phone, TV, fridge	None

These four households demonstrate how poverty cannot be understood through a single lens of income. Each family's unique combination of educational access, health conditions, housing quality, and basic infrastructure reveals the multidimensional nature of economic hardship. The intricate interplay of these factors challenges simplistic definitions of poverty, showing why researchers have developed more comprehensive measurement approaches.

The MPI calculation functions as a comprehensive assessment of each household's situation across 10 key indicators spanning 3 main dimensions: education, health, and living standards. To ensure balanced evaluation, each dimension receives equal weight, and within each dimension, specific indicators are carefully weighted to provide a nuanced view of household deprivations, as shown in Table 2.

The process of determining poverty status extends far beyond examining income alone. The Global Multidimensional Poverty Index approaches this challenge by carefully examining how different aspects of deprivation interconnect. Each major dimension—health,

Table 2. Deprivation matrix

Indicator (weight)	**Household**			
	1	**2**	**3**	**4**
Deprived: Years of schooling? (1/6)	0	1	0	1
Deprived: Child attendance? (1/6)	1	1	0	1
Deprived: Nutrition? (1/6)	0	1	0	1
Deprived: Child mortality? (1/6)	0	0	0	0
Deprived: Electricity? (1/18)	0	1	0	1
Deprived: Water? (1/18)	0	1	0	1
Deprived: Sanitation? (1/18)	1	1	0	1
Deprived: Housing? (1/18)	0	1	0	1
Deprived: Fuel? (1/18)	0	1	0	1
Deprived: Assets? (1/18)	0	1	0	1

education, and living standards—receives equal importance in the assessment. Within these dimensions, specific indicators are weighted to ensure comprehensive evaluation. Health examines both nutrition and child mortality with equal emphasis, while education balances years of schooling with current attendance. Living standards encompass six distinct aspects, from electricity access to asset ownership, each contributing to the overall assessment.

The MPI employs a sophisticated "dual cutoff" method that extends beyond simple binary classifications. This approach first identifies specific deprivation thresholds for each indicator, then determines poverty status by examining the total weighted deprivations a household experiences. To illustrate this process, we can examine Household 2's situation in detail.

In the education dimension, Household 2 faces two significant deprivations: insufficient years of schooling and a child not attending school. These educational deprivations together contribute one-third ($2 \times 1/6$) to their total deprivation score. The health dimension reveals one deprivation—undernourishment—contributing one-sixth ($1 \times 1/6$) to their score. In living standards, they face deprivation in all six indicators, adding another one-third ($6 \times 1/18$) to their total. Combined, these deprivations sum to $1/3 + 1/6 + 1/3 = 5/6$ or equivalently 0.833, reflecting severe multidimensional poverty.

The other households present contrasting situations. Household 1 experiences only two deprivations—child attendance and sanitation—resulting in a significantly lower score of 0.222 (calculated as $0.167 + 0.056$). Household 3 stands out with no deprivations, yielding a score of zero. Household 4 mirrors Household 2's severe deprivation level with an identical score of 0.833, though arising from a slightly different combination of challenges. Thus, all the deprivation scores are as follows:

- HH1: $(0 \times 1/6) + (1 \times 1/6) + (0 \times 1/6) + (0 \times 1/6) + (0 \times 1/18) + (0 \times 1/18) + (1 \times 1/18) + (0 \times 1/18) + (0 \times 1/18) + (0 \times 1/18) = 1/6 + 1/18 = 0.222$

- HH2: (1 × 1/6) + (1 × 1/6) + (1 × 1/6) + (0 × 1/6) + (1 × 1/18) + (1 × 1/18) + (1 × 1/18) + (1 × 1/18) + (1 × 1/18) + (1 × 1/18) = 3/6 + 6/18 = 0.833
- HH3: All zeros = 0.000
- HH4: (1 × 1/6) + (1 × 1/6) + (1 × 1/6) + (0 × 1/6) + (1 × 1/18) + (1 × 1/18) + (1 × 1/18) + (1 × 1/18) + (1 × 1/18) + (1 × 1/18) = 3/6 + 6/18 = 0.833

To transform these household-level assessments into a comprehensive poverty measure, we apply a poverty cutoff of one-third (approximately 0.333). Any household with a deprivation score exceeding this threshold is classified as multidimensionally poor. Under this criterion, both Households 2 and 4 are identified as poor, while Households 1 and 3 fall below the poverty threshold.

- HH1: 0.222 < 1/3 → Not poor
- HH2: 0.833 > 1/3 → Poor
- HH3: 0.000 < 1/3 → Not poor
- HH4: 0.833 > 1/3 → Poor

The final MPI calculation combines two essential measurements that together capture both the prevalence and intensity of poverty. First, we calculate the headcount ratio (H), which measures the proportion of people living in poor households. In our sample of 18 total people, 11 individuals (6 from Household 2 and 5 from Household 4) live in households classified as poor, yielding a headcount ratio of

$$H = 11/18 = 0.611 \text{ or } 61.1\%.$$

The second component, the intensity of poverty (A), reveals the average share of deprivations experienced by poor households. Both poor households in our sample face identical deprivation scores of 0.833. When we weight these scores by household size—multiplying 0.833 by 6 people for Household 2 and by 5 people for Household 4, then dividing by the total of 11 poor people—we arrive at an intensity measure of

$$A = (0.833 \times 6 + 0.833 \times 5)/11 = 0.833 \text{ or } 83.3\%.$$

Multiplying these two components together yields our final MPI value:

$$MPI = H \times A = 0.611 \times 0.833 = 0.509$$

This number represents a comprehensive assessment of poverty that accounts for both its spread across the population and its depth within affected households.

The framework allows us to delve deeper through various decomposition analyses. A striking geographic pattern emerges when we examine urban versus rural locations. The urban households (Households 1 and 3) show an MPI of zero, while rural households (Households 2 and 4) exhibit a severe MPI of 0.833, highlighting profound spatial disparities in poverty experience.

We can further understand the structure of poverty by examining how different dimensions contribute to overall deprivation. The education dimension, with a censored headcount ratio of 0.611, contributes 40 percent to total poverty (calculated as $(11/18 \times 1/3)/0.509$). The health dimension, where only nutrition shows significant deprivation, accounts for 20 percent of total poverty ($(11/18 \times 1/6)/0.509$). Living standards match education's contribution at 40 percent, reflecting the comprehensive nature of deprivation among poor households.

This detailed decomposition reveals that education and living standards jointly account for four-fifths of observed multidimensional poverty in our sample. Such insights prove invaluable for policy design, suggesting where interventions might have the greatest impact in reducing poverty's multiple manifestations. The analysis demonstrates how the MPI methodology captures nuances of poverty that income-based measures alone would miss, providing a richer understanding of how different aspects of deprivation combine to shape the lived experience of poverty. ∇

Example A-1 demonstrates how the MPI provides a nuanced understanding of poverty beyond traditional monetary-based measures, capturing the overlapping deprivations that characterize the experience of poverty. It shows how multiple deprivations are combined using weights to determine the extent of each household's deprivation, as well as how the dual cutoff approach classifies households as multidimensionally poor. It further illustrates how summary measures capture both the incidence of poverty (the proportion of people who are poor) and the intensity of poverty (the average share of deprivations among the poor). Finally, the example highlights how the measure can be decomposed by different dimensions (such as education, health, and living standards) and by various subgroups (such as rural versus urban areas).

By merging multiple deprivations into a single index and applying the dual cutoff, the MPI not only identifies who is poor but also shows how they are poor, offering a nuanced picture that combines incidence and intensity. This dual perspective, combined with flexibility in decomposing results, provides policymakers with powerful insights to design targeted interventions aimed at reducing multidimensional poverty.

The Global MPI's design offers several important strengths. Its standardized methodology allows for meaningful international comparisons, while its ability to be decomposed by subgroups helps identify which populations face the greatest disadvantages. The measure directly captures actual deprivations rather than relying on indirect proxies, and its specific, actionable indicators provide clear guidance for policy interventions.

However, the Global MPI also faces important limitations. Available survey data often constrain which indicators can be included, potentially missing important aspects of poverty. The equal weighting across dimensions, while transparent, may not reflect local priorities or circumstances. The use of binary cutoffs for each indicator might miss important gradations in deprivation severity. Perhaps most importantly, measuring at the household level may mask significant inequalities between household members, particularly along gender lines.

Despite these limitations, the Global MPI has proven remarkably influential, both as a direct measurement tool and as a model for countries developing their own multidimensional measures. Its success demonstrates the value of systematic approaches to measuring poverty's multiple dimensions, while its limitations have spurred important innovations in national and regional adaptations of multidimensional poverty measurement.

3A.3. FGT Extension to Multidimensional Measures

The Global MPI framework builds on the FGT class of poverty measures, adapting them for multidimensional analysis. Just as the FGT measures capture different aspects of income poverty through increasingly sophisticated metrics (headcount, poverty gap, squared gap), the Global MPI can be extended beyond the basic adjusted headcount ratio or MPI (M_0) to create adjusted versions of the FGT measures. The adjusted poverty gap (M_1), for instance, measures the average depth of deprivation across all dimensions for poor households. For example, if a poor household has children who dropped out after completing four years of schooling when six years is the threshold, their education deprivation gap would be 2/6. The adjusted poverty gap M_1 averages such gaps across all dimensions and all poor households. Similarly, the adjusted squared gap (M_2) squares these gaps before averaging, giving greater weight to households facing more severe deprivations.

To understand how M1 and M2 provide deeper insights into poverty measurement, let us return to Example A-1 where we identified Households 2 and 4 as multidimensionally poor. While the poverty headcount H or M_0 told us that these households were poor and in how many dimensions, M_1 and M_2 will reveal how far these households are from the deprivation cutoffs in each dimension.

Example A-1 (continued): For the education dimension, we begin by examining years of schooling, where the threshold is six years. Household 2, with three years of schooling, falls halfway short of this threshold, giving us a normalized gap of 0.5 (calculated as (6 – 3)/6). Household 4's situation is even more severe, with only one year of schooling resulting in a larger gap of 0.833. For school attendance, both households are simply marked as fully deprived since this is a binary indicator, giving a gap of 1.

- Years of schooling: Threshold is 6 years
  - HH2: Has 3 years → gap = (6 – 3)/6 = 0.5
  - HH4: Has 1 year → gap = (6 – 1)/6 = 0.833
- School attendance: Binary indicator, so gap is 1 when deprived
  - HH2: Deprived → gap = 1
  - HH4: Deprived → gap = 1

In the health dimension, both households are deprived in nutrition (giving a gap of 1) but neither experienced child mortality (gap of 0).

- Nutrition: Binary indicator
  - HH2: Deprived → gap = 1
  - HH4: Deprived → gap = 1
- Child mortality: Binary indicator
  - Neither household deprived → gap = 0

The living standards dimension comprises six binary indicators where both households face complete deprivation, resulting in gaps of 1 for each indicator. This pattern of gaps provides our first indication that while both households are poor, they experience different depths of poverty in certain dimensions.

- HH2: Deprived in all six → gaps = 1 for each
- HH4: Deprived in all six → gaps = 1 for each

To calculate M_1 (the adjusted poverty gap), we combine these gaps using the same weighting structure as before—1/6 for each education and health indicator, and 1/18 for each living standards indicator. For Household 2, this weighted sum of gaps comes to 0.778, while Household 4's slightly deeper deprivation in education pushes its weighted sum to 0.806. The average of these gaps (G) is 0.792, indicating that poor households face gaps that are, on average, about 79.2% of the maximum possible deprivation.

- For each poor household:
  - HH2: Weighted sum of gaps = $(0.5 \times 1/6) + (1 \times 1/6) + (1 \times 1/6) + (0 \times 1/6) + 6(1 \times 1/18) = 0.778$
  - HH4: Weighted sum of gaps = $(0.833 \times 1/6) + (1 \times 1/6) + (1 \times 1/6) + (0 \times 1/6) + 6(1 \times 1/18) = 0.806$
- Average gap (G) = $(0.778 + 0.806)/2 = 0.792$

The final M_1 calculation combines this average gap with our previous measures of poverty's breadth and incidence. Recall that H (headcount ratio) was 0.611 and A (average intensity) was 0.833. Multiplying these three components—H × A × G—gives us

$$M_1 = 0.611 \cdot 0.833 \cdot 0.792 = 0.403$$

This lower value than M_0 (0.509) reflects how M_1 accounts for partial deprivations rather than treating all deprivations as complete.

The adjusted squared gap M_2 follows a similar process but squares the gaps before aggregating them, thereby giving greater weight to larger deprivations. When we square Household 2's education gap, for instance, 0.5 becomes 0.25, while Household 4's 0.833 gap becomes 0.694, magnifying the difference between them. Following through with the weighted sums using these squared gaps, we find that Household 2's aggregate squared gap is 0.736 and Household 4's is 0.785, averaging to 0.761. ∇

The final M_2 calculation, again using H and A, gives us 0.387. The progression from M_0 (0.509) to M_1 (0.403) to M_2 (0.387) tells an important story about poverty in our sample. The declining values indicate that while our poor households face many deprivations (captured by M_0), some of these deprivations are partial rather than complete (shown by M_1), and there is meaningful variation in deprivation depth across dimensions (revealed by M_2). This more nuanced understanding of poverty's structure can help policymakers better target interventions—for instance, highlighting the particularly deep educational deprivation in Household 4 that might require special attention.

3A.4. Comparative Analysis of Measurement Frameworks

The theoretical foundation of effective multidimensional poverty measurement rests on several axioms that ensure measures behave appropriately under different conditions. These properties can be formalized mathematically and illustrated through specific examples.

Focus Axiom

Formally, let P(X) denote a poverty measure applied to a distribution matrix X, where each row represents a household, and each column represents an indicator. Let x_i represent the achievement vector for household i. The focus axiom requires

$$\mathbf{P(X) = P(X') \text{ where } X' \text{ differs from } X \text{ only in that for some non-poor household } j, x\_j \neq x'\_j}$$

Using our five-family example, consider the Gomez family with income above the poverty line but deprived in education and sanitation. If their income doubles from \$400 to \$800 monthly while their education and sanitation deprivations remain unchanged, a properly focused poverty measure should show $P(X) = P(X')$. This ensures that improvements among the non-poor (those not classified as multidimensionally poor) do not artificially reduce measured poverty.

Mathematically, if household j is classified as non-poor ($c_j = 0$ under the counting approach), then any change in j's achievement vector should leave the overall poverty measure unchanged:

$$\partial P/\partial x_{jk} = 0 \text{ for all } k, \text{ when } c_j = 0$$

Monotonicity Axiom

The monotonicity axiom requires that poverty measures increase when poor households become more deprived. Formally,

If household i is poor ($c_i = 1$) and experiences a deterioration in indicator k (x_{ik} decreases), then $P(X') > P(X)$.

Consider the Martinez family experiencing loss of healthcare access while maintaining their other characteristics. If $c_{Martinez} = 1$ (classified as poor), then the reduction in their healthcare achievement $x_{Martinez,health}$ should result in

$$P(X') = P(X_{original} \text{ with deteriorated healthcare}) > P(X_{original})$$

For the Alkire–Foster class of measures, this translates to

$$\partial M_\alpha/\partial x_{ik} < 0 \text{ for all } k \text{ when } c_i = 1 \text{ and } \alpha \geq 0$$

where M_α represents the general class of AF measures with parameter α.

Decomposability

Decomposability requires that overall poverty can be expressed as a weighted sum of subgroup poverty levels. For population partition $\{G_1, G_2, ..., G_m\}$ with population shares n_j/n:

$$P(X) = \Sigma(j = 1 \text{ to } m)\ (n\_j/n)\ P(X\_j)$$

Using our example, if we partition households into urban (Households 1, 3, 5) and rural (Households 2, 4) groups:

$$P\_total = (3/5)P\_urban + (2/5)P\_rural$$

For the Perez family example regarding disability, decomposability allows us to calculate

$$P\_total = (n\_disabled/n)P\_disabled + (n\_non\text{-}disabled/n)\ P\_non\text{-}disabled$$

This property proves essential for policy targeting, as it enables identification of subgroups contributing disproportionately to overall poverty. The mathematical requirement ensures

$$\partial P/\partial P\_j = n\_j/n \text{ for all subgroups } j$$

Transfer Principles

Advanced poverty measures often satisfy transfer principles. The weak transfer principle requires that a progressive transfer from a richer to a poorer individual should not increase poverty:

$$\text{If } x\_i > x\_j \text{ and we transfer } \delta \text{ from } i \text{ to } j \text{ such that } x\_i - \delta \geq x\_j + \delta, \text{ then } P(X') \leq P(X)$$

The strong transfer principle requires strict inequality $P(X') < P(X)$ when both individuals remain on the same side of the poverty line.

Dimensional Monotonicity

Specific to multidimensional measures, dimensional monotonicity requires that poverty increases when an already poor person becomes deprived in an additional dimension:

If $c_i = 1$ and household i becomes deprived in previously non-deprived indicator k, then $P(X') > P(X)$.

These axioms provide the theoretical foundation ensuring that multidimensional poverty measures respond appropriately to changes in deprivation patterns while maintaining analytical tractability for policy applications.

3A.5. Comparative Analysis of Measurement Frameworks

Example A-2: Let us analyze our four sample households in Example A-1 using both the World Bank MPM and EU approaches to see how different measurement frameworks lead to different conclusions about who is poor. First, we will gather comprehensive information about each household:

- Household 1 (four members):
  - Daily income per person: \$3.33
  - Education: All adults completed primary school
  - Basic infrastructure: Has electricity and water, lacks improved sanitation
  - Can afford seven of nine EU standard items
  - Cannot afford holiday, unexpected expenses
- Household 2 (six members):
  - Daily income per person: \$1.67
  - Education: No adult completed primary school
  - Basic infrastructure: Lacks all three services

  - Can afford three of nine EU standard items
  - Cannot afford holiday, unexpected expenses, adequate meals, heating, car, washing machine
- Household 3 (three members):
  - Daily income per person: $6.67
  - Education: All adults completed secondary school
  - Basic infrastructure: Has all three services
  - Can afford all nine EU standard items
- Household 4 (five members):
  - Daily income per person: $2.00
  - Education: One adult completed primary school
  - Basic infrastructure: Lacks electricity and sanitation, has water
  - Can afford four of nine EU standard items
  - Cannot afford holiday, unexpected expenses, heating, car, washing machine

Let us examine how the World Bank MPM evaluates poverty across three key dimensions. In the monetary dimension, the World Bank uses the international poverty line of $2.15 per day as its threshold. Applying this criterion to our sample, we find that Households 2 and 4, with daily per person incomes of $1.67 and $2.00, respectively, fall below this threshold and are thus considered monetarily poor.

The education dimension focuses on basic educational attainment within households. A household is considered education-deprived if none of its adult members has completed primary education. In our sample, only Household 2 faces this deprivation, as it is the only household where no adult has completed primary schooling. This reflects the World Bank's emphasis on basic education as a fundamental aspect of poverty.

For the infrastructure dimension, the World Bank considers access to three basic services: electricity, water, and sanitation. A household is marked as infrastructure-deprived if it lacks access to any of these services. This criterion identifies three households—1, 2, and 4—as infrastructure-deprived, though for different reasons. Household 1 lacks only sanitation, while Household 2 lacks all three services, and Household 4 lacks electricity and sanitation but has water access.

The World Bank's approach to identifying the multidimensionally poor differs significantly from the Global MPI's methodology. A household can be classified as poor through two routes: either by being monetarily poor (below $2.15/day) or by being deprived in both non-monetary dimensions (education and infrastructure). This creates a broader conception of poverty than approaches requiring deprivation in multiple dimensions.

Applying these criteria to our sample produces clear results. Household 1, despite lacking sanitation infrastructure, is not classified as poor because it is above the monetary poverty line and faces only one non-monetary deprivation. Household 2 is identified as poor through both pathways—it is monetarily poor and faces both non-monetary deprivations. Household 3 escapes poverty classification entirely, having no deprivations in any dimension. Household 4 is classified as poor primarily due to its monetary poverty and infrastructure deprivation, though it avoids education deprivation by having one adult who completed primary school.

The European Union's approach to measuring material deprivation takes a markedly different path. Rather than focusing on absolute deprivations, it examines whether households can afford items and activities considered normal in European society. The EU considers nine specific items, ranging from basic needs like adequate heating to social participation indicators like the ability to take an annual holiday. A household lacking access to four or more of these items is considered severely materially deprived.

When we apply the EU's criteria to our sample households, we see a pattern that partially aligns with but also differs from the World Bank's results. Household 1, missing only two items (holiday and unexpected expenses capacity), escapes classification as materially deprived. Household 2, unable to afford six of the nine items, is clearly identified as severely deprived. Household 3 maintains its non-poor status, having access to all nine items. Household 4 joins Household 2 in the severely deprived category, lacking five items, namely holiday, unexpected expenses capacity, heating, car ownership, and a washing machine.

Comparison of results:

	Global MPI	World Bank MPM	EU approach
Household 1	Not poor	Not poor	Not deprived
Household 2	Poor	Poor	Severely deprived
Household 3	Not poor	Not poor	Not deprived
Household 4	Poor	Poor	Severely deprived

This comparison reveals several important insights about different approaches to multidimensional poverty measurement. The World Bank's MPM includes monetary poverty as a direct criterion, meaning any household below the international poverty line is automatically classified as poor, regardless of other dimensions—an approach that contrasts with the Global MPI's omission of monetary criteria. Meanwhile, the EU's focus on social inclusion through access to common goods and activities represents a relative approach to measuring poverty, differing significantly from the absolute deprivation focus of both the Global MPI and World Bank MPM measures. Despite these methodological differences, all three frameworks converge in identifying Households 2 and 4 as poor or deprived, suggesting some alignment in pinpointing the most disadvantaged households despite varying conceptual foundations. ∇

CHAPTER 4

The Collective Household Model on Assignable Goods

"Like slavery and apartheid, poverty is not natural. It is man-made and it can be overcome and eradicated by the action of human beings."
—NELSON MANDELA

SUMMARY

This chapter explores how poverty measurement can be significantly improved through the collective household model with assignable goods. Traditional poverty measures assume that resources are shared equally within households, but this assumption often does not reflect reality and can result in misclassifying many poor individuals. By analyzing consumption patterns of items that can be clearly attributed to specific household members (like clothing or food), researchers can now reveal who is truly poor, even within households that appear non-poor overall.

The collective household model builds on the pioneering work by Chiappori and others, recognizing that families consist of individuals with distinct preferences and varying bargaining power rather than functioning as single decision-making units.

A key concept is "resource shares"—the proportion of total household spending allocated to each person. These shares help translate household-level expenditure into individual well-being, which is crucial for accurate poverty identification.

Since resource shares are not directly observable in most surveys, researchers have developed innovative methods to estimate them by analyzing spending patterns on assignable goods. Recent methodological breakthroughs have made these techniques more accessible, allowing researchers to see beyond household averages and identify individuals experiencing poverty despite living in nominally non-poor households.

Empirical evidence consistently shows that women typically receive smaller resource shares than men, children receive less than adults, later-born children receive less than firstborns, and resources often decline with age, particularly for women. These findings have profound implications for poverty measurement, with studies showing that approximately one-third of poor individuals may live in non-poor households, and accounting for intrahousehold inequality can substantially increase measured poverty rates.

Policy implications include the need for individual-level targeting of anti-poverty programs, careful consideration of who receives transfers within households, and complementary interventions addressing social norms and power dynamics. While implementation challenges remain, methodological innovations continue to make these approaches more accessible for routine poverty monitoring and program design. By revealing who might be poor even within non-poor households, the collective household model offers valuable insights for designing more effective poverty reduction strategies that ensure no individual is left behind.

4.1. Introduction: Looking Inside a Household

4.1.1. Why this matters: A real family example

Imagine the Rodriguez family: father Miguel, mother Carmen, and their two children, Sofia (8) and Diego (12). According to government statistics, this family earns $600 per month, which puts them just above the poverty line of $150 per person. Therefore, the family is classified as "not poor".

But let us look closer at how this $600 is actually used. Miguel receives $280 (47 percent) for his personal needs and interests, while Carmen receives $180 (30 percent) for her expenses. Diego receives $90 (15 percent) for school and personal items, and Sofia receives only $50 (8 percent) for her needs.

Now we see a different picture. While Miguel lives comfortably above the poverty line, both children—especially Sofia—are actually living in poverty with resources below $150 per person per month. Carmen is also close to the poverty line. Traditional poverty measurement would completely miss this reality.

4.1.2. The problem with traditional poverty measurement

Traditional approaches to measuring poverty make a simple but problematic assumption: They divide the total household income or spending by the number of people and assume everyone gets an equal share. Using this "per capita" approach, the Rodriguez family's calculation would be $600 ÷ 4 people = $150 per person, making the family "not poor" in official statistics.

Traditional approaches to measuring poverty make a simple but problematic assumption about how resources are shared within households. The conventional per capita approach assumes that individual consumption can be calculated as

$$x_i = \frac{C_h}{n_h}$$

where

- x_i is the consumption of individual i (in household h)
- C_h is the total consumption of household h
- n_h is the number of members in household h

This formula implicitly assumes that every individual receives an identical share ($\frac{1}{n_h}$) of the total household resources (Deaton, 1997). However, a growing body of evidence suggests that this assumption is often far from reality. Intrahousehold allocation of resources may be influenced by factors such as gender, age, earning capacity, social norms, and bargaining power (Browning and Chiappori, 1998; Browning et al., 2013).

4.1.3. What this chapter will teach you

This chapter introduces the "collective household model with assignable goods", a framework that recognizes households as collections of individuals with different needs (and preferences) and different amounts of (bargaining) power to get resources, rather than single decision-making units. We can estimate how resources are shared by analyzing spending patterns on items clearly attributable to specific people (like children's clothing vs. adult clothing), revealing hidden poverty that traditional measures miss entirely. Ultimately, this helps design better policies to help those who truly need assistance

4.2. How Families Really Make Decisions

4.2.1. Moving beyond the "household as a single unit" idea

Traditional economic models treated households as if they were single individuals with unified preferences—an approach known as the "unitary household model" (Becker, 1981). Think of it like imagining families as single-minded teams where everyone agreed on how to spend money, like a perfectly coordinated sports team where every player has identical goals. In this framework, household decisions can be represented as maximizing a single household utility function:

$$\max U(x_1, x_2, \ldots, x_n)$$

subject to a household budget constraint:

$$\sum_{i=1}^{n} p_i x_i \leq Y$$

where

- U is the household utility function
- x_i are the consumption goods
- p_i are the prices
- Y is the total household income

While mathematically convenient, this approach fails to capture the complex dynamics of real families. Families are more like groups of individuals who care about each other but have different wants, needs, and amounts of influence over decisions. Think of a family planning a vacation where parents might want relaxation, teenagers might want adventure, and young children might just want fun. The final decision reflects negotiation and the relative influence of each family member.

Furthermore, this "unitary household model" cannot explain, for instance, why giving cash transfers to mothers rather than fathers often leads to different spending patterns and child welfare outcomes—a phenomenon observed in numerous studies of conditional cash transfer programs (Duflo, 2003).

4.2.2. The collective household model: A more realistic approach

Recognizing these limitations, researchers developed "collective" or "bargaining" models, which incorporate the idea that household outcomes result from negotiation among members with varying degrees of power (Browning and Chiappori, 1998; Chiappori, 1988, 1992).

Collective models recognize that households consist of multiple individuals with distinct preferences who need to reach decisions together. Under the collective approach, household decisions are Pareto efficient—meaning no household member's welfare can be improved without reducing another's. This framework can be represented as

$$\max \sum_{j=1}^{m} \mu_j U^j \left(x_1^j, x_2^j, \ldots, x_n^j \right)$$

subject to the household budget constraint

$$\sum_{j=1}^{m} \sum_{i=1}^{n} p_i \, x_i^j \leq Y$$

where

- U^j is the utility function of household member j
- x_{ij} is the consumption of good i by household member j
- μ_j represents the bargaining power or the "Pareto weight" of each household member
- m is the number of household members

The weights μ_j represent the bargaining power of each household member and may depend on factors like income contribution, education, age, social norms, and outside options (Apps and Rees, 1988).

This approach has proven particularly valuable in understanding gender- and age-based disparities within households, which often remain hidden in traditional poverty measures. As Browning, Chiappori, and Lewbel (2013) note,

> "The collective setting provides a natural framework for analyzing intra-household inequality and for evaluating policies targeted at specific household members."

4.2.3. Resource shares: The key concept

A "resource share" is simply the portion of the family's total spending that goes to each person. For example, if a family spends \$1,000 per month total and the father gets goods and services worth \$400, then the father's resource share is 40 percent (400/1,000).

Formally, the resource share for individual j in household h can be defined as

$$\eta_j^h = \frac{x_j^h}{C_h}$$

where

- η_j^h is the resource share of individual j in household h
- x_j^h is the consumption of individual j in household h
- C_h is the total household consumption

Resource shares tell us who really gets what in the household. They help us move from knowing the family's total income to understanding each person's actual living standard. Consider the Kumar family with total monthly spending of \$800: father Dev gets \$320 (40 percent share), mother Priya gets \$240 (30 percent share), son Raj gets \$160 (20 percent share), and daughter Mira gets only \$80 (10 percent share). Even though this family is not poor on average (\$200 per person), Mira is living on much less than her brother or parents. If the poverty line is \$120 per person, Mira is actually poor even though her family appears non-poor in traditional statistics.

An individual would be classified as poor in traditional poverty measurement if his/her individual consumption falls below the poverty line:

$$x_j^h < z$$

where z is the poverty line. Under the equal sharing assumption, all members of a household are either poor or non-poor together. But with unequal resource shares, some members may be poor while others are not, even within the same household.

Resource shares may vary significantly based on factors like

- Gender (men often receive larger shares than women)
- Age (adults typically receive more than children, but elderly members may receive less than working-age adults)
- Education (more educated members may command larger shares)
- Employment status (earning members often receive larger shares)
- Cultural and social norms (which influence bargaining power)

Understanding these patterns helps explain why certain individuals may experience poverty even in households that appear non-poor on average.

4.3. Estimating Individual Consumption Through Assignable Goods

4.3.1. The challenge of measurement

While resource shares are conceptually important, they cannot be directly observed in most household surveys. Standard surveys collect data at the household level, with limited information on who consumes what within the household. This creates a fundamental identification challenge: how can we estimate individual-level consumption from household-level data?

4.3.2. Solution: Assignable goods

The innovative breakthrough involves using "assignable goods"—items that can be clearly attributed to specific household members (Browning et al., 1994; Deaton, 1989). Common assignable goods include

- Clothing and footwear designed specifically for men, women, and children (Dunbar et al., 2013)
- Gender-specific personal care items
- Individual food items like infant formula consumed exclusively by infants
- Adult-only items such as alcohol, tobacco, or personal electronics used solely by certain adults (Bargain et al., 2014)
- Educational expenses for specific household members

By tracking the household's expenditure on these goods and relating it to the presence (or characteristics) of specific members (e.g., the number of children, older adults, or working-age men), researchers can infer how much is being diverted to or withheld from these subgroups (Brown et al., 2021; Lewbel and Pendakur, 2008). In turn, these patterns can illuminate hidden intrahousehold poverty.

Some national statistics offices conduct detailed household expenditure surveys that include itemized spending on

- **Food** (often not assignable unless it is child-specific, like infant formula)
- **Clothing and footwear**, sometimes broken down by gender/age (children's vs. adult's attire)
- **Leisure and personal care** (alcohol, tobacco, personal electronics)
- **Education** (school uniforms, tuition fees, textbooks)
- **Healthcare** (child vs. adult prescriptions)

When these national surveys allow for disaggregation by individual data users, the data analysts can apply the assignable-goods method (Bose-Duker et al., 2021). However, data quality varies across surveys.

Some surveys lump all clothing expenditures into one category, whereas others may separate men's, women's, and children's clothing in monthly or quarterly budgets. Also, underreporting can occur, especially for goods considered private or stigmatized (e.g., alcohol, tobacco).

4.3.3. From Engel curves to resource shares

The pathway from observed expenditure on assignable goods to estimated resource shares relies on the analysis of Engel curves—the relationships between total household expenditure and expenditure on specific goods. For assignable goods, these Engel curves can be represented as

$$w_j^h = \frac{p_j \, q_j^h}{C^h}$$

where

- w_j^h is the budget share of the assignable good for person type j in household h
- p_j is the price of the assignable good
- q_j^h is the quantity consumed
- C^h is the total household expenditure

In the Dunbar, Lewbel, and Pendakur (2013) framework, these household-level Engel curves for assignable goods can be related to individual-level Engel curves through resource shares:

$$w_j^h\left(C^h\right) = \eta_j^h \; w_j\left(\frac{\eta_j^h C^h}{n_j^h}\right)$$

where

- $w_j^h\left(C^h\right)$ is the observed household-level budget share for the assignable good of type j

- η_j^h is the resource share for type j individuals
- w_j is the individual-level Engel curve function
- n_j^h is the number of type j individuals in the household

This equation establishes a relationship between observable household-level budget shares and unobservable resource shares.

To see this intuitively, consider a simple example where men and women have identical preferences for their respective clothing. If we observe that men's clothing budget shares increase more rapidly with household expenditure than women's clothing budget shares, this suggests men command larger resource shares than women.

4.3.4. Recent methodological advances

Lechene, Pendakur, and Wolf (2021) introduced a linear reframing of the Dunbar–Lewbel–Pendakur model (L-DLP). This approach simplifies estimation by allowing for the use of ordinary least squares techniques:

$$W_j^h = a_j^h + b_j^h \ln C_h + \varepsilon_j^h$$

where resource shares can be estimated as

$$\eta_j^h = \frac{b_j^h}{\sum_k b_k^h}$$

This linear approach makes the model more accessible for practical applications in poverty measurement.

Example: Estimating Resource Shares in Bangladesh

Using data from Bangladesh, Brown, Calvi, and Penglase (2021) estimated resource shares using both food and clothing as assignable goods. For a typical household with one man, one woman, one boy, and one girl, they found that

- Men consumed 36 percent of household resources.
- Women consumed 30 percent of household resources.
- Boys and girls each consumed approximately 17 percent of household resources.

This unequal distribution would be completely hidden in traditional poverty measures that assume equal sharing.

Interestingly, they found that resource shares estimated from clothing versus food were similar for adults but differed for children, with food-based estimates showing larger resource shares for children. This discrepancy highlights the importance of using multiple assignable goods to validate results.

To see how this works in practice, let us walk through a simplified example using data from a small sample of Bangladeshi households. Imagine we have data on clothing expenditure for different household members and total household expenditure.

First, we estimate Engel curves for men's clothing, women's clothing, and children's clothing as functions of log household expenditure. For men's clothing, we might find these regressions:

$$\widehat{W_m^h} = 0.02 + 0.04 \ln C_h$$

For women's clothing:

$$\widehat{W_f^h} = 0.015 + 0.03 \ln C_h$$

And for children's clothing:

$$\widehat{W_c^h} = 0.01 + 0.02 \ln C_h$$

The coefficients on $\ln C_h$ are 0.04, 0.03, and 0.02 for men, women, and children, respectively. Using the L-DLP approach, we would estimate resource shares as

$$\eta_m^h = \frac{0.04}{0.04+0.03+0.02} = \frac{0.04}{0.09} = 0.44 \text{ or } 44 \text{ percent}$$

$$\eta_f^h = \frac{0.03}{0.04+0.03+0.02} = \frac{0.03}{0.09} = 0.33 \text{ or } 33 \text{ percent}$$

$$\eta_c^h = \frac{0.02}{0.04+0.03+0.02} = \frac{0.02}{0.09} = 0.22 \text{ or } 22 \text{ percent}$$

This means that in the average household, men get 44 percent of resources, women get 33 percent, and children get 22 percent. If there are two children in the household, each child would receive 11 percent of household resources.

Now, suppose a household has total expenditure of $400 per month. Under the equal sharing assumption with two adults and two children, each person would be assigned $100. But using our estimated resource shares, the man would receive $176 (44 percent of $400), the woman would receive $132 (33 percent of $400), and each child would receive $44 (11 percent of $400).

If the poverty line were $90 per person per month, the household as a whole would not be considered poor under the equal sharing assumption since everyone would have $100. But when we account for unequal sharing, both children would be classified as poor since they only receive $44 each, well below the poverty line. The woman and man, with $132 and $176, respectively, would not be classified as poor.

This simple example demonstrates how accounting for intrahousehold inequality can fundamentally change our understanding of who is poor, even within the same household.

4.4. Key Findings on Intrahousehold Resource Allocation

Studies applying the collective household model across diverse contexts have revealed several consistent patterns in how resources are allocated within households.

4.4.1. Gender disparities among adults

Women typically receive smaller resource shares than men, though the magnitude of this gap varies across contexts. The relative resource share of women compared to men can be expressed as

$$\frac{\eta_f^h}{\eta_m^h}$$

In Bangladesh, Brown et al. (2021) found that women's resource shares are about 20 percent smaller than men's in many household types: $\frac{\eta_f^h}{\eta_m^h} \approx 0.8$. In Malawi, Dunbar et al. (2013) found even larger gender gaps, with women's resource shares approximately 30 percent smaller than men's: $\frac{\eta_f^h}{\eta_m^h} \approx 0.7$.

These gender gaps often reflect broader social and economic inequalities. However, the gap typically narrows with women's education and employment status. Calvi (2020) found that in India, women with secondary education command resource shares closer to men's compared to women with no education.

4.4.2. Age patterns

Resource shares often decline with age, particularly for women. Calvi (2020) modeled this relationship in India using age-specific resource shares:

$$\eta_f^h(a) = \eta_f^h \times f(a)$$

where a is age and $f(a)$ is an age adjustment function. She found that women's resource shares decrease substantially after reproductive age (approximately age 45), potentially contributing to excess female mortality among older women. At advanced ages (70+), women's resource shares were approximately 60 percent of their peak values at prime working age.

4.4.3. *Children's resource shares*

Children typically receive smaller resource shares than adults, with the per-child share declining as the number of children increases. For a household with n_c children, the resource share per child can be expressed as

$$\frac{\eta_c^h}{n_c}$$

Dunbar et al. (2013) found that in Malawian households with one man, one woman, and one child, the child received approximately 23 percent of household resources. In similar households with three children, each child received only about 15 percent of resources.

The relationship between the number of children and the total resources allocated to children often follows a concave pattern:

$$\eta_j^h = \alpha + \beta \ln(n_c)$$

where α and β are the parameters. This functional form captures the empirical regularity that while total resources allocated to children increase with the number of children, they do so at a decreasing rate.

4.4.4. *Birth order and gender effects among children*

Several studies have found that a child's birth order significantly affects their resource share. Denoting the resource share of the ith child as $\eta_{c,i}^h$, research typically finds

$$\eta_{c,1}^h > \eta_{c,2}^h > \eta_{c,3}^h > \ldots >$$

This pattern may reflect evolutionary strategies, declining household resources, or decreasing parental investment in later-born children. In societies with strong son preference, this pattern can interact with gender discrimination:

$$\eta^{h}_{c,i,\text{male}} > \eta^{h}_{c,i,\text{female}}$$

However, the evidence on gender disparities among children is mixed. While some studies have found that boys receive larger shares than girls, others—including Brown et al. (2021) in Bangladesh—found minimal gender differences among children. The presence and magnitude of such differences appear to vary substantially across cultural contexts.

4.4.5. Education and employment effects

Higher educational attainment, particularly for women, is associated with more equal resource allocation. This relationship can be modeled as

$$\eta^{h}_{f} = \alpha_0 + \alpha_1 \mathrm{E}_f + \alpha_2 \mathrm{E}_m + \alpha_3 \mathbf{X} + \varepsilon$$

where

- E_f is the woman's education level
- E_m is the man's education level
- $\mathbf{X}$ is a vector of other household characteristics

Typically, $\alpha_1 > 0$, indicating that women's resource shares increase with their education. Brown et al. (2021) found that in more educated households in Bangladesh, resources are shared more equitably between women and children.

Similarly, women's participation in income-generating activities often increases their resource shares:

$$\eta^{h}_{f} = \beta_0 + \beta_1 \mathrm{Y}_f + \beta_2 \mathrm{Y}_m + \alpha_3 \mathbf{X} + \varepsilon$$

where

- Y_f is the woman's income or earnings
- Y_m is the man's income or earnings

Typically $\beta_1 > 0$, indicating that women's resource shares increase with their income contribution. However, the relationship is not always straightforward. Bargaining power appears linked to both current earnings and outside options in case of household dissolution.

These patterns have important implications for understanding who is poor even within non-poor households and for designing policies to address intrahousehold inequality.

4.5. Implications for Poverty Measurement and Policy

4.5.1. *Misclassification of poverty status*

When resource shares are combined with household expenditure data, they reveal striking patterns of individual-level poverty. A significant proportion of poor individuals live in non-poor households, and conversely, some non-poor individuals live in poor households.

The poverty status under equal sharing versus actual resource shares can be expressed as

- Under equal sharing: Poor if $\frac{C_h}{n_h} < z$
- Under actual sharing: Poor if $\eta_j^h C_h < z$

where z is the poverty line. Misclassification occurs when these two approaches yield different results:

- False negative: $\frac{C_h}{n_h} \geq z$ but $\eta_j^h C_h < z$
- False positive: $\frac{C_h}{n_h} < z$ \$ but $\eta_j^h C_h \geq z$

Brown et al. (2021) found that in Bangladesh, a third of individuals with consumption below the extreme poverty line live in households with per-capita consumption above the poverty line.

The misclassification rate can be quantified as

$$M = \frac{N_{FN} + N_{FP}}{N}$$

where

- N_{FN} is the number of false negatives
- N_{FP} is the number of false positives
- N is the total population

Brown et al. (2021) found misclassification rates of approximately 17 percent in Bangladesh, indicating that nearly one in five individuals is incorrectly classified by standard poverty measures.

4.5.2. Higher overall poverty rates

Accounting for unequal resource allocation typically increases estimated poverty rates compared to household per-capita measures. The individual-level poverty rate can be calculated as

$$P_{\text{individual}} = \frac{1}{N}\sum_{j=1}^{N} I(\eta_j^h C_h < z)$$

where $I(.)$ is an indicator function equal to 1 if the condition is true and 0 otherwise.

The per-capita poverty rate, in contrast, is

$$P_{\text{per-capita}} = \frac{1}{N}\sum_{h=1}^{H} n_h \, I(\frac{C_h}{n_h} < z)$$

where H is the number of households.

In Malawi, Dunbar et al. (2013) found that accounting for intra-household inequality increases the child poverty rate from 40 percent to nearly 60 percent. Similar patterns have been found in other contexts, such as in the Philippines (Albert et al., 2024), suggesting that standard poverty measures may significantly underestimate the true extent of poverty.

4.5.3. *Policy applications*

Individual-level targeting

Traditional targeting approaches based on household characteristics may miss many poor individuals living in non-poor households. Individual-level targeting using information on demographic characteristics and household composition may achieve higher efficiency.

Transfer recipient identity

The impact of a transfer on individual consumption can be modeled as

$$\Delta c_j = \frac{\partial \eta_j^h}{\partial y_r} C_h + \eta_j^h \, \Delta C_h$$

where

- y_r is the income of the transfer recipient
- $\frac{\partial \eta_j^h}{\partial y_r}$ captures how resource shares change in response to recipient income
- ΔC_h is the change in total household consumption

When transfers are directed to women or other vulnerable household members, the first term may be positive for those individuals, leading to larger increases in their consumption than would occur if transfers were directed to household heads.

Program conditions

Program conditions can influence intrahousehold allocation by affecting the relative bargaining power of different household members or by directly targeting specific consumption categories. For instance, conditional cash transfers that require children's school attendance may increase children's resource shares. The effectiveness of conditions depends on their enforceability and relevance to household decision-making processes.

4.5.4. Case studies: Intrahousehold allocation and poverty

The Philippine Context

The Philippines provides a compelling case study of how intrahousehold inequality affects poverty measurement in a Southeast Asian context. Recent work by Albert et al. (2024) applies the collective household model to Filipino households, revealing significant disparities in resource allocation that remain hidden in official income poverty statistics.

The Philippine Statistics Authority (PSA) reported that the country's poverty incidence declined from 18.1 percent in 2021 to 15.5 percent in 2023. These statistics, however, are based on the standard assumption of equal resource sharing within households. When researchers examined resource allocation using the assignable goods approach, they found substantial evidence of intrahousehold inequality.

Using data from the Family Income and Expenditure Survey (FIES), Albert et al. (2024) estimated resource shares for different household members by examining expenditure patterns on clothing and food items. They found that in a typical Filipino household with two parents and two children, resources were allocated approximately as follows:

- The father received 35–40 percent of household resources.
- The mother received 30–35 percent of household resources.

- Each child received 12–18 percent of household resources, with estimates varying depending on which assignable good was used.

The researchers found several important patterns in resource allocation within Filipino households:

1. Rural–urban differences: Intrahousehold inequality was more pronounced in rural areas than in urban areas. The gender gap in resource shares was approximately 10–15 percentage points in rural households compared to 5–10 percentage points in urban settings.
2. Basic sector patterns: The study examined resource allocation across the Philippines' officially recognized "basic sectors"—vulnerable groups including farmers, fisherfolk, and informal sector workers. Farmers and fisherfolk showed particularly high levels of intrahousehold inequality, with women and children in these households receiving significantly smaller resource shares.
3. Age-related inequality: Elderly women were found to receive substantially smaller resource shares than elderly men, paralleling findings from India and other contexts. This age–gender interaction creates particularly high vulnerability for older women.
4. Education effects: Women's education had a significant positive impact on their resource shares. Women with secondary education commanded resource shares much closer to men's compared to women with no formal education.

These patterns of unequal resource allocation have profound implications for poverty measurement in the Philippines. When Albert et al. (2024) calculated individual poverty rates using their estimated resource shares rather than the standard per capita approach, they found the following:

- The overall poverty rate increased by 7–8 percentage points.
- Child poverty rates were nearly twice as high as official estimates based on equal sharing.

- Women's poverty rates were 9–12 percentage points higher than men's.
- The elderly poverty rate increased by about 10 percentage points overall, with especially large increases for elderly women.

These findings suggest that the Philippines may be making less progress in reducing poverty than official statistics indicate, particularly for vulnerable household members. They also have important implications for the country's social protection programs, such as the conditional cash transfer program called *Pantawid Pamilyang Pilipino* Program (4Ps), which traditionally targets households rather than individuals. The study suggests that programs might reach more poor individuals by accounting for demographic factors associated with smaller resource shares.

The Philippines' experience demonstrates how the collective household model can reveal important patterns of poverty hidden by conventional measures, even in a country that has made significant progress in economic development and poverty reduction in recent years.

The Bangladesh Example

To provide another illustration of how accounting for intrahousehold inequality affects our understanding of poverty, let us examine a case study from Bangladesh based on Brown, Calvi, and Penglase (2021). This research combines detailed household survey data with methodological innovations to reveal patterns of individual poverty hidden by conventional measures.

Bangladesh's official statistics showed substantial progress in reducing poverty, with the national poverty rate declining from 48.9 percent in 2000 to 24.3 percent in 2016. However, these impressive figures rely on the standard assumption of equal sharing within households. When researchers examined individual-level consumption using the assignable goods approach, a different picture emerged.

Using data from the Bangladesh Integrated Household Survey, which uniquely collected information on individual food consumption, researchers estimated resource shares for men, women, and children. They found that in a typical Bangladeshi household with one man, one woman, and two children, resources were allocated approximately as follows:

- The man received 38 percent of household resources.
- The woman received 30 percent of household resources.
- Each child received 16 percent of household resources.

These unequal shares have dramatic implications for poverty measurement. When the researchers calculated poverty rates based on these individual-level consumption estimates, they found that

1. The overall poverty rate increased from 17 to 27 percent when accounting for intrahousehold inequality.
2. The poverty rate for women was 13 percent higher than for men.
3. The child poverty rate more than doubled compared to conventional measures.
4. About one-third of poor individuals lived in households classified as non-poor by conventional measures.

This pattern of hidden poverty was particularly pronounced for certain vulnerable groups. Elderly women, for instance, had poverty rates nearly twice as high as elderly men due to their smaller resource shares. Similarly, later-born children faced significantly higher poverty risks than firstborn children, reflecting parents' tendency to allocate more resources to older children.

The Bangladesh case study also revealed important patterns in how resource shares vary with household characteristics. Women's resource shares increased with their education level and labor force participation, suggesting that empowering women economically can help reduce intrahousehold inequality. Similarly, children's shares were larger in households where mothers had more education, indicating that maternal empowerment benefits children as well.

These findings have important policy implications. Bangladesh's flagship poverty reduction programs, like the Vulnerable Group Development program, traditionally target households based on aggregate poverty measures. The research suggests that such programs could reach more poor individuals by accounting for demographic factors associated with smaller resource shares—targeting households with elderly women or multiple children, for instance, even if those households are not classified as poor by conventional measures.

Additionally, the evidence on how women's education and employment increase their resource shares suggests that programs promoting female education and labor force participation could reduce intrahousehold inequality directly. These structural interventions might complement direct transfers in creating more equitable resource allocation within families.

The Bangladesh case illustrates how the collective household model with assignable goods can reveal important patterns of poverty hidden by conventional measures. Similar patterns have been documented in other contexts, suggesting that accounting for intrahousehold inequality is crucial for understanding and addressing poverty globally.

4.6. Practical Applications and Future Directions

4.6.1. *Current applications*

Several countries have begun incorporating insights from this approach into their poverty measurement and program design:

- **Mexico** uses detailed information on individual-level deprivations to tailor social assistance programs. Their conditional cash transfer program, *Progresa/Oportunidades* (now called Prospera), provides transfers directly to mothers and includes conditions related to children's education and health, explicitly acknowledging and addressing intrahousehold allocation issues.

- **Colombia** has experimented with multidimensional poverty measures that consider individual-level education and health outcomes. Their program Red Unidos assigns social workers to develop personalized strategies for each family member, recognizing that household members may face different types of deprivation.

These applications demonstrate the practical value of looking beyond household averages to understand individual experiences of poverty.

4.6.2. *Methodological advances for practical implementation*

The linear Dunbar–Lewbel–Pendakur (L-DLP) model developed by Lechene, Pendakur, and Wolf (2021) significantly simplifies the estimation of resource shares. Under this approach, resource shares can be estimated using standard OLS regression of budget shares on log household expenditure:

$$W_j^h = a_j^h + b_j^h \ln(C_h) + \varepsilon_j^h$$

with resource shares calculated as

$$\eta_j^h = \frac{b_j^h}{\sum_i b_i^h}$$

This linear approach makes implementation more feasible for statistical agencies and policy analysts without specialized econometric expertise.

Brown, Calvi, and Penglase (2021) showed that using multiple assignable goods can reduce the restrictiveness of identification assumptions while providing a check on the robustness of results. Their approach allows preferences for assignable goods to vary more freely across individuals while maintaining identification power.

If we observe budget shares for two assignable goods (indexed by k) for each person type, we have

$$W_{j,k}^{h} = \eta_j^h \, w_{j,k}\left(\frac{\eta_j^h C_h}{n_j^h}\right)$$

This provides additional equations that can help identify resource shares under weaker assumptions.

Browning, Chiappori, and Lewbel (2013) developed methods to account for economies of scale in household consumption, recognizing that some goods are partially or fully shared within households. Their approach introduces a consumption technology function that maps private consumption to household purchases:

$$z = F\left(x_1, x_2, \ldots, x_m\right)$$

where z represents household purchases, and x_j represents private consumption of individual j.

While sophisticated, these approaches help provide more accurate assessments of individual welfare, particularly for goods like housing that exhibit significant economies of scale.

4.6.3. Challenges and limitations

Implementation requires detailed data on assignable goods expenditures, which may not be available in all contexts. The statistical methods are more complex than traditional approaches. Patterns of resource sharing vary across societies. Programs explicitly aimed at redistributing resources within households may face political resistance.

4.7. Conclusion

The collective household model with assignable goods represents a significant advancement in poverty measurement. By moving beyond the assumption of equal resource allocation, this approach reveals important patterns of individual deprivation hidden in conventional measures.

Key findings show that significant intrahousehold inequality exists, with women, children, and elderly often receiving smaller resource shares than prime-age men. This inequality means that substantial numbers of poor individuals live in households not classified as poor under standard measures.

Mathematically, the relationship between individual poverty and household poverty can be expressed as

$$P_{\text{individual}} = P_{\text{household}} + P_{\text{misclassified}} + P_{\text{misclassified}'}$$

where

- $P_{\text{individual}}$ is the true individual-level poverty rate
- $P_{\text{household}}$ is the poverty rate based on household per-capita measures
- $P_{\text{misclassified}}$ is the rate of poor individuals in non-poor households
- $P_{\text{misclassified}'}$ is the rate of non-poor individuals in poor households

Studies consistently find that $P_{\text{misclassified}} > P_{\text{misclassified}''}$, leading to $P_{\text{individual}} > P_{\text{household}}$. This underestimation of poverty has significant implications for policy design and targeting.

The collective household model offers both diagnosis and a solution framework. By understanding which individuals are most likely poor within different household types, policymakers can design more targeted interventions. Successful programs address both immediate needs and underlying power dynamics determining resource allocation.

As we work toward eliminating poverty, the collective household model provides essential framework for ensuring no individual is left behind. By looking inside households, we can design more effective strategies recognizing that even within families, some members may experience deprivation while others thrive.

References

Albert, J. R. G., Dacuycuy, C. B., Agdeppa, I., Punongbayan, J. C., Cabalfin, D. L. D., Vargas, A. R. P., Duante, C., Ferrer, E. B., & Fernandez-Patalen, C. M. (2024). *Measuring poverty within Filipino households: Examining of resource sharing and economies of scale*. Philippine Institute for Development Studies. https://www.pids.gov.ph/publication/discussion-papers/measuring-poverty-within-filipino-households-examining-of-resource-sharing-and-economies-of-scale

Apps, P. F., & Rees, R. (1988). Taxation and the household. *Journal of Public Economics, 35*(3), 355–369. http://sciencedirect.com/science/article/abs/pii/0047272788900370

Bargain, O., Donni, O., & Kwenda, P. (2014). Intrahousehold distribution and poverty: Evidence from Côte d'Ivoire. *Journal of Development Economics, 107*, 262–276. https://www.sciencedirect.com/science/article/abs/pii/S0304387813001806

Bose-Duker, T., Gaddis, I., Kilic, T., Lechene, V., & Pendakur, K. (2021). *Diamonds in the rough? Repurposing multi-topic surveys to estimate individual-level consumption poverty* (World Bank Policy Research Working Paper 9661). World Bank. https://documents1.worldbank.org/curated/en/354631620913886186/pdf/Diamonds-in-the-Rough-Repurposing-Multi-Topic-Surveys-to-Estimate-Individual-Level-Consumption-Poverty.pdf

Brown, C., Calvi, R., & Penglase, J. (2021). Sharing the pie: An analysis of undernutrition and individual consumption in Bangladesh. *Journal of Public Economics, 200*, 104460. https://www.sciencedirect.com/science/article/abs/pii/S0047272721000967

Browning, M., Bourguignon, F., Chiappori, P. A., & Lechene, V. (1994). Income and outcomes: A structural model of intrahousehold allocation. *Journal of Political Economy, 102*(6), 1067–1096. https://www.journals.uchicago.edu/doi/10.1086/261964

Browning, M., & Chiappori, P. A. (1998). Efficient intra-household allocations: A general characterization and empirical tests. *Econometrica, 66*(6), 1241–1278. https://www.jstor.org/stable/2999616

Browning, M., Chiappori, P. A., & Lewbel, A. (2013). Estimating consumption economies of scale, adult equivalence scales, and household bargaining power. *Review of Economic Studies, 80*(4), 1267–1303. https://www.jstor.org/stable/43551559

Calvi, R. (2020). Why are older women missing in India? The age profile of bargaining power and poverty. *Journal of Political Economy, 128*(7), 2453–2501. https://www.journals.uchicago.edu/doi/10.1086/706983

Chiappori, P. A. (1988). Rational household labor supply. *Econometrica, 56*(1), 63–90. https://www.jstor.org/stable/1911842

Chiappori, P. A. (1992). Collective labor supply and welfare. *Journal of Political Economy, 100*(3), 437–467. https://www.jstor.org/stable/2138727

Deaton, A. (1989). Looking for boy-girl discrimination in household expenditure data. *World Bank Economic Review, 3*(1), 1–15. https://academic.oup.com/wber/article-abstract/3/1/1/1650128

Deaton, A. (1997). *The analysis of household surveys: A microeconometric approach to development policy*. World Bank Publications.

Duflo, E. (2003). Grandmothers and granddaughters: Old-age pensions and intrahousehold allocation in South Africa. *World Bank Economic Review, 17*(1), 1–25.

Dunbar, G. R., Lewbel, A., & Pendakur, K. (2013). Children's resources in collective households: Identification, estimation, and an application to child poverty in Malawi. *American Economic Review, 103*(1), 438–471. https://www.aeaweb.org/articles?id=10.1257/aer.103.1.438

Lechene, V., Pendakur, K., & Wolf, A. (2021). *OLS estimation of the intra-household distribution of consumption* (IFS Working Paper W21/19). Institute for Fiscal Studies. https://ifs.org.uk/publications/ols-estimation-intra-household-distribution-expenditure

Lewbel, A., & Pendakur, K. (2008). Estimation of collective household models with Engel curves. *Journal of Econometrics, 147*(2), 350–358. https://www.sciencedirect.com/science/article/abs/pii/S0304407608001498

CHAPTER 5

Determinants of Poverty

"Poverty entails fear and stress and sometimes depression. It meets a thousand petty humiliations and hardships. Climbing out of poverty by your own efforts, that is something on which to pride yourself, but poverty itself is romanticized only by fools."
—J.K. ROWLING

SUMMARY

Poverty has multiple, interlocking causes that operate at different levels of society. This chapter provides a framework for understanding these determinants, essential for designing effective poverty reduction strategies.

At the regional level, geographical factors significantly influence poverty. Remote areas with difficult terrain, limited resources, or vulnerability to disasters typically experience higher poverty rates. Research from Ethiopia shows households in remote areas are 7.5 percentage points more likely to remain poor. Governance quality represents another critical regional determinant, with evidence from Indonesia demonstrating that better-governed districts achieve nearly twice the poverty reduction despite similar growth rates. Inequality further shapes regional poverty patterns, with Latin American data showing high-inequality countries experience 25 percent less poverty reduction per percentage point of growth.

Community-level characteristics create the immediate context for households. Infrastructure access significantly affects poverty outcomes, as highlighted by Rwanda's rural electrification program, which reduced poverty by 5–7 percentage points in electrified villages. Market access represents another crucial factor, with Tanzanian research showing households with better market access were 18 percentage points more likely to sell crops commercially and received 23 percent higher prices. Social capital also influences community resilience during economic shocks.

At the household level, demographic characteristics strongly influence poverty risk. Research from Bangladesh shows demographic transition explained approximately 22 percent of poverty reduction over 25 years. Employment quality strongly affects poverty transitions, with South African data revealing households gaining formal employment were 4.3 times more likely to exit poverty than those gaining informal employment. Education, health, and housing quality directly impact both income-generating capacity and expenditure needs.

The chapter discusses methodological approaches, highlighting advanced techniques including panel data methods and machine-learning approaches that reveal complex interaction patterns among poverty determinants.

The challenge remains in identifying deeper causes beyond proximate determinants. Historical institutions, as demonstrated in research on colonial land systems in India, can create structural causes of poverty that persist across generations. Political economy factors also fundamentally shape outcomes, with Kenyan evidence showing local elite interests strongly influence service delivery effectiveness.

Effective poverty reduction strategies must address multiple determinants simultaneously, as exemplified by Mexico's

Progresa/Oportunidades program, which combined household-level transfers with community investments. This integrated approach achieved 37 percent poverty reduction compared to 21 percent for cash transfers alone.

5.1. Introduction

Poverty profiles describe patterns of poverty, but they are not primarily concerned with explaining its causes. Yet a satisfactory explanation of why some people are poor is essential if we want to tackle the roots of poverty rather than just its manifestations. While a poverty profile tells us who is poor, understanding the determinants of poverty helps us understand why they are poor—information critical for crafting effective poverty reduction strategies.

Understanding poverty's causes requires analyzing factors operating at multiple levels, from individual characteristics to household dynamics, community infrastructure, and broader regional environments. This multidimensional nature of poverty determinants makes analysis complex but also creates multiple potential entry points for policy interventions.

The conventional approach to measuring poverty typically focuses on household-level data, often masking important variations within those households. A subsistence farmer might experience poverty differently than an urban day laborer, even if their income levels are similar. Likewise, economic shocks like illness or unemployment can quickly push vulnerable households into poverty, while lack of education or exclusion from networks may keep others trapped in chronic deprivation.

This chapter presents a comprehensive framework for understanding poverty determinants, beginning with region-level characteristics before examining community, household, and individual-level factors. We explore both immediate and deeper causes of poverty, recognizing that some factors (like low education) may be both consequences and causes of poverty—part of self-reinforcing poverty traps.

The challenge, as Howard White and David Booth (2003) argue, lies in addressing the "missing middle"—the gap between macro-level development goals and the micro-level interventions used to achieve them. This requires a clear understanding of the causal pathways linking development policies to poverty outcomes. Since the causes of poverty are context-specific, country-level diagnostics are essential. By systematically identifying and analyzing the determinants of poverty, policymakers can design more targeted and effective strategies that address not only the symptoms but also the structural roots of poverty.

5.2. Region-Level Characteristics

Regional factors create the broader context in which poverty occurs and can significantly influence poverty rates across entire populations. These characteristics operate at national or sub-national levels and shape the overall environment in which households and individuals function.

5.2.1. Geography and natural resources

Geographical characteristics significantly influence poverty rates. Remote areas often experience higher poverty rates due to limited market access, higher transportation costs, and reduced economic opportunities. Mountain regions in countries like Nepal and Peru face particular challenges due to difficult terrain that limits infrastructure development and raises the costs of service delivery.

Bahru et al. (2019) investigated the impact of drought on child undernutrition in rural Ethiopia using longitudinal household survey data and structural equation modeling. The study found that drought exposure significantly reduces children's height-for-age z-scores (HAZ), indicating an increase in chronic malnutrition or stunting. These negative effects were most pronounced in food-insecure and geographically remote regions, where access to markets, healthcare, and safety nets is limited. The analysis highlights how environmental shocks interact with geographic disadvantage to intensify household vulnerability. Drought not only directly affects nutrition through reduced food availability but also indirectly affects it by lowering household income and food consumption. The findings suggest that geographic isolation and climatic stressors can jointly contribute to poverty traps, where structural barriers and recurring shocks hinder long-term improvements in child health and household welfare.

Beyond the Ethiopian context, resource endowments and environmental risk factors are critical determinants of poverty persistence. Areas with poor soil quality, limited access to water, or frequent exposure to natural disasters often experience development setbacks. For example, Bangladesh's low-lying geography leaves it highly vulnerable to annual flooding, disrupting livelihoods and damaging infrastructure. Similarly, Thua Thien Hue province in Vietnam faces recurrent typhoons that regularly erode household assets and hinder recovery, especially among poor farming communities (Tan et al., 2023). These environmental constraints reduce household resilience and contribute to chronic poverty.

Climate patterns introduce further spatial variation in poverty dynamics. Regions experiencing erratic rainfall, frequent droughts, or extreme temperatures often suffer from lower agricultural productivity and food insecurity. As climate change continues to intensify weather variability, the interaction between geography and environmental stress is becoming an increasingly important dimension of poverty analysis. Addressing these challenges will require more than general economic growth—it calls for targeted investments in climate adaptation, rural infrastructure, and safety net systems tailored to the most vulnerable and geographically disadvantaged communities.

5.2.2. Governance and institutions

Regional governance quality strongly influences poverty outcomes. Areas with effective governance typically provide better public services, more accountable institutions, and environments more conducive to economic growth. Conversely, regions suffering from corruption, weak rule of law, or political instability often experience higher poverty rates as resources are misallocated and economic activity is disrupted.

Sumarto, Vothknecht, and Wijaya (2014) conducted a district-level analysis of poverty outcomes across Indonesia during the early years of decentralization, using panel data from 2005 to 2010 covering over 400 districts. Their study examined how local economic, demographic, and institutional factors influenced regional poverty reduction. While economic growth and education levels were positively associated with poverty decline, the study found that institutional characteristics also played a crucial role. In particular, the presence of active local poverty reduction coordination teams (TKPKDs) was associated with better poverty outcomes, suggesting that local governance structures can facilitate more effective implementation of poverty programs. The authors concluded that regional disparities in poverty reduction were not only a function of economic performance but also linked to variations in local administrative capacity and institutional engagement.

Market institutions also play a crucial role. The experience of transition, especially in countries of the former Soviet Union, demonstrates that market reforms without effective supporting institutions may fail to deliver growth and poverty reduction. Functioning financial markets, clear property rights, and effective contract enforcement all create environments where economic opportunity can flourish.

Political stability represents another critical regional factor. Conflict-affected regions typically experience significantly higher poverty rates as violence disrupts economic activity, destroys infrastructure, and diverts resources from development. In the extreme, vicious cycles of social division and failed development erupt into internal conflict, as seen in places like the Balkans and Liberia, with devastating consequences for people.

5.2.3. *Inequality and social divisions*

Social, economic, and ethnic divisions within regions often contribute to poverty by excluding certain groups from opportunities. High levels of inequality can undermine the poverty-reducing effects of economic growth, as the benefits accrue primarily to the already advantaged. Evidence suggests that more unequal societies often experience lower poverty reduction from a given amount of growth compared to more equitable societies.

Lucchetti, Vakis, and Rigolini (2016) analyzed chronic poverty and mobility patterns across 18 Latin American and Caribbean countries from 2000 to 2012 using harmonized household survey data and synthetic panel methods. Their findings emphasize that high initial levels of inequality constrained the poverty-reducing impact of economic growth. Countries with lower inequality and those that implemented redistributive policies experienced faster poverty reduction and greater upward mobility. For example, Bolivia and Ecuador saw substantial declines in chronic poverty following significant expansions in social protection and inclusive policy reforms. Brazil's experience during the 2000s also illustrates this trend: Targeted cash transfer programs like Bolsa Família, combined with rising labor incomes among the poor, contributed to substantial poverty and inequality reductions even during periods of moderate growth. The study underscores that inequality reduction is not just a consequence of poverty reduction—it can also be a powerful driver, amplifying the impact of economic growth on improving welfare for the poor.

Gender inequality represents a particularly important dimension of social division that affects poverty. In regions where women face significant discrimination in education, employment, and asset ownership, overall poverty rates tend to be higher. This pattern reflects both the direct impoverishment of women and the broader economic inefficiencies that gender discrimination creates.

Ethnic and racial inequalities similarly contribute to poverty through mechanisms of exclusion and discrimination. When certain groups face systematic barriers to education, employment, or political representation, their ability to escape poverty is severely constrained. These patterns of exclusion often persist across generations, contributing to the intergenerational transmission of poverty.

5.3. Community-Level Characteristics

Community characteristics create the immediate context in which households function and can significantly influence poverty outcomes even among households with similar individual characteristics. These factors operate at the village, neighborhood, or local community level.

5.3.1. Infrastructure and services

Access to basic infrastructure significantly affects poverty at the community level. Communities with good road connections to markets typically experience lower poverty rates, as farmers can sell their produce at better prices and access a wider range of economic opportunities. Similarly, access to electricity enables productive activities and extends working hours, contributing to higher incomes.

IEG (2008) revisited the welfare effects of rural electrification, challenging the assumption that access to electricity alone automatically leads to significant poverty reduction. Drawing on evidence from multiple impact evaluations in sub-Saharan Africa, including Ethiopia, the authors found that while electrification can improve quality of life and access to information, its effects on income, employment, and poverty are often modest without complementary investments. The study emphasized that electrification benefits tend to materialize only when households have the means, skills, and infrastructure to translate access into productive use. In areas where local economies are underdeveloped, or where markets and roads are poorly connected, the impact of electrification on poverty remains limited. The findings suggest that to realize the full potential of rural electrification, programs must be integrated with broader development strategies, including infrastructure upgrades, business support services, and skill development.

Basic infrastructure beyond electricity—such as water and sanitation—also plays a crucial role in shaping poverty outcomes. Communities lacking access to clean water face higher rates of illness, increased care burdens, and reduced productivity, all of which contribute to income losses and greater vulnerability. In rural Cambodia, for instance, the absence of reliable public services and poorly developed markets has hindered poverty reduction efforts, particularly in remote areas where time burdens for water collection and illness-related absences from work or school are common.

Access to quality education and health services at the community level remains foundational for long-term poverty reduction. Functioning schools and health facilities not only improve individual human capital outcomes but also enhance intergenerational mobility. When these services are accessible and of adequate quality, children from low-income households are more likely to escape poverty cycles through better learning and improved health outcomes. These findings support an integrated approach to rural development, where infrastructure investments are coupled with service delivery improvements and economic inclusion measures to ensure sustained poverty reduction.

5.3.2. Market access

Proximity to markets represents a crucial community-level factor affecting poverty. Remote communities often face higher prices for purchased goods and receive lower prices for their products due to transportation costs. This "price scissors" effect can significantly reduce real incomes even when productive capacity is similar to less remote areas.

Research by Minot (2006) explored the relationship between market access and rural poverty in Tanzania using geo-referenced household survey data and travel time estimates to regional markets. The study found that households with better market access were more likely to participate in agricultural markets and exhibited lower poverty rates. Improved market connectivity was associated with increased commercialization, particularly in regions producing high-value or perishable crops. However, the analysis also suggested that proximity alone was not sufficient—poor road infrastructure and high transport costs could limit the benefits of market access. The findings underscore the importance of investments in rural infrastructure as a means of promoting agricultural income and poverty reduction, especially for communities dependent on smallholder farming.

Local labor market conditions also significantly influence poverty outcomes. Communities with diverse employment opportunities typically experience lower poverty rates than those dependent on a single economic sector. When local economies offer only seasonal or unstable employment, households may struggle to maintain consistent incomes throughout the year.

Financial service access at the community level affects households' ability to save, invest, and manage risk. Communities without banking services or microfinance institutions may rely on informal lenders charging high interest rates, limiting capital accumulation and investment potential. Successful microfinance programs in Bangladesh and elsewhere have demonstrated how improved financial access can help reduce poverty at the community level.

5.3.3. Social capital and institutions

Social capital—the networks, norms, and trust that facilitate cooperation—represents an important community characteristic affecting poverty. Research on the roles of different types of social networks in poor communities confirms their importance. An analysis of poor villages in north India shows that social groups play an important role in protecting the basic needs of poor people and in reducing risk (Kozel and Parker, 2000).

Research by Gaillard et al. (2009) examined how livelihood strategies and social structures influence vulnerability and resilience among coastal communities in the Philippines, particularly in the face of recurrent natural disasters. Drawing on fieldwork across several disaster-prone areas, the study emphasized that people's ability to reduce and recover from poverty is shaped not just by economic assets but also by access to social, cultural, and institutional resources. Households with diversified livelihoods, strong local support networks, and connections to external assistance were found to be better positioned to withstand the adverse impacts of typhoons and other hazards. However, the study also cautioned that while local coping strategies—such as relying on kinship and neighborhood networks—offered short-term protection, they often failed to address the root causes of vulnerability or enable long-term poverty reduction. In some cases, these community-based safety nets led to stagnation or "resilience without transformation", where households repeatedly recovered from shocks but remained trapped in a cycle of chronic poverty.

Community-level institutions and power structures were also central to shaping vulnerability outcomes. The study noted that inclusive governance, where all segments of the community—including women, the poor, and ethnic minorities—had a voice in decision-making, enhanced equitable access to post-disaster recovery resources. In contrast, in areas with hierarchical or exclusionary power dynamics, disaster relief and development interventions often disproportionately favored better-connected households, exacerbating inequalities. These findings highlight that poverty dynamics in hazard-prone areas are deeply intertwined with local social and political relations.

Strong community organizations and networks can also play a critical role in facilitating recovery and resilience. As seen in other contexts, such as agricultural trading communities in Madagascar (Fafchamps and Minten, 1999), dense social networks help lower transaction costs and offer informal insurance mechanisms. In the Philippines, effective community mobilization—particularly when supported by NGOs and government programs—can increase collective bargaining power and improve access to basic services, infrastructure, and livelihood opportunities. However, for such efforts to be transformative rather than merely protective, they must address deeper structural issues, including inequality in resource access and the unequal distribution of power within communities.

5.4. Household and Individual-Level Characteristics

While regional and community factors create the context for poverty, household and individual characteristics often most directly determine whether a particular person experiences poverty. These characteristics can be grouped into demographic, economic, and social categories.

In the Philippine context, Albert and Collado (2004) conducted comprehensive analysis of poverty determinants using data from the 2000 Family Income and Expenditure Survey. Their multivariate regression analysis confirmed that household-level characteristics strongly correlate with poverty outcomes in the Philippines. They found that the likelihood of being poor increased significantly with household size, while decreasing with higher educational attainment of the household head. Their findings also revealed that households involved in agriculture were at substantially higher risk of poverty, with those headed by self-employed agricultural workers showing particularly high poverty rates. These findings align with broader regional patterns but highlight the specific configuration of poverty determinants in the Philippine setting.

5.4.1. *Demographic characteristics*

Household composition significantly influences poverty risk. Larger households typically experience higher poverty rates, as resources must be spread among more members. In Cambodia, the 1993–1994 Socio-Economic Survey showed that the average family size was 6.6 persons in the poorest quintile compared to 4.9 in the richest quintile. This pattern appears in most countries, though it weakens somewhat when household welfare is measured on a per adult equivalent rather than a per capita basis.

An assessment of the World Bank (2019) identified the drivers of Bangladesh's impressive poverty reduction from the mid-1990s to 2016, during which national poverty declined from over 50 percent to around 24 percent. The assessment attributes this progress in poverty reduction to a combination of sustained economic growth, rising labor incomes, and favorable demographic changes. A key element of this demographic transition was a significant decline in fertility—from an average of over six children per woman in the 1970s to around 2.1 by 2016—which reduced household dependency ratios. Smaller household sizes meant that income was distributed among fewer dependents, allowing for increases in per capita consumption. This trend was especially pronounced in rural areas, where reductions in poverty were strongly correlated with falling dependency burdens and increased investments in human capital, such as education and health.

The age structure of households emerged as a critical factor shaping poverty outcomes. Households with lower dependency ratios—meaning more working-age adults relative to children or the elderly—were more likely to escape poverty. These households were better positioned to take advantage of rising labor market opportunities, especially in sectors like manufacturing and services that expanded during Bangladesh's structural transformation. Moreover, the combination of declining fertility and rising female labor force participation further enhanced household resilience. The report highlights that when women enter the workforce, particularly in garment and export sectors, household income gains tend to translate into more diversified spending on children's health, nutrition, and schooling—creating long-term poverty-reducing effects.

The role of gender dynamics in poverty is also nuanced. While female-headed households are often assumed to be more vulnerable, the World Bank (2019) report finds that in Bangladesh, these households do not uniformly experience higher poverty. In many cases, women heading households were recipients of remittances or engaged in formal sector work, which improved their economic standing. However, gender disparities remain significant in labor force participation rates and access to decent work. Addressing these gaps—particularly through investments in female education, vocational training, and child care services—remains essential to ensuring that women can fully participate in and benefit from Bangladesh's development progress.

5.4.2. Economic characteristics

Employment characteristics strongly influence household poverty status. Unemployment or underemployment directly reduces income, while employment quality—whether jobs are stable, well-paid, and offer benefits—affects long-term economic security. Households relying on casual labor or highly seasonal employment typically face greater poverty risks than those with stable, formal sector employment.

Foster (2023) analyzed employment transitions in South Africa using panel data from the Post-Apartheid Labour Market Series (PALMS), focusing on how labor market dynamics affect worker outcomes during both stable and recessionary periods. Rather than treating employment as a binary state, the study disaggregated worker flows across formal employment, informal employment, and unemployment. The findings highlight that transitions into formal employment are more stable and associated with longer employment spells, while informal sector employment tends to be transient and less protective during economic downturns. During recessionary periods, including the COVID-19 pandemic, many workers exited both formal and informal employment entirely, underscoring limited labor market resilience. Importantly, Foster observed that the informal sector in South Africa is relatively small and does not function as a strong buffer against unemployment, unlike in many other developing countries. These results suggest that improving access to and retention in formal employment is essential for ensuring labor market security and enhancing household resilience to economic shocks. The study emphasizes the need for labor policies that go beyond job creation to also address job quality, employment stability, and inclusion within the formal sector.

Asset ownership represents another critical economic factor. The property of a household includes its tangible goods (land, cultivated areas, livestock, agricultural equipment, machinery, buildings, household appliances, and other durable goods) and its financial assets (liquid assets, savings, and other financial assets). Land ownership is particularly important in rural areas, where it provides both a productive asset and collateral for accessing credit. In some contexts, households may be income-poor but asset-wealthy, complicating poverty measurement.

Income diversification affects vulnerability to poverty. Households with multiple income sources typically face lower poverty risks, as they can better withstand shocks affecting any single source. Rural households combining farming with non-farm enterprises or wage employment, for instance, often demonstrate greater resilience than those relying exclusively on agriculture.

The Asian Development Bank (2009) provided further insight into economic determinants of poverty in the Philippines, finding that access to productive assets represented a critical factor separating poor from non-poor households. Their analysis showed that only 3.3 percent of poor households had access to formal financial markets compared to 16.5 percent of non-poor households. This asset poverty extended beyond financial resources to physical capital, with poor households having significantly lower access to agricultural equipment, reliable transportation, and income-generating assets that could buffer against economic shocks. The ADB study emphasized that addressing these asset constraints requires more than income-based interventions, highlighting the importance of expanding poor households' access to credit, land, and essential infrastructure.

5.4.3. Social characteristics

Education levels significantly influence poverty risk at both individual and household levels. More educated individuals typically command higher wages and have greater adaptability to changing economic conditions. At the household level, the education of the household head often strongly predicts poverty status. In Cambodia, adults in the poorest quintile averaged 3.1 years of schooling compared with 5.3 years among the richest quintile.

Recent empirical work underscores the importance of both education quantity and quality in shaping poverty outcomes in India. Agrawal (2011), using nationally representative data, finds that the average returns to education in India are positive and significant but vary considerably across different population groups and education levels. In particular, returns are highest for individuals completing secondary and higher education, while returns to primary education remain relatively low. These patterns suggest that simply expanding years of schooling may not be sufficient to reduce poverty unless it leads to tangible improvements in skills and labor market outcomes. Complementing these findings, Kingdon and Unni (2001) highlight the critical role of education in improving women's labor market participation and earnings. Their analysis shows that female labor force participation is strongly influenced by education level and quality, with better-educated women more likely to access formal sector jobs and earn higher wages. This, in turn, contributes to overall household income growth and improved welfare outcomes.

These findings point to a key policy implication: enhancing education quality—particularly in terms of learning outcomes and relevance to labor market needs—is as crucial as expanding school access. For women, in particular, better education not only improves individual empowerment but also strengthens household resilience and poverty reduction pathways. The studies suggest that targeted investments in secondary and tertiary education, as well as vocational training, can amplify the economic returns to education and have sustained impacts on poverty alleviation.

Health status remains another critical determinant of poverty. Poor health reduces earning potential and increases household spending on care, compounding economic vulnerability. Malnutrition, disease burden, and limited access to quality health services all undermine productivity. These effects are especially severe for poorer households, where lost labor income and out-of-pocket medical expenses can quickly lead to further deprivation.

Similarly, housing quality and access to basic services like clean water and sanitation directly affect household wellbeing. Poor living conditions increase exposure to environmental hazards and disease, while inadequate infrastructure places time and labor burdens—often disproportionately on women and children. In Cambodia, for example, just 4 percent of the poorest quintile had access to piped water compared to over 17 percent of the richest quintile, with sanitation disparities just as stark. These conditions reinforce poverty by limiting health, productivity, and time available for income-generating activities.

5.5. Analyzing the Determinants of Poverty: Regression Techniques

While descriptive statistics and simple cross-tabulations provide valuable insights into poverty correlates, more sophisticated analytical techniques help identify the relative importance of different factors and disentangle complex relationships. Regression analysis represents the most widely used approach for this purpose.

5.5.1. Regression approaches to analyzing poverty determinants

Regression analysis allows researchers to examine how closely an independent variable relates to poverty or welfare indicators, holding other factors constant. This statistical model helps isolate the contribution of specific variables beyond their correlation with other factors. For example, tabulated data from Vietnam showed higher per capita expenditure in female-headed households, but regression analysis revealed that this effect became statistically insignificant after controlling for other factors like location and household size.

A methodological study by Sohnesen and Stender (2016) assessed whether machine-learning approaches—specifically random forest—could outperform traditional econometric methods in predicting poverty status using household survey data from Rwanda. Drawing on a nationally representative dataset with over 200 potential predictor variables, the authors compared the predictive performance of ordinary least squares (OLS), logistic regression, and random forest models. Their findings showed that random forest substantially outperformed traditional regression models in classifying household poverty status, particularly for households near the poverty line. While logistic regression achieved moderate predictive accuracy, random forest offered superior performance due to its ability to capture non-linear relationships and complex variable interactions. The study also found that variable importance rankings differed notably between methods: traditional models emphasized variables such as education and household size, whereas the random forest model revealed a more diverse set of important predictors, including housing quality, asset ownership, and access to services. The authors concluded that machine-learning approaches like random forest can enhance poverty targeting by providing more accurate and nuanced classification of household welfare.

Two main regression approaches dominate the poverty analysis literature:

1. **Welfare regressions**: These explain the level of expenditure (or income) per capita as a function of various household and individual characteristics. This approach preserves more information by using the continuous welfare measure rather than the binary poor/non-poor classification. A typical specification might be

$$\ln\left(\frac{y_i}{z}\right)=\alpha+\sum_{j=1}^{k}\beta_j X_{ji}+\epsilon_i$$

where y_i represents per the traditional welfare indicator capita income or consumption for household i, z is the poverty line, X_{ji} are explanatory variables for household i, and ϵ_i is the model error term.

2. **Poverty status regressions**: These explain whether a household is poor using logit or probit models[1] where the dependent variable is binary (1 if poor, 0 if non-poor). While this approach loses some information by collapsing the welfare distribution into a binary variable, it can be useful for understanding factors specifically associated with crossing the poverty threshold.

Most researchers prefer welfare regressions for general analysis of poverty determinants, as they use the full distribution of the welfare measure rather than just the binary poor/non-poor distinction. However, poverty status regressions can be valuable when designing targeted interventions that require clear eligibility criteria.

Albert and Collado's (2004) regression analysis of Philippine poverty represents an instructive application of the welfare regression approach. Their model explained approximately 60 percent of the variability in household per capita income relative to the poverty line, with separate regressions for different geographical areas revealing

[1] Logit and probit models are statistical models used when analyzing binary dependent variables (those with only two possible outcomes, such as "poor" or "not poor"). The logit model uses the logistic function to estimate the probability of an outcome based on predictor variables, producing coefficients that can be interpreted as log-odds. The probit model uses the cumulative normal distribution function instead. While both models typically yield similar results, they differ in their mathematical formulations and the interpretation of their coefficients. These models are particularly useful in poverty analysis when researchers want to identify factors that influence whether a household falls below the poverty line, rather than examining variations in income or consumption levels across the entire distribution.

important structural differences in poverty determinants. For example, while the marginal effect of additional employed household members was positive across all areas, it was substantially larger in Metro Manila (32 percent increase in per capita income) compared to areas outside Metro Manila (26 percent increase), highlighting the higher economic returns to labor in urban areas. Such region-specific analyses provide crucial insights for tailoring poverty reduction strategies to local contexts.

5.5.2. Model specification and interpretation issues

When developing regression models for poverty analysis, several specification issues require careful attention:

- **Variable selection**: The independent variables should be exogenous to current consumption or income levels. Including variables like current income in a model explaining consumption would create endogeneity problems. Researchers typically focus on predetermined characteristics like education, demographic composition, location, and physical assets.
- **Functional form**: The relationship between explanatory variables and welfare may be non-linear. Log transformations of the dependent variable are common, reflecting the typically log-normal distribution of consumption or income. Researchers may also include squared terms or interaction effects to capture non-linear relationships and structural differences across subgroups.
- **Structural differences**: The determinants of poverty may differ across regions or between rural and urban areas. Researchers often estimate separate models for different subpopulations or include interaction terms to capture these structural differences. Testing for equality of parameter estimates across regions can indicate whether pooling data is appropriate.
- **Endogeneity concerns**: Some apparent determinants of poverty may themselves be influenced by poverty status, creating reverse causality problems. For instance, asset ownership might influence

current consumption, but past consumption likely influenced asset accumulation. Researchers must carefully consider the potential for such endogeneity and employ appropriate techniques like instrumental variables when necessary.

- **Interpreting logistic regression results**: Logistic regression is particularly useful in poverty analysis because it directly estimates the probability of a household being poor. The model can be specified as

$$\log\left(\frac{p}{1-p}\right) = \beta_0 + \beta_1 X_1 + \beta_2 X_2 + \ldots + \beta_k X_k$$

where p is the probability of being poor, and the β coefficients represent the change in log-odds associated with a one-unit change in the corresponding explanatory variable.

These coefficients can be difficult to interpret directly, so researchers typically convert them to more intuitive measures:

- **Odds ratios**: The odds ratio represents the ratio of the odds of being poor when an explanatory variable increases by one unit relative to the original odds. Odds ratios are a fundamental way to interpret results from logistic regression models in poverty analysis. The odds ratio is calculated by exponentiating the logistic regression coefficient (e^{β}). For example, if the coefficient for household size is 0.403, the corresponding odds ratio is $e^{0.403} = 1.50$, indicating that each additional household member increases the odds of being poor by 50 percent. For binary variables, the odds ratio compares the odds of poverty between the two groups. An odds ratio greater than 1 indicates an increased likelihood of poverty, while a value less than 1 indicates a decreased likelihood. Unlike probabilities, which are bounded between 0 and 1, odds can range from 0 to infinity, making odds ratios multiplicative rather than additive. This property allows for symmetric treatment of positive and negative effects—an odds ratio of 2 represents the same magnitude of effect (in the opposite direction) as an odds ratio of 0.5.

Odds ratios are preferred in some applications because they are not dependent on the values of other variables in the model and remain constant across the entire range of the probability distribution.

- **Marginal effects**: These represent the change in the probability of an outcome occurring for a unit change in an explanatory variable, holding all other variables constant at specified values (typically their means). In poverty analysis using logistic regression, the marginal effect shows how much the probability of being poor changes when an independent variable increases by one unit. For continuous variables like age or income, the marginal effect is calculated as the partial derivative of the probability function with respect to that variable: $\frac{\partial p}{\partial x^k} = \beta^k p(1-p)$, where p is the probability of being poor and β^k is the logistic regression coefficient. For binary variables (like male = 1/female = 0), the marginal effect represents the difference in predicted probabilities when the variable changes from 0 to 1. Marginal effects are particularly valuable in policy contexts because, unlike logistic regression coefficients, which represent changes in log-odds, they can be directly interpreted as percentage point changes in the probability of poverty. For instance, a marginal effect of 0.046 for household size indicates that each additional household member increases the probability of being poor by 4.6 percentage points, providing policymakers with an intuitive measure of the variable's practical significance.

Interpreting regression results requires understanding both statistical and practical significance. A coefficient may be statistically significant (unlikely to occur by chance) but have a small magnitude that implies limited practical importance for poverty reduction. Both the p-values (indicating statistical significance) and the magnitude of coefficients (indicating practical significance) deserve attention.

5.5.3. *Example: Determinants of household income in the Philippines*

Table 5.1 presents regression results adapted from an analysis of poverty determinants in the Philippines, which reveals important variations in how different factors affect household welfare across areas (Albert and Collado, 2004). The table presents selected results from their regression models for Metro Manila (National Capital Region), other regions, and the national level.

In all areas, household demographic characteristics strongly influence welfare. Each additional household member significantly reduces per capita welfare, with children having a larger negative impact than adults. The age of the household head shows a positive association with welfare, suggesting accumulation of assets and experience over time. Male-headed households show significantly lower welfare when controlling for other factors—an unexpected finding that may reflect household composition differences or greater vulnerability among certain types of male-headed households.

Infrastructure access shows important regional variations. While electricity access significantly improves welfare across regions, the effect is substantially stronger in Metro Manila (33.9 percent increase in welfare) compared to other regions (about 21 percent increase). Similarly, urban residence is associated with approximately 6.6 percent higher welfare nationwide. Access to water shows regional variation, with distance to water source having significant negative effects on welfare mainly in Visayas and Mindanao.

For education and employment, the level of education consistently shows strong positive effects on welfare across all regions. However, self-employment status reveals an interesting pattern—it has no significant effect in Metro Manila but shows a significant negative association with welfare in other regions. This suggests that the nature of self-employment opportunities differs substantially between the capital region and the rest of the country.

Table 5.1. Selected determinants of household welfare in the Philippines

Variable	Coefficient (t-stat)		
	NCR (Metro Manila)	**Other areas**	**National**
Household demographic characteristics			
Age of household head	0.005 (5.62)**	0.003–0.004 (10.8)**	0.003 (12.31)**
Sex of household head (1 = male, 0 = female)	-0.117 (-4.98)**	-0.091 to -0.093 (-7.56)**	-0.091 (-10.69)**
Additional household member (by age group)	-0.098 to -0.196 (-9.75 to 1-9.94)**	-0.075 to -0.178 (-14.91 to -47.1)**	-0.097 to -0.174 (-22.26 to 67.56)**
Infrastructure and access			
Urban residence (1 versus 0 = rural)	(dropped since NCR is fully urban)	0.065–0.066 (7.4)**	0.066 (10.74)**
Distance of water source from house	0.0001 (0.41)	-0.0001 (-0.85) to -0.0001 (-2.99)**	-0.0001 (-2.99)**
Electricity access (indicator 1 = yes, 0 = no)	0.339 (2.47)*	0.208–0.219 (16.61–27.71)**	0.219 (27.71)**
Education and employment			
Highest education of household head	0.152 (23.69)**	0.134–0.141 (50.85–72.31)**	0.134 (72.31)**
Self-employed household head (indicator 1 = yes, 0 = no)	0.019 (1.58)	-0.020 to -0.023 (-3.14 to -5.27)**	-0.023 (-5.27)**

Source: Modified from Albert and Collado (2004).

Notes:

(i) ** significant at 1 percent level; * significant at 5 percent level.

(ii) The dependent variable is the natural logarithm of household expenditure per capita relative to the poverty line.

(iii) R^2 values: NCR = 53.9 percent, other regions = 57.8–60.2 percent, National = 60.2 percent.

These findings highlight how poverty determinants can vary significantly across regions within a country.

5.5.4. Using regression to analyze poverty in Kenya

Otieno (2015) provides an instructive example of how regression analysis can be applied to understand poverty determinants at the household level in Kenya. The study provides insight into how such models directly estimate the probability of being poor rather than modeling welfare levels. Unlike linear regression that models welfare levels directly, logistic regression estimates the probability of a household being poor. This approach is particularly useful for directly informing targeting criteria in poverty reduction programs. Using data from the 2005/2006 Kenya Integrated Household Budget Survey, Otieno employed a logistic regression model to estimate the probability of a household being poor based on various characteristics. Otieno's model can be expressed as

$$P(\text{poor}=1)=\frac{1}{\left(1+e^{-X\beta}\right)}$$

where X represents the vector of household characteristics, and β represents the vector of regression coefficient estimates. The study included variables such as land holding, household size, literacy rates, sector of employment, and water source access. Table 5.2 presents marginal effects, which show how the probability of being poor changes with a unit change in each explanatory variable, holding other factors constant. This approach provides highly interpretable results for policy purposes.

The findings reveal several important patterns. Household size is a significant determinant of poverty, with each additional member increasing the probability of poverty by 4.6 percentage points. Age shows a non-linear relationship with poverty—each additional year initially reduces poverty probability by 0.4 percentage points, but the

Table 5.2. Determinants of poverty in Kenya: Marginal effects from logistic regression

Variable	Marginal effect	P value
Household characteristics		
Household size	0.046**	0.000
Age of household member	−0.004**	0.000
Age squared	0.00005**	0.000
Household head (1 = male, 0 = female)	−0.019*	0.029
Infrastructure and access		
Urban residence (1 = urban, 0 = rural)	−0.055**	0.000
Time to collect water (minutes)	0.0009**	0.000
Time to reach workplace (minutes)	−0.0006**	0.000
Regional variables (relative to Kakamega County)		
Nairobi County	0.050**	0.000
Mombasa County	0.067**	0.000
Kisumu County	−0.030	0.299
Nyeri County	0.004	0.831
Nakuru County	−0.095**	0.000
Embu County	0.031	0.125
Garissa County	0.115**	0.000

Source: Modified from Otieno (2015).
Notes:
(i) ** significant at 1 percent level; * significant at 5 percent level.
(ii) Dependent variable is the probability of a household being poor.
(iii) Number of observations = 9,681 LR chi2(23) = 1,292.43, Prob > chi2 = 0.0000.

positive coefficient on age-squared indicates that this benefit diminishes for older individuals.

The sex of the household head also matters, with male-headed households having a 1.9 percentage point lower probability of poverty compared to female-headed households, contradicting the findings from the Philippines study in Table 5.1. This highlights how poverty determinants can vary across different country contexts.

Infrastructure and access variables show strong effects. Urban households have a 5.5 percentage point lower probability of being poor compared to rural households. Time spent collecting water—a proxy for service access—increases poverty probability by 0.09 percentage points per additional minute, reflecting the opportunity costs of limited infrastructure.

Perhaps most notably, the analysis reveals that county of residence significantly affects poverty probability, even after controlling for household characteristics. Relative to Kakamega County, living in Garissa County increases poverty probability by 11.5 percentage points, while residence in Nakuru County reduces it by 9.5 percentage points. These geographic effects point to structural differences in economic opportunities across regions.

The power of regression analysis lies in its ability to isolate the effect of each factor while controlling for other variables. This helps policymakers prioritize interventions—showing, for example, that both household-level factors (like family size) and structural factors (like geographic location and infrastructure) significantly influence poverty outcomes in Kenya.

A key advantage of the logistic approach is the interpretability of results through marginal effects and odds ratios. For example, Otieno's (2015) marginal effect of -0.055 for urban residence indicates that urban households have a 5.5 percentage point lower probability of being poor compared to rural households.

Both approaches provide valuable insights, but the choice between modeling welfare levels (as in Albert and Collado, 2004) versus directly modeling poverty status (as in Otieno, 2015) depends on research objectives. Welfare regressions provide more information about the full distribution but may be less directly applicable to targeting programs. Poverty status models are more intuitive for policy targeting but sacrifice information about the degree of poverty or affluence.

5.5.5. Advanced techniques for poverty analysis

While standard regression approaches dominate poverty analysis literature, researchers have increasingly employed more sophisticated techniques to address complex relationships and modeling challenges.

Case study: Panel data analysis of poverty dynamics in Indonesia

Research by Sami'ani et al. (2024) employed dynamic panel data modeling to analyze poverty levels across Indonesian provinces from 2013 to 2022. Using the Generalized Method of Moments (GMM) estimator, the study controlled for unobserved heterogeneity and dynamic effects in provincial-level poverty determinants. Their findings show that the Human Development Index (HDI) has a robust and significant negative effect on poverty, underscoring the central role of education, health, and living standards in long-term poverty reduction. The study also found that exports are associated with lower poverty levels, while imports had a counterintuitive positive effect—likely reflecting reduced purchasing power from imported goods and services. By accounting for dynamic interactions and endogeneity, the analysis provided more precise estimates of causal relationships than standard cross-sectional models. These results highlight the value of panel data techniques in clarifying how structural development indicators and trade openness shape poverty dynamics over time.

Panel data methods: When multiple surveys track the same households over time, panel data techniques allow researchers to control for unobserved household characteristics and better identify causal relationships. Fixed-effects models, for instance, can help distinguish whether education causes higher income or whether unobserved factors influence both education and income.

Decomposition techniques: These methods analyze changes in poverty over time by separating the contributions of changes in household characteristics versus changes in returns to those characteristics. Such decompositions help understand whether poverty reduction resulted from households acquiring more assets (like education) or from increased returns to existing assets.

Quantile regression: This approach examines how determinants of welfare may differ across the welfare distribution. Some factors might strongly influence welfare for the poorest households but show weaker effects for better-off households, information that mean regression cannot capture.

Non-parametric techniques: Methods like Classification and Regression Trees (CART) and Multiple-Adaptive Regression Splines (MARS) offer more flexible approaches for identifying complex, non-linear relationships without imposing strong functional form assumptions. These techniques can help uncover important threshold effects or interaction patterns that traditional regression might miss.

While these advanced techniques offer analytical advantages, they also typically require stronger data, more complex implementation, and more nuanced interpretation. Researchers must balance methodological sophistication with practical applicability when analyzing poverty determinants for policy purposes.

5.6. From Proximate to Fundamental Causes

The regression approaches discussed above excel at identifying proximate determinants of poverty—factors that directly influence welfare levels. However, they often struggle to identify deeper, more fundamental causes. Understanding these deeper causes requires moving beyond statistical associations to analyze causal mechanisms and structural factors.

5.6.1. The challenge of identifying fundamental causes

Regression analysis might show that lacking education causes poverty, but it cannot easily explain why some people lack education in the first place. The deeper causes might include inadequate school infrastructure, high direct or opportunity costs of schooling, poor quality education, or discriminatory practices that exclude certain groups.

Case study: Colonial institutions and contemporary poverty in India

Banerjee and Iyer's (2005) seminal research investigated the long-term impacts of British colonial land tenure systems in India, uncovering how institutional legacies shape contemporary economic outcomes. Using detailed district-level data, they compared regions historically governed under three systems: landlord-based, where elites collected taxes from tenant farmers; ryotwari, where cultivators paid taxes directly to the state; and village-based communal systems. They found that areas with landlord-based systems had significantly lower agricultural productivity and public investments—particularly in education and infrastructure—decades after independence. These effects persist due to entrenched inequalities in political power and elite capture, which limit collective investments in public goods.

This research illustrates the need to move beyond proximate poverty correlates—such as low productivity—and to interrogate their deeper institutional roots. The enduring underdevelopment of landlord regions cannot be explained solely by present-day economic variables; rather, it reflects historical patterns of exclusion and weak state capacity. These findings echo the "missing middle" described by White and Booth (2003)—the analytical gap between observed poverty outcomes and the institutional mechanisms that produce them. Bridging this gap requires integrating econometric analysis with historical and institutional inquiry to uncover the deeper constraints on inclusive development.

5.6.2. Approaches to identifying deeper causes

Several approaches can help researchers move beyond proximate causes to understand deeper determinants of poverty:

Historical analysis: Examining how poverty patterns evolved over time can reveal deeper structural factors. Historical analysis might show how colonial patterns of land distribution created persistent inequality, or how discriminatory institutions excluded certain groups from economic opportunities across generations.

Institutional analysis: Examining how formal and informal institutions shape incentives and opportunities can reveal deeper causes of poverty. For instance, weak property rights might discourage agricultural investment, or discriminatory hiring practices might limit employment opportunities for certain groups regardless of their skills.

Political economy analysis: Understanding how power relations influence resource allocation and policy implementation helps identify why some poverty-reducing policies succeed while others fail. Even well-designed programs may prove ineffective if they threaten powerful interests or if implementing agencies lack accountability mechanisms.

Case study: Political economy of service delivery in Kenya

Muwonge et al. (2022) examined how political economy dynamics influence public service delivery outcomes under Kenya's devolved system of governance. Using a mixed-methods approach—including quantitative assessments of service delivery and qualitative institutional analysis across eight counties—the study highlighted stark differences in performance among counties with similar levels of resources and formal institutional structures. These differences were often shaped by local political incentives, elite interests, and the strength of accountability mechanisms. Counties where local leadership and elites were incentivized by development-linked interests, such as economic growth or infrastructure expansion, tended to invest more effectively in service delivery. In contrast, where political control was dominated by patronage or rent-seeking incentives, services were often unevenly distributed or underfunded. Additionally, stronger civil society engagement and local oversight were associated with more equitable and responsive service provision. The study emphasized that development interventions are more likely to succeed when they account for the political and institutional context, cautioning that technically sound reforms may underperform if they ignore underlying power structures and incentive systems.

Comparative analysis: Comparing regions or countries with similar initial conditions but different poverty outcomes can help identify deeper causal factors. Such analysis might reveal, for instance, how different policy choices or institutional arrangements led to divergent development paths despite similar resource endowments.

These approaches complement rather than replace regression analysis. By combining statistical identification of proximate causes with deeper analysis of causal mechanisms, researchers can develop more comprehensive understanding of poverty determinants and more effective strategies for poverty reduction.

5.6.3. *Examples of deeper causes*

Several fundamental factors have emerged from research as deeper causes of poverty across multiple contexts.

Institutional quality: Countries and regions with stronger institutions—effective property rights, rule of law, control of corruption, and accountable governance—typically achieve greater poverty reduction over time. These institutions create environments where economic activity can flourish and where public resources are more likely directed toward development priorities.

Case study: Institutional reform and poverty reduction in developing Asia

Perera and Lee (2013) examined the role of institutional quality in shaping poverty and inequality outcomes across nine developing countries in Asia between 1985 and 2009. Their analysis found that certain aspects of institutional development—such as improvements in government stability and law and order—were significantly associated with poverty reduction. In contrast, other dimensions, including corruption control, bureaucratic quality, and democratic accountability, were paradoxically linked with higher poverty and worsening income distribution.

Using panel data and institutional quality indicators, the study revealed that the effects of institutional reforms on poverty are complex and multifaceted. While sound institutions can improve the targeting and efficiency of social protection, foster legal environments conducive to business development, and reduce barriers to public services, these effects are not uniform across all governance dimensions. The findings emphasize that the impact of institutional quality on poverty is context-dependent, and reforms must be tailored to enhance inclusivity and efficiency in service delivery.

Rather than being peripheral, institutional quality emerged as a key factor mediating the relationship between economic growth and poverty outcomes. The study underscores the need for nuanced institutional reforms that not only promote economic growth but also ensure that the benefits of growth reach the poor.

In a broader context, historical legacies and power relations often shape the quality and inclusivity of institutions. Colonial histories, patterns of state formation, and past conflicts have produced persistent structural inequalities in many countries. These historical factors shape contemporary governance arrangements and often determine which groups have voice in policymaking or access to public resources. Environmental factors—such as vulnerability to natural hazards or uneven resource distribution—also play a role, compounding structural disadvantage and exposing certain populations to recurrent shocks. An understanding of these intersecting dynamics is essential for designing poverty reduction strategies that are equitable, effective, and resilient to institutional and environmental stressors.

Case study: Climate vulnerability and poverty traps in Bangladesh

Research by Leichenko and Silva (2014) explores how climate change interacts with poverty to create and reinforce vulnerability, particularly in regions like coastal Bangladesh that face recurrent environmental shocks. The authors synthesize evidence showing that climate-induced events such as flooding and cyclones can erode household assets, disrupt livelihoods, and deepen existing socioeconomic inequalities. These shocks often trigger what the authors term "climate-related poverty traps", wherein affected households are unable to recover their prior welfare levels due to limited access to credit, markets, or social protection. In areas with high exposure and weak institutional support, even households that were previously non-poor may experience downward mobility. A particularly concerning pattern discussed is the shift toward lower-risk, lower-return livelihood strategies in response to repeated shocks—an adaptive response that reduces vulnerability in the short term but entrenches chronic poverty over time. This research highlights the need for poverty alleviation strategies that go beyond conventional economic measures and address the structural and environmental dimensions of vulnerability.

By combining analysis of these deeper causes with identification of proximate determinants, researchers and policymakers can develop more comprehensive strategies for addressing poverty at multiple levels.

5.7. Conclusion

Understanding the determinants of poverty requires analyzing factors operating at multiple levels, from individual and household characteristics to community infrastructure and regional environments. This multidimensional nature creates analytical challenges but also provides multiple potential entry points for policy interventions.

At the regional level, geographical factors, governance quality, and social divisions significantly influence poverty outcomes. These factors create the broader context in which more local determinants operate. At the community level, infrastructure, service access, market conditions, and social capital shape the opportunities available to households regardless of their individual characteristics.

Household and individual characteristics—including demographic composition, employment status, asset ownership, education, and health—more directly determine whether specific people experience poverty. Regression analysis helps identify which of these factors most strongly influence welfare levels in particular contexts and how their effects may differ across subpopulations.

While identifying these proximate determinants provides valuable guidance for policy, understanding deeper structural and institutional causes remains challenging. The "missing middle" in poverty analysis—the gap between statistical correlates and fundamental causes—requires complementary approaches that combine quantitative analysis with historical, institutional, and political economy perspectives.

Despite these challenges, the growing body of research on poverty determinants offers important insights for policy design. Effective poverty reduction strategies typically address factors at multiple levels, combining interventions targeted at household-level constraints with broader initiatives to improve community infrastructure and address regional inequalities. By understanding both proximate and deeper causes of poverty, policymakers can design more comprehensive approaches with greater potential for sustainable poverty reduction.

Case study: Integrated approach to poverty reduction in Mexico

Mexico's *Oportunidades* program (formerly *Progresa* and later renamed *Prospera*) stands as a leading case of how comprehensive anti-poverty interventions can generate long-term development gains. As analyzed by Debowicz and Golan (2013), the program used a combination of conditional cash transfers and complementary social investments to address both immediate income deprivation and structural barriers to human capital development. Through a combination of top-down policy planning and bottom-up community engagement, *Oportunidades* linked cash assistance to requirements for school attendance and regular health checkups, thereby incentivizing human capital accumulation among the poorest households. The analysis found that the program contributed significantly to improvements in educational attainment and reductions in income inequality, with notable long-term benefits that extended to second-generation participants.

The impact was especially strong when viewed through the lens of income distribution: The program helped compress the lower tail of the income distribution while improving intergenerational mobility. While the direct effects on household consumption were modest, the indirect impacts through enhanced education and better health outcomes proved substantial. Households that remained in the program over time saw meaningful improvements in children's school completion rates, nutritional status, and eventual labor market outcomes. These findings highlight that the success of *Oportunidades* was not solely due to income supplementation but to its integrated design that combined demand-side incentives with targeted service delivery.

The broader lesson from *Oportunidades* is that effective poverty reduction requires attention to both the proximate and structural causes of deprivation. Programs that simultaneously address multiple dimensions of poverty—such as access to education, health, and income—are more likely to generate sustainable results than those that focus on a single factor. Moreover, strategic alignment between policy design and local implementation, as well as ongoing investments in service infrastructure, are essential to ensure that households can take full advantage of the opportunities created by such interventions.

Key determinants of poverty

Level	Key determinants
Regional	Geography and remoteness
	Resource base and climate conditions
	Quality of governance and institutions
	Social divisions and inequality patterns
Community	Infrastructure (roads, electricity, water)
	Service availability (education, health)
	Market access and conditions
	Social capital and local institutions
Household	Demographic composition and dependency ratio
	Asset ownership and economic activities
	Education levels of household members
	Health status and access to healthcare

The most effective poverty reduction strategies typically address multiple determinants simultaneously, recognizing both the immediate constraints facing poor households and the broader structural factors that perpetuate poverty across generations.

References

Agrawal, T. (2011). *Returns to education in India: Some recent evidence* (IGIDR Working Paper No. WP-2011-017). Indira Gandhi Institute of Development Research. http://www.igidr.ac.in/pdf/publication/WP-2011-017.pdf

Albert, J. R. G., & Collado, P. M. (2004). *Profile and determinants of poverty in the Philippines*. Paper presented at the 9th National Convention on Statistics (NCS), EDSA Shangri-La Hotel, Manila, Philippines. https://www.academia.edu/63168748/Profile_and_Determinants_of_Poverty_in_the_Philippines

Asian Development Bank (ADB). (2009). *Poverty in the Philippines: Causes, constraints, and opportunities.* Mandaluyong City, Philippines: ADB. https://www.adb.org/publications/poverty-philippines-causes-constraints-and-opportunities

Bahru, B. A., Bosch, C., Birner, R., & Zeller, M. (2019). Drought and child undernutrition in Ethiopia: A longitudinal path analysis. *PLOS ONE, 14*(6), Article e0217821. https://doi.org/10.1371/journal.pone.0217821

Banerjee, A., & Iyer, L. (2005). History, institutions, and economic performance: The legacy of colonial land tenure systems in India. *American Economic Review, 95*(4), 1190–1213. https://www.aeaweb.org/articles?id=10.1257/0002828054825574

Debowicz, D., & Golan, J. (2013). *The impact of Oportunidades on human capital and income distribution: A top-down/bottom-up approach* (IFPRI Discussion Paper No. 01257). International Food Policy Research Institute. https://papers.ssrn.com/sol3/papers.cfm?abstract_id=2249810

Fafchamps, M., & Minten, B. (1999). Relationships and traders in Madagascar. *Journal of Development Studies, 35*(6), 1–35. https://doi.org/10.1080/00220389908422600

Foster, S. (2023). *Employment transitions with high unemployment and a small informal sector: Examining worker flows during normal and recessionary periods in South Africa* (WIDER Working Paper No. 2023/56). United Nations University World Institute for Development Economics Research (UNU-WIDER). https://doi.org/10.35188/UNU-WIDER/2023/364-2

Gaillard, J. C., Maceda, E. A., Stasiak, E., Le Berre, I., & Espaldon, M. V. O. (2009). Sustainable livelihoods and people's vulnerability in the face of coastal hazards. *Journal of Coastal Conservation, 13*(2–3), 119–129. https://doi.org/10.1007/s11852-009-0054-y

Independent Evaluation Group (IEG). (2008). *The welfare impact of rural electrification: A reassessment of the costs and benefits.* Washington, DC: World Bank. https://openknowledge.worldbank.org/entities/publication/3fab2298-5cec-52aa-b6c8-1dd4c45d9d33

Kingdon, G. G., & Unni, J. (2001). Education and women's labour market outcomes in India. *Education Economics, 9*(2), 173–195. https://www.tandfonline.com/doi/10.1080/09645290110056994

Kozel, V., & Parker, B. (2000). Integrated approaches to poverty assessment in India. In M. Bamberger (Ed.), *Integrating quantitative and qualitative research in development projects* (pp. 53–74). Washington, DC: World Bank. https://openknowledge.worldbank.org/entities/publication/5e37109a-6b22-5d22-942c-7a3c40461145

Leichenko, R., & Silva, J. A. (2014). Climate change and poverty: Vulnerability, impacts, and alleviation strategies. *WIREs Climate Change, 5*(4), 539–556. https://doi.org/10.1002/wcc.287

Lucchetti, L., Vakis, R., & Rigolini, J. (2016). *Left behind: Chronic poverty in Latin America and the Caribbean.* World Bank. https://openknowledge.worldbank.org/handle/10986/21552

Minot, N. (2006). *Market access and rural poverty in Tanzania* (Conference Paper No. 25603). International Association of Agricultural Economists. https://ageconsearch.umn.edu/record/25603/files/cp060705.pdf

Muwonge, A., Williamson, T. S., Owuor, C., & Kinuthia, M. (2022). *Making devolution work for service delivery in Kenya.* International Development in Focus. World Bank. https://hdl.handle.net/10986/37017

Otieno, O. G. (2015). *Determinants of poverty in Kenya* (Unpublished master's thesis). University of Nairobi. https://erepository.uonbi.ac.ke/bitstream/handle/11295/94549/Otieno%20George%20O_Determinants%20of%20Poverty%20in%20Kenya.pdf?sequence=1

Perera, L. D. H., & Lee, G. H. Y. (2013). *Have economic growth and institutional quality contributed to poverty and inequality reduction in Asia?* (MPRA Paper No. 52763). Munich Personal RePEc Archive. https://mpra.ub.uni-muenchen.de/52763/

Sami'ani, S., Endang, E., Susilo, J. H., & Astuti, H. (2024). Dynamic panel data modeling of Indonesia's poverty level 2013–2022. *Jurnal Ekonomi & Studi Pembangunan, 25*(1), 130–147. https://doi.org/10.18196/jesp.v25i1.21079

Sohnesen, T. P., & Stender, N. (2016). *Is Random Forest a superior methodology for predicting poverty? An empirical assessment* (Policy Research Working Paper No. 7612). World Bank. https://hdl.handle.net/10986/24154

Sumarto, S., Vothknecht, M., & Wijaya, L. (2014). *Explaining the regional heterogeneity of poverty: Evidence from decentralized Indonesia* (SMERU Working Paper, April 2014). The SMERU Research Institute. https://www.smeru.or.id/sites/default/files/publication/regionalheterogeneity_eng_0_0.pdf

Tan, N. Q., Dinh, N. C., Linh, N. H. K., Hung, P. X., Kien, N. D., Phuong, T. T., & Tinh, B. D. (2023). Climate change vulnerability and poverty nexus: Evidence from coastal communities in central Vietnam. *Journal of Agriculture and Environment for International Development (JAEID), 117*(1), 61–84. https://doi.org/10.36253/jaeid-13966

White, H., & Booth, D. (2003). Using development goals to design country strategies. In R. Black & H. White (Eds.), *Targeting development: Critical perspectives on the Millennium Development Goals* (pp. 53–74). Routledge.

https://www.taylorfrancis.com/chapters/edit/10.4324/9780203403235-12/using-development-goals-design-country-strategies-1-howard-white-david-booth

World Bank. (2019). *Bangladesh poverty assessment: Facing old and new frontiers in poverty reduction.* World Bank. https://documents1.worldbank.org/curated/en/793121572582830383/pdf/Bangladesh-Poverty-Assessment-Facing-Old-and-New-Frontiers-in-Poverty-Reduction.pdf

CHAPTER 6
Measuring Inequality

"It is not great wealth in a few individuals that proves a country is prosperous, but great general wealth evenly distributed among the people."
—VICTORIA WOODHULL

SUMMARY

Inequality is a broader concept than poverty, as it considers the entire distribution of economic resources, not just the share below a specific threshold. This chapter introduces key measures and analytical approaches used to quantify economic inequality.

A basic approach involves dividing the population into groups by economic status and comparing their shares of total resources. Quintile analysis typically shows that the poorest fifth of the population receives only 5–10 percent of total income, while the richest fifth commands 40–60 percent. When illustrated graphically, these disparities are depicted using the Lorenz curve, which shows the cumulative distribution of income or consumption across the population.

The Gini coefficient—the most widely used measure of inequality—quantifies the area between the Lorenz curve and the line of perfect equality. It ranges from 0 (perfect equality) to 1 (perfect inequality). While the Gini coefficient is easy to interpret and satisfies key properties such as scale independence and the Pigou–Dalton transfer principle, it lacks full decomposability into within-group and between-group components, limiting its use in certain types of disaggregated analysis.

Entropy-based measures, such as Theil's T and Theil's L (mean log deviation), offer stronger analytical capabilities through their decomposability. These measures enable researchers to assess how much of total inequality stems from differences between groups—such as urban versus rural areas or among educational categories. Empirical evidence from many countries shows that within-group inequality typically accounts for 75–85 percent of overall inequality, highlighting the limitations of group-based targeting strategies for reducing inequality.

More recent measures include the Palma ratio, which compares the income share of the richest 10 percent to that of the poorest 40 percent, reflecting a growing concern with top-end inequality. The Atkinson index incorporates explicit value judgments through an inequality aversion parameter, allowing policymakers to assign greater weight to disparities in different parts of the income distribution.

Dynamic analysis of inequality examines how the distribution of economic resources evolves over time and across generations. Tools such as growth incidence curves reveal how income growth is distributed across different population segments, while decomposition methods allow researchers to isolate the roles of demographic shifts, changes in returns to education, occupational transitions, and policy reforms in shaping inequality trends.

The chapter concludes by exploring the relationship between economic growth, inequality, and poverty reduction. Although high inequality generally weakens the poverty-reducing effect of growth, this relationship is nuanced and context-specific. Evidence suggests that reducing asset inequality, improving access to quality education, and adopting progressive fiscal policies can foster more inclusive growth that simultaneously reduces both poverty and inequality.

6.1. Introduction: Understanding Inequality

Inequality refers to the uneven distribution of economic resources, opportunities, and outcomes across a population. While poverty focuses on those falling below a defined threshold, inequality examines disparity across the entire distribution. Inequality is fundamentally concerned with relative wellbeing, considering how resources are distributed among different individuals, households, or groups within society (Cowell, 2000; Haughton and Khandker, 2009).

Economic inequality typically refers to differences in income or consumption, but can also encompass disparities in wealth, assets, human capital, or opportunities. These various dimensions of inequality, while often correlated, can exhibit distinct patterns and dynamics. For instance, wealth inequality is typically more pronounced than income inequality in most societies, reflecting the cumulative nature of asset accumulation across time and generations.

The conceptual distinction between poverty and inequality is important. Poverty reduction might occur without reducing inequality if living standards rise across the distribution while relative gaps remain similar. Conversely, inequality might decrease while poverty remains unchanged if compression occurs in the middle or upper portions of the distribution. Understanding these distinct concepts helps clarify policy objectives and evaluate outcomes more precisely.

Measuring inequality serves several important purposes. First, it provides a descriptive picture of how economic resources are distributed, which many consider intrinsically important for social justice and societal wellbeing. Second, inequality trends help explain broader economic and social phenomena, including patterns of economic growth, social mobility, and political dynamics. Third, inequality measures inform policy design, helping to target interventions and evaluate their distributional impact.

This chapter introduces key approaches to measuring inequality, from simple comparisons of income shares to more sophisticated decomposable indices. We examine the properties of different measures, their interpretation, and their applications in analyzing the sources and consequences of economic disparity. The chapter also explores how inequality relates to poverty and economic growth, providing a foundation for understanding the distributional dynamics of development.

6.2. Basic Inequality Measurement

6.2.1. Comparing income shares

The simplest approach to measuring inequality divides the population into groups ordered by economic status and compares their respective shares of total resources. This method provides an intuitive starting point for understanding distributional patterns.

Percentile divisions

Population groups are typically divided into fifths (quintiles), tenths (deciles), or hundredths (percentiles), from the poorest to the richest based on per capita income or consumption. Table 6.1 illustrates a quintile breakdown for the Philippines in the period 2018–2023, showing the proportion of total expenditure accruing to each fifth of the population.

The quintile analysis reveals substantial disparity: the poorest 20 percent of Filipinos receive only about 4 to 7 percent of total income, while the richest 20 percent capture around half (48 to 56 percent) of all income. This pattern, though varying in magnitude, is found consistently across countries and time periods. Inequality in the Philippines appears to have increased in the aftermath of the pandemic.

Quintile ratios

These distributional shares can be used to construct simple ratio measures of inequality. The "20:20 ratio" divides the income share of the richest quintile by that of the poorest. In the Philippines example, this

Table 6.1. Per capita income distribution by quintile, Philippines: 2018–2023

Income quintile	2018		2021		2023	
	Share of total income (%)	Cumulative share (%)	Share of total income (%)	Cumulative share (%)	Share of total income (%)	Cumulative share (%)
Poorest 20%	5.6	5.6	4.1	4.1	6.5	6.5
Second 20%	9.3	14.9	7.7	11.8	10.3	16.8
Middle 20%	13.6	28.5	12.1	23.9	14.4	31.2
Fourth 20%	20.7	49.2	19.7	43.7	21.1	52.3
Richest 20%	50.9	100.2	56.4	100.0	47.7	100.0

Source: *Family Income and Expenditure Survey 2018, 2021 and 2023,* Philippine Statistics Authority.

ratio is approximately 7.5 (46.4/6.2), indicating that the richest fifth claims 7.5 times more economic resources than the poorest fifth.

Decile ratios

For finer analysis, decile ratios compare income or consumption at different points in the distribution. Common decile ratios include the following:

- P90/P10: Compares the 90th percentile to the 10th percentile, showing the full range of the distribution excluding extreme outliers
- P90/P50: Compares the upper end to the median, showing upper-tail inequality
- P50/P10: Compares the median to the lower end, showing lower-tail inequality

In Vietnam, for instance, the P90/P10 ratio for income increased from 5.95 to 6.06 between 2014 and 2016, indicating widening inequality across the bulk of the distribution (Nguyen et al., 2021).

6.2.2. The Lorenz curve

The Lorenz curve provides a graphical representation of distribution, plotting the cumulative percentage of the population (from poorest to richest) on the horizontal axis against the cumulative percentage of income or consumption on the vertical axis.

Figure 6.1 displays the Lorenz curve for per capita income data in the Philippines (in both urban and rural areas) for 2023. The 45-degree line represents perfect equality—where each population percentile would receive exactly that same percentage of total income. The actual distribution creates a curve that falls below this line of equality. The greater the distance between the Lorenz curve and the line of equality, the greater the inequality.

The Lorenz curve provides several insights:

1. The curve always begins at the origin (0,0) and ends at the point (100,100).
2. If everyone had exactly the same income, the Lorenz curve would follow the 45-degree line.

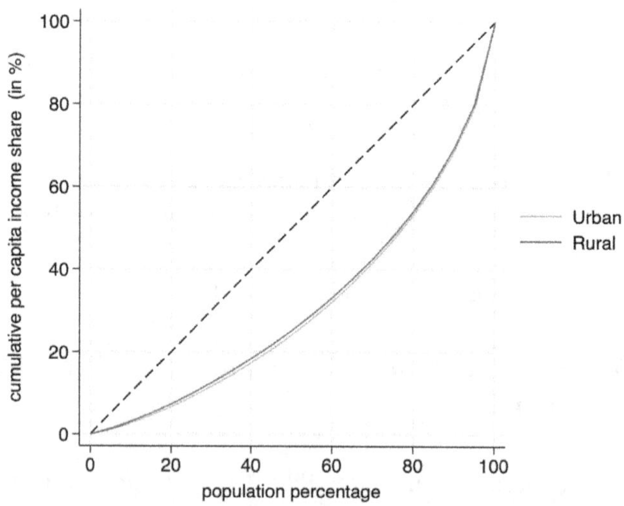

Figure 6.1. Lorenz curve for per capita income distribution (in urban and rural areas), Philippines, 2023.

3. If one person received all income, the Lorenz curve would follow the bottom and right edges of the graph.
4. The area between the line of equality and the Lorenz curve indicates the degree of inequality.

For any population subgroup (for example, the bottom 40 percent), we can use the Lorenz curve to identify their share of total resources. In the Philippines example, the bottom 40 percent receive approximately 16.7 percent of the total expenditure—less than half their proportional share in a perfectly equal distribution.

The Lorenz curve allows for intuitive visual comparisons across time or between different societies. When Lorenz curves for two distributions do not cross, we can make unambiguous statements about their relative inequality—the distribution with the Lorenz curve closer to the line of equality is unambiguously more equal.

6.2.3. The Gini coefficient

The Gini coefficient translates the graphical information of the Lorenz curve into a single numerical measure of inequality. It represents the ratio of the area between the line of equality and the Lorenz curve (Area A in Figure 6.1) to the total area under the line of equality ($A + B$).

Formally, the Gini coefficient can be defined as

$$\text{Gini} = \frac{A}{A+B} = 2A = 1 - 2B$$

The Gini coefficient ranges from 0 to 1:

- A value of 0 represents perfect equality (everyone has the same income).
- A value of 1 represents perfect inequality (one person has all income).

In practice, Gini coefficients for income typically range from about 0.25 (relatively equal societies like Denmark or Finland) to around 0.60 (highly unequal countries like South Africa or Brazil).

When working with individual data points, the Gini coefficient can be calculated as

$$\text{Gini} = \frac{1}{2n^2\mu}\sum_{i=1}^{n}\sum_{j=1}^{n}\left|y_i - y_j\right|$$

where

- n is the number of observations
- μ is the mean income
- y_i and y_j are individual income observations

For grouped data (such as deciles), the Gini can be approximated using the formula

$$\text{Gini} \approx 1 - \sum_{i=1}^{k}\left(X_i - X_{i-1}\right)\left(Y_i + Y_{i-1}\right)$$

where

- X_i is the cumulative proportion of the population
- Y_i is the cumulative proportion of income
- k is the number of groups

Table 6.2 presents Gini coefficients for selected countries, illustrating the wide variation in income inequality across regions and development levels. It provides pre-pandemic and post-pandemic data for various countries, showcasing how inequality levels shifted over time. Gini coefficients remain high in South American countries such as Brazil (52.0 in 2022), reflecting persistent income inequality driven by factors like informal labor markets, unequal access to education,

Table 6.2. Gini coefficients for selected countries, 2015–2020

Country	Gini coefficient	Year
Brazil	53.5	2019
	52	2022
Cote d'Ivoire	37.2	2018
	35.3	2021
Finland	27.3	2018
	27.7	2021
India	34.5	2018
	32.8	2021
Netherlands	28.1	2018
	25.7	2021
Philippines	42.3	2018
	40.7	2021
Senegal	38.3	2018
	36.2	2021
Thailand	34.9	2019
	34.9	2021
Vietnam	35.7	2018
	36.1	2022

Source: World Bank, World Development Indicators.

and segmented economic opportunities. In contrast, European countries such as Finland (27.7 in 2021) and the Netherlands (25.7 in 2021) exhibit lower levels of inequality, attributed to progressive taxation, strong social safety nets, and well-developed public services that facilitate income redistribution. These regional contrasts highlight the need for targeted policy approaches to address structural inequalities and promote inclusive growth.

The Gini coefficient offers several advantages as a measure of inequality:

1. **Mean independence**: The measure remains unchanged if all incomes are multiplied by a constant.
2. **Population size independence**: The measure is invariant to population size.
3. **Symmetry**: The measure is unchanged if people swap incomes.
4. **Pigou–Dalton transfer sensitivity**: Transfers from rich to poor reduce measured inequality.

Despite these advantages, the Gini coefficient has limitations. It cannot be neatly decomposed into inequality between and within population subgroups—a significant analytical constraint. The Gini coefficient also gives equal weight to gaps throughout the distribution, whereas alternative measures can place greater emphasis on disparities at the bottom or top of the distribution, depending on normative priorities.

6.3. Entropy-Based Inequality Measures

6.3.1. Generalized entropy measures

The generalized entropy (GE) class of inequality measures offers powerful analytical advantages, particularly through their decomposability properties. These measures derive from information theory and measure the divergence of a distribution from perfect equality.

The general formula for the GE class is

$$\mathrm{GE}(\alpha)=\frac{1}{\alpha(\alpha-1)}\left[\frac{1}{n}\sum_{i=1}^{n}\left(\frac{y_i}{\bar{y}}\right)^{\alpha}-1\right]$$

where

- y_i is the income of individual i
- $\bar{y}$ is the mean income

- n is the population size
- α is a parameter that determines sensitivity to different parts of the distribution

The parameter α reflects the weight given to distances between incomes at different parts of the distribution. Lower values make the measure more sensitive to changes in the lower tail of the distribution, while higher values increase sensitivity to the upper tail.

The most commonly used entropy measures are

1. **Mean log deviation (MLD)**: GE(0) or Theil's L
2. **Theil's T index**: GE(1)
3. **Half the squared coefficient of variation**: GE(2)

6.3.2. Theil's T index or GE(1)

Theil's T index, GE(1), is perhaps the most widely used entropy measure (Theil, 1969). Its formula simplifies to

$$\mathrm{T} = \mathrm{GE}(1) = \frac{1}{n}\sum_{i=1}^{n}\left(\frac{y_i}{\bar{y}}\right)\ln\left(\frac{y_i}{\bar{y}}\right)$$

This formula represents a weighted average of the logarithm of the ratio of each individual's income to mean income, with the weights being the relative incomes themselves. Theil's T gives more weight to transfers at the upper end of the distribution.

The values of Theil's T range from 0 (perfect equality) to $\ln(n)$ (maximum inequality). Unlike the Gini coefficient, the upper bound depends on the population size, making direct comparisons across populations of different sizes somewhat problematic.

Figure 6.2 presents Theil T estimates from Mercado et al. (2023) for three Southeast Asian countries. The data show modest declines in Theil T for the Philippines and Thailand between 2015 and 2021, and a slight increase for Vietnam. Among these countries, the Philippines

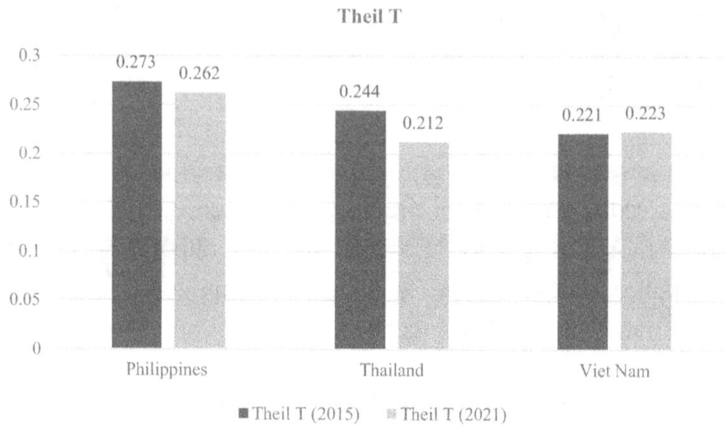

Figure 6.2. Theil T in select ASEAN member states: 2015 and 2021.
Source: Mercado et al. (2023).

had the highest level of inequality as measured by Theil T in both years.

6.3.3. Mean log deviation (GE(0))

The mean log deviation (MLD), or Theil's L, is GE(0), which is calculated as

$$L = GE(0) = \frac{1}{n}\sum_{i=1}^{n} \ln\left(\frac{\bar{y}}{y_i}\right)$$

This measure represents the average of the logarithm of the ratio of mean income to individual incomes. The MLD gives more weight to transfers at the lower end of the distribution, making it particularly useful for analyzing poverty-related inequality.

Like Theil's T, the MLD equals zero for perfect equality but has a variable upper bound of $\ln(n)$.

Research by Akita and Miyata (2018) applied the MLD to study urban–rural disparities in Indonesia. Their findings indicate that inequality in urban areas was consistently higher, with the MLD increasing from 0.25 in 1999 to 0.37 in 2005. This upward trend reflects widening dispersion among lower-income groups in urban areas, likely driven by uneven access to labor market opportunities and public services. Their decomposition approach highlighted that much of Indonesia's overall inequality stemmed from within-group rather than between-group differences, reinforcing the importance of localized, intra-regional inequality interventions.

6.3.4. Decomposition properties

The key advantage of entropy measures is their decomposability into between-group and within-group components. For any mutually exclusive population subgroups, total inequality can be expressed as

$$\mathrm{GE}(\alpha) = \mathrm{GE}_B(\alpha) + \mathrm{GE}_W(\alpha)$$

where

- $\mathrm{GE}_B(\alpha)$ represents the inequality between groups
- $\mathrm{GE}_W(\alpha)$ represents the weighted average of inequality within each group

For Theil's T specifically, the decomposition formula is

$$\mathrm{T} = \sum_{j=1}^{m} s_j \mathrm{T}_j + \sum_{j=1}^{m} s_j \ln\left(\frac{\mu_j}{\mu}\right)$$

where

- m is the number of groups
- s_j is group j's share of total income

- T_j is the Theil index within group j
- μ_j is the mean income in group j
- μ is the overall mean income

The first term represents within-group inequality, while the second term measures between-group inequality.

Similarly, for the mean log deviation (MLD):

$$L = \sum_{j=1}^{m} f_j L_j + \sum_{j=1}^{m} f_j \ln\left(\frac{\mu}{\mu_j}\right)$$

where f_j is the population share of group j.

These decomposition properties allow researchers to assess how much inequality stems from differences between groups (such as urban–rural gaps) versus disparities within groups. Table 6.3 presents decomposition results for the Philippines and other countries (taken

Table 6.3. Decomposition of inequality by regions/provinces (MLD measure)

Country/area	Year	Within-group (%)	Between-group (%)	Source
Philippines	2009	76–80	20–24	PSA (2010)
Philippines	2012	86–89	11–14	PSA (2013)
China	1998	62	38	Akita (2003)
Vietnam	1999	64	36	Minot et al. (2003)
Italy	1995	87	13	Förster and Mira (2005)
Russia	1995	91	9	Förster and Mira (2005)
Canada	1997	98	2	Gray et al. (2003)

Source: Chua et al. (2015).

from Chua et al., 2015), highlighting the relative contributions of within-region and between-region inequalities to total inequality.

The decomposition results show that the Philippines exhibits a relatively high proportion of within-region inequality, contributing 76 to 80 percent of total inequality in 2011 and increasing to 86 to 89 percent by 2012. The between-group component declined from 20 to 24 percent in 2011 to 11 to 14 percent in 2012, indicating a reduction in regional disparities. Compared to other countries, China and Vietnam show higher between-group inequality, contributing 38 and 36 percent, respectively. In contrast, wealthier and more integrated countries such as Italy (13 percent), Russia (9 percent), and Canada (2 percent) exhibit significantly lower between-group inequality. Interestingly, the urban–rural decomposition for the Philippines in 2012 reveals that the urban–rural share of total inequality was around 10 percent, which is almost equal to the regional between-region share of 11 percent.

These decompositions reveal that even though between-group disparities (such as urban–rural gaps) often receive significant policy attention, the majority of inequality—typically 75–85 percent—occurs within these groups. This finding has important implications for targeting strategies, suggesting that effective inequality reduction requires addressing disparities within localities, not just between them.

6.3.5. *Temporal decomposition*

Entropy measures also allow decomposition of changes in inequality over time. For the MLD, the change between two periods can be expressed as

$$\Delta L = \sum_{j=1}^{m} \bar{f}_j \, \Delta L_j + \sum_{j=1}^{m} \bar{L}_j \, \Delta f_j + \sum_{j=1}^{m} \Delta \ln\left(\frac{\mu}{\mu_j}\right) \bar{f}_j + \sum_{j=1}^{m} \ln\left(\frac{\bar{\mu}}{\bar{\mu}_j}\right) \Delta f_j$$

This decomposition separates the change in inequality into

1. Changes in within-group inequality
2. Changes in population shares
3. Changes in relative mean incomes
4. Interaction effects

Such decompositions can reveal, for instance, whether rising inequality stems from increasing disparities within urban areas, migration patterns, or growing urban–rural income gaps.

6.4. Alternative Inequality Measures

6.4.1. *The Palma ratio*

The Palma ratio, proposed by economist José Gabriel Palma, measures the ratio of the income share of the top 10 percent to that of the bottom 40 percent. This measure emerged from Palma's observation that the middle 50 percent (deciles 5–9) tend to capture a relatively stable share of national income across countries (approximately 50 percent), while the main variation occurs in how the remaining income is split between the richest 10 percent and the poorest 40 percent (Palma, 2011).

The formula is simple:

$$\text{Palma ratio} = \frac{S_{10}}{S_{1-4}}$$

where

- S_{10} is the income share of the top decile
- S_{1-4} is the combined income share of the bottom four deciles

The Palma ratio typically ranges from about 1.0 in relatively equal societies (Scandinavian countries) to over 7.0 in the most unequal countries (South Africa). The Philippines' Palma ratio stands at approximately 3.0, indicating that the richest 10 percent receive about three times the income of the poorest 40 percent combined.

This measure has gained traction in policy circles for several reasons:

1. It focuses attention on the extremes of the distribution where most variation occurs.
2. It is easily understood and communicated.
3. It aligns with growing concern about top-end inequality and its economic and political consequences.

The United Nations Development Programme and some development agencies have incorporated the Palma ratio into their inequality monitoring frameworks alongside traditional measures.

6.4.2. *Atkinson's inequality index*

The Atkinson index, developed by economist Anthony Atkinson, explicitly incorporates normative judgments about inequality through an inequality aversion parameter (ε). This parameter reflects how much a society values equality—higher values indicate greater societal concern for inequality (Atkinson, 1970).

The Atkinson index is defined as

$$A_\varepsilon = 1 - \left[\frac{1}{n}\sum_{i=1}^{n}\left(\frac{y_i}{\bar{y}}\right)^{1-\varepsilon}\right]^{\left(\frac{1}{1-\varepsilon}\right)} \quad \text{for } \varepsilon \neq 1$$

$$A_1 = 1 - \frac{\prod_{i=1}^{n}(y_i)^{1/n}}{\bar{y}} \quad \text{for } \varepsilon = 1$$

where

- ε is the inequality aversion parameter
- y_i is the income of individual i

- $\bar{y}$ is the mean income
- n is the population size

The inequality aversion parameter ε typically ranges from 0.5 (low aversion) to 2.0 (high aversion). As ε increases, the measure becomes more sensitive to inequalities at the bottom of the distribution.

The Atkinson index has an intuitive interpretation: it represents the proportion of total income that could be sacrificed with no loss of social welfare if the remaining income were distributed equally. For example, an Atkinson index of 0.3 with $\varepsilon = 1$ implies that society could achieve the same level of welfare with 70 percent of the current total income if that reduced amount were distributed equally. The increasing values as ε rises reflect greater sensitivity to inequality at the bottom of the distribution. The large differences between $A(0.5)$ and $A(2.0)$ highlight how normative judgments about the importance of equality can dramatically affect perceptions of how unequal a society is.

Table 6.4 presents the Atkinson indices for selected countries using an aversion parameter of $\varepsilon = 1.0$, which is commonly used in inequality analyses.

Table 6.4. Atkinson indices with aversion parameter $\varepsilon = 1.0$

Country	Year	Atkinson Index (ε = 1.0)
Denmark	2022	0.11
	2018	0.11
Vietnam	2022	0.21
	2018	0.20
Philippines	2022	0.24
	2018	0.25
Brazil	2022	0.44
	2018	0.43

Source: *Our World in Data*, based on UNDP Human Development Report (2024).

As of 2022, Denmark exhibits a relatively low Atkinson index of 0.11, indicating a more equal income distribution. Vietnam has a moderate Atkinson index of 0.21, suggesting moderate income inequality. The Philippines shows a higher Atkinson index of 0.24, reflecting greater income inequality compared to Denmark and Vietnam. Brazil records a high Atkinson index of 0.44, indicating significant income inequality. These figures illustrate the varying degrees of income inequality across different countries, as measured by the Atkinson index with an aversion parameter of $\varepsilon = 1.0$.

6.4.3. *Percentile ratios and shares*

Simple percentile ratios provide intuitive measures that focus on specific parts of the distribution. Common variants include

- **P90/P10 ratio**: The ratio of income at the 90th percentile to that at the 10th percentile
- **P90/P50 ratio**: The ratio of income at the 90th percentile to the median
- **P50/P10 ratio**: The ratio of median income to that at the 10th percentile
- **Top 1% income share**: The proportion of total income accruing to the richest 1 percent
- **Top 10% income share**: The proportion of total income accruing to the richest 10 percent

These measures have gained prominence in recent inequality debates, particularly those focusing on top incomes. Research by Piketty and Saez (2003) and others has highlighted dramatic increases in top income shares in many advanced economies since the 1980s.

In the United States, for instance, the income share of the top 1 percent increased from about 10 percent in the 1970s to approximately 20 percent by 2019. Such concentration has significant implications for economic opportunity, political influence, and social cohesion.

6.5. Inequality Dynamics and Analysis

6.5.1. Growth incidence curves

The growth incidence curve (GIC) provides a graphical representation of how economic growth is distributed across income percentiles. This tool helps evaluate whether growth has been "pro-poor" or has disproportionately benefited certain segments of the distribution.

The GIC plots income growth rates for each percentile of the distribution between two time periods:

$$g_p = \frac{y_{p,t+1}}{y_{p,t}} - 1$$

where

- g_p is the growth rate for percentile p
- $y_{p,t}$ is the income at percentile p in period t
- $y_{p,t+1}$ is the income at percentile p in period $t+1$

Figure 6.3, sourced from the *2022 Vietnam Poverty and Equity Assessment* (WB, 2022), provides a growth incidence curve (GIC) for Vietnam between 2010 and 2020, showing household consumption growth across the welfare distribution.

The pattern in Vietnam shows higher growth rates in the middle of the distribution compared to either end, creating an inverted-U shape in the entire period 2010–2020. This pattern differs from many developing countries where growth often benefits the upper end of the distribution the most, producing an upward-sloping GIC.

Growth is considered "pro-poor" in an absolute sense if incomes of the poor grow in real terms. In a relative sense, growth is "pro-poor" if the growth rates for poorer segments exceed the average growth rate, reducing inequality. The GIC allows visual assessment of both concepts.

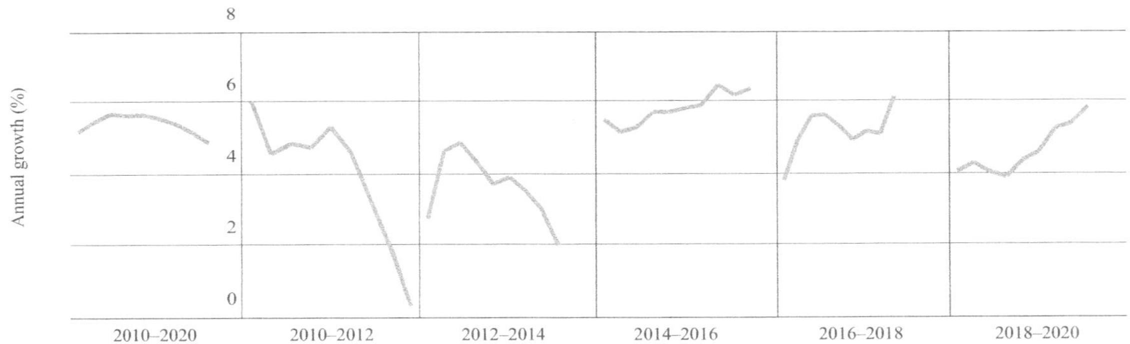

Figure 6.3. Growth incidence curve for Vietnam, 2010–2020.
Note: Due to the small sample size of the household survey, and also less precision in the tails, these curves are constructed from 10 points, each representing a welfare decile.
Source: World Bank staff calculations using VHLSS.

Ravallion and Chen (2003) propose the "rate of pro-poor growth" as the mean growth rate of the poor (those below the poverty line). This can be calculated as the area under the GIC up to the headcount poverty rate, divided by the headcount rate.

Figure 6.3 also illustrates that between 2010 and 2014, growth rates were higher for the lower end of the distribution, while in the later periods (2014–2016, 2016–2018, and 2018–2020), the highest rates of growth were observed among households at the upper end of the distribution. This indicates that the pattern of growth in Vietnam during this period was pro-poor initially, but later shifted toward benefiting higher-income households.

6.5.2. Mobility and dynamics

Cross-sectional inequality measures provide a snapshot of distribution at a given time but reveal nothing about movement within that distribution. Panel data, which track the same households over time, allow the analysis of economic mobility—how individuals move up or down the economic ladder.

Common mobility measures include the following:

1. **Transition matrices**: Show movement between income quintiles over time
2. **Mobility indices**: Single-value measures of overall positional change
3. **Shorrocks' rigidity index**: Compares inequality of average income over time to average of period-specific inequality measures

The transition matrix for income mobility in the Philippines between 2003 and 2009, as shown in Table 6.5, provides insights into the dynamics of poverty transitions that will be discussed in more detail in the next chapter. Based on "panel data", i.e., households that were surveyed across several years, for the period 2003 to 2009 from the Family Income and Expenditure Survey (FIES), the table reveals

Table 6.5. Five-year income quintile transition matrix, Philippines, 2003–2009

2003 Quintile	Q1 (poorest)	Q2	Q3	Q4	Q5 (richest)
Q1 (poorest)	64.3%	25.3%	7.5%	2.3%	0.6%
Q2	25.0%	34.2%	27.0%	10.5%	3.3%
Q3	7.8%	24.6%	36.9%	23.5%	7.2%
Q4	2.0%	9.0%	22.3%	45.0%	21.7%
Q5 (richest)	0.9%	2.3%	6.1%	19.8%	70.9%

that a substantial proportion of households remained in the same income quintile during this period. However, there is notable movement across income groups, with nearly 8.6 percent of households escaping poverty by 2009, while 9.2 percent slipped into poverty during the same period. The largest movements were observed among households in the middle quintiles, reflecting moderate income mobility in the Philippines. Despite some upward mobility, large movements between the extreme quintiles (from poorest to richest or vice versa) remain rare, indicating the persistence of structural barriers to economic advancement.

Albert (2023) highlights that while a significant proportion of poor households transitioned out of poverty, many remained vulnerable to slipping back into poverty. Approximately 64.3 percent of the poorest households in 2003 remained in the lowest quintile by 2009, while only 0.6 percent managed to reach the richest quintile. Similarly, a large proportion of households in the richest quintile in 2003 (70.9 percent) stayed in the top quintile by 2009, indicating relatively low mobility across the extremes of the distribution.

Income mobility patterns provide important context for interpreting inequality measures. A society with high inequality but substantial mobility may offer more economic opportunity than one with moderate inequality but rigid class structures.

6.5.3. Inequality decomposition by income source

Income inequality can be decomposed by source to understand which income components drive overall inequality. For any income measure composed of multiple sources (labor, capital, transfers, etc.), we can calculate the contribution of each source to total inequality. Shorrocks (1982), for instance, discusses how to break down overall income inequality into contributions from different income sources, such as wages, capital income, transfers, etc.

For the Gini coefficient, the decomposition formula is

$$\text{Gini} = \sum_{k=1}^{K} S_k C_k$$

where

- S_k is the share of source k in total income
- C_k is the concentration ratio of source k

The concentration ratio measures how source k is distributed relative to total income. The contribution of source k to total inequality is $\frac{S_k C_k}{\text{Gini}}$, expressed as a percentage.

Table 6.6 presents a decomposition of income inequality by source for Indonesia, using a regression-based inequality decomposition approach, where income is regressed on various explanatory variables (Wicaksono et al., 2017). The predicted income from this regression is then decomposed using the Shapley value approach, which assigns the contribution of each variable to overall inequality based on its marginal effect on the predicted outcome. This method allows for a more nuanced understanding of the drivers of inequality and highlights the differential impact of various income sources. The results, derived from household survey data for 2014, illustrate the relative contributions of education, wealth, and other factors to income inequality in Indonesia.

The decomposition in Table 6.6. highlights that education and wealth contribute significantly to income inequality in Indonesia.

Table 6.6. Decomposition of income inequality by source, Indonesia, 2014

Income source	Share (in %) of total income	Concentration ratio	Contribution (in %) to Gini
Education	16.7	0.46	12.84
Wealth	19.2	0.48	20.33
Wage earners	20.2	0.45	15.11
Household size	1.3	-0.03	0.91
Age	14.7	0.36	4.74
Male-headed households	0.87	0.04	0.04
Rural location	3.7	0.22	2.48
Eastern Indonesia	0.61	0.10	0.18
Residuals	22.7	–	42.18
Total	100.0	0.38	100.0

Source: Wicaksono et al. (2017).

Wealth accounted for the largest share of inequality, contributing 20.33 percent to the Gini despite representing only 19.2 percent of total income. Similarly, education contributed 12.84 percent to inequality, reflecting disparities in access to quality education across different socioeconomic groups. Wage earners contributed 15.11 percent to overall inequality, which suggests that differences in labor market outcomes remain an important source of inequality. Interestingly, household size and male-headed households had minimal impacts on inequality, with contributions below 1 percent. Rural location and being in Eastern Indonesia contributed modestly to overall inequality, highlighting the geographical dimensions of income disparity. Residuals, which capture unobserved factors not included in the model, accounted for the largest share of inequality at 42.18 percent, underscoring the importance of unmeasured variables in explaining income disparities.

Such decompositions provide valuable insights for policy interventions. For instance, reforms targeting the distribution of property income might have a significant inequality-reducing effect despite its relatively small income share. Conversely, expanding transfer programs could increase equality by growing the share of this already equally distributed income source.

6.5.4. *Microdecomposition methods*

Advanced microdecomposition methods allow researchers to identify the factors driving changes in inequality over time or differences across countries. These approaches typically involve counterfactual simulations that isolate the effects of specific factors while holding others constant.

The Oaxaca–Blinder decomposition and its extensions separate observed changes into

1. **Endowment effects**: Changes in the distribution of characteristics (education levels, age structure, etc.)
2. **Returns effects**: Changes in how characteristics translate into income (returns to education, etc.)
3. **Residual effects**: Unexplained changes in distribution

More sophisticated approaches include

- **Semi-parametric decompositions** (DiNardo et al., 1996)
- **Regression-based methods** (Wan 2002; Wicaksono et al., 2017)
- **Recentered influence function decompositions** (Firpo et al., 2018)

These methods have revealed that rising inequality in many countries stems from a combination of technological change, globalization, weakening labor market institutions, and changes in tax and transfer policies—though their relative importance varies by context.

6.6. Inequality, Growth, and Poverty Reduction

6.6.1. *The growth–inequality–poverty nexus*

The relationship between economic growth, inequality, and poverty reduction forms a critical nexus in development economics. While growth is generally necessary for substantial poverty reduction, its impact depends significantly on both initial inequality and how the benefits of growth are distributed.

The mathematical relationship between these factors can be expressed through the poverty-growth-inequality triangle. For a given poverty line, the change in poverty (P) can be approximated as

$$\Delta P \approx \eta_g \times g + \eta_I \times \Delta I$$

where

- η_g is the growth elasticity of poverty (the percentage change in poverty for a 1 percent increase in mean income)
- η_I is the inequality elasticity of poverty (the percentage change in poverty for a 1 percent increase in inequality)
- g is the growth rate of mean income
- ΔI is the change in inequality

Research consistently shows that higher initial inequality reduces the poverty-reducing impact of a given growth rate. Ravallion (2007) found that for countries with very high inequality (Gini above 0.6), even 1 percent growth produces little poverty reduction. Conversely, for countries with low inequality (Gini around 0.3), the same growth rate can reduce poverty by 4–5 percent.

6.6.2. *The Kuznets hypothesis and beyond*

Simon Kuznets hypothesized in the 1950s that inequality follows an inverted U-shaped pattern during economic development—first rising and then falling as countries industrialize (Kuznets, 1955). His theory suggested that in early stages of development, inequality increases as labor shifts from low-productivity agriculture to higher-productivity industry, creating wider wage dispersions. As development continues, education expands, social protections strengthen, and progressive taxation emerges, reducing inequality.

Empirical evidence has not consistently supported this deterministic pattern. While some countries showed Kuznets-like trajectories, many others did not:

1. **East Asian "growth with equity"**: Japan, South Korea, and Taiwan achieved rapid growth while keeping inequality relatively low through land reform, education investments, and labor-intensive industrialization.
2. **Rising inequality in advanced economies**: Since the 1980s, many high-income countries have experienced increasing inequality, contradicting the downward portion of the Kuznets curve.
3. **Mixed patterns in developing regions**: Latin America has seen high inequality persist through different stages of development, while parts of Africa show various patterns depending on resource endowments and institutions.

Modern understanding recognizes that the growth–inequality relationship depends critically on policies and institutions, not just stages of development. Economic growth creates opportunities for both greater equality and inequality—the outcome depends on how growth processes are structured and how resources are distributed.

6.6.3. *Inclusive growth and shared prosperity*

The concept of "inclusive growth" has emerged as an approach that integrates equity considerations directly into growth strategies. While traditional measures focus on poverty reduction or aggregate growth, inclusive growth metrics examine how economic gains are distributed across the population.

The World Bank's "shared prosperity" indicator measures the income growth of the bottom 40 percent compared to the overall population. For growth to be considered inclusive under this definition, the income growth rate of the bottom 40 percent must equal or exceed the average growth rate.

Table 6.7 presents shared prosperity data for selected countries between 2012 and 2017 (WB, 2020). It reveals that Vietnam and China experienced inclusive growth, where the income growth of the bottom 40 percent was comparable to or slightly higher than that of the overall population. However, in Indonesia, the overall growth rate of 6.18 percent exceeded the bottom 40 percent growth of 5.06 percent, indicating that growth was less inclusive during this period. Similarly, in Thailand, growth for the bottom 40 percent was almost equal to the overall growth rate, implying neutral growth distribution. The Philippines saw higher growth among the bottom 40 percent (5.12 percent) than the overall population (4.03 percent), suggesting modestly inclusive growth.

Alternative inclusive growth measures include:

1. **Growth incidence curves**: Examining growth rates across all income percentiles
2. **Poverty-adjusted growth rates**: Weighting growth by its impact on poverty reduction

Table 6.7. Shared prosperity indicators for selected countries, 2012–2017

Country	Bottom 40% growth	Overall growth	Difference
Vietnam	4.91%	5.16%	–0.25%
Indonesia	5.06%	6.18%	–1.12%
Thailand	1.45%	1.40%	+0.05%
Philippines	5.12%	4.03%	+1.09%
China	8.38%	7.86%	+0.52%

Source: WB (2020).

3. **Distribution-adjusted growth indices**: Incorporating inequality penalties into growth measures
4. **Generalized means approach**: Using lower-parameter generalized means to give greater weight to lower incomes

6.6.4. Poverty elasticity of growth

The poverty elasticity of growth measures how responsive poverty reduction is to economic growth, quantifying the percentage change in poverty rates associated with a 1 percent change in mean income or GDP per capita. This metric is crucial for understanding the inclusiveness of growth and designing effective poverty reduction strategies.

Formally, the poverty elasticity of growth (PEG) can be expressed as

$$\text{PEG} = \frac{\Delta \text{Poverty}}{\Delta \text{Income}}$$

where a higher absolute value indicates greater poverty reduction for a given rate of economic growth.

The magnitude of poverty elasticity is significantly influenced by initial conditions. Several empirical studies have identified key determinants of poverty elasticity. Bourguignon (2003) demonstrated that both initial levels of inequality and average income strongly affect how growth translates into poverty reduction. Countries with lower initial inequality tend to have higher poverty elasticities, while those with higher initial average incomes typically have lower elasticities as the "low-hanging fruit" of poverty reduction has already been achieved.

Ravallion (2001) estimated that for countries with very low inequality (Gini of 0.25), the poverty elasticity might be around –3.0, meaning a 1 percent increase in average incomes reduces poverty by 3 percent. However, for highly unequal countries (Gini of 0.60), the elasticity could be as low as –0.6. This relationship helps explain why some rapidly growing economies have struggled to translate that growth into proportional poverty reduction.

Evidence from Southeast Asia provides instructive contrasts. Vietnam achieved remarkably high poverty elasticity between 2002 and 2018, with estimates ranging from –2.0 to –2.6, reflecting its relatively equitable growth pattern and effective poverty-focused policies (Nguyen et al., 2021). In contrast, the Philippines has historically demonstrated lower poverty elasticity despite periods of strong economic growth.

The World Bank's recent Poverty and Equity Assessment for the Philippines (2025) offers compelling evidence of changing poverty elasticity over time. The assessment (Figure 6.4) shows that before 2015, the Philippines exhibited relatively low responsiveness of poverty to growth, with elasticity estimates around –0.2 to –0.5. However, from 2015 onward, poverty became significantly more responsive to economic growth, with elasticity improving to approximately –1.5 to –2.6 by the 2021–2023 period. This dramatic improvement suggests structural changes in how growth benefits are distributed across Philippine society.

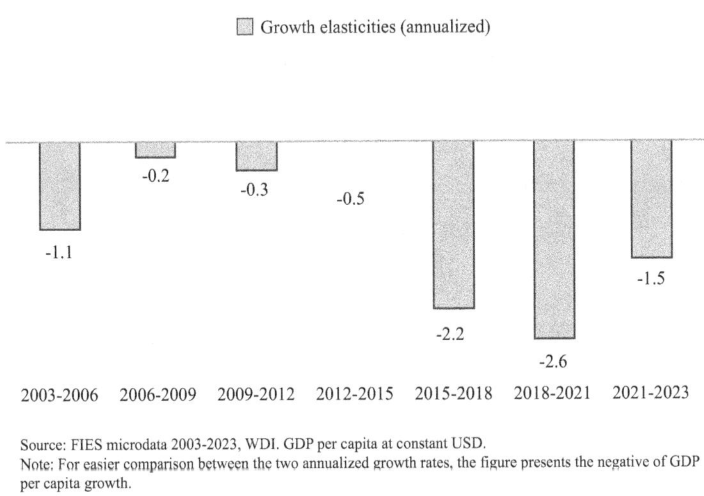

Figure 6.4. Growth elasticities of poverty in the Philippines, 2003–2023
Source: WB (2025).

Several factors can explain variations in poverty elasticity across countries and time periods:

1. **Sectoral composition of growth**: Growth in sectors where the poor are concentrated (such as agriculture in many developing countries) tends to have higher poverty elasticity than growth concentrated in capital-intensive sectors with limited employment generation.
2. **Geographic distribution of growth**: Growth concentrated in regions with higher poverty rates typically yields greater poverty reduction than growth in already prosperous areas.
3. **Labor market conditions**: When growth expands employment opportunities for the poor and raises wages at the lower end of the distribution, poverty elasticity tends to be higher.
4. **Policy environment**: Progressive fiscal policies, targeted social protection programs, and investments in human capital can enhance the poverty-reducing impact of growth.
5. **Initial inequality**: Lower initial inequality generally leads to higher poverty elasticity, creating a more favorable starting point for inclusive growth strategies.

The Philippines case study illustrates how these factors can evolve over time. The World Bank (2025) attributes the increased poverty elasticity after 2015 primarily to changes in the labor market, with growth creating more wage employment opportunities for lower-income households. The assessment shows that from 2015 to 2023, income from wage employment contributed substantially more to poverty reduction than other income sources, including government transfers and remittances.

Understanding poverty elasticity has important policy implications. Rather than pursuing growth at any cost, policymakers can focus on enhancing the quality of growth to maximize poverty reduction. This might involve targeting investments toward labor-intensive sectors, improving access to productive assets and credit for the poor, strengthening human capital formation, and implementing redistributive policies that increase the poor's capacity to participate in and benefit from economic growth.

The evidence suggests that poverty elasticity is not a fixed parameter but can be influenced by deliberate policy choices that make growth more inclusive. Countries seeking to accelerate poverty reduction would benefit from regularly monitoring not just growth rates but also how effectively that growth translates into improved living standards for their poorest citizens.

6.6.5. Inequality and economic efficiency

Traditional economic theory often presented a tradeoff between equity and efficiency, suggesting that redistribution harms economic performance. More recent evidence presents a more nuanced view, finding that certain types and levels of inequality may actually impede growth and economic efficiency through several mechanisms:

1. **Human capital underinvestment**: When inequality limits educational opportunities for lower-income individuals, society fails to develop its full productive potential.
2. **Credit market imperfections**: High inequality combined with imperfect financial markets prevents capable but resource-constrained individuals from making productive investments.
3. **Political economy effects**: Extreme inequality can lead to policies that protect entrenched interests rather than promoting broad-based growth.
4. **Social cohesion and stability**: High inequality may undermine social trust and increase political instability, deterring investment.
5. **Demand-side effects**: Excessive concentration of income can reduce aggregate demand when wealthy individuals save larger portions of their income.

The IMF and OECD have found that beyond certain thresholds, inequality negatively affects growth sustainability. IMF research suggests that lower net inequality is robustly correlated with faster and more durable growth. This evidence challenges simplistic equity-efficiency tradeoffs and suggests that well-designed policies can promote both objectives simultaneously.

6.7. Policy Approaches to Inequality

6.7.1. Pre-distribution policies

"Pre-distribution" policies address inequality by changing how market incomes are generated before taxes and transfers. These policies focus on equalizing opportunity and market outcomes rather than relying solely on after-the-fact redistribution. Key approaches include the following:

1. **Human capital development**: Expanding access to quality education and healthcare to equalize productive opportunities
2. **Labor market institutions**: Strengthening collective bargaining, minimum wages, and employment protections to improve earnings at the bottom of the distribution
3. **Competition policy**: Reducing monopoly power and market concentration that allow firms to capture excessive profits
4. **Financial inclusion**: Expanding access to financial services and capital for small businesses and underserved populations
5. **Spatial policies:** Addressing regional disparities through infrastructure investment and place-based development strategies

The World Bank's Human Capital Index reveals substantial disparities in how countries translate economic resources into human development outcomes. Vietnam, for instance, achieves significantly better education and health outcomes than countries with similar income levels, creating the foundation for more equitable growth.

6.7.2. Redistribution policies

Redistribution policies modify the distribution of income and wealth after-market outcomes through taxes and transfers. Fiscal systems vary dramatically in their redistributive impact, with Scandinavian countries typically achieving much greater inequality reduction than most developing nations.

Key redistributive approaches include

1. **Progressive taxation**: Income, wealth, and capital gains taxes that take higher percentages from those with greater resources
2. **Social transfers**: Cash and in-kind benefits targeted toward lower-income households
3. **Social insurance**: Programs that protect against economic shocks and life-cycle risks (unemployment, old age, disability)
4. **Public services**: Universal or means-tested access to education, healthcare, and other services that reduce out-of-pocket costs for essential needs

The redistributive impact of fiscal systems can be measured by comparing inequality of market income (pre-tax, pre-transfer) to inequality of disposable income (post-tax, post-transfer). In OECD countries, fiscal redistribution typically reduces the Gini coefficient by 0.15–0.25 point (or approximately 30–40 percent). In contrast, many developing countries achieve much smaller reductions, often just 0.02–0.05 Gini points.

To illustrate specifically, the redistributive impact of fiscal systems in Vietnam has been analyzed in detail in the 2022 Vietnam Poverty and Equity Assessment (PEA) by the World Bank (2022). The findings show that fiscal policies, including taxes and transfers, have a significant impact on reducing income inequality. According to the assessment, direct transfers (such as cash transfers) and personal income taxes (PITs) are the most effective instruments in reducing inequality. Personal income taxes reduce inequality by about 0.5 point, while other direct taxes contribute a reduction of around 0.2 point. The largest impact is attributed to social insurance contributions (such as social security, health, and unemployment insurance), which reduce inequality by 1.6 points. Indirect subsidies (such as electricity subsidies) and indirect taxes (such as VAT and

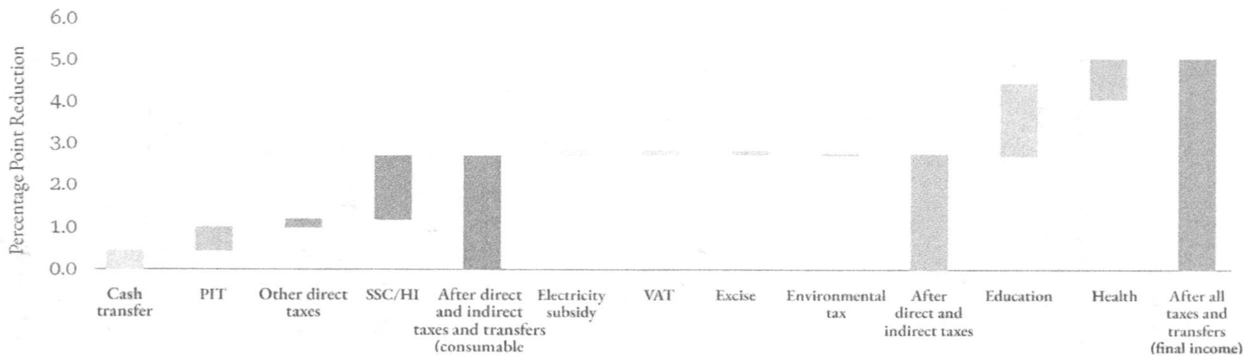

Note: Marginal effects on poverty reduction are presented. A positive bar represents contribution to poverty reduction. A negative bar represents an increase in poverty. Individual subcomponents are scaled to the marginal effect of each fiscal category. For example, the marginal effects of VAT, excises and environmental taxes are scaled to sum to the marginal effect of indirect taxes as a category.

Figure 6.5. The impact of fiscal policy on inequality by fiscal instrument, Vietnam (2018).
Source: WB (2022).

excises) have a minimal redistributive effect, with limited impact on reducing inequality (Figure 6.5).

When all taxes and transfers are combined, fiscal policies in Vietnam reduce the Gini coefficient by approximately 5 points after including non-cash health and education spending. Moreover, the cost-effectiveness of fiscal instruments varies, with personal income taxes emerging as the most cost-effective method of reducing inequality per unit of revenue raised. In contrast, social insurance contributions—though generating the largest share of revenue—are the least cost-effective in terms of inequality reduction. Direct cash transfers are almost three times more effective at reducing inequality than indirect subsidies, although spending on subsidies remains nearly equal to that of transfers. The assessment suggests that a shift in Vietnam's revenue mix toward direct taxes and well-targeted transfers could further enhance the redistributive impact without increasing fiscal costs (WB, 2022).

6.7.3. Asset-based policies

Asset inequality is typically more extreme than income inequality and more persistent across generations. Asset-based policies aim to broaden ownership of productive resources and build wealth among lower-income households. Approaches include

1. **Land reform**: Redistributing or formalizing land ownership to provide productive assets to rural households
2. **Housing assistance**: Subsidies, community land trusts, and other mechanisms to promote affordable homeownership
3. **Individual development accounts**: Matched savings accounts that help lower-income households build assets
4. **Baby bonds or universal capital grants**: Endowments provided at birth or adulthood to ensure all citizens have some minimum capital
5. **Worker ownership**: Policies promoting employee stock ownership, cooperatives, and other forms of shared ownership

Asset-based policies can address wealth inequality directly while also improving income distribution over time as assets generate returns. Research suggests that more equal asset distribution contributes to more sustainable and equitable growth patterns, as seen in the developmental success of countries that implemented substantial land reforms, such as South Korea and Taiwan.

6.8. Conclusion

Inequality measurement provides essential insights into how economic resources are distributed across society. The various measures described in this chapter—from simple comparisons of income shares to sophisticated decomposable indices—offer complementary perspectives on disparities within and between groups.

Beyond measurement, understanding inequality dynamics and their relationship to economic growth and poverty reduction is critical for designing effective development strategies. The evidence suggests that extreme inequality can undermine both economic efficiency and poverty reduction efforts, while moderate inequality with strong social mobility may be consistent with dynamic, inclusive growth.

Policy approaches to inequality should reflect context-specific factors, including the level and structure of inequality, institutional capacity, and societal preferences. Most successful approaches combine elements of pre-distribution, redistribution, and asset-based policies, recognizing that inequality has multiple, interconnected dimensions requiring comprehensive responses.

As societies continue to debate appropriate levels and types of inequality, rigorous measurement and analysis remain essential for informing these discussions with evidence rather than ideology. The methods and insights presented in this chapter provide a foundation for this ongoing inquiry into one of the most fundamental aspects of economic systems.

References

Akita, T. (2003). Decomposing regional income inequality in China and Indonesia using two-stage nested Theil decomposition method. *The Annals of Regional Science, 37*(1), 55–77.

Akita, T., & Miyata, S. (2018). Spatial inequalities in Indonesia, 1996–2010: A hierarchical decomposition analysis. *Social Indicators Research, 138*, 829–852. https://www.jstor.org/stable/48715204

Albert, J. R. G. (2023). *Poverty transitions and the near-poor in the Philippines* (PIDS Discussion Paper Series No. 2023-27). Philippine Institute for Development Studies. https://www.pids.gov.ph/publications/7926

Atkinson, A. B. (1970). On the measurement of inequality. *Journal of Economic Theory, 2*(3), 244–263. https://www.sciencedirect.com/science/article/pii/0022053170900396

Bourguignon, F. (2003). The growth elasticity of poverty reduction: Explaining heterogeneity across countries and time periods. In T. Eicher & S. Turnovsky (Eds.), *Inequality and growth: Theory and policy implications* (pp. 3–26). MIT Press.

Chua, K. K., Limkin, L., Nye, J., & Williamson, J. G. (2015). Urban-rural income and wage gaps in the Philippines: Measurement error, unequal endowments, or factor market failure? *The Philippine Review of Economics, 52*(2), 1–21. https://pre.econ.upd.edu.ph/index.php/pre/article/viewFile/921/821

Cowell, F. A. (2000). Measurement of inequality. In A. B. Atkinson & F. Bourguignon (Eds.), *Handbook of income distribution* (Vol. 1, pp. 87–166). Amsterdam: Elsevier. https://ssrn.com/abstract=1094782

DiNardo, J., Fortin, N. M., & Lemieux, T. (1996). Labor market institutions and the distribution of wages, 1973–1992: A semiparametric approach. *Econometrica, 64*(5), 1001–1044. https://www.jstor.org/stable/2171954

Firpo, S., Fortin, N. M., & Lemieux, T. (2018). Decomposing wage distributions using recentered influence function regressions. *Econometrics, 6*(2), 28. https://www.mdpi.com/2225-1146/6/2/28

Förster, M. and Mira, D. E. M. (2005). Income distribution and poverty in OECD countries in the second half of the 1990s. Oecd Social, Employment and Migration Working Papers 22:1–7.

Gray, D., Mills, J. A., & Zandvakili, S. (2003). Statistical analysis of inequality with decompositions: The Canadian experience. *Empirical Economics, 28*(2), 291–302.

Haughton, J., & Khandker, S. R. (2009). *Handbook on poverty and inequality*. Washington, DC: World Bank. https://documents1.worldbank.org/curated/en/488081468157174849/pdf/483380PUB0Pove101OFFICIAL0USE0ONLY1.pdf

Kuznets, S. (1955). Economic growth and income inequality. *American Economic Review, 45*(1), 1–28. https://www.jstor.org/stable/1811581

Mercado, R., Park, C.-Y., & Zhuang, J. (2023). *Trends and drivers of income inequality in the Philippines, Thailand, and Viet Nam: A decomposition analysis* (ADB Economics Working Paper Series No. 692). Asian Development Bank. https://www.adb.org/sites/default/files/publication/901481/ewp-692-income-inequality-philippines-thailand-viet-nam.pdf

Minot, N., Baulch, B., & Epprecht, M. (2003). *Poverty and inequality in Vietnam: Spatial patterns and geographic determinants*. Washington, DC: International Food Policy Research Institute.

Nguyen, L. T. (2021). The determinants of poverty and inequality in Vietnam (Doctoral dissertation, University X). Lincoln University, New Zealand. https://core.ac.uk/download/587085664

Our World in Data. (2025, May 7). Human Development Index (HDI) [dataset]. Global Change Data Lab. Data adapted from United Nations Development Programme (2024), Human Development Report 2024: Breaking the Gridlock. https://ourworldindata.org/grapher/human-development-index

Palma, J. G. (2011). Homogeneous middles vs. heterogeneous tails, and the end of the 'Inverted-U': It's all about the share of the rich. *Development and Change, 42*(1), 87–153. https://onlinelibrary.wiley.com/doi/abs/10.1111/j.1467-7660.2011.01694.x

Philippine Statistics Authority (PSA). (2013). 2012 Family Income and Expenditure Survey (FIES) [microdata file]. Quezon City, Philippines: PSA. https://psada.psa.gov.ph/index.php/catalog/38

PSA. (2010). 2009 Family Income and Expenditure Survey (FIES) [microdata file]. Quezon City, Philippines: PSA. https://psada.psa.gov.ph/catalog/39

Piketty, T., & Saez, E. (2003). Income inequality in the United States, 1913–1998. *Quarterly Journal of Economics, 118*(1), 1–39. https://academic.oup.com/qje/article-abstract/118/1/1/1917000?redirectedFrom=fulltext

Ravallion, M. (2001). Growth, inequality and poverty: Looking beyond averages. *World Development, 29*(11), 1803–1815. https://doi.org/10.1016/S0305-750X(01)00072-9

Ravallion, M. (2007). Inequality is bad for the poor. In J. Micklewright & S. Jenkins (Eds.), *Inequality and poverty re-examined* (pp. 49–74). Oxford:

Oxford University Press. https://global.oup.com/academic/product/inequality-and-poverty-re-examined-9780199218110

Ravallion, M., & Chen, S. (2003). Measuring pro-poor growth. *Economics Letters, 78*(1), 93–99. https://www.sciencedirect.com/science/article/pii/S0165176502002057

Shorrocks, A. F. (1982). Inequality decomposition by factor components. *Econometrica, 50*(1), 193–211. http://jstor.org/stable/1912537

Theil, H. (1969). The measurement of inequality by components of income. *The Economic Journal, 79*(315), 601–609. https://doi.org/10.2307/2236977

Wan, G. (2002). *Regression-based inequality decomposition: Pitfalls and a solution procedure* (UNU-WIDER Discussion Paper No. 2002/101). United Nations University World Institute for Development Economics Research. https://www.wider.unu.edu/sites/default/files/dp2002-101.pdf

Wicaksono, E., Amir, H., & Nugroho, A. (2017). *The sources of income inequality in Indonesia: A regression-based inequality decomposition* (ADBI Working Paper 667). Tokyo: Asian Development Bank Institute. https://www.adb.org/sites/default/files/publication/229411/adbi-wp667.pdf

World Bank. (2020). *Global database of shared prosperity and median income/consumption, circa 2012–2017*. Washington, DC: World Bank. https://thedocs.worldbank.org/en/doc/803811601320694951-0090022020/render/GPSPandMedianincome20122017.pdf

World Bank. (2022). *Vietnam poverty and equity assessment: From the last mile to the next mile*. Washington, DC: World Bank. https://documents1.worldbank.org/curated/en/099115004242216918/pdf/P176261155e1805e1bd6e14287197d61965ce02eb562.pdf

World Bank. (2025, March). *Philippines poverty and equity assessment: Consultations* [PowerPoint slides]. World Bank East Asia and the Pacific, Poverty and Equity Global Practice.

CHAPTER 7
Poverty Dynamics

"Once poverty is gone, we'll need to build museums to display its horrors to future generations. They'll wonder why poverty continued so long in human society – how a few people could live in luxury while billions dwelt in misery, deprivation and despair."
—Muhammad Yunus

SUMMARY

While cross-sectional poverty analysis provides a snapshot of poverty at a specific point in time, poverty dynamics examines how poverty evolves over time for the same individuals or households. This chapter introduces the analytical approaches used to study poverty transitions and the persistence of poverty over time.

Panel data—which track the same units over multiple periods—are essential for studying poverty dynamics. Such data allow researchers to distinguish between persistent poverty (affecting households continuously over time) and transient poverty (involving temporary episodes of poverty). Panel surveys face challenges, including attrition bias, representativeness issues, and difficulties in tracking household compositional changes, but provide invaluable insights impossible to obtain from cross-sectional data.

Poverty transition matrices reveal substantial mobility into and out of poverty over time. Research consistently shows that in many countries, the proportion of people experiencing poverty at some point exceeds the poverty rate at any single time point, highlighting the importance of distinguishing between the chronically poor, the transiently poor, and those who have never experienced poverty.

The chapter examines methodological approaches for analyzing chronic poverty, including the spells approach (focusing on continuous periods in poverty) and the components approach (examining average welfare over time). Statistical methods such as regression models help identify key factors associated with poverty transitions while controlling for measurement error that might otherwise create spurious transitions.

Recent advances in measuring multidimensional poverty dynamics extend beyond income or consumption to capture deprivations across multiple dimensions simultaneously, revealing that different dimensions often follow distinct temporal patterns. The analysis of intergenerational poverty transmission further broadens our temporal perspective, examining how poverty status transmits across generations through channels including human capital investment, asset inheritance, and social networks.

The determinants of poverty transitions reflect both structural factors (including educational attainment, assets, and location) and stochastic events (such as health shocks, natural disasters, and economic crises). Understanding these patterns helps policymakers design interventions that not only alleviate current poverty but also prevent vulnerable households from falling into poverty and help the chronically poor achieve sustainable escapes from poverty.

The chapter concludes by highlighting that persistent and transient poverty may require different policy responses—the former demanding structural interventions to build assets and capabilities, while the latter necessitates risk management tools and social protection systems to help households weather temporary shocks.

7.1. Introduction: Understanding Poverty over Time

Poverty is inherently dynamic. Individuals and households move in and out of poverty over time in response to life-cycle changes, economic shifts, health events, natural disasters, and other shocks. Some experience short spells of poverty before returning to better circumstances, while others remain entrapped in persistent deprivation for extended periods. Understanding these dynamics is crucial for designing effective policies that address both chronic and transient forms of poverty.

Traditional poverty measures based on cross-sectional data provide important information about the prevalence and depth of poverty at specific points in time. However, they cannot reveal whether the same or different households constitute the poor from one period to the next. Cross-sectional analysis might show stable poverty rates over time, obscuring significant underlying churn—with some households escaping poverty while others fall into it. This limitation restricts our understanding of poverty persistence and vulnerability, potentially leading to misguided policies that fail to address the specific needs of different poverty trajectories.

Poverty dynamics research addresses these limitations by examining how poverty status changes for the same individuals or households over time. This approach distinguishes between persistent or chronic poverty (affecting households continuously over extended periods) and transient poverty (involving temporary episodes of poverty). Such distinctions have profound policy implications, as interventions to address persistent poverty (such as building human capital and productive assets) may differ from those addressing transient poverty (such as risk management and social protection).

This chapter introduces the analytical approaches used to study poverty dynamics. We begin by examining panel data—the primary data source for poverty dynamics research—and their methodological challenges. We then explore methods for analyzing persistent and transient poverty, including the use of poverty transition matrices and more sophisticated measures of chronic poverty. The discussion extends to multidimensional poverty dynamics, which consider deprivations across multiple dimensions beyond income or consumption. Finally, we examine the determinants of poverty transitions and discuss their implications for policy design.

7.2. Panel Data for Poverty Analysis

7.2.1. Types of data for measuring poverty dynamics

Studying poverty dynamics requires information about the same individuals or households over multiple time periods. Researchers use various approaches to collect such data, each with strengths and limitations:

- **Panel surveys** track the same units (households, individuals, or dwellings) over time, providing the most direct measure of welfare dynamics. Common examples include the Panel Study of Income Dynamics (PSID) in the United States, the German Socio-Economic Panel (SOEP), and various national Living Standards Measurement Studies (LSMS) panels in developing countries. These surveys typically collect comprehensive information on income, consumption, assets, employment, health, education, and other welfare indicators.
- **Rotating panels** replace a portion of the sample in each wave while retaining others, allowing both longitudinal analysis (for units that remain) and continued representativeness of the population.

Examples include Indonesia's National Socioeconomic Survey (SUSENAS) and the Philippines' Family Income and Expenditure Survey (FIES) rotating panel.

- **Pseudo-panels** construct synthetic cohorts by grouping individuals with similar time-invariant characteristics (such as birth year) across repeated cross-sectional surveys. This approach approximates genuine panel data when true panels are unavailable, but cannot track specific individuals over time.
- **Retrospective questions** in cross-sectional surveys ask respondents about past conditions, providing partial insights into dynamics despite limitations in recall accuracy and detail. This approach is often used to collect information on past shocks or welfare status when panel data are unavailable.

Among these approaches, genuine panel surveys provide the most reliable basis for poverty dynamics research, as they allow direct observation of changes in individuals' circumstances over time. However, their implementation faces several methodological challenges.

7.2.2. Panel survey challenges and solutions

Panel surveys face distinct challenges that can affect the reliability of poverty dynamics analysis:

- **Attrition bias** occurs when respondents drop out of the panel non-randomly over time, potentially making the remaining sample unrepresentative. Attrition rates vary widely across panels—from under 5 percent per wave in well-established panels with effective tracking protocols to over 20 percent in more challenging contexts. Attrition often correlates with mobility (as migrating households are harder to relocate) and socioeconomic status (with both the poorest and wealthiest respondents more likely to drop out). Statistical corrections for attrition include inverse probability weighting and imputation methods.
- **Tracking protocol decisions** determine which members of the original sample to follow when households split or recombine,

creating complex tradeoffs between maintaining representativeness and controlling costs. Different protocols include following all original household members, following only designated respondents, or tracking only those who remain in the original dwelling. Each approach has different implications for the types of mobility and household changes that can be analyzed.

- **Measurement error** in welfare indicators can significantly distort poverty dynamics analysis, potentially creating spurious transitions. For instance, random errors in measuring consumption might incorrectly suggest that households have crossed the poverty line when their true welfare has remained stable. Approaches to mitigate measurement error include using multiple welfare indicators, averaging welfare measures across waves, or employing statistical methods that explicitly model measurement error.
- **Representativeness over time** becomes challenging as panel samples age and new population groups (such as young households or immigrants) are not incorporated. Some panels address this by periodically refreshing the sample to maintain representativeness of the current population.

Despite these challenges, panel data remain indispensable for poverty dynamics research. Sophisticated research designs and analytical techniques can mitigate many of these limitations, allowing meaningful insights into how poverty evolves over time.

7.2.3. Examples of panel surveys for poverty analysis

Several influential panel surveys have contributed significantly to our understanding of poverty dynamics:

- The **Indonesia Family Life Survey (IFLS)** has tracked the same households across five waves from 1993 to 2014, achieving remarkably low attrition rates (under 10 percent cumulative attrition over 21 years) through intensive tracking of migrants. This survey provided crucial evidence on household adaptations to the

1997–1998 Asian Financial Crisis, showing substantial resilience in food consumption despite large income shocks.

- The **Young Lives Study** follows cohorts of children in Ethiopia, India, Peru, and Vietnam from early childhood into adulthood, focusing on the dynamics of child poverty and its long-term consequences. This study combines quantitative panel surveys with qualitative research, offering nuanced insights into poverty trajectories and their determinants.
- The **Philippines' Family Income and Expenditure Survey (FIES)** panel component tracked the same households across 2003, 2006, and 2009, revealing substantial movement into and out of poverty despite relatively stable aggregate poverty rates. Analysis of this panel showed that many near-poor households—those with incomes just above the poverty line—remained vulnerable to falling into poverty, with about one-third of the near-poor in 2003 becoming poor by 2009.
- The **Tanzania National Panel Survey** collects detailed agricultural data alongside standard household welfare indicators, enabling analysis of how agricultural productivity changes relate to poverty transitions. This integration of agricultural and welfare data is particularly valuable for understanding rural poverty dynamics.

These diverse panel surveys illustrate both the potential and the practical challenges of collecting longitudinal data for poverty analysis. While resource-intensive, such datasets provide invaluable insights that cannot be obtained through cross-sectional analysis alone.

7.3. Approaches to Analyzing Poverty Dynamics

7.3.1. Poverty transition matrices

The simplest approach to analyzing poverty dynamics is through poverty transition matrices, which tabulate poverty status in an initial period against poverty status in a subsequent period. These matrices reveal both the persistence of poverty (diagonal elements) and movements into and out of poverty (off-diagonal elements).

Consider Table 7.1, which shows poverty transitions in the Philippines between 2003 and 2009, based on the FIES panel data.

This matrix reveals significant mobility despite seemingly stable cross-sectional poverty rates (19.8 percent in 2003, 20.3 percent in 2009). While 9.3 percent of households remained poor across both periods (the "chronically poor"), 10.5 percent escaped poverty (the "upwardly mobile"), and 11.0 percent fell into poverty (the "downwardly mobile"). The majority (69.2 percent) remained non-poor throughout. These patterns highlight that cross-sectional poverty rates—which changed little over this period—mask substantial underlying churn.

Transition matrices can be refined by incorporating finer welfare categories—such as distinguishing between extreme poor, moderate poor, vulnerable non-poor, and secure non-poor—or by extending to more than two time periods. Such refinements provide more nuanced pictures of welfare mobility beyond simple poverty transitions.

The Philippines example also demonstrates the vulnerability of near-poor households—those with incomes just above the poverty line. When analyzing the 2003–2009 panel, Albert (2023) found that while 56.2 percent of near-poor households remained non-poor throughout the period, 31.2 percent had fallen into poverty by 2009. This vulnerability rate was substantially higher than for households

Table 7.1. Poverty transition matrix, Philippines, 2003–2009 (percentage of 2003 households)

	2009 status		
2003 status	**Poor**	**Non-poor**	**Total**
Poor	9.3	10.5	**19.8**
Non-poor	11.0	69.2	**80.2**
Total	**20.3**	**79.7**	**100.0**

Source: Albert (2023), based on the 2003–2009 FIES panel data.

with incomes well above the poverty line, highlighting the precarious position of the near-poor.

While transition matrices provide valuable initial insights into poverty dynamics, they have limitations. They typically focus on transitions between discrete states (poor versus non-poor) rather than capturing changes in the depth of poverty. They also potentially overstate mobility if measurement error causes some households to appear to cross the poverty line when their true welfare remains unchanged. These limitations motivate more sophisticated approaches to analyzing persistent and transient poverty.

7.3.2. Measuring chronic and transient poverty: Conceptual approaches

Beyond simple transitions, researchers have developed more sophisticated approaches to distinguish between chronic and transient components of poverty. Two main conceptual approaches have emerged in the literature:

The **spells approach** focuses on the duration of poverty episodes. It classifies individuals as chronically poor if they experience poverty for an extended period or for a minimum number of time periods. For instance, households might be considered chronically poor if they are poor in all periods observed or in at least a specified number of periods (e.g., at least two out of three survey waves). This approach emphasizes the persistence of poverty over time.

The **components approach** examines average welfare over time relative to the poverty line. It identifies individuals as chronically poor if their average consumption or income over all periods falls below the poverty line, regardless of their poverty status in any specific period. This approach emphasizes the permanence of low welfare rather than the continuity of the poverty experience.

These approaches reflect different conceptualizations of chronic poverty. The spells approach focuses on the persistence of the poverty state itself, while the components approach emphasizes the persistence of low welfare levels. The choice between them has both theoretical and practical implications for how we understand and measure chronic poverty.

The conceptual approaches to chronic and transient poverty can be illustrated with empirical data from the Philippines. Table 7.2 presents the poverty trajectories of Filipino households across three survey waves (2003, 2006, and 2009) based on panel data from the Family Income and Expenditure Survey (FIES). The table categorizes households into five distinct trajectories, revealing the dynamic nature of poverty in the Philippines. It reveals that while 73.0 percent of households never experienced poverty during this period, 9.3 percent were chronically poor (poor in all three waves), 6.9 percent became impoverished (moving from non-poor to poor), 1.2 percent experienced transitory poverty (poor, then non-poor, then poor again), and 9.5 percent demonstrated resilience by escaping poverty (moving from poor to non-poor).

These patterns illustrate that while the aggregate poverty rate in the Philippines remained relatively stable over this period (around 20 percent), this apparent stability masked substantial underlying churn. The fact that over a quarter of Filipino households experienced poverty at some point during these six years—despite only about a fifth being

Table 7.2. Poverty trajectories of households in the Philippines, 2003–2009

Poverty trajectory	Description	Percentage of households
Chronic poor	Poor in all three waves (2003, 2006, 2009)	9.3%
Impoverished	Non-poor in 2003 and 2006, poor in 2009	6.9%
Transitory poor	Poor in 2003, non-poor in 2006, poor again in 2009	1.2%
Resilient	Poor in 2003 and 2006, non-poor in 2009	9.5%
Never poor	Non-poor in all three waves	73.0%

Source: Albert (2023), based on the 2003–2009 FIES panel data.

poor at any single point in time—demonstrates the importance of distinguishing between persistent and transient forms of poverty. Such distinctions have significant implications for policy design, as households in different trajectories may require different types of interventions to effectively address their specific challenges.

7.3.3. Operationalizing chronic poverty measurement

Building on these conceptual approaches, researchers have developed various methods to measure chronic and transient poverty. We outline several influential operational approaches below:

- **Jalan and Ravallion's components approach** (1998) decomposes total poverty into chronic and transient components. The chronic component represents poverty that would exist if consumption were equalized across all periods at its intertemporal average value for each household. The transient component captures additional poverty due to consumption fluctuations around this average. Formally, total poverty (P) can be expressed as

$$P = P^{C} + P^{T}$$

  where P^{C} is chronic poverty (based on average consumption over time) and P^{T} is transient poverty (the difference between total observed poverty and chronic poverty). This approach allows the calculation of the share of total poverty attributable to chronically low consumption versus consumption volatility.
- **Foster's duration-adjusted chronic poverty measures** (2009) incorporate both the spells and components approaches. These measures identify the chronically poor based on both the duration of their poverty spells and the average depth of their poverty. They satisfy desirable properties including decomposability (allowing analysis by population subgroups) and dimensional monotonicity (reflecting that poverty becomes more severe as more periods are spent in poverty). This approach yields indices measuring the prevalence, depth, and severity of chronic poverty.

- **Calvo and Dercon's intertemporal poverty indices** (2009) explicitly incorporate time preference and risk aversion parameters, reflecting that poverty experienced earlier might be weighted differently than later poverty, and that variability in consumption might matter beyond its average level. These indices accommodate different normative perspectives on how poverty should be aggregated across time.

Each of these approaches offers distinct insights into chronic poverty while involving different data requirements and assumptions. The choice among them depends partly on the specific research or policy questions being addressed, as well as on practical constraints related to data availability and quality.

7.3.4. *Empirical evidence on chronic and transient poverty*

Empirical research applying these approaches has yielded several important insights about the prevalence and determinants of chronic and transient poverty across contexts.

Studies consistently find that the proportion of people experiencing transient poverty—being poor in some periods but not others—often exceeds the proportion experiencing chronic poverty. For instance, research in China using panel data from 1985 to 1990 found that only 6.2 percent of the population was poor in all six years, while 47.8 percent experienced poverty in at least one year (Jalan and Ravallion, 1998). Similarly, in rural Pakistan, about 3 percent of households were chronically poor over a five-year period, while 55.3 percent experienced transient poverty (McCulloch and Baulch, 2000b).

However, these patterns vary substantially across contexts. In countries with higher overall poverty rates, chronic poverty typically constitutes a larger share of total poverty. In sub-Saharan Africa, for example, research in Ethiopia found that 21 percent of rural households were chronically poor over a five-year period compared to 30 percent experiencing transient poverty (Dercon and Porter, 2011).

The duration of panel data affects estimates of chronic poverty. Longer panels typically reveal lower rates of chronic poverty (defined as being poor in all periods) but higher rates of ever experiencing poverty. This reflects both genuine welfare mobility over longer timeframes and the statistical reality that the probability of observing consecutive periods in poverty decreases with the number of periods observed.

These findings underscore that poverty is not a static condition for many households. Understanding the dynamic nature of poverty—including both entries into and exits from poverty—is essential for designing appropriate policy responses that address both persistent deprivation and vulnerability to temporary shocks.

Table 7.3, drawn from Jalan and Ravallion's (1998) research in China, compares the cost efficiency of different approaches to eliminating poverty across four provinces. It demonstrates that perfect targeting—directing resources specifically to the chronically poor—would cost just 6.94 yuan per capita, while uniform transfers to everyone or targeting based on current consumption would cost 361 and

Table 7.3. Cost of poverty elimination under different targeting scenarios, China 1985–1990

Region	Perfect targeting (yuan per capita)	Uniform transfer (yuan per capita)	Targeting based on current consumption (yuan per capita)
All four provinces	6.94 (100%)	25.07 (361%)	24.88 (358%)
Guangdong	0.33 (100%)	0.88 (267%)	0.72 (218%)
Guangxi	6.30 (100%)	24.00 (379%)	18.89 (300%)
Guizhou	14.35 (100%)	46.23 (322%)	44.44 (310%)
Yunnan	7.62 (100%)	26.20 (344%)	22.21 (292%)

Source: Jalan and Ravallion (1998).
Note: Figures in parentheses show percentages of the total budget required to eliminate chronic poverty under perfect targeting.

358 percent more, respectively. The provincial breakdown reveals significant regional variations, with elimination of chronic poverty in poorer Guizhou requiring over 40 times more resources per capita than in wealthier Guangdong under perfect targeting. These findings highlight the potential efficiency gains from accurately identifying the chronically poor, while also demonstrating the practical challenges of doing so.

7.3.5. Further evidence from the Philippines FIES panel

The Philippines FIES panel data provide valuable insights into poverty transitions in the country. Beyond the basic transitions discussed earlier, more nuanced analyses by Filipino researchers reveal complex patterns of poverty dynamics.

Martinez (2016) conducted a thorough analysis of the 2003–2006–2009 FIES panel data, incorporating appropriate weights to ensure the panel's representativeness. He used different poverty trajectories based on various poverty lines and broken down by urban and rural areas (Table 7.4).

This detailed analysis by Martinez (2016) reveals significant differences in poverty dynamics depending on how poverty is measured and where households are located.

- Using the government poverty line, 15.50 percent of the Philippine population was chronically poor (i.e., poor in all three survey waves), with striking disparities between urban areas (6.12 percent) and rural areas (26.36 percent). The proportion of never-poor households (NP,NP,NP) was 61.08 percent nationwide but dramatically different between urban (80.29 percent) and rural (44.03 percent) settings. These findings highlight the persistently higher vulnerability of rural populations.
- When using the international $2/day poverty line, chronic poverty affected 28.33 percent of Filipinos, with an alarming 43.84 percent of the rural population remaining poor throughout all three waves. Only 27.47 percent of rural households remained consistently

Table 7.4. Population share by intertemporal poverty status, poverty line type and location, 2003–2009

Poverty status (2003, 2006, 2009)	$1.25 poverty line			$2 poverty line		
	PHI	Urban	Rural	PHI	Urban	Rural
P, P, P	7.75	1.91	13.4	28.33	12.33	43.84
P, P, NP	4.55	1.67	7.33	5.97	4.10	7.78
P, NP, P	1.29	0.42	2.14	2.18	1.56	2.78
P, NP, NP	4.70	2.53	6.81	4.05	3.70	4.39
NP, P, P	2.97	1.57	4.33	4.32	3.42	5.32
NP, P, NP	3.98	2.17	5.74	4.42	4.26	4.58
NP, NP, P	3.38	2.64	4.11	3.86	3.87	3.84
NP, NP, NP	71.37	87.08	56.15	46.37	65.86	27.47

Poverty status (2003, 2006, 2009)	Half of median poverty line			Government poverty line		
	PHI	Urban	Rural	PHI	Urban	Rural
P, P, P	5.91	1.33	10.34	15.50	6.12	26.36
P, P, NP	3.58	1.07	6.00	4.05	1.93	6.24
P, NP, P	1.39	0.33	2.42	2.72	1.32	4.25
P, NP, NP	4.52	1.95	7.00	5.20	3.68	6.83
NP, P, P	2.80	1.67	3.88	5.02	3.48	6.68
NP, P, NP	3.38	1.67	5.03	4.13	3.19	5.57
NP, NP, P	2.91	1.99	3.81	5.69	5.00	6.52
NP, NP, NP	75.53	89.98	61.52	61.08	80.29	44.03

Source: Martinez (2016) analysis of 2003–2006–2009 FIES panel data.

non-poor under this more stringent measure compared to 65.86 percent in urban areas. This demonstrates how poverty line choices significantly impact our understanding of poverty persistence and transitions.

Furthermore, the results of Martinez (2016) suggest that between 46 and 76 percent of the Philippine population never experienced poverty during this period (depending on the choice of the poverty line), while 12 to 15 percent were poor for only one survey year, 9 to 13 percent were poor for two years, and 6 to 28 percent were consistently poor throughout all three survey years (Table 7.5). Defining persistent poverty as experiencing poverty for at least two survey years, Martinez estimates that between 16 and 41 percent of the population were persistently poor. Following the spells approach, total poverty—defined as experiencing poverty in at least one time period—affected approximately 29 to 54 percent of the population. These wide ranges of estimates reflect the sensitivity of poverty dynamics measures to methodological choices (in the poverty line), including the treatment of attrition and the application of weights. The lower bounds generally emerge from analyses that exclude households with missing data in any wave, while the upper bounds come from analyses that use

Table 7.5. Intertemporal poverty status in the Philippines, 2003–2009

Number of years in poverty	Martinez (2016) estimates
Never poor (0 years)	46–76%
Poor for 1 year	12–15%
Poor for 2 years	9–13%
Poor for all 3 years	6% - 28%
Total poor (≥1 year)	29–54%
Persistently poor (≥2 years)	16–41%

Source: Martinez (2016) analysis of 2003–2006–2009 FIES panel data.

imputation methods to account for likely patterns among households that dropped out of the panel.

Reyes et al. (2011) tracked movements in and out of poverty using the same 2003–2006–2009 FIES panel data. This study, which does not incorporate survey weights, reports remarkably stable transition patterns, with approximately 68 percent of households remaining non-poor across each period, while around 11 percent remained poor (Table 7.6). The proportion of households escaping poverty ranged from 9.2 to 11.1 percent, roughly matching those falling into poverty (9.2 to 11.1 percent). These balanced entries into and exits from poverty explain why the aggregate poverty rate remained relatively stable at around 20 percent throughout the period, despite significant movement of individual households across the poverty line.

Table 7.7 presents a more granular view of poverty dynamics from Reyes et al. (2011), showing the distribution of Filipino households across all eight possible poverty trajectories over the three survey waves (2003, 2006, 2009). The largest group (62.3 percent) consisted of households that remained non-poor throughout all periods (NNN), while 11.1 percent were chronically poor across all waves (PPP). The remaining 26.6 percent of households experienced some transition, with various patterns of entry into and exit from poverty. Notably, 5.4 percent were poor only in 2003 (PNN), 4.6 percent only in 2006 (NPN), and 5.6 percent only in 2009 (NNP), while 4.6 percent were

Table 7.6. Poverty transitions between periods in the Philippines (as % of households)

Period	Remained non-poor	Fell into poverty	Escaped poverty	Remained poor
2003–2006	67.9%	11.1%	9.2%	11.8%
2006–2009	68.8%	9.2%	11.1%	10.9%
2003–2009	67.9%	11.1%	9.2%	11.8%

Source: Reyes et al. (2011) based on 2003–2006–2009 FIES panel data.

Table 7.7. Detailed poverty trajectories in the Philippines, 2003–2009

Pattern code*	Description	Percentage of households
NNN	Never poor	62.3%
NNP	Transient poor (fell into poverty in 2009)	5.6%
NPN	Previously poor (poor only in 2006)	4.6%
NPP	Impoverished (non-poor in 2003, poor after)	4.6%
PNN	Previously poor (poor only in 2003)	5.4%
PNP	Transient poor (poor in 2003 and 2009)	2.1%
PPN	Previously poor (poor in 2003 and 2006)	4.4%
PPP	Chronic poor (poor in all periods)	11.1%

Source: Reyes et al. (2011) based on 2003–2006–2009 FIES panel data.
*Note: Pattern code refers to poverty status in 2003, 2006, and 2009, respectively, where P = Poor and N = Non-poor.

non-poor only in 2003 (NPP), 4.4 percent non-poor only in 2009 (PPN), and 2.1 percent non-poor only in 2006 (PNP). This detailed breakdown illustrates the diverse pathways households follow through poverty and non-poverty states.

Reyes et al. (2011) also shows the clear relationship between household size and poverty trajectories in the Philippines (Table 7.8). Chronically poor households (PPP) had the largest average family size of 6.6 members, while those who were never poor (NNN) had the smallest at 4.3 members. Households that became impoverished (NPP) averaged 5.8 members, transitory poor households (PNP) averaged 5.6 members, and previously poor households (including PNN, PPN, and NPN) averaged 5.1 members. This gradient in family size across different poverty trajectories highlights household composition as a key factor associated with poverty persistence and transitions, though the direction of causality remains complex—large families may cause poverty through higher dependency ratios, or poverty may lead to higher fertility through limited access to family planning and education.

Table 7.8. Average family size by poverty trajectory in the Philippines, 2003–2009

Poverty trajectory	Average family size
Chronic poor (PPP)	6.6
Impoverished (NPP)	5.8
Transitory (PNP)	5.6
Previously poor (PNN, PPN, NPN)	5.1
Never poor (NNN)	4.3

Source: Adapted from Reyes et al. (2011) based on 2003–2006–2009 FIES panel data.

Furthermore, Reyes et al. (2011) also reported that households that exited poverty often showed substantial increases in non-agricultural employment, particularly among female members. Conversely, non-poor households that fell into poverty typically experienced increasing shares of employment in agriculture and decreased food expenditures (in real terms). Those experiencing income shocks often coped by selling assets such as cell phones or, more disturbingly, by removing children from school.

All these studies on the FIES panel data by Reyes et al. (2011), Martinez (2016), and Albert (2023) highlight that poverty in the Philippines is not a static condition but a dynamic process with substantial movement both into and out of poverty. They also underscore that different poverty trajectories are associated with distinct household characteristics and experiences, suggesting the need for tailored policy approaches to address different types of poverty.

7.4. Multidimensional Poverty Dynamics

7.4.1. Extending dynamic analysis beyond monetary measures

The approaches discussed thus far focus primarily on monetary poverty dynamics based on income or consumption. However, as discussed in earlier chapters, poverty encompasses deprivations across multiple dimensions beyond just income. Multidimensional poverty analysis has gained prominence in recent years, but extending this approach to dynamic analysis introduces additional conceptual and methodological challenges.

Multidimensional poverty dynamics research examines how deprivations across multiple dimensions evolve over time for the same individuals or households. This approach recognizes that people may move into or out of deprivation in different dimensions at different times—for instance, gaining access to education while losing access to healthcare, or improving housing conditions while experiencing deteriorating income.

Early approaches to multidimensional poverty dynamics simply tracked transitions in each dimension separately, without aggregating across dimensions. While informative, this approach does not provide an integrated measure of multidimensional poverty dynamics. More recent approaches have sought to develop comprehensive frameworks that capture both the multidimensionality of poverty and its dynamics over time.

7.4.2. Frameworks for analyzing multidimensional poverty dynamics

Several frameworks have been developed to analyze multidimensional poverty dynamics:

- **The Oxford Poverty and Human Development Initiative (OPHI) approach** extends the Alkire–Foster method for measuring multidimensional poverty to dynamic contexts. This approach identifies individuals as multidimensionally poor in each period based on a dual-cutoff method: They must be deprived in a sufficient number of dimensions, each with its own deprivation threshold. Chronic multidimensional poverty is then measured as a function of the duration and intensity of multidimensional poverty experienced over time.

Formally, the chronic multidimensional poverty measure (M_0^C) decomposes into three intuitive components:

- H^C (the incidence of chronic multidimensional poverty—the percentage of people who are chronically multidimensionally poor)
- A^C (the average intensity of poverty among the chronically poor—the average share of weighted deprivations they experience in periods when they are multidimensionally poor)
- D^C (the average duration of poverty among the chronically poor—the average proportion of periods in which they experience multidimensional poverty)

Together, these components yield

$$M_0^C = H^C \times A^C \times D^C$$

providing a measure that is sensitive to the breadth, depth, and persistence of multidimensional poverty.

- **Gradin, del Rio, and Canto's approach** (2012) focuses on measuring multidimensional chronic poverty using both "union" and "intersection" approaches to aggregation across dimensions. Under the union approach, an individual is considered deprived if they experience deprivation in any dimension; under the intersection approach, deprivation must occur in all dimensions simultaneously. Their framework yields bounds on multidimensional chronic poverty measurements.
- **Nicholas and Ray's approach** (2012) applies intertemporal analysis directly to a multidimensional poverty index, rather than first identifying the multidimensionally poor in each period. This approach treats time as an additional dimension of wellbeing, allowing direct incorporation of time preferences into the measurement of multidimensional poverty.

These frameworks offer different perspectives on how to integrate temporal and dimensional aspects of deprivation. Their relative merits depend on normative judgments about how to conceptualize persistent deprivation across multiple dimensions, as well as on practical considerations about data availability and measurement precision.

7.4.3. Empirical Evidence on Multidimensional Poverty Dynamics

Research applying these frameworks has revealed important insights about multidimensional poverty dynamics.

Studies consistently find imperfect correlation between dynamics in different dimensions. For instance, research in Chile using 1996–2006 panel data found that improvements in income poverty did not necessarily coincide with improvements in non-monetary dimensions such as housing quality or access to education (Alkire et al., 2014). These findings highlight that pathways out of multidimensional poverty may involve progress in some dimensions before others.

Different dimensions show different patterns of persistence. In Chile, for example, access to education showed more rapid improvement over time than overcrowding in housing, reflecting the different timeframes required for interventions in different dimensions to yield results (Alkire et al., 2017).

In many contexts, non-income dimensions of poverty show greater persistence than income poverty. This reflects both the longer time horizon typically required for structural changes in areas like education and health, and the fact that income may fluctuate more rapidly in response to short-term shocks.

The relationship between chronic income poverty and chronic multidimensional poverty varies across contexts. In some settings, the chronically income poor and chronically multidimensionally poor are largely the same households; in others, there is limited overlap. These patterns have important implications for targeting of poverty interventions.

These findings underscore the value of examining poverty dynamics from a multidimensional perspective. By tracking deprivations across multiple dimensions over time, researchers and policymakers gain a more comprehensive understanding of pathways into and out of poverty, facilitating more effective intervention design.

While empirical evidence reveals important patterns in multidimensional poverty dynamics across dimensions, deeper methodological approaches are needed to fully capture the persistence of multidimensional deprivation over time. Building on these empirical insights, researchers have developed increasingly sophisticated frameworks that specifically address the temporal aspects of multidimensional poverty. These chronic poverty measurement approaches move beyond simple transitions to incorporate both the duration and breadth of deprivations in unified analytical frameworks.

Measuring chronic multidimensional poverty requires frameworks that incorporate both the duration and breadth of deprivations. Several approaches have been developed to conceptualize and measure the persistence of multidimensional deprivation over time.

Alkire, Apablaza, Chakravarty, and Yalonetzky (2017) proposed a duration-adjusted multidimensional poverty index that extends the Alkire–Foster methodology to incorporate time explicitly. Their measure identifies the chronically poor as those experiencing a sufficient breadth of deprivations for a minimum duration. Applied to Chilean panel data, they found that while 8.2 percent of the population was chronically multidimensionally poor between 2006 and 2009, this figure rose to 16.5 percent when using a more comprehensive set of indicators spanning health, education, and living standards.

Porter and Quinn (2013) developed an alternative approach based on the "components method", which identifies chronic poverty based on average wellbeing over time rather than continuous spells of poverty. Their method avoids the "censoring" of shorter poverty spells while capturing the cumulative burden of deprivation. Using panel data from Ethiopia, they found that chronic multidimensional poverty affects a substantially larger proportion of the population

(27 percent) than would be identified using spell-based approaches (18 percent).

Nicholas and Ray (2012) proposed yet another framework that treats time directly as an additional dimension in the multidimensional measure, rather than as a separate filtering mechanism. Their approach allows for explicit modeling of time preferences and risk aversion in chronic poverty measurement. Applied to Australian panel data, they found that incorporating time preferences significantly affects chronic poverty estimates, with stronger preferences for current wellbeing reducing estimated chronic poverty rates by up to 15 percent.

7.4.4. Changes over time by dynamic subgroups

Exits, entries, and the ongoing poor: A two-period panel

When examining multidimensional poverty dynamics, understanding the movement of households in and out of poverty provides crucial insights beyond what static measures reveal. Using two-period panel data, we can categorize households into distinct dynamic subgroups: those who exit poverty, those who enter poverty, and those who remain poor across both periods.

Alkire et al. (2017) developed a framework for analyzing these transitions in multidimensional poverty. Their study of 34 developing countries showed that behind seemingly modest net changes in multidimensional poverty indices often lie substantial gross flows both into and out of poverty. For instance, in Indonesia between 2007 and 2014, while the overall reduction in multidimensional poverty was 8 percentage points, this modest net change masked that approximately 15 percent of households exited poverty while 7 percent entered it.

Suppa (2018) extended this approach by examining dimension-specific transitions, finding that exits from multidimensional poverty often begin with improvements in particular dimensions (typically education and basic services) before other deprivations are addressed. His analysis of Peruvian panel data revealed that households frequently escaped deprivation in electricity and sanitation before exiting overall multidimensional poverty, suggesting that these dimensions might serve as "leading indicators" of poverty exits.

Table 7.9 illustrates the dynamic transitions between different multidimensional poverty states. It shows that while 72.4 percent of households remained non-poor across both periods, significant movement occurred among the remaining population. Of particular note, 10.3 percent of households exited multidimensional poverty (moving from poor to non-poor), while 7.3 percent entered poverty (moving from non-poor to poor). The table also reveals differences in mobility patterns between moderately and severely poor households, with moderately poor households showing higher exit rates.

A key advantage of this dynamic subgroups approach is its policy relevance. As Baulch (2011) argues, understanding which households are entering poverty versus remaining chronically poor enables more targeted interventions—with social protection programs directed toward those at risk of falling into poverty—while structural interventions address the needs of the chronically poor.

Table 7.9. Multidimensional poverty transition matrix, Chile 1996–2006

1996 status	2006 status			Total (1996)
	Non-poor	Moderately poor	Severely poor	
Non-poor	72.4%	6.3%	1.0%	79.7%
Moderately poor	8.2%	3.1%	1.6%	12.9%
Severely poor	2.1%	3.2%	2.1%	7.4%
Total (2006)	82.7%	12.6%	4.7%	100.0%

Source: Adapted from Suppa (2018) based on Chilean panel data.
Note: Multidimensional poverty status determined using Alkire–Foster method with dimensions including education, health, housing, and basic services. Moderately poor defined as deprived in 20–33 percent of weighted indicators; severely poor as deprived in >33 percent of weighted indicators.

Decomposition by incidence and intensity for cross-sectional data

When genuine panel data are unavailable, researchers have developed innovative approaches to analyze poverty dynamics using repeated cross-sectional surveys. These methods attempt to decompose changes in poverty into those driven by changes in the incidence of poverty (the headcount ratio) versus changes in the intensity of poverty (the average deprivation score among the poor).

Apablaza and Yalonetzky (2013) proposed a formal decomposition method for the Alkire–Foster multidimensional poverty index (MPI) that has been widely applied. Their approach decomposes changes in the MPI (M_0) into three components: a pure incidence effect (changes in the percentage of poor people), a pure intensity effect (changes in the average deprivation score among those who remain poor), and an interaction effect.

Employing this methodology, Alkire and Seth (2015) analyzed multidimensional poverty reduction in India between 1999 and 2006. They found that while the national MPI fell from 0.300 to 0.251, about 60 percent of this reduction came from decreasing the incidence of poverty, with the remaining 40 percent attributable to reduced intensity among those who remained poor. Importantly, they observed significant regional variation—in some states like Kerala, poverty reduction was predominantly driven by reducing intensity, while in others like Andhra Pradesh, the incidence effect dominated.

Seth and Villar (2017) further refined these decomposition techniques by developing methods that account for changes in population size across survey periods. Their approach distinguishes between the "growth effect" (changes in poverty due to population growth) and the "redistribution effect" (genuine changes in poverty rates), providing more accurate assessments in contexts with significant demographic changes.

These methods offer valuable insights even without panel data, but as Alkire and Roche (2017) caution, they cannot identify which individuals or households are moving into or out of poverty, limiting our understanding of poverty trajectories at the household level.

Theoretical incidence–intensity decompositions

Formal theoretical frameworks for decomposing changes in multidimensional poverty measures have advanced our understanding of poverty dynamics. These approaches provide rigorous mathematical foundations for distinguishing different components of poverty changes over time.

Apablaza and Yalonetzky (2013) developed one of the most influential theoretical decompositions, showing that for the Alkire–Foster family of measures, changes in M_0 can be expressed as

$$\Delta M_0 = A_1(H_2 - H_1) + H_1(A_2 - A_1) + (H_2 - H_1)(A_2 - A_1)$$

where H represents the headcount ratio, and A represents average intensity, with subscripts indicating time periods. This decomposition clearly separates the incidence effect, the intensity effect, and their interaction.

Building on this work, Roche (2013) proposed a Shapley value decomposition following Shorrocks' (1999) approach, which allocates the interaction term proportionally between the incidence and intensity components. This method has been particularly useful in policy contexts because it produces a complete two-part decomposition:

$$\Delta M_0 = [(A_2 + A_1)/2](H_2 - H_1) + [(H_2 + H_1)/2](A_2 - A_1)$$

Vaz (2014) extended these theoretical frameworks to incorporate dimensional decompositions, allowing researchers to simultaneously analyze how changes in specific dimensions (education, health, living standards) contribute to overall poverty dynamics. Applied to Mozambique, this approach revealed that improvements in school attendance and access to clean water were the primary drivers of multidimensional poverty reduction between 2003 and 2011.

Alkire et al. (2020) further refined these theoretical decompositions by incorporating demographic shifts through statistical reweighting techniques, enabling more accurate analysis in contexts with significant population change or migration. Their approach has been particularly valuable for analyzing long-term trends where demographic composition changes substantially between survey waves.

7.4.5. *Chronic poverty measurement with panel data*

Panel data: Advantages and disadvantages

Panel data provide unique advantages for chronic poverty measurement but also present significant methodological challenges. Understanding these tradeoffs is essential for robust analysis of multidimensional poverty dynamics.

Among the key advantages, McKay and Lawson (2003) highlight panel data's unique ability to distinguish between structural and stochastic components of poverty, allowing researchers to separate persistent disadvantage from temporary fluctuations. This distinction is particularly important for multidimensional poverty, where different dimensions may exhibit varying levels of volatility over time.

Dercon and Shapiro (2007) emphasize another critical advantage: panel data enable the identification of causal mechanisms behind poverty transitions, distinguishing between factors that prevent poverty entries and those that facilitate poverty exits. Their review of panel studies across developing countries found that different sets of assets and capabilities influence these distinct transition types, with education being more important for facilitating exits while health shocks predominantly trigger entries.

However, as Baulch (2011) notes, panel data collection faces several significant challenges. Attrition bias presents perhaps the most serious threat to validity, as households that drop out of panels between waves are often systematically different from those that remain. In a meta-analysis of panel surveys from 17 developing countries, they found attrition rates ranging from 3.5 to 50 percent between waves, with attrition commonly correlated with mobility, urban residence, and baseline poverty status—potentially biasing dynamic analyses.

Jenkins and Van Kerm (2017) identify additional challenges including measurement error, which can create spurious poverty transitions, and representativeness concerns, as panels become less representative of current populations over time due to demographic changes and migration. They recommend various statistical corrections including inverse probability weighting and multiple imputation techniques to address these issues.

Despite these challenges, Dang and Lanjouw (2018) argue that the unique insights from panel data justify the additional costs and complexities of collection and analysis, particularly for understanding the dynamic nature of multidimensional poverty. As they demonstrate through Vietnamese panel data, the policy implications of understanding poverty dynamics often differ substantially from those derived from static measures alone.

Chronic poverty measurement using panel data

Panel data enable the implementation of sophisticated approaches to measure chronic multidimensional poverty. These methods capture both the persistence and multidimensionality of deprivation, providing richer insights than either cross-sectional multidimensional measures or longitudinal monetary-only approaches.

Alkire et al. (2017) developed a framework specifically for measuring chronic multidimensional poverty using panel data. Their approach first identifies the multidimensionally poor in each period using the Alkire–Foster method, then classifies individuals as chronically poor if they experience multidimensional poverty for a minimum duration. Applying this to Chilean panel data (1996–2006), they found that while 20.3 percent of the population experienced multidimensional poverty at some point, only 5.5 percent were chronically poor (experienced multidimensional poverty in at least two of three survey waves). Their measure decomposes into three intuitive components:

1. The incidence of chronic multidimensional poverty (the percentage of people who are chronically poor)
2. The average intensity of poverty among the chronically poor (the average share of weighted deprivations they experience when poor)
3. The average duration of poverty among the chronically poor (the average proportion of periods in which they experience multidimensional poverty)

Apablaza and Yalonetzky (2013) extended this framework by incorporating sensitivity to the distribution of deprivations across dimensions and time. Their measure penalizes cases where deprivations are concentrated in particular dimensions or time periods, reflecting evidence that such concentration often indicates more severe or entrenched disadvantage. Applied to data from the Young Lives study, their approach identified additional chronically poor households compared to methods that ignore distributional concerns.

Dotter and Klasen (2017) proposed an alternative "welfare-trajectory" approach that tracks dimension-specific deprivation trajectories over time. This method captures the sequencing of deprivations, distinguishing between households experiencing simultaneous multidimensional deprivations versus sequential deprivations in different dimensions. Their analysis of Indonesian panel data revealed that approximately 30 percent of households followed "divergent" trajectories—improving in some dimensions while deteriorating in others—highlighting the complex, non-linear nature of multidimensional poverty dynamics.

Chronic poverty in Ethiopia is severe whether measured in monetary or multidimensional terms. Analysis of the Ethiopian Rural Household Survey (1994–2004) by Porter and Quinn (2008) found that about one-fifth of households were persistently poor—poor in at least three of five survey waves—while only 2.6 percent remained poor throughout. Duration-adjusted measures confirm similar results, underscoring long-term vulnerability in rural areas (Table 7.10a).

Table 7.10a. Chronic monetary poverty under alternative duration-based approaches, Ethiopia 1994–2004

Approach	Data source / coverage	Parameter choices	Chronic poverty rate (%)	Nature of estimate	Interpretation / salient characteristics
Spells (income)	*Ethiopian Rural Household Survey 1994–2004* (Porter and Quinn, 2008)	Poor in ≥ 3 of 5 waves	**≈ 21**	*Empirical*	Households poor in most rounds; rural, low-education, asset-poor.
Duration-adjusted (Foster measure)	Same as above	$\tau = ⅔$ duration parameter	**≈ 21.5**	*Empirical*	Adjusts headcount by length of poverty spell; nearly identical to spells result.
Always poor	Same as above	Poor in all 5 rounds	**≈ 2.6**	*Empirical*	Households continuously below poverty line; chronically destitute.

Source: Porter and Quinn (2008).
Note: The ERHS covers five rounds (1994, 1995, 1997, 1999, 2004). Households poor in at least three rounds are classified as *persistently poor*; only 2.6 percent remained poor throughout all rounds.

Using multidimensional frameworks and the Young Lives panel for 2002–2009, Apablaza and Yalonetzky (2013) estimated chronic multidimensional poverty between 25 and 32 percent (Table 7.10b), depending on the approach. Households that remained multidimensionally poor throughout were typically those deprived in education, housing, and basic services. Ethiopia displayed the highest chronic poverty rates among the four Young Lives countries, reflecting the persistence of overlapping deprivations despite periods of income mobility. Together, these studies demonstrate that chronic poverty—monetary

Table 7.10b. Chronic multidimensional poverty under alternative methodological frameworks, Chile 2006–2009

Approach	Data source / coverage	Main parameter choices	Chronic poverty rate (%)	Nature of estimate	Interpretation / salient characteristics
Components approach	*Chile 2006–2009* (Apablaza and Yalonetzky, 2013)	Average MPI > 0.33	≈ **27**	*Illustrative*	Households whose average deprivation score exceeds threshold; includes those with transient escapes.
Time as dimension	Same as above	Equal weights across time	≈ **26**	*Illustrative*	Treats time as an explicit dimension; sensitive to timing of deprivations.
Dimensional duration	Same as above	Persistent in ≥ 2 dimensions	≈ **31**	*Illustrative*	Identifies households repeatedly deprived in key dimensions despite income mobility.

Source: Apablaza and Yalonetzky (2013).
Note: Illustrative results using Chilean household panel data demonstrate how incorporating persistence across dimensions raises measured chronic-poverty incidence relative to income-based approaches.

or multidimensional—remains a defining feature of Ethiopian deprivation, with roughly one in four households facing sustained poverty over time.

Poverty transitions using panel data

Panel data allow for detailed analysis of transitions between different poverty states over time, revealing patterns of mobility that cannot be observed with cross-sectional data. This approach is particularly valuable for understanding the dynamic pathways into and out of multidimensional poverty.

Suppa (2018) utilized Chilean panel data (1996–2006) to construct multidimensional poverty transition matrices, revealing substantial mobility beneath seemingly stable aggregate poverty rates. While approximately 14 percent of households remained multidimensionally poor across all three survey waves ("chronic poor"), 16 percent moved out of poverty ("ascending"), 12 percent fell into poverty ("descending"), and 6 percent experienced transitory poverty (poor in the middle wave only). Importantly, he found different dimensional patterns associated with these transitions—education improvements typically preceded exits from poverty, while health deterioration often preceded entries.

Addressing the challenge of potentially spurious transitions due to measurement error, Vaz, Alkire, and Amarante (2022) developed a methodology to distinguish genuine poverty transitions from statistical noise. Applied to Uruguayan panel data, their approach reduced estimated transition rates by approximately 15–20 percent, suggesting that conventional methods may overstate poverty mobility. They found that genuine transitions were most strongly associated with changes in employment status and household composition, while smaller changes in housing conditions often reflected measurement issues rather than substantive welfare changes.

Taking a different approach, Notten and Guio (2021) examined transitions using overlapping measures of monetary and multidimensional poverty in European longitudinal data. They identified four distinct groups: (1) the "consistent poor" (deprived on both measures), (2) the "only materially deprived", (3) the "only income poor", and (4) the "non-poor". Their analysis revealed different transition patterns for these groups—the consistent poor showed the highest persistence (70 percent remaining in poverty after one year), while the "only income poor" demonstrated the highest exit rates (45 percent becoming nonpoor within one year). These findings suggest that multidimensional measures capture more structural forms of disadvantage that are less volatile than income-only measures.

Building on these insights, Dang and Lanjouw (2018) developed synthetic panel methods that approximate poverty transition analysis when genuine panel data are unavailable. By modeling the joint distribution of welfare indicators across repeated cross-sections, their approach provides bounds on mobility estimates that can be calculated for many more countries and time periods than genuine panels allow. Applied to contexts where both panel and cross-sectional data exist, they found that their method typically estimates transition rates within 2–3 percentage points of those from actual panel data, offering a valuable alternative when panels are unavailable.

7.4.6. Evidence from multidimensional poverty dynamics research

Recent research by the Oxford Poverty and Human Development Initiative (OPHI) has significantly advanced the measurement and analysis of multidimensional poverty dynamics. This work extends beyond monetary measures to capture changes in multiple dimensions of deprivation over time.

Alkire, Roche, and Vaz (2015) analyzed changes in the Global Multidimensional Poverty Index (MPI) across 34 countries and 338 sub-national regions. Their study revealed both the breadth of multidimensional poverty reduction and its composition across dimensions and regions (Table 7.11). While Nepal, Rwanda, Bangladesh, Ghana, and Tanzania all achieved statistically significant reductions in multidimensional poverty, with annualized relative reductions ranging from 5.0 percent in Tanzania to 14.2 percent in Ghana, Senegal showed a contrasting pattern with a slight increase in its MPI (a 0.4 percent annualized relative increase). Nepal, Rwanda, and Bangladesh achieved the fastest absolute reductions in MPI, with annualized absolute reductions of 0.027, 0.026, and 0.024 points, respectively. Their approach disaggregated these overall changes into reductions in

Table 7.11. Reduction in multidimensional poverty index and component indices in selected countries

Country	Period	Initial MPI	Final MPI	Annualized absolute change	Annualized relative change (%)	Initial H (%)	Final H (%)	Initial A (%)	Final A (%)
Nepal	2006–2011	0.350	0.217	−0.027*	−9.1*	64.7	44.2	54.0	49.0
Rwanda	2005–2010	0.461	0.330	−0.026*	−6.4*	81.4	66.1	56.6	50.0
Bangladesh	2004–2007	0.365	0.292	−0.024*	−7.1*	67.1	57.8	54.3	50.4
Ghana	2003–2008	0.309	0.144	−0.033*	−14.2*	58.7	31.2	52.5	46.2
Tanzania	2008–2010	0.371	0.335	−0.018*	−5.0*	70.3	65.8	52.7	50.9
Senegal	2005–2011	0.439	0.450	+0.002	0.4	74.4	76.3	59.0	59.0

Source: Alkire, Roche, and Vaz (2015).

Notes: (i) * indicates statistical significance at $\alpha = 0.05$. (ii) H represents headcount ratio; A represents intensity of poverty.

both the incidence (*H*) and intensity (*A*) of multidimensional poverty. This decomposition reveals that countries experienced multidimensional poverty dynamics through different combinations of changing the number of poor people and changing the deprivation level among those who remained poor. Nepal, for instance, reduced its multidimensional headcount ratio by 4.1 percentage points annually while also reducing the intensity of poverty among the poor by 1.0 percentage point annually. In contrast, Senegal's headcount ratio increased by 0.3 percentage points annually while its intensity remained unchanged.

A particularly valuable contribution of this research is the analysis of dimensional changes. In Nepal, the authors found statistically significant reductions in all indicators between 2006 and 2011, with the largest absolute annual reductions in electricity deprivation (5.0 percentage points), followed by improvements in assets (4.8 percentage points), cooking fuel (4.3 percentage points), and sanitation (3.8 percentage points). This dimensional analysis reveals which aspects of multidimensional poverty are changing most rapidly, providing crucial information for policy prioritization.

To achieve a decline in the absolute number of poor people, the reduction in the headcount ratio must exceed the rate of population growth. Among the countries highlighted in the study, Nepal recorded the fastest absolute reduction in multidimensional poverty, followed closely by Rwanda and Bangladesh. Ghana achieved the steepest relative decline, while Tanzania posted more modest progress. In contrast, Senegal experienced an increase in both its MPI and the proportion of people identified as multidimensionally poor, despite maintaining the same intensity level among the poor. These diverse outcomes across countries reflect different pathways through which multidimensional poverty can evolve, highlighting the importance of monitoring both positive and negative changes over time.

Alkire and Seth (2015) applied similar methods to analyze changes in multidimensional poverty in India. They decomposed these changes by sub-national regions and social groups, revealing important variations in poverty reduction patterns. For instance, their analysis showed that while multidimensional poverty decreased in both rural and urban areas between 1999 and 2006, the reduction was significantly faster in urban areas. Similarly, they found that poverty reduction was slower among the most disadvantaged social groups, such as Scheduled Tribes and Scheduled Castes, compared to the General category population.

Alkire and Roche (2017) focused specifically on child poverty dynamics, recognizing that children experience poverty differently than adults. Their cross-country analysis revealed that in many countries, multidimensional child poverty was reducing at different rates than adult poverty, highlighting the need for age-disaggregated analysis. In some countries, such as Bangladesh, improvements in child-specific indicators like school attendance and child mortality were driving overall poverty reduction, while in others, adult-focused indicators showed more progress.

These multidimensional approaches to poverty dynamics offer several advantages over analyses focused solely on monetary measures. They reveal that deprivations in different dimensions often change at different rates, reflecting both variation in policy effectiveness across sectors and differences in how quickly improvements in various dimensions can be achieved. They also show that overall poverty reduction may mask significant variation across population subgroups, with some groups experiencing much slower improvements than others.

Furthermore, multidimensional analysis helps identify situations where improvements in monetary wellbeing do not translate into improvements in other crucial dimensions of welfare. For instance, Alkire and Seth (2015) found regions in India where consumption poverty decreased while nutritional indicators showed little improvement, highlighting the imperfect correlation between monetary and non-monetary dimensions of poverty.

This growing body of research on multidimensional poverty dynamics represents an important frontier in poverty analysis, providing a more comprehensive understanding of how deprivation evolves across multiple dimensions and population groups over time. Such insights are crucial for designing policies that address the multifaceted nature of poverty and ensure that no one is left behind in poverty reduction efforts.

7.5. Determinants of Poverty Transitions

7.5.1. Conceptual framework for understanding poverty transitions

Understanding what factors drive movements into and out of poverty is crucial for designing effective anti-poverty policies. A conceptual framework for analyzing poverty transitions should consider both structural determinants (factors that influence long-term welfare prospects) and stochastic elements (shocks and events that trigger specific transitions).

Structural determinants include household characteristics and assets that affect long-term productive potential, such as

- Human capital (education, skills, health status)
- Physical assets (land, livestock, equipment)
- Financial assets (savings, access to credit)
- Social capital (networks, group memberships)
- Location characteristics (remoteness, agro-ecological conditions, infrastructure access)

Stochastic elements encompass various shocks that can trigger poverty transitions:

- Health shocks (illness, injury, disability, death)
- Natural disasters (droughts, floods, earthquakes)
- Economic shocks (price changes, job loss, business failure)
- Social/political shocks (conflict, violence, discrimination)
- Demographic events (births, marriages, household splits)

The interaction between structural determinants and stochastic elements shapes poverty dynamics. Households with stronger asset bases and capabilities are better positioned to withstand negative shocks without falling into poverty (resilience) and to take advantage of positive opportunities to escape poverty (agency). Conversely, households with limited assets face both higher vulnerability to negative shocks and greater constraints in seizing opportunities for upward mobility.

This framework highlights that poverty transitions often result from the interaction between longer-term processes of asset accumulation or depletion and specific trigger events that precipitate changes in welfare status. Empirical research has sought to disentangle and quantify the relative importance of these factors across different contexts.

7.5.2. Empirical evidence on determinants of poverty transitions

Extensive research across diverse contexts has identified several consistent patterns in the determinants of poverty transitions:

Factors associated with poverty exits typically include the following:

- Education and skills acquisition, particularly completion of secondary education
- Asset accumulation, especially productive assets like land, livestock, and equipment
- Diversification into non-farm income sources
- Migration to areas with better economic opportunities
- Demographic changes that improve dependency ratios (e.g., children growing up and entering the workforce)
- Access to networks and social capital that provide information and opportunities

Factors associated with poverty entries commonly include

- Health shocks requiring high out-of-pocket expenditures or reducing earning capacity

- Natural disasters destroying assets or livelihoods
- Loss of employment or business failure
- Food price increases affecting net food buyers
- Household division or dissolution (e.g., through death or divorce)
- Conflict and violence causing displacement or asset destruction

The relative importance of these factors varies across contexts. In settings with limited social protection systems, health shocks often emerge as leading triggers of descents into poverty. Quisumbing (2007), using longitudinal household data from rural Bangladesh, shows that repeated exposure to shocks—including illness, flooding, and price volatility—significantly increases the likelihood of households entering or remaining in poverty. Her findings highlight how idiosyncratic and covariate shocks interact with household vulnerabilities to influence poverty transitions. In Cambodia, health shocks were identified as the primary cause of 22 percent of documented cases of impoverishment (Krishna et al., 2006). Similarly, across multiple countries in Africa and South Asia, studies using participatory methods have consistently identified health-related expenses as major causes of impoverishment (Krishna, 2010).

The role of assets in facilitating poverty exits has been documented across diverse contexts. In rural Kenya, households that escaped poverty typically doubled their asset holdings over a 25-year period (Krishna et al., 2006). Similarly, in Vietnam, increases in productive assets were strongly associated with sustained poverty exits during the period of rapid economic growth from 1993 to 2004 (Baulch and Dat, 2011).

Education consistently emerges as a critical factor influencing long-term poverty dynamics. Panel studies across multiple countries find that households headed by individuals with secondary education are significantly less likely to experience poverty and more likely to achieve sustained escapes from poverty when they do experience it. For instance, in Indonesia, households headed by someone with upper secondary education were 75 percent less likely to be chronically poor compared to those headed by someone with no education (McCulloch and Baulch, 2000a).

These empirical patterns highlight that poverty transitions reflect both structural factors and idiosyncratic events. Effective policies must therefore address both the underlying determinants of long-term welfare (through investments in education, health, and productive assets) and the specific shocks that trigger movements into poverty (through social protection systems and risk management tools).

7.5.3. Near-poor vulnerability and poverty dynamics

A particularly important insight from poverty dynamics research concerns the vulnerability of the near-poor—those with incomes just above the poverty line. Panel data consistently show that these households face significant risk of falling into poverty over time, highlighting the importance of policies that address vulnerability alongside current poverty.

Analysis of panel data from the Philippines for 2003–2009 found that of households classified as near-poor in 2003 (with incomes between 100 and 125 percent of the poverty line), about 31 percent had fallen into poverty by 2009 compared to just 8 percent of households with incomes well above the poverty line (Albert, 2023). Similar patterns have been documented in other contexts, including Indonesia, where the near-poor were three times more likely than the secure non-poor to fall into poverty following the 1997–1998 Asian Financial Crisis (Pritchett et al., 2000).

This vulnerability reflects several factors:

- Near-poor households typically have limited asset buffers to withstand shocks.
- They often remain dependent on precarious livelihoods with high income volatility.
- They may lack access to formal risk management tools like insurance.

- They frequently fall outside the targeting of social protection programs focused on the current poor.

The high vulnerability of the near-poor has important policy implications. It suggests that poverty reduction strategies should extend beyond those currently identified as poor to include preventive interventions for vulnerable non-poor households. Such interventions might include extending social protection coverage, providing access to risk management tools (such as weather insurance or health insurance), and supporting asset accumulation to build resilience.

7.6. Policy Implications of Poverty Dynamics Research

7.6.1. Differentiating policies for chronic and transient poverty

A central insight from poverty dynamics research is that different types of poverty may require different policy responses. While some interventions may address both chronic and transient poverty, the primary policy emphases differ between these types.

Addressing chronic poverty typically requires interventions that build households' productive capacity and address structural constraints:

- Investments in human capital through education, skills training, and health services
- Asset transfers and support for asset accumulation (land, livestock, equipment)
- Infrastructure development to improve market access and public service delivery
- Addressing social exclusion and discrimination that limit opportunity structures
- Long-term social assistance for those unable to participate in productive activities (e.g., elderly, severely disabled)

Addressing transient poverty focuses more on risk management and consumption smoothing:

- Social insurance mechanisms (health insurance, unemployment insurance, weather insurance)
- Flexible safety nets that can expand during crises (e.g., scalable cash transfer programs)
- Improved access to savings and credit markets to facilitate consumption smoothing
- Early warning systems and disaster preparedness measures
- Diversification of income sources to reduce covariate risk

The balance between these approaches depends on the relative prevalence of chronic and transient poverty in a given context. In settings where chronic poverty dominates, structural interventions to build assets and capabilities should receive primary emphasis. Where transient poverty is more prevalent, risk management tools may yield greater returns.

In practice, comprehensive poverty reduction strategies typically incorporate elements addressing both chronic and transient poverty, recognizing that many households experience both forms at different times or simultaneously. For instance, Ethiopia's Productive Safety Net Program combines predictable transfers to chronically food-insecure households with temporary support during crises, while also incorporating public works components that build community assets and graduation pathways to sustainable livelihoods.

7.6.2. Preventing poverty through vulnerability reduction

Poverty dynamics research highlights the importance of preventive interventions that reduce vulnerability to poverty among non-poor households. Such interventions are particularly relevant for the near-poor, who face substantial risk of falling into poverty over time.

Effective vulnerability reduction strategies include the following.

Risk management tools that help households cope with shocks without depleting productive assets:

- Health insurance to prevent catastrophic health expenditures
- Weather-indexed insurance for agricultural producers
- Unemployment insurance or employment guarantees
- Fire, theft, and other property insurance

Livelihood diversification support to reduce exposure to sector-specific shocks:

- Training and capital for non-farm enterprises
- Support for migration and remittances
- Access to markets for new products or services

Early warning systems and preventive measures for foreseeable risks:

- Weather and climate information services
- Disease surveillance and preventive health measures
- Market information systems to anticipate price shocks

Inclusive growth strategies that expand economic opportunities for vulnerable groups:

- Labor market policies promoting quality employment
- Financial inclusion initiatives
- Support for small and medium enterprises
- Reduction of spatial disparities in infrastructure and services

By preventing descents into poverty, such interventions can be highly cost-effective components of poverty reduction strategies. They also recognize that the boundary between "poor" and "non-poor" is permeable, with households moving across this threshold in both directions over time.

7.6.3. Facilitating sustainable poverty exits

Another key policy insight from poverty dynamics research concerns the factors that facilitate not just exits from poverty but also sustainable exits that reduce the risk of future poverty re-entry. Evidence suggests that sustainable poverty exits typically involve the following.

Progressive accumulation of diverse assets that provide both income generation and risk management capabilities:

- Human capital (education, skills, health)
- Physical and natural assets (land, equipment, housing)
- Financial assets (savings, access to credit)
- Social capital (networks, group membership)

Engagement with higher-return livelihood activities that offer more stable income streams:

- Skilled wage employment
- Higher-value agricultural production
- Profitable non-farm enterprises

Access to markets and services that enhance returns to assets and provide risk management tools:

- Output markets with fair prices
- Input markets for productivity-enhancing technologies
- Financial services for savings, credit, and insurance
- Public services including healthcare, education, and infrastructure

Policies promoting sustainable poverty exits should therefore focus not just on immediate income improvement but also on supporting these longer-term processes of asset accumulation and livelihood transformation. This may involve sequenced interventions that address immediate needs while building pathways to sustainable livelihoods.

For instance, "graduation" approaches to extreme poverty combine time-bound consumption support with productive asset transfers, skills training, savings promotion, and coaching to facilitate sustainable exits from extreme poverty. Evaluations across multiple countries have found that such integrated approaches can achieve lasting improvements in consumption, assets, and psychological wellbeing (Banerjee et al., 2015).

7.7. Statistical Methods for Analyzing Poverty Transitions

7.7.1. Regression models for analyzing poverty transitions

Beyond descriptive analysis of poverty transitions, researchers employ various regression techniques to identify determinants of poverty status changes while controlling for multiple factors simultaneously. These approaches help disentangle the relative importance of different household characteristics and external conditions in shaping poverty dynamics.

Binary outcome models analyze transitions into or out of poverty using discrete dependent variables. Common approaches include:

- Probit or logit models examining the probability of exiting poverty (for initially poor households) or entering poverty (for initially non-poor households) as a function of household characteristics and experiences. For example, Albert et al. (2015) used logistic regression on Philippine panel data to identify factors associated with escaping poverty, finding that higher education, smaller household size, and non-agricultural employment significantly increased exit probabilities.
- Hazard models analyzing the duration of poverty spells and factors affecting transition probabilities. These models account for right-censored observations (poverty spells that continue beyond the observation period) and can incorporate time-varying covariates.

Using such models, McCulloch and Baulch (2000b) showed that household size and education level significantly influenced poverty exit rates in rural Pakistan.

Multinomial models recognize that households may follow multiple distinct poverty trajectories over longer periods. These models simultaneously examine the determinants of different trajectory types, such as

- Chronic poverty (poor throughout the observation period)
- Transitory poverty (moving in and out of poverty)
- Upward mobility (escaping poverty)
- Downward mobility (falling into poverty)
- Never poor (non-poor throughout)

For instance, using multinomial logit models on Vietnam panel data, Baulch and Dat (2011) found that ethnic minority status strongly predicted chronic poverty even after controlling for education, assets, and location. Such findings highlight potentially discriminatory factors that perpetuate poverty for specific population groups.

Fixed-effects models exploit the panel structure to control for unobserved time-invariant household characteristics that might otherwise bias results. By focusing on changes within households over time, these models provide more robust estimates of how changes in specific variables (such as asset holdings or employment) affect poverty status. This approach helps address the potential endogeneity that arises when unobserved factors (such as ability or motivation) correlate with both explanatory variables and poverty outcomes.

Each of these regression approaches has strengths and limitations. The appropriate choice depends on the specific research question, the nature of available data (especially the number of time periods), and assumptions about the poverty generation process. In practice, researchers often employ multiple complementary methods to ensure robust conclusions.

7.7.2. Addressing measurement error in poverty dynamics analysis

A significant methodological challenge in poverty dynamics research is measurement error in welfare indicators, which can create spurious poverty transitions. Random errors in measuring consumption or income might erroneously suggest that households have crossed the poverty line when their true welfare remained stable.

Several approaches help address this challenge:

- Error-correction models explicitly incorporate measurement error in estimating true transitions. For example, Glewwe (2012) developed a method that uses repeated observations to distinguish genuine welfare changes from measurement noise, finding that conventional approaches overestimated poverty mobility in Vietnam by 12–35 percent. Similarly, Lee et al. (2017) used latent variable models to correct for measurement error in South African panel data, revealing substantially lower genuine mobility than apparent transitions suggested.
- Asset-based approaches complement income or consumption measures with information on asset holdings, which typically exhibit less measurement error and greater stability over time. Discrepancies between asset trajectories and consumption-based poverty transitions can help identify likely measurement errors. Additionally, assets provide insights into structural dimensions of welfare that might not be captured in current consumption alone.
- Mixed methods approaches combine quantitative panel data with qualitative research on poverty dynamics. Participatory methods such as life histories or wellbeing rankings can provide valuable validation of transitions identified in panel surveys while offering deeper insights into causal mechanisms. For instance, the "Stages of Progress" methodology developed by Krishna (2010) combines community-based recall methods with household interviews to identify genuine poverty transitions and their causes.
- Multiple welfare indicators reduce reliance on any single measure. Examining transitions across various indicators—consumption,

income, food security, and subjective assessments—provides a more robust picture of genuine welfare changes. Concordance across multiple measures suggests more reliable transitions, while discordance may indicate measurement issues in particular indicators.

These approaches highlight that measurement precision is crucial for valid inferences about poverty dynamics. Ignoring measurement error can lead to significant overestimation of poverty mobility and potentially misguided policy conclusions.

7.8. Intergenerational Poverty Dynamics

7.8.1. Conceptualizing intergenerational poverty transmission

While much poverty dynamics research focuses on changes in household welfare over relatively short periods, a broader temporal perspective examines how poverty status transmits across generations. Intergenerational poverty dynamics address questions of social mobility—specifically, to what extent does being born into poverty determine one's economic prospects throughout life?

Intergenerational poverty transmission operates through multiple channels:

- Human capital transmission occurs when children in poor households receive inadequate investments in health, nutrition, and education, limiting their future productivity and earnings. For instance, malnourished children may experience cognitive impairments that persist into adulthood, while limited educational attainment restricts access to higher-paying occupations. These effects can create "poverty traps" where low parental human capital begets low child human capital across generations.
- Asset inheritance determines the physical and financial resources available to children as they begin adult life. In agrarian societies,

land inheritance patterns strongly influence children's economic prospects, while in urban settings, housing wealth and financial assets play similar roles. Unequal inheritance systems may concentrate assets among particular children (often sons), creating divergent welfare trajectories among siblings.

- Aspirations and psychological factors shape how individuals perceive their opportunities and make decisions about education, employment, and family formation. Growing up in chronic poverty can induce "aspirational poverty" where limited exposure to success models and repeated experiences of constraint lead to reduced educational and occupational aspirations. These psychological factors can perpetuate poverty even when objective opportunities improve.
- Social capital and networks determine access to information, opportunities, and support. Poor households often have networks concentrated among other poor households, limiting access to information about educational opportunities, job openings, and productive innovations. These network effects can perpetuate social segregation across generations.

Understanding these transmission mechanisms helps identify potential intervention points to break cycles of intergenerational poverty. Depending on which mechanisms predominate in a given context, effective interventions might focus on early childhood development, education access, asset redistribution, aspiration-building, or social integration.

7.8.2. Measuring intergenerational poverty persistence

Researchers use various approaches to measure intergenerational poverty persistence:

- Intergenerational income elasticity (IGE) measures the strength of the relationship between parents' and children's incomes. An IGE of 0 would indicate complete mobility (no relationship between parental and child income), while an IGE of 1 would indicate perfect persistence (children's relative income position exactly matching their parents'). Empirical estimates of IGE vary substantially across countries, from around 0.2 in some Scandinavian countries to over 0.6 in certain developing countries, indicating vastly different levels of economic mobility (Corak, 2013).

- Poverty transition matrices across generations examine specific transitions between poverty states rather than continuous income measures. These matrices show the probability of children being poor conditional on their parents' poverty status. For example, data from the United States show that 45 percent of children born to persistently poor parents remain poor as adults, compared to just 4 percent of children whose parents were never poor (Ratcliffe and McKernan, 2010).
- Sibling correlation studies estimate the proportion of outcome variance attributable to factors shared by siblings, including both observable characteristics (like parental education and income) and unobservable family and community factors. High sibling correlations indicate strong family influence on economic outcomes. Research consistently finds higher sibling correlations in developing countries, suggesting stronger family background effects on economic mobility in these contexts (Emran and Shilpi, 2015).
- Multigenerational approaches extend beyond parent–child relationships to examine persistence across three or more generations. Recent research suggests that conventional two-generation approaches may underestimate long-run persistence, as some factors (such as wealth or certain human capital dimensions) exhibit significant "dynastic" effects across multiple generations (Mare, 2011).

These measurement approaches face substantial data challenges, particularly in developing countries where long-term longitudinal data following families across generations remain scarce. Nevertheless, creative use of retrospective data, administrative records, and innovative survey designs has expanded our understanding of intergenerational mobility patterns across diverse contexts.

7.8.3. Policy approaches to breaking intergenerational poverty cycles

Policies to disrupt intergenerational poverty transmission typically focus on critical intervention points in the life cycle where investments can generate long-term returns:

- Early childhood development programs target the critical period when brain architecture and foundational skills are established. Programs providing nutrition support, healthcare, stimulation, and early education show particularly strong returns for disadvantaged children. For instance, Jamaica's home visiting program for stunted toddlers increased adult earnings by 25 percent two decades later (Gertler et al., 2014). Such programs address the early divergence in cognitive and non-cognitive skills that can perpetuate poverty across generations.
- Education quality and access initiatives reduce barriers to human capital accumulation throughout childhood and adolescence. Interventions span from conditional cash transfers that increase school enrollment to pedagogical reforms that improve learning outcomes. Evidence consistently shows that completion of quality secondary education substantially increases intergenerational mobility, particularly for girls.
- Asset-building approaches help disadvantaged youth begin adulthood with resources that facilitate economic advancement. These include individual development accounts (matched savings), child trust funds, and inheritance reforms. Such approaches recognize that initial asset endowments strongly influence subsequent economic trajectories, helping break the intergenerational transmission of asset poverty.
- Residential mobility and neighborhood integration initiatives address the spatial dimension of opportunity. Programs like Moving to Opportunity in the United States demonstrate that relocating families from high-poverty to low-poverty neighborhoods can significantly improve children's long-term outcomes, particularly when moves occur during early childhood (Chetty et al., 2016).

- Labor market inclusion policies improve employment opportunities for disadvantaged workers through job training, placement services, anti-discrimination enforcement, and minimum wage regulations. Such policies address the perpetuation of labor market disadvantage across generations, ensuring that enhanced human capital translates into improved economic outcomes.

Effective strategies to break intergenerational poverty cycles typically combine multiple approaches, recognizing that poverty transmission operates through interrelated channels requiring coordinated intervention. They also recognize the importance of timing, with early interventions generally yielding higher returns while still maintaining support throughout the life course to reinforce initial investments.

7.9. Conclusion: Advancing Research and Policy on Poverty Dynamics

Poverty dynamics research has transformed our understanding of poverty as a dynamic process rather than a static condition. By tracking welfare changes for the same individuals or households over time, this research reveals substantial movement into and out of poverty, distinguishes between persistent and transient forms of deprivation, and identifies factors associated with different poverty trajectories.

Key insights from poverty dynamics research include the following:

- The proportion of people experiencing poverty at some point typically exceeds the poverty rate at any single time point, highlighting the importance of addressing both current poverty and vulnerability to future poverty.
- Chronic and transient poverty may require different policy responses—the former demanding structural interventions to build assets and capabilities, the latter necessitating risk management tools to help households weather temporary shocks.
- Multidimensional approaches to poverty dynamics reveal that deprivations across different dimensions often follow distinct

temporal patterns, with some dimensions showing greater persistence than others.

- The near-poor face substantial vulnerability to falling into poverty, underscoring the importance of preventive interventions alongside those addressing current poverty.
- Intergenerational poverty transmission operates through multiple channels including human capital investment, asset inheritance, psychological factors, and social networks, requiring coordinated interventions at critical points in the life cycle.

Future research directions in poverty dynamics include the following:

- Developing more integrated approaches to measuring multidimensional poverty dynamics that capture both the breadth and persistence of deprivations
- Expanding the temporal scope of analysis to better understand both short-term volatility and long-term intergenerational processes
- Incorporating new dimensions of wellbeing, including psychological and relational aspects that may exhibit distinct dynamic patterns
- Leveraging new data sources, including high-frequency mobile phone surveys and administrative data, to capture poverty dynamics over shorter timeframes and longer periods
- Strengthening causal analysis of poverty transitions through experimental and quasi-experimental approaches that identify the effects of specific interventions on poverty trajectories

Translating these research insights into effective policies requires both technical innovations in program design and political commitment to addressing the diverse needs of those experiencing or vulnerable to poverty. It demands policies that are responsive to the dynamic nature of poverty—supporting both sustainable escapes from current poverty and prevention of future poverty entries.

As poverty dynamics research continues to advance, it offers an increasingly nuanced foundation for designing, implementing, and evaluating policies aimed at the sustainable reduction of poverty in all its forms and dimensions. By understanding poverty not as a fixed state but as a dynamic process, we gain powerful insights for creating more effective pathways to lasting prosperity for all.

References

Albert, J. R. G. (2023). *Poverty transitions and the near-poor in the Philippines* (PIDS Discussion Paper Series No. 2023-27). Philippine Institute for Development Studies. https://www.pids.gov.ph/publication/discussion-papers/poverty-transitions-and-the-near-poor-in-the-philippines

Albert, J. R. G., Dumagan, J., & Martinez, A., Jr. (2015). *Inequalities in income, labor, and education: The challenge of inclusive growth* (Discussion Paper Series 2015-01). Philippine Institute for Development Studies. https://www.pids.gov.ph/publication/discussion-papers/inequalities-in-income-labor-and-education-the-challenge-of-inclusive-growth

Alkire, S., Apablaza, M., & Jung, E. (2014). *Multidimensional poverty measurement for EU-SILC countries* (OPHI Research in Progress 36c). Oxford University. https://ophi.org.uk/sites/default/files/RP36b.pdf

Alkire, S., Apablaza, M., Chakravarty, S., & Yalonetzky, G. (2017). Measuring chronic multidimensional poverty. *Journal of Policy Modeling, 39*(6), 983–1006. https://www.sciencedirect.com/science/article/abs/pii/S0161893817300625

Alkire, S., Kanagaratnam, U., Nogales, R., & Suppa, N. (2020). Revising the global Multidimensional Poverty Index: Empirical insights and robustness. *Oxford Development Studies, 48*(4), 395–415. https://doi.org/10.1080/13600818.2020.1854209

Alkire, S., & Roche, J. M. (2017). Monitoring progress in reducing multidimensional poverty. In *Measuring multidimensional poverty and deprivation* (pp. 69–101). Palgrave Macmillan. https://doi.org/10.1057/978-1-137-51327-0_4

Alkire, S., Roche, J. M., & Vaz, A. (2017). Changes over time in multidimensional poverty: Methodology and results for 34 countries. *World Development, 94*, 232–249. https://doi.org/10.1016/j.worlddev.2017.01.011

Alkire, S., & Seth, S. (2015). Multidimensional poverty reduction in India between 1999 and 2006: Where and how? *World Development, 72*, 93–108. https://doi.org/10.1016/j.worlddev.2015.02.009

Alkire, S., Roche, J. M., and Vaz, A. (2015). *Changes over time in multidimensional poverty: Methodology and results for 34 countries* (OPHI Working Paper No. 76). Oxford Poverty & Human Development Initiative. https://ophi.org.uk/sites/default/files/OPHIWP076.pdf

Apablaza, M., & Yalonetzky, G. (2013). *Decomposing multidimensional poverty dynamics* (Young Lives Working Paper 101). Young Lives. https://www.younglives.org.uk/sites/www.younglives.org.uk/files/YL-WP101_Apablaza-Yalonetzky-Multidimensional-Poverty-Dynamics.pdf

Banerjee, A., Duflo, E., Goldberg, N., Karlan, D., Osei, R., Parienté, W., Shapiro, J., Thuysbaert, B., & Udry, C. (2015). A multifaceted program causes lasting progress for the very poor: Evidence from six countries. *Science, 348*(6236), 1260799. https://www.science.org/doi/10.1126/science.1260799

Baulch, B., & Dat, V. H. (2011). Poverty dynamics in Vietnam, 2002 to 2006. In B. Baulch (Ed.), *Why poverty persists: Poverty dynamics in Asia and Africa* (pp. 219–254). Edward Elgar Publishing. https://www.elgaronline.com/edcollchap/edcoll/9780857930248/9780857930248.00014.xml

Baulch, B. (Ed.). (2011). *Why poverty persists: Poverty dynamics in Asia and Africa*. Cheltenham, UK: Edward Elgar Publishing. https://doi.org/10.4337/9780857930255

Calvo, C., & Dercon, S. (2009). Chronic poverty and all that: The measurement of poverty over time. In T. Addison, D. Hulme, & R. Kanbur (Eds.), *Poverty dynamics: Interdisciplinary perspectives* (pp. 29–58). Oxford University Press. https://academic.oup.com/book/11989/chapter-abstract/161233963?redirectedFrom=fulltext

Chetty, R., Hendren, N., & Katz, L. F. (2016). The effects of exposure to better neighborhoods on children: New evidence from the Moving to Opportunity experiment. *American Economic Review, 106*(4), 855–902. https://www.aeaweb.org/articles?id=10.1257/aer.20150572

Corak, M. (2013). Income inequality, equality of opportunity, and intergenerational mobility. *Journal of Economic Perspectives, 27*(3), 79–102. https://www.aeaweb.org/articles?id=10.1257/jep.27.3.79

Dang, H. A., & Lanjouw, P. F. (2018). Welfare dynamics measurement: Two definitions of a vulnerability line and their empirical application. *Review of Income and Wealth, 64*(3), 633–660. https://doi.org/10.1111/roiw.12294

Dercon, S., & Porter, C. (2011). A poor life? Chronic poverty and downward mobility in rural Ethiopia, 1994 to 2004. In B. Baulch (Ed.), *Why poverty persists: Poverty dynamics in Asia and Africa* (pp. 65–91). Edward Elgar Publishing. https://www.elgaronline.com/edcollchap/edcoll/9780857930248/9780857930248.00010.xml

Dercon, S., & Shapiro, J. (2007). *Moving on, staying behind, getting lost: Lessons on poverty mobility from longitudinal data* (Global Poverty Research Group Working Paper 075). Oxford: Global Poverty Research Group. https://www.gov.uk/research-for-development-outputs/moving-on-staying-behind-getting-lost-lessons-on-poverty-mobility-from-longitudinal-data

Dotter, C., & Klasen, S. (2017). *The multidimensional poverty index: Achievements, conceptual and empirical issues* (Discussion Papers 233). Courant Research Centre PEG. https://www.econstor.eu/handle/10419/157267

Emran, M. S., & Shilpi, F. (2015). Gender, geography, and generations: Intergenerational educational mobility in post-reform India. *World Development, 72*, 362–380. https://www.sciencedirect.com/science/article/abs/pii/S0305750X15000686

Foster, J. E. (2009). A class of chronic poverty measures. In T. Addison, D. Hulme, & R. Kanbur (Eds.), *Poverty dynamics: Interdisciplinary perspectives* (pp. 59–76). Oxford University Press. https://academic.oup.com/book/11989/chapter-abstract/161235446

Gertler, P., Heckman, J., Pinto, R., Zanolini, A., Vermeersch, C., Walker, S., Chang, S. M., & Grantham-McGregor, S. (2014). Labor market returns to an early childhood stimulation intervention in Jamaica. *Science, 344*(6187), 998–1001. https://www.science.org/doi/10.1126/science.1251178

Glewwe, P. (2012). How much of observed economic mobility is measurement error? IV methods to reduce measurement error bias, with an application to Vietnam. *The World Bank Economic Review, 26*(2), 236–264. https://academic.oup.com/wber/article-abstract/26/2/236/1664433

Gradin, C., del Rio, C., & Canto, O. (2012). Measuring poverty accounting for time. *Review of Income and Wealth, 58*(2), 330–354. https://onlinelibrary.wiley.com/doi/abs/10.1111/j.1475-4991.2011.00458.x

Jalan, J., & Ravallion, M. (1998). Transient poverty in postreform rural China. *Journal of Comparative Economics, 26*(2), 338–357. https://www.sciencedirect.com/science/article/abs/pii/S0147596798915268

Jenkins, S. P., & Van Kerm, P. (2017). How does attrition affect estimates of persistent poverty rates? The case of EU-SILC. In A. B. Atkinson, A.-C. Guio, & E. Marlier (Eds.), *Monitoring social inclusion in Europe* (pp. 401–417).

Luxembourg: Publications Office of the European Union. https://ec.europa.eu/eurostat/documents/3217494/8031566/KS-05-14-075-EN-N.pdf

Krishna, A. (2010). *One illness away: Why people become poor and how they escape poverty*. Oxford University Press. https://academic.oup.com/book/4086

Krishna, A., Lumonya, D., Markiewicz, M., Mugumya, F., Kafuko, A., & Wegoye, J. (2006). Escaping poverty and becoming poor in 36 villages of Central and Western Uganda. *The Journal of Development Studies, 42*(2), 346–370. https://www.tandfonline.com/doi/abs/10.1080/00220380500405634#:~:text=Twenty%2Dfour%20per%20cent%20of,have%20simultaneously%20fallen%20into%20poverty

Lee, N., Ridder, G., & Strauss, J. (2017). Estimation of poverty transition matrices with noisy data. *Journal of Applied Econometrics, 32*(1), 37–55. https://onlinelibrary.wiley.com/doi/abs/10.1002/jae.2506

Mare, R. D. (2011). A multigenerational view of inequality. *Demography, 48*(1), 1–23. https://link.springer.com/article/10.1007/s13524-011-0014-7

Martínez Jr., A. (2016, March). *Analytical tools for measuring poverty dynamics: An application using panel data in the Philippines* (ADB Economics Working Paper Series No. 477). Asian Development Bank.

McCulloch, N., & Baulch, B. (2000a). *Tracking pro-poor growth* (ID21 Insights No. 31). Sussex: Institute of Development Studies.

McCulloch, N., & Baulch, B. (2000b). Simulating the impact of policy upon chronic and transitory poverty in rural Pakistan. *The Journal of Development Studies, 36*(6), 100–130. https://www.ids.ac.uk/files/jdsrevpap7.pdf

McKay, A., & Lawson, D. (2003). Assessing the extent and nature of chronic poverty in low income countries: Issues and evidence. *World Development, 31*(3), 425–439. https://doi.org/10.1016/S0305-750X(02)00221-8

Nicholas, A., & Ray, R. (2012). Duration and persistence in multidimensional deprivation: Methodology and Australian application. *Economic Record, 88*(280), 106–126. https://doi.org/10.1111/j.1475-4932.2011.00760.x

Notten, G., & Guio, A. C. (2021). The impact of social transfers on income poverty and material deprivation. In Z. Hass & A. Chzhen (Eds.), *Improving the understanding of poverty and social exclusion in Europe* (pp. 83–99). Publications Office of the European Union. https://doi.org/10.2785/50266

Porter, C., & Quinn, N. N. (2013). Measuring intertemporal poverty: Policy options for the poverty analyst. In G. Betti & A. Lemmi (Eds.), *Poverty and social exclusion: New methods of analysis* (pp. 166–193). London: Routledge. https://doi.org/10.4324/9780203085172-11

Pritchett, L., Suryahadi, A., & Sumarto, S. (2000). *Quantifying vulnerability to poverty: A proposed measure, applied to Indonesia* (World Bank Policy Research Working Paper No. 2437). Washington, DC: World Bank. http://hdl.handle.net/10986/21355

Quisumbing, A. R. (2007). *Poverty transitions, shocks, and consumption in rural Bangladesh: Preliminary results from a longitudinal household survey* (CPRC Working Paper No. 105). Chronic Poverty Research Centre. http://crsps.net/wp-content/downloads/BASIS/Inventoried%203.2/13-2007-7-216.pdf

Ratcliffe, C., & McKernan, S. (2010). *Childhood poverty persistence: Facts and consequences* (Urban Institute Brief 14). Washington, DC: Urban Institute. https://www.urban.org/sites/default/files/publication/32926/412126-childhood-poverty-persistence-facts-and-consequences.pdf

Reyes, C. M., Tabuga, A. D., Mina, C. D., Asis, R. D., & Datu, M. B. (2011). *Dynamics of poverty in the Philippines: Distinguishing the chronic from the transient poor* (PIDS Discussion Paper No. 2011-31). Philippine Institute for Development Studies. https://pidswebs.pids.gov.ph/CDN/PUBLICATIONS/pidsdps1131.pdf

Roche, J. M. (2013). Monitoring progress in child poverty reduction: Methodological insights and illustration to the case of Bangladesh. *Social Indicators Research, 112*(2), 363–390. https://doi.org/10.1007/s11205-013-0252-8

Seth, S., & Villar, A. (2017). *Measuring human development and human deprivations* (OPHI Working Paper No. 110). University of Oxford. https://ophi.org.uk/wp-content/uploads/OPHIWP110.pdf

Shorrocks, A. F. (1999). Decomposition procedures for distributional analysis: A unified framework based on the Shapley value. *Journal of Economic Inequality, 11*(1), 99–126. https://doi.org/10.1007/s10888-011-9214-z

Suppa, N. (2018). Transitions in poverty and deprivations: An analysis of multidimensional poverty dynamics. *Social Indicators Research, 140*(2), 523–555. https://doi.org/10.1007/s11205-017-1793-z

Vaz, A. (2014). *Are children among the poorest?* (Discussion Paper No. 91). OPHI, University of Oxford. https://ophi.org.uk/wp-content/uploads/OPHIWP091.pdf

Vaz, A., Alkire, S., & Amarante, V. (2022). Poverty dynamics and intertemporal multidimensional deprivation. *Journal of Development Studies, 58*(5), 954–973. https://doi.org/10.1080/00220388.2021.2001129

CHAPTER 8

Policy and Program Interventions: What Works and What Doesn't

"Give a man a fish, and you feed him for a day. Teach a man to fish, and you feed him for a lifetime... But first, check whether he has a fishing rod, access to a pond, rights to fish there, a market to sell his catch, and isn't being exploited by the fishing industry."

—ADAPTED PROVERB

SUMMARY

This chapter examines the effectiveness and sustainability of various poverty reduction strategies implemented globally. It begins by explaining impact evaluation methodologies, emphasizing their critical role in distinguishing between correlation and causation when assessing anti-poverty programs. The chapter explores diverse intervention approaches including social safety nets, conditional cash transfers, microfinance, sustainable livelihoods, and community development initiatives, presenting evidence from rigorous impact evaluations across multiple contexts.

The analysis reveals that conditional cash transfers have demonstrated consistent positive impacts on education, health, and nutrition outcomes, though their long-term effects on poverty reduction remain mixed. Microfinance shows more modest and heterogeneous impacts that depend significantly on local contexts and implementation quality. Graduation programs that combine multiple interventions in sequence have shown promising results for the ultra-poor, though their cost-effectiveness and scalability present ongoing challenges. Community-driven development approaches demonstrate varied success, with stronger outcomes in infrastructure delivery but more limited impact on governance and social capital.

Throughout the chapter, case studies illuminate both successes and failures, emphasizing that context matters tremendously in poverty reduction efforts. The evidence suggests that no single intervention works universally; rather, effective poverty reduction requires tailored approaches that address multiple dimensions of poverty simultaneously while adapting to local conditions. The most sustainable interventions build local capacity, integrate with existing systems, establish appropriate exit strategies, and move beyond treating symptoms to address underlying structural causes of poverty.

The chapter concludes that successful poverty reduction requires not just technically sound interventions but also enabling policy environments, strong institutions, and adaptive approaches that evolve based on evidence. The field of poverty reduction continues to build empirical knowledge about what works, challenging policymakers to move beyond ideological positions to evidence-based approaches that can be sustained financially, institutionally, and environmentally over time.

8.1. Introduction: The Search for Effective Poverty Reduction

Throughout the previous chapters, we have explored the multidimensional nature of poverty, its measurement, and its dynamics over time. This foundation brings us to a critical question: What can actually be done to reduce poverty effectively and sustainably? Governments, international organizations, NGOs, and communities have implemented countless programs and policies aimed at poverty reduction, with varying degrees of success. This chapter examines what we know about which interventions work, which do not, and why.

Over the past few decades, the approach to poverty reduction has evolved considerably. Early efforts often focused on economic growth as the primary pathway out of poverty, based on the assumption that benefits would naturally "trickle down" to the poor (Kanbur & Vines, 2000). When this approach showed limited success, attention shifted to more direct interventions targeting poor households and communities. More recently, there has been growing recognition that effective poverty reduction requires addressing multiple dimensions simultaneously, combining economic opportunities with social protections and structural reforms (Alkire et al., 2015).

At the same time, the methods used to evaluate poverty interventions have become increasingly sophisticated. The rise of rigorous impact evaluation methods has transformed our understanding of what works by enabling policymakers to distinguish between correlation and causation (Duflo, Glennerster, & Kremer, 2007). These methods help us determine whether observed improvements in people's lives are actually caused by specific interventions, or whether they might have occurred anyway due to other factors.

This chapter begins by explaining impact evaluation approaches and why they matter for poverty reduction efforts. We then examine evidence on the effectiveness of various intervention types, including social safety nets, conditional cash transfers, microfinance, sustainable livelihood approaches, and community-driven development.

Throughout, we emphasize not just what works but also under what conditions, for whom, and—critically—whether positive impacts can be sustained over time.

Several themes emerge across these diverse interventions. First, context matters tremendously—what works in one setting may fail in another due to differences in local conditions, institutions, and social dynamics. Second, implementation quality often determines success or failure, regardless of how well designed an intervention is theoretically. Third, sustainable poverty reduction typically requires addressing multiple constraints simultaneously rather than focusing narrowly on a single dimension of poverty.

As we explore the evidence on various intervention types, we will encounter important tensions and tradeoffs. For instance, more comprehensive interventions often show stronger impacts but are more expensive and difficult to scale. Similarly, programs that show impressive short-term impacts may not lead to sustained poverty reduction if they do not address underlying structural causes.

Throughout, our focus remains on building a nuanced understanding of what approaches have the greatest potential to create lasting improvements in the lives of poor people across diverse contexts. By critically examining what we know about poverty interventions—both their strengths and limitations—we aim to provide a foundation for more effective, sustainable approaches to poverty reduction.

8.2. Understanding Impact Evaluation: Measuring What Works

Before diving into specific poverty reduction approaches, we must understand how researchers and policymakers determine whether an intervention actually works. Impact evaluation is the systematic process of assessing the changes that can be attributed to a particular intervention, such as a project, program, or policy. The central challenge is establishing causality—determining whether observed changes were actually caused by the intervention rather than by other factors.

8.2.1. The challenge of attributing impact

Consider a scenario where a government implements a microfinance program in certain villages, and two years later, incomes in these villages have increased by 15 percent. Can we conclude that the microfinance program caused this improvement? Not necessarily. Many other factors could be responsible: maybe these villages were already on an upward economic trajectory; perhaps favorable weather boosted agricultural yields; or possibly other development programs were operating in the same areas.

The fundamental problem in impact evaluation is that we cannot simultaneously observe what happens to the same people both with and without the intervention—what economists call the "counterfactual" (Gertler et al., 2016). To address this challenge, impact evaluations attempt to create or identify a valid comparison group that approximates what would have happened to program participants had they not received the intervention.

8.2.2. Approaches to impact evaluation

Various methodologies help establish causality in impact evaluations, each with strengths and limitations:

- **Randomized controlled trials (RCTs)** are considered the gold standard for impact evaluation. In an RCT, eligible individuals or communities are randomly assigned to either receive the intervention (treatment group) or not receive it (control group). This randomization ensures that the two groups are statistically identical on average before the intervention, so any differences observed afterward can be attributed to the program (Duflo, Glennerster, & Kremer, 2007). For example, in Mexico's PROGRESA conditional cash transfer program (later renamed Oportunidades), the program was initially rolled out randomly across eligible communities, allowing researchers to compare outcomes between communities that received the program and those that did not (Gertler, 2004).

- **Quasi-experimental methods** are used when randomization is not feasible. These include
  - **Difference-in-differences**, which compares changes over time between program recipients and non-recipients
  - **Regression discontinuity design**, which compares individuals just above and below program eligibility thresholds
  - **Matching methods** like Propensity Score Matching, which create comparison groups with similar observable characteristics
  - **Instrumental variables**, which use factors that affect participation but not outcomes directly (White & Raitzer, 2017)
- **Non-experimental methods** include before–after comparisons, which measure outcomes before and after an intervention without a comparison group, and qualitative approaches that use interviews, focus groups, and observation to understand program impacts in depth.

8.2.3. Beyond average effects: Heterogeneity and mechanisms

Modern impact evaluations increasingly look beyond program effects, called average treatment effects (ATEs), to understand how impacts vary across different subgroups and contexts. For example, the same microcredit program might benefit entrepreneurs with existing businesses but have little impact on households starting new enterprises. Similarly, a conditional cash transfer might have larger effects on school enrollment for girls than boys, or work better in communities with better school infrastructure (Duflo, 2012).

Understanding these variations helps policymakers tailor interventions to contexts where they will be most effective. Similarly, exploring the mechanisms through which programs achieve their effects—the causal chains linking intervention to outcomes—provides insights for program improvement.

8.2.4. *From efficacy to effectiveness to sustainability*

As the field of impact evaluation has matured, focus has shifted from merely establishing whether interventions work under ideal circumstances ("efficacy") to whether they work in real-world contexts ("effectiveness") and whether their impacts persist over time ("sustainability"). This evolution reflects recognition that many promising approaches show positive results in small, carefully managed pilot projects but struggle when implemented at scale or fail to produce lasting change after the intervention ends (Bold et al., 2013).

This shift has prompted greater attention to implementation quality, cost-effectiveness, and program sustainability. Researchers increasingly track outcomes not just immediately after program completion but also years later, seeking to understand whether interventions create enduring pathways out of poverty or merely temporary relief.

8.2.5. *Limitations and ethical considerations*

Despite their value, impact evaluations have limitations. They typically focus on quantifiable, shorter-term outcomes rather than complex, long-term changes. They may not fully capture spillover effects on non-participants or broader systemic changes. And they sometimes struggle to incorporate more qualitative dimensions of poverty and wellbeing (Ravallion, 2009).

Impact evaluations also raise ethical questions about withholding potentially beneficial interventions from control groups and about the role of affected communities in research design. Many evaluations now incorporate mixed methods, combining quantitative measurement of impacts with qualitative exploration of experiences and mechanisms, and increasingly involve local stakeholders in design and interpretation (Barrett & Carter, 2010).

8.2.6. The evidence revolution in poverty reduction

The proliferation of rigorous impact evaluations over the past two decades has transformed our understanding of what works in poverty reduction. Organizations like the Abdul Latif Jameel Poverty Action Lab (J-PAL), Innovations for Poverty Action (IPA), and the International Initiative for Impact Evaluation (3ie) have catalyzed hundreds of evaluations across diverse contexts. This has created an unprecedented evidence base that challenges conventional wisdom and informs more effective approaches.

For example, early assumptions about microfinance as a silver bullet for poverty reduction have been tempered by evidence showing more modest and heterogeneous impacts (Banerjee, Karlan, & Zinman, 2015). Similarly, evaluations have revealed that removing small barriers to service utilization—like providing free deworming medication in schools—can have outsized effects relative to their costs (Miguel & Kremer, 2004).

As we examine specific poverty reduction approaches in subsequent sections, we will draw heavily on this growing evidence base, recognizing both its strengths and limitations in guiding more effective poverty reduction efforts.

8.3. Social Safety Nets: Providing Protection and Promotion

Social safety nets are programs that protect vulnerable populations from destitution and help the poor invest in their future. These programs have become a cornerstone of poverty reduction strategies worldwide, operating under the premise that providing basic income support and essential services can both alleviate immediate suffering and create conditions for longer-term advancement. Safety nets, however, are not supposed to be permanent measures, and thus it is important for the design of these programs to incorporate a graduation out of the program.

8.3.1. Types of social safety net programs

Social safety nets encompass various interventions designed to provide protection, facilitate access to essential services, and promote livelihoods:

- **Unconditional cash transfers** provide direct monetary assistance without requiring specific actions from recipients. These programs operate on the principle that poor households can make appropriate decisions about resource allocation.
- **Food and in-kind transfers** deliver essential goods directly to beneficiaries, including food rations, nutritional supplements, school supplies, or agricultural inputs.
- **Public works programs** provide temporary employment on infrastructure or community projects, offering income while creating public assets.
- **Fee waivers and subsidies** reduce the cost of essential services like healthcare, education, or utilities for vulnerable populations.
- **Social pensions** provide regular cash payments to elderly or disabled individuals regardless of their formal employment history.

8.3.2. Evidence on effectiveness

Rigorous evaluations have yielded insights into the impacts of various social protection approaches meant to improve the plight of the poor.

Unconditional cash transfers (UCTs) have been extensively studied, with evidence challenging early concerns about dependency or misuse. A systematic review of studies from Latin America, Africa, and Asia found that UCTs consistently increased household consumption, reduced food insecurity, and improved child health and education outcomes (Bastagli et al., 2016). Contrary to common stereotypes, studies in Kenya, Uganda, and other settings have found little evidence that cash transfers increase spending on temptation goods like alcohol or tobacco; instead, they are typically invested in nutrition, education, and productive assets (Evans & Popova, 2017).

Kenya's Give Directly program, which provides substantial one-time cash transfers to extremely poor households, has been extensively evaluated through RCTs. Results show increased assets, earnings, food security, and psychological wellbeing among recipients, with effects persisting several years after the transfers (Haushofer & Shapiro, 2016). These impacts extended beyond recipient households, with positive spillover effects on non-recipients in the same communities through increased economic activity.

Similarly, Zambia's Child Grant Program, which provides regular cash transfers to households with young children, increased food consumption, productive asset ownership, and agricultural output. An evaluation found that each dollar transferred generated 1.79 dollars in local economic benefits through multiplier effects (Handa et al., 2018).

Public works programs show mixed results. Ethiopia's Productive Safety Net Program (PSNP), one of Africa's largest social protection initiatives, combines seasonal employment on public works projects with direct support for those unable to work. Evaluations show that the program has improved food security, increased livestock holdings, and reduced the need for distress sales of assets during droughts (Berhane et al., 2014). However, the program's impacts on graduating participants from food insecurity have been more modest.

India's Mahatma Gandhi National Rural Employment Guarantee Act (MGNREGA), which guarantees up to 100 days of wage employment annually to rural households, has demonstrated positive impacts on rural wages, food security, and women's labor force participation. However, implementation challenges including delayed payments, corruption, and limited job creation in some regions have constrained its effectiveness (Subbarao et al., 2013).

Social pensions have expanded rapidly, particularly in middle-income countries. South Africa's Old Age Pension reaches over 3 million elderly citizens, with evaluations showing positive impacts extending beyond recipients to household members, particularly grandchildren. Girls in households with pension-eligible grandmothers show better nutritional status and educational outcomes (Duflo,

2003). However, pension eligibility also reduced labor supply among working-age household members in South Africa, suggesting potential for both positive intergenerational transfers and some dependency effects.

8.3.3. Design and implementation challenges

Despite demonstrated successes, social protection interventions, particularly safety nets, face significant implementation deficits and challenges that can undermine their effectiveness.

Targeting accuracy remains contentious. Methods include means testing (based on income verification), proxy means testing (using observable household characteristics), geographic targeting, categorical targeting (to specific groups like children or elderly), and community-based targeting where local leaders identify beneficiaries. Each method involves tradeoffs between inclusion errors (including non-poor), exclusion errors (missing the poor), administrative costs, and social acceptability. Research in Indonesia, Mexico, and Niger shows that different targeting approaches reach different segments of the poor, suggesting the need for context-specific approaches (Coady, Grosh, & Hoddinott, 2004).

Administrative capacity often constrains program effectiveness. Many programs struggle with unreliable payment systems, weak monitoring, and limited capacity to verify eligibility or track outcomes. The expansion of digital identification systems, mobile banking, and biometric verification has created opportunities to strengthen delivery systems, though these technologies bring their own challenges regarding privacy, accessibility, and potential exclusion.

Fiscal sustainability presents a persistent challenge, particularly in low-income countries with limited tax bases. While evidence increasingly shows that well-designed safety nets represent investments rather than merely expenditures, securing adequate, stable financing remains difficult. Some countries have addressed this by reallocating funds from less efficient subsidies; for example, Indonesia expanded its safety net programs partly by reducing fuel subsidies that disproportionately benefited the non-poor (World Bank, 2017).

8.3.4. From protection to promotion: Building sustainable pathways

A key evolution in safety net design has been the shift from purely protective functions toward "productive" safety nets that aim to help poor households graduate from poverty permanently. This approach recognizes that sustainable poverty reduction requires addressing both immediate needs and underlying constraints to income generation.

Ethiopia's PSNP exemplifies this evolution, combining regular transfers with complementary interventions including agricultural extension, credit access, and irrigation development. Similarly, Rwanda's Vision 2020 Umurenge Programme (VUP) provides both direct support to the extremely poor and public works employment while linking beneficiaries to financial services and skills training.

The evidence on whether safety nets alone can facilitate sustainable exits from poverty remains mixed. A systematic review of graduation rates from various programs found substantial heterogeneity, with more success in contexts of economic growth and when programs explicitly incorporate livelihood enhancement components (Banerjee et al., 2015). This has led to growing interest in "graduation" approaches that sequentially layer multiple interventions, as we will discuss in a later section.

8.4. Conditional Cash Transfers: Incentivizing Human Capital Investment

Conditional cash transfers (CCTs) represent an innovative approach to social assistance that provides cash payments to poor households contingent on their fulfillment of specific conditions, typically related to children's education, healthcare utilization, or nutrition. These programs aim to address both current poverty (through the cash component) and future poverty (by incentivizing human capital investments).

8.4.1. *The conceptual framework*

CCTs emerged from recognition that poor households face both resource constraints and potential underinvestment in human capital due to information gaps, behavioral biases, or intra-household decision dynamics. By attaching conditions to transfers, these programs attempt to address both immediate consumption needs and longer-term capability development (Fiszbein & Schady, 2009).

The specific conditions (which are sometimes euphemistically called "co-responsibilities") vary across programs but typically include

- **Education requirements** such as minimum school attendance rates for children (usually 80–85 percent)
- **Health requirements** including regular checkups, growth monitoring, and vaccinations for young children
- **Nutrition components** such as attendance at health education sessions for parents or participation in supplementary feeding programs

8.4.2. *Evidence from major CCT programs*

CCTs represent one of the most extensively evaluated social policy innovations. Several landmark programs have provided robust evidence on their impacts.

Mexico's PROGRESA/Oportunidades/Prospera (the program has been renamed over time) began in 1997 and became a model for CCTs globally. The program's randomized phase-in design allowed for rigorous evaluation, showing significant positive impacts on school enrollment, progression to secondary school, and health service utilization. Children in participating households experienced reduced stunting, improved nutrition, and fewer sick days. Long-term follow-up studies have found that children who benefited from the program completed more years of education and had higher labor market earnings as adults (Parker & Todd, 2017).

Brazil's Bolsa Família, the world's largest CCT program, reaches over 14 million households. Studies show that the program reduced poverty and inequality while increasing school enrollment and attendance, particularly for older children at risk of dropping out. The program is credited with contributing significantly to Brazil's reduction in income inequality during the 2000s, though disentangling its effects from broader economic and social policies remains challenging (Soares, Ribas, & Osório, 2010).

Colombia's Familias en Acción has demonstrated positive impacts on both demand and supply sides. Beyond increasing school enrollment and healthcare utilization among beneficiaries, the program stimulated improvements in service quality as providers responded to increased demand. The program also increased local economic activity through multiplier effects as beneficiaries spent their transfers locally (Attanasio et al., 2010).

Philippines' Pantawid Pamilyang Pilipino Program (4Ps) has shown strong compliance with conditions and positive impacts on education and health utilization. However, impacts on final outcomes like learning achievement and nutritional status have been more modest, highlighting the importance of service quality alongside access (World Bank, 2020).

8.4.3. Design variations and tradeoffs

While sharing a common conceptual framework, CCT programs vary significantly in design features, with important implications for their effectiveness.

Transfer size ranges from as little as 4 percent of pre-program household consumption in Honduras to over 20 percent in Mexico and Nicaragua. Research suggests that larger transfers typically generate larger impacts, particularly on consumption and poverty reduction, though the relationship is not strictly linear. Programs must balance adequacy against fiscal constraints and potential labor market disincentives (Fiszbein & Schady, 2009).

Targeting mechanisms include proxy means tests (using observable household characteristics to estimate poverty), geographic targeting, categorical targeting (to specific demographic groups), and combinations thereof. Each approach involves tradeoffs between inclusion errors, exclusion errors, administrative complexity, and social acceptability. Brazil's approach of combining multiple methods has achieved reasonable targeting accuracy with administrative feasibility (Soares, Ribas, & Osório, 2010).

Conditionality strictness varies substantially. Some programs (like Mexico's) strictly enforce conditions and reduce payments for non-compliance, while others (like Brazil's) view conditions more as co-responsibilities and emphasize support for compliance rather than punishment. Evidence suggests that stricter enforcement increases compliance with conditions but may exclude the most vulnerable households who face the greatest barriers to fulfilling requirements (Baird et al., 2013).

Payment mechanisms have evolved from cash disbursements at designated payment points to electronic transfers through bank accounts, mobile money, or specialized payment cards. Digitalization has reduced administrative costs and leakage while improving timeliness, though it requires adequate infrastructure and financial literacy among recipients.

8.4.4. Emerging evidence and debates

As CCTs have matured, research has progressed beyond asking whether they "work" to more nuanced questions about optimal design, long-term impacts, and comparative effectiveness.

The value of conditionality itself remains debated. Several studies comparing conditional and unconditional versions of the same program have found that conditions enhance impacts on the behaviors they target (particularly school enrollment), but unconditional transfers may be more cost-effective for some outcomes like consumption (Baird et al., 2013). The optimal approach likely depends on program objectives and context-specific barriers to human capital investment.

Long-term and intergenerational impacts are increasingly studied as early CCT recipients reach adulthood. Evidence from Mexico suggests that children who benefited from PROGRESA completed more schooling and earned higher wages as adults, though the magnitude of labor market impacts has been moderate rather than transformative (Parker & Todd, 2017). These findings highlight that human capital investments alone may not guarantee economic mobility without complementary efforts to improve labor market opportunities.

Graduation strategies for CCT programs have gained attention as policymakers seek sustainable exits rather than indefinite support. Approaches include time limits on participation, progressive reduction of benefits, and links to complementary programs like skills training or productive inclusion initiatives. Evaluations of these approaches are ongoing, with preliminary evidence suggesting that abrupt exits without adequate preparation often lead to reversal of gains.

8.4.5. Limitations and criticisms

Despite their demonstrated successes, CCTs face several important limitations and criticisms.

Supply-side constraints often limit program effectiveness. When schools or health facilities are absent, understaffed, or low quality, increasing demand through CCTs yields limited improvements in final outcomes like learning or health status. This highlights the need for complementary investments in service quality and accessibility (Fiszbein & Schady, 2009).

Limited impact on extreme poverty emerges in contexts where the poorest households face barriers beyond those addressed by CCTs. For instance, when children must contribute economically to household survival, transfer amounts may be insufficient to offset opportunity costs of schooling. Similarly, when geographic isolation or discrimination creates structural barriers, CCTs alone may prove insufficient.

Administrative complexity and costs present challenges, particularly in low-capacity settings. Effective CCT implementation requires systems for targeting, registering beneficiaries, monitoring compliance, delivering payments, and addressing grievances. Building these systems represents a significant investment, though costs typically decline as a percentage of transfers over time.

Potential for dependency remains a concern, though evidence suggests that it is often overstated. Studies generally find limited negative effects on adult labor supply, with some programs actually increasing productive activities through eased credit constraints or improved health. Nevertheless, the question of how to facilitate sustainable graduation from CCTs remains prominent.

8.5. Microfinance: Small Loans, Big Expectations

Microfinance—the provision of small-scale financial services to people excluded from traditional banking—emerged as one of the most celebrated approaches to poverty reduction in the late 20th century. Popularized by Bangladesh's Grameen Bank and its founder Muhammad Yunus (who received the Nobel Peace Prize in 2006), microfinance promised to transform the lives of the poor through entrepreneurship and self-employment. However, as rigorous evidence has accumulated, a more nuanced picture has emerged about what microfinance can and cannot achieve.

8.5.1. Understanding microfinance

The microfinance sector encompasses various financial services tailored to low-income populations:

- **Microcredit** provides small loans, typically for income-generating activities, using innovative mechanisms like group lending, progressive loan sizes, or frequent repayment schedules to overcome traditional barriers to lending to the poor.
- **Microsavings** offers secure savings facilities with low minimum balances or alternative arrangements like savings groups.
- **Microinsurance** provides coverage against common risks like illness, crop failure, or livestock death.
- **Payment services** enable money transfers and bill payments.

While early microfinance focused primarily on credit, the field has evolved toward a more comprehensive view of financial inclusion that recognizes poor households' diverse financial needs beyond business loans (Collins et al., 2009).

8.5.2. Evidence on impacts

Microfinance's reputation soared based largely on compelling anecdotes and observational studies showing that microfinance clients often experienced improved welfare. However, these studies could not distinguish whether microfinance caused these improvements or whether already-improving households were more likely to participate. Beginning in the mid-2000s, randomized evaluations provided more rigorous evidence of impacts.

Microcredit has shown more modest and heterogeneous effects than early advocates claimed. A series of RCTs across six countries (Bosnia and Herzegovina, Ethiopia, India, Mexico, Mongolia, and Morocco) found that while access to microcredit typically increased business activity, effects on household income, consumption, women's empowerment, and children's education were minimal or non-existent for the average borrower (Banerjee, Karlan, & Zinman, 2015).

However, these studies also revealed important nuances. Households with existing businesses or strong entrepreneurial abilities often benefited substantially, using loans to expand profitable enterprises.

Other households sometimes reduced consumption or casual labor to invest in businesses that generated returns only over longer periods. These patterns suggest that microcredit works more as a business development tool for those with entrepreneurial capacity than as a general poverty reduction strategy.

Microsavings interventions have demonstrated more consistently positive effects. In Kenya, providing market vendors (mostly women) with simple savings accounts led to higher business investment, greater resilience to health shocks, and increased household expenditures (Dupas & Robinson, 2013). Similarly, village savings and loan associations (VSLAs) in Malawi, Ghana, and Uganda have shown positive impacts on food security, asset accumulation, and women's decision-making power.

Microinsurance, particularly weather-indexed crop insurance, has shown promise in helping farmers manage risk and invest in higher-return but riskier activities. In Ghana, farmers offered rainfall insurance increased investments in agriculture and achieved higher yields in normal rainfall years (Karlan et al., 2014). However, uptake of microinsurance products often remains low without significant subsidies or bundling with other services.

Digital financial services including mobile money have demonstrated significant potential for improving financial inclusion and welfare. In Kenya, access to M-PESA mobile money services strengthened risk-sharing networks, increased savings, and contributed to women's economic advancement through greater occupational choice (Suri & Jack, 2016). These digital approaches lower transaction costs dramatically, making it economically viable to serve previously excluded populations.

8.5.3. Implementation deficits and innovations

The microfinance sector has encountered several implementation challenges that have prompted innovative responses.

Interest rates remain contentious. Providing small loans entails high administrative costs relative to loan amounts, necessitating interest rates that appear high in absolute terms (often 20–40 percent annually) but may be lower than informal alternatives. Critics argue that these rates exploit the poor, while proponents maintain that they are necessary for institutional sustainability. Some organizations have reduced rates through operating efficiencies, technology, or cross-subsidization from other products (Rosenberg et al., 2013).

Client protection concerns emerged as the sector commercialized and grew rapidly in the 2000s. In Andhra Pradesh, India, aggressive lending practices and over-indebtedness contributed to a crisis in 2010, including reports of suicide among borrowers unable to repay. This prompted the development of client protection principles, including transparent pricing, appropriate product design, prevention of over-indebtedness, and ethical collection practices.

Women's empowerment has been a stated goal of many microfinance programs, which often target female clients. Evidence on empowerment impacts is mixed and context-dependent. Group-based approaches that combine financial services with social support and training have shown more consistent empowerment effects than standalone credit, though even these vary substantially based on local gender norms and women's baseline status (Kabeer, 2005).

Reaching the poorest remains challenging for traditional microfinance, as the extremely poor often lack the skills, confidence, or stability to use credit effectively. In response, some organizations have developed "graduation" approaches that provide consumption support and asset transfers before introducing financial services, or ultra-poor programs that combine highly subsidized services with intensive coaching.

8.5.4. From microfinance to financial inclusion

The microfinance sector has evolved significantly from its early focus on group-based microcredit toward a broader financial inclusion approach. This evolution reflects both accumulating evidence and changing market conditions.

Product diversification recognizes that poor households need diverse financial tools beyond business loans. Savings facilities help manage irregular income streams; insurance products provide protection against common shocks; and payment services enable safer, cheaper fund transfers including remittances. Leading microfinance institutions now typically offer multiple products tailored to different client needs (Collins et al., 2009).

Individual lending has increasingly supplemented or replaced group lending as microfinance institutions develop better screening and monitoring mechanisms. While group lending effectively leveraged social capital to reduce default risk in early microfinance, it sometimes imposed significant costs on borrowers through lengthy meetings and joint liability requirements.

Digital transformation has dramatically reduced transaction costs, enabling outreach to previously unviable markets including rural areas. Mobile banking, agent networks, and simplified Know-Your-Customer requirements have expanded access while reducing costs. In Kenya, M-PESA mobile money reached 60 percent of adults within four years of launch, demonstrating the potential for rapid expansion through digital channels (Suri & Jack, 2016).

Integration with non-financial services reflects recognition that financial services alone may not enable sustained poverty reduction, particularly for the most disadvantaged. Many organizations now combine financial services with training in financial literacy, business skills, or health education, though the cost-effectiveness of these integrated approaches remains debated.

8.5.5. Reassessing microfinance's role in poverty reduction

The accumulated evidence on microfinance suggests a reassessment of its role in poverty reduction strategies. Rather than a transformative solution to poverty, microfinance appears more effective as one component of broader development strategies.

Microfinance works best when

- Targeting populations with entrepreneurial capacity and opportunities
- Providing appropriate products beyond just credit
- Operating in contexts with adequate infrastructure and markets
- Setting realistic expectations about impacts
- Integrating with complementary services where needed

This more modest but realistic view acknowledges microfinance's meaningful contribution while recognizing its limitations. Financial inclusion remains a valuable goal, but sustainable poverty reduction requires addressing multiple constraints simultaneously, often including non-financial barriers related to health, education, infrastructure, and market access.

8.6. Graduation Programs: A Multi-Faceted Approach to Ultra-Poverty

While single-intervention approaches show mixed results in addressing extreme poverty, a more comprehensive model known as the "graduation approach" has demonstrated promising impacts for the ultra-poor. These programs recognize that the poorest households face multiple, overlapping constraints that require coordinated interventions to create sustainable pathways out of poverty.

8.6.1. The graduation model

The graduation approach originated with the Challenging the Frontiers of Poverty Reduction (CFPR) program in Bangladesh, implemented by the Bangladesh Rural Advancement Committee (BRAC). The CFPR has been adapted globally. The model typically includes a carefully sequenced package of interventions delivered over 18–36 months:

1. **Consumption support** provides regular cash or food transfers to ensure that basic needs are met and stabilize consumption.
2. **Asset transfer** of a productive asset (livestock, inventory for a store, equipment for a trade).
3. **Technical skills training** related to managing the asset and associated livelihood activities.
4. **Financial literacy and access** through savings groups, financial education, and sometimes access to credit.
5. **Life skills coaching** with regular home visits addressing health, nutrition, social issues, and household management.
6. **Healthcare access** through linkages to health services or health education.

These components address different constraints simultaneously: consumption support meets immediate needs and reduces pressure to sell productive assets; asset transfers and skills training build productive capacity; financial inclusion facilitates savings and risk management; and coaching supports behavior change while addressing psychosocial dimensions of poverty (Banerjee et al., 2015).

8.6.2. Evidence from multi-country evaluations

The graduation approach has been evaluated through randomized controlled trials across multiple countries, producing some of the most compelling evidence for poverty reduction interventions:

A landmark six-country RCT (in Ethiopia, Ghana, Honduras, India, Pakistan, and Peru) found that the graduation approach produced consistent positive impacts across diverse contexts. One year after the program concluded (three years after it began), participating households experienced

- 5.8 percent increase in consumption
- 15 percent increase in assets
- 96 percent increase in savings

- Improvements in food security, physical and mental health, and women's empowerment
- Positive returns on investment in five of six countries, ranging from 133 to 433 percent (Banerjee et al., 2015)

Importantly, follow-up studies in India and Bangladesh found that many of these impacts persisted seven years after the program ended, with continued increases in consumption, assets, and income-generating activities. This suggests the graduation approach created sustainable change rather than merely temporary improvements (Banerjee et al., 2016).

8.6.3. Adaptations and implementations

Since these promising results emerged, the graduation approach has expanded substantially with adaptations to diverse contexts.

Government adoptions have scaled the model significantly. Ethiopia integrated graduation components into its Productive Safety Net Program (PSNP) reaching hundreds of thousands of households. Similarly, Peru's Ministry of Development and Social Inclusion incorporated the graduation approach into its national poverty reduction strategy through the Haku Wiñay program, which combines asset transfers with technical training and financial inclusion for rural households (Escobal & Ponce, 2016). Pakistan's Benazir Income Support Programme (BISP) added graduation elements to its core cash transfer program, providing productive assets and training to beneficiaries ready to transition to sustainable livelihoods (Cheema et al., 2016).

Contextual adaptations have tailored the model to diverse settings. In urban contexts, programs have shifted from agricultural assets toward microenterprises and wage employment pathways. In fragile and conflict-affected settings, implementing organizations have incorporated conflict sensitivity and social cohesion elements. In refugee contexts, graduation programs have been adapted to address both refugees' immediate needs and longer-term self-reliance, though legal barriers to employment often constrain effectiveness.

Cost variations across implementations highlight important tradeoffs. Per-household costs typically range from $1,000 to $2,000, which appears high compared to single-intervention programs but has proven cost-effective based on long-term impacts (Banerjee et al., 2015). Attempts to reduce costs by eliminating components or reducing their intensity have yielded mixed results—some streamlined versions maintain effectiveness, while others show diminished impacts, suggesting careful consideration of essential elements versus potential efficiencies (Sulaiman et al., 2016).

8.6.4. *Challenges and limitations*

Despite its demonstrated effectiveness, the graduation approach faces several implementation challenges and limitations.

Targeting complexity arises from the need to identify the ultra-poor accurately while excluding those who would not benefit from the specific package offered. Targeting errors can lead to either program inefficiency (including non-poor) or exclusion of vulnerable populations. Most implementations use multiple targeting methods, including community-based identification, asset and consumption verification, and sometimes psychological assessments of motivation (Hashemi & de Montesquiou, 2011).

Implementation quality significantly affects outcomes. The intensity, duration, and quality of coaching emerge as particularly critical, requiring well-trained frontline workers who can establish trust with participating households. In contexts with limited implementation capacity, maintaining this quality at scale becomes challenging. Evidence from Rwanda and Ghana suggests that high-quality implementation may be more important than specific design variations in determining program success (Sengupta, 2018).

Asset selection and market linkages present ongoing challenges. Identifying appropriate productive assets requires careful assessment of local markets, household capabilities, and vulnerability contexts. When programs select assets unsuited to local conditions or fail to establish adequate market connections, participants struggle to maintain livelihoods after program completion. These challenges increase in economically depressed regions where market opportunities are inherently limited.

Scalability concerns persist despite expansion. The comprehensive, high-touch nature of the graduation approach makes it more complex to administer than single-component programs. Government adoptions sometimes struggle to maintain the intensity and quality of original models, particularly the coaching component. Finding the right balance between fidelity to the proven model and pragmatic adaptations for scale remains an ongoing challenge (Devereux & Sabates-Wheeler, 2015).

8.6.5. Toward sustainable graduation

The graduation approach represents a promising model for addressing ultra-poverty, but its continued evolution focuses on several key questions.

Long-term sustainability of impacts remains partially answered. While follow-up studies in Bangladesh and India show impressive persistence of effects up to seven years post-intervention, even longer-term monitoring is needed to understand whether these programs truly break poverty traps permanently or require periodic reinforcement (Banerjee et al., 2016).

Integration with broader social protection systems presents both opportunities and challenges. Rather than standalone interventions, graduation approaches increasingly function as components within comprehensive social protection frameworks. This integration can enhance sustainability through institutional embeddedness but raises questions about maintaining programmatic integrity within larger bureaucratic structures (Roelen et al., 2017).

Cost-effectiveness versus alternatives deserves continued scrutiny. While benefit–cost analyses show strong returns, comparing graduation approaches against alternative uses of the same resources (such as unconditional transfers, infrastructure development, or market-strengthening interventions) remains important for optimal resource allocation in resource-constrained environments.

The graduation approach illustrates a broader trend in poverty reduction toward more comprehensive, sequenced interventions that address multiple constraints simultaneously. This trend acknowledges the complex, multidimensional nature of extreme poverty while recognizing that effective interventions must match this complexity with appropriately multifaceted responses.

8.7. Community-Driven Development: Empowering Local Action

Community-Driven Development (CDD) represents an approach to poverty reduction that empowers communities to identify, implement, and manage development initiatives. This model shifts decision-making power and resources to local communities, operating on the principle that community members best understand their own needs and priorities while building capacity for collective action.

8.7.1. Core principles and mechanisms

CDD approaches typically incorporate several defining features:

- **Community control** over key project decisions, including identification of priorities, resource allocation, implementation oversight, and sometimes management of funds
- **Participatory processes** designed to ensure inclusive decision-making, often with special provisions for marginalized groups
- **Transparency mechanisms** like public meetings, community notice boards, or social audits

- **Capacity building** to strengthen community organizations' ability to plan, implement, and sustain development initiatives
- **External facilitation and technical support** from government agencies or NGOs

These features aim to enhance project relevance, effectiveness, and sustainability while strengthening local governance and social capital that can support ongoing development beyond specific project interventions (Mansuri & Rao, 2013).

8.7.2. Evidence from major CDD programs

CDD has been implemented at significant scale across diverse contexts, with several flagship programs providing evidence about its effectiveness.

Indonesia's Kecamatan Development Program (KDP) and its successor, the National Program for Community Empowerment (PNPM), represent one of the world's largest and longest-running CDD initiatives. These programs provided block grants to thousands of villages for infrastructure, economic activities, and social services based on community priorities. Rigorous evaluations found that KDP/PNPM successfully delivered infrastructure at lower costs than comparable government projects, improved household welfare through increased consumption, and reduced poverty in participating communities (Voss, 2008). The program also showed positive impacts on social capital and local problem-solving capacity that persisted beyond the program period.

Afghanistan's National Solidarity Program (NSP) established democratically elected Community Development Councils (CDCs) and provided block grants for community-prioritized infrastructure. A randomized evaluation found that NSP improved access to drinking water, electricity, education, and healthcare, with corresponding gains in economic welfare and reduction in the acceptability of violence against women. However, effects on broader governance indicators and social cohesion were more limited, and institutional sustainability faced challenges after external support ended (Beath, Christia, & Enikolopov, 2013).

The Philippines' KALAHI-CIDSS program demonstrated positive impacts on basic service access, household consumption, and social capital measures including trust and collective action. Particularly notable were stronger positive effects in more remote, poorer municipalities, suggesting the approach successfully reached otherwise neglected areas. However, impacts on governance quality beyond the program showed limited evidence of transformation (Labonne & Chase, 2011).

8.7.3. Patterns in CDD effectiveness

Looking across these and other CDD evaluations, several consistent patterns emerge regarding where and how CDD delivers positive impacts.

Infrastructure and service delivery represent CDD's clearest successes. Communities generally select and successfully implement small infrastructure projects that respond to local priorities. These projects typically cost less than comparable contractor-built infrastructure and achieve reasonable technical quality, though with some variation based on technical complexity (Wong, 2012).

Economic welfare impacts are positive but modest in magnitude. Improved infrastructure and services contribute to increased household consumption and income, though the pathways vary by context and selected investments. Effects on the poorest households within communities are heterogeneous, depending partly on how inclusive decision-making processes actually function (Mansuri & Rao, 2013).

Social capital and collective action impacts show mixed results. Some programs demonstrate enhanced trust, increased participation in community organizations, and improved problem-solving capacity. However, these effects often remain localized to program activities rather than transforming broader community dynamics, and they may not persist after external support ends (Casey, Glennerster, & Miguel, 2012).

Governance transformation represents CDD's most ambitious and least consistently achieved objective. Despite creating parallel governance structures (like development committees), evidence for spillover effects on local government performance, accountability, or inclusiveness remains limited. Programs generally show stronger impacts on community capacity to implement projects than on deeper institutional change (Casey, 2018).

8.7.4. Design and implementation challenges

Despite its widespread adoption, CDD faces several persistent challenges that limit its effectiveness.

Elite capture poses an ongoing risk, as more powerful community members can dominate ostensibly participatory processes. Evidence on elite capture is mixed—while some studies find benefits disproportionately flowing to elites, others show relatively equitable distribution. Program design features including transparency requirements, quotas for marginalized groups, and effective facilitation can mitigate but not eliminate this risk (Platteau, 2004).

Participation costs for community members can be substantial, particularly for the poorest who can least afford to divert time from survival activities. When participation requires multiple meetings, travel to central locations, or contribution of labor, disadvantaged community members may self-exclude or participate nominally without meaningful influence (White, 1996).

Technical capacity constraints limit the range and quality of projects communities can effectively implement. While communities generally manage simple infrastructure well, more complex projects often require technical support that may be unavailable or insufficient. Balancing community control with necessary technical input represents an ongoing tension in program design (Wong, 2012).

Sustainability challenges emerge after external support ends. Many CDD initiatives struggle to maintain infrastructure, continue collective activities, or preserve institutional arrangements once project funding and facilitation conclude. Programs that establish linkages to local government systems, build maintenance capacity, and create sustainable financing mechanisms show better but still mixed success in this regard (Casey, 2018).

8.7.5. Evolving approaches to CDD

As evidence has accumulated on both strengths and limitations, CDD approaches have evolved in several directions.

Integration with government systems marks a shift from standalone projects toward embedding CDD principles within permanent governance structures. Examples include Indonesia's Village Law, which institutionalized participatory planning and budgeting processes within the regular village governance system, and the Philippines' effort to mainstream CDD principles in local government operations. This evolution aims to enhance sustainability while recognizing that parallel systems rarely transform mainstream governance (Wong & Guggenheim, 2018).

Adaptive implementation responds to recognition that standardized CDD "templates" often fail to accommodate local contexts. Newer approaches emphasize flexible facilitation responsive to community dynamics, tailored capacity building based on existing strengths and weaknesses, and iterative learning during implementation. Problem-Driven Iterative Adaptation (PDIA) represents one framework for this more context-sensitive approach (Andrews, Pritchett, & Woolcock, 2017).

Issue-specific applications have emerged in areas like disaster recovery, climate adaptation, and conflict resolution. These applications tailor CDD principles to specific challenges, recognizing that community agency matters particularly in contexts of uncertainty, rapid change, or contested legitimacy. Evidence from post-disaster contexts in Indonesia and the Philippines suggests that CDD mechanisms can effectively support community-led recovery processes when appropriately adapted (Thorburn, 2009).

CDD's evolution reflects both its demonstrated potential and recognized limitations. The approach continues to offer valuable mechanisms for enhancing community agency in development, but increasingly as part of broader, integrated strategies rather than as a standalone solution to poverty or governance challenges.

8.8. Sustainable Livelihood Approaches: Frameworks, Successes, and Failures

Many critics of CCTs point out that the poor need jobs now. Sustainable livelihood approaches represent a holistic framework for analyzing and addressing poverty through understanding how people combine various assets and capabilities to create survival strategies. These approaches gained prominence in the 1990s as a reaction to narrowly economic perspectives on poverty, emphasizing instead the diverse ways poor households construct livelihoods in response to their particular constraints and opportunities.

8.8.1. Conceptual framework

The sustainable livelihoods framework analyzes poverty through several interconnected components:

- **Livelihood assets** or "capitals" that households can draw upon, including
  - Human capital (skills, knowledge, health, labor capacity)
  - Social capital (networks, group membership, relationships of trust)
  - Natural capital (land, water, forests, biodiversity)
  - Physical capital (infrastructure, tools, equipment)
  - Financial capital (savings, credit, remittances, pensions)

- **Vulnerability context** including shocks (sudden disruptions like natural disasters or illness), trends (longer-term changes like environmental degradation or technological development), and seasonality (cyclical changes affecting livelihoods)
- **Transforming structures and processes** including institutions, policies, cultural norms, and power relations that shape how assets can be deployed
- **Livelihood strategies** that households adopt to convert assets into outcomes within their particular context
- **Livelihood outcomes** such as increased income, reduced vulnerability, improved food security, or enhanced wellbeing (Scoones, 1998; DFID, 1999)

This framework emphasizes that sustainable poverty reduction requires understanding the complex, dynamic ways households navigate constraints and opportunities, rather than focusing narrowly on single interventions or pathways.

8.8.2. Implementation approaches

The sustainable livelihoods framework has informed diverse implementation approaches.

Integrated rural development programs apply livelihood principles by addressing multiple constraints simultaneously. For example, the International Fund for Agricultural Development (IFAD) has implemented projects combining agricultural extension, market access, infrastructure development, and financial services based on participatory analysis of local livelihood systems. In Vietnam, such integrated approaches contributed to significant rural poverty reduction by enhancing multiple livelihood assets simultaneously (IFAD, 2015).

Natural resource management initiatives use livelihood perspectives to reconcile conservation with poverty reduction. In Namibia's community conservancy program, rural communities gained rights to manage wildlife while developing tourism enterprises and other sustainable natural resource-based livelihoods. This approach increased household incomes while improving conservation outcomes by aligning incentives (Hoole, 2010).

Market systems development (also called "Making Markets Work for the Poor" or M4P) focuses on transforming how market systems function for poor producers, workers, and consumers. These approaches analyze market constraints and intervene strategically to improve information flows, strengthen supportive services, or reform policies that disadvantage poor participants. In Bangladesh, Katalyst supported growth of agricultural input markets serving small farmers, leading to increased productivity and incomes across multiple crops (Taylor, 2013).

Climate resilience programs increasingly apply livelihood frameworks to strengthen communities' ability to withstand, adapt to, and recover from climate-related shocks. These approaches emphasize diversification of livelihood strategies, strengthening of community institutions, and sustainable management of natural resources. In Ethiopia, the Climate Resilient Green Economy strategy has supported watershed management, diversified agricultural practices, and alternative livelihoods to reduce vulnerability to increasing drought frequency (World Bank, 2016).

8.8.3. Successes in sustainable livelihood approaches

Evidence on livelihood approaches shows several consistent patterns of success.

Diversification benefits are well established. Households with more diverse livelihood strategies—spanning agricultural production, off-farm employment, microenterprises, and migration—typically demonstrate greater resilience to shocks and higher average incomes. In Tanzania, households that diversified from purely agricultural livelihoods into non-farm enterprises experienced both higher consumption and reduced vulnerability to drought (Ellis & Freeman, 2004).

Asset accumulation shows strong correlations with sustainable poverty reduction. Programs that help households build and protect productive assets demonstrate persistent poverty impacts. In Bangladesh, studies of BRAC's early livelihood-focused programs found that asset transfers combined with supportive services enabled sustained improvements in consumption and wellbeing (Hulme & Moore, 2010).

Collective action components often enhance effectiveness. When livelihood programs strengthen group-based action—through producer organizations, natural resource management committees, or savings groups—they typically achieve more sustained impacts. In Kenya, dairy farmer cooperatives supported through livelihood programs increased members' incomes while improving their bargaining position in value chains (Devaux et al., 2018).

Adaptability to shocks demonstrates the value of resilience-focused approaches. Programs emphasizing flexible, adaptive livelihood strategies rather than narrow productivity increases often show better outcomes during crises. During drought periods in Ethiopia, participants in livelihood programs emphasizing diversification and social capital showed fewer negative coping strategies like distress asset sales compared to non-participants (Sabates-Wheeler et al., 2013).

8.8.4. The challenge of employment-focused livelihood programs

Despite the conceptual soundness of sustainable livelihood approaches, many employment and livelihood programs have struggled in implementation. These difficulties highlight the gap between theoretical frameworks and practical application, especially when programs focus narrowly on employment or income generation without addressing broader livelihood constraints.

Mismatch between program offerings and labor market realities represents a fundamental challenge. Many employment initiatives train participants for jobs that do not exist locally in sufficient numbers or for skills that do not match employer requirements. In Kenya, a vocational training program showed minimal employment impacts partly because the training focused on saturated traditional sectors rather than emerging opportunities (Hicks et al., 2016).

Implementation by agencies lacking appropriate expertise undermines many programs. Social welfare ministries often lead poverty reduction efforts but may lack experience in labor market analysis, enterprise development, or sectoral expertise. Similarly, agricultural ministries may have technical knowledge but limited experience working with vulnerable populations or facilitating market linkages.

Supply-side focus neglects demand constraints that often limit employment opportunities. Programs frequently emphasize skills development without addressing limited job creation, market access barriers, or structural constraints in local economies. Even well-trained participants struggle to find employment when jobs are scarce or inaccessible (McKenzie, 2017).

Inadequate duration and intensity characterize many employment interventions. Short training courses or limited support periods often prove insufficient to overcome the multiple barriers facing the chronically poor. Programs typically achieve better results when providing longer-term, more intensive support, but these approaches cost more per beneficiary and reach fewer people (Blattman & Ralston, 2015).

8.8.5. Case study: The Philippines' Sustainable Livelihood Program

The Philippines' Sustainable Livelihood Program (SLP) illustrates the challenges faced in translating livelihood frameworks into effective interventions. Implemented by the Department of Social Welfare and Development (DSWD), this program aims to reduce poverty by providing employment facilitation and microenterprise development to poor households, including beneficiaries of the Pantawid Pamilyang Pilipino Program (4Ps) conditional cash transfer.

Multiple evaluations by the Philippine Institute for Development Studies (PIDS) have found limited impact on household income, employment rates, or sustainable poverty exits. Orbeta et al. (2021) found that while many participants reported receiving program inputs like skills training or capital seed funds, these rarely translated into sustainable livelihood improvements or measurable welfare gains. The program showed better results for microenterprise development than for employment facilitation, but even these impacts were modest and often temporary.

A comprehensive process evaluation by Ballesteros et al. (2021) identified significant implementation issues, including lengthy disbursement processes for microenterprise assistance, limited monitoring and enforcement of compliance conditions, and lack of coordination with local government units that could provide complementary support. These operational challenges severely constrained the program's effectiveness despite substantial resource allocation.

Further research by Tabuga and Cabaero (2021) on the SLP's role in helping 4Ps beneficiaries "graduate" from social assistance found that the program's approach to livelihood development lacked sufficient depth, duration, and customization to participants' specific constraints. The study concluded that while the concept of linking cash transfer beneficiaries to livelihood opportunities was sound, the specific implementation approach failed to address the multiple barriers facing chronically poor households.

Institutional capacity constraints significantly limited effectiveness. DSWD operations staff predominantly have backgrounds in social work rather than economic development, business management, or labor market analysis. This mismatch between staff expertise and program requirements led to challenges in providing appropriate technical guidance, forming effective market linkages, or adapting interventions to local economic contexts.

Mina and Reyes (2017) examined governance aspects of the SLP, finding that insufficient technical expertise among implementers led to inadequate business development support. Many participants received capital grants for simple retail enterprises in already saturated local markets, with limited assessment of market viability or growth potential. As a result, many microenterprises failed within the first year, representing poor return on substantial public investment.

Coordination challenges further constrained impact. Despite its name suggesting comprehensive livelihood development, the SLP operated largely in isolation from complementary initiatives in other agencies. Albert et al. (2025) identified over 50 employment programs, activities, and projects (PAPs) spread across the Philippine bureaucracy—including many in the Department of Agriculture—with minimal coordination or strategic alignment. This fragmentation led to duplication, gaps in service provision, and missed opportunities for synergy.

Implementation inconsistencies resulted from ambitious scale-up without proportionate capacity development. As the program expanded nationwide, quality and approach varied significantly across locations. Some areas emphasized quick distribution of capital grants with limited follow-up, while others focused on training without adequate market analysis or linkage to employment opportunities (Acosta & Velarde, 2015).

The experience of the SLP highlights a broader pattern observed in many employment-focused livelihood programs. Despite solid conceptual frameworks and genuine commitment to improving livelihoods, these initiatives often struggle with the complexity of implementation in resource-constrained environments.

8.8.6. The problem of fragmented employment and livelihood initiatives

The limitations of programs like the Philippines' SLP reflect broader patterns observed in employment and livelihood initiatives worldwide.

Fragmentation across multiple agencies undermines coherence and effectiveness. Many countries, like the Philippines with its more than 50 employment-related programs, spread interventions across numerous ministries and departments with limited coordination. This fragmentation creates confusion for potential beneficiaries, administrative inefficiencies, and missed opportunities for complementary support (Albert et al., 2025). A review of employment initiatives in Latin America similarly found that countries with more fragmented institutional arrangements typically achieved lower program effectiveness and higher implementation costs (Levy & Schady, 2013).

Lack of sustainable exit pathways from social assistance represents a persistent challenge. Employment programs often aim to help social assistance recipients "graduate" to self-reliance, but without addressing structural barriers or providing adequate transition support, these expectations frequently prove unrealistic. As observed with the Philippines' 4Ps beneficiaries attempting to transition through the SLP, abrupt exits from social assistance without established alternative livelihoods can lead to renewed vulnerability rather than sustainable graduation (Orbeta et al., 2021).

Poor targeting and sequencing limit effectiveness. Employment interventions often target beneficiaries based on poverty status or social assistance receipt rather than readiness for specific livelihood activities. Without proper assessment and sequencing, programs may attempt to promote entrepreneurship among participants who lack basic literacy or numeracy, or offer job placement to individuals facing multiple barriers beyond skills deficits (such as care responsibilities or transportation constraints) (Banerjee et al., 2015).

Inadequate monitoring and adaptation prevent learning and improvement. Many programs collect limited data on outcomes beyond immediate outputs (number of people trained, amount of capital distributed), making it difficult to assess the actual impact or identify implementation improvements. Without rigorous evaluation and feedback mechanisms, ineffective approaches persist despite limited results (McKenzie, 2017).

8.8.7. Promising improvements in livelihood programming

Despite these widespread challenges, evidence points toward several promising approaches that address common limitations in livelihood programs.

Market systems development addresses both supply and demand constraints by analyzing and strengthening the markets within which poor people operate. Rather than directly providing jobs or skills, these approaches identify and address key constraints in market systems that prevent inclusive growth. In Kenya, the Financial Sector Deepening program analyzed constraints preventing banks from serving small farmers, then helped develop appropriate financial products and delivery channels, ultimately reaching over 200,000 previously unbanked farmers (Sinha, Holmberg, & Thomas, 2013).

Graduation approaches show promise for transitioning safety net beneficiaries to sustainable livelihoods. As discussed earlier in this chapter, these sequenced, multi-faceted interventions address multiple constraints simultaneously through consumption support, asset transfers, skills training, savings promotion, and coaching. Recent efforts to adapt graduation approaches to the Philippines context show potential for more effective transitions from the 4Ps, though questions about cost-effectiveness and scalability remain (Acosta & Velarde, 2015; ADB, 2022).

Private sector partnerships leverage market demand and business expertise. Programs that engage employers directly in designing training curricula, providing internships, or committing to hiring graduates typically show better employment outcomes than supply-driven approaches. In the Dominican Republic, the Juventud y Empleo program combines classroom training with internships at private firms, showing significant positive impacts on formal employment and earnings (Ibarrarán et al., 2014).

Adaptive implementation allows programs to evolve based on learning. Rather than rigid adherence to predefined approaches, more successful employment initiatives incorporate structured learning and adaptation. In Bangladesh, BRAC's Ultra-Poor Graduation program continuously refined its model based on implementation experience and evaluation findings, significantly enhancing effectiveness and cost-efficiency over time (Bandiera et al., 2017).

8.8.8. Key lessons from livelihood program experiences

The mixed record of sustainable livelihood approaches in practice yields several important lessons for future poverty reduction efforts.

Institutional capacity matters as much as program design. Even well-conceived interventions fail when implementing agencies lack appropriate expertise, systems, or resources. Rather than assigning programs to agencies based solely on their poverty reduction mandate (like welfare departments), successful implementation requires matching program requirements with institutional capabilities or investing significantly in capacity development.

Economic analysis must inform program design to ensure interventions address actual constraints and opportunities. Market assessments, value chain analyses, and labor market studies should precede rather than follow program design, ensuring skills development and enterprise promotion align with economic realities.

Coordination mechanisms need strengthening to overcome fragmentation. Rather than adding more standalone programs, governments should rationalize existing initiatives, strengthen coordination platforms, and develop integrated implementation strategies that leverage complementary strengths across agencies.

Realistic expectations about graduation timeframes and pathways are essential. Sustainable transitions from social assistance to self-reliance typically require longer timeframes and more comprehensive support than many programs provide. Setting realistic expectations and designing appropriate transition pathways prevent premature exits that lead to renewed vulnerability.

Context-specific adaptations of conceptual frameworks are necessary for effectiveness. While sustainable livelihood frameworks provide valuable organizing principles, their application must be tailored to specific contexts, considering local economic structures, cultural factors, institutional capacities, and livelihood patterns.

These lessons highlight that while sustainable livelihood approaches offer a compelling conceptual framework for understanding and addressing poverty, translating this framework into effective interventions requires careful attention to implementation realities. When well-designed and implemented, livelihood approaches can create sustainable pathways out of poverty by building assets, capabilities, and resilience. However, narrowly conceived employment or enterprise promotion programs that neglect broader livelihood constraints frequently fall short of their objectives.

The accumulated evidence on sustainable livelihood approaches suggests that their effectiveness depends not on whether they adopt the terminology or conceptual framework of sustainable livelihoods but on whether they successfully address the multiple, interconnected constraints that poor households face in constructing resilient, dignified livelihoods in their specific contexts.

8.9. Integrated Social Protection Systems: Building Comprehensive Approaches

As evidence accumulates on various intervention types, many countries have moved toward building integrated social protection systems that combine multiple programs within coherent frameworks. These systems aim to address different dimensions of poverty and vulnerability while creating synergies between previously isolated interventions.

8.9.1. The systems approach

Integrated social protection systems typically encompass multiple program types organized within a coherent architecture:

- **Social assistance** including cash transfers, in-kind support, and subsidies
- **Social insurance** covering health, unemployment, disability, and old age
- **Labor market interventions** such as skills training, employment services, and wage subsidies
- **Social care services** for vulnerable populations including children, elderly, and people with disabilities
- **Complementary programs** in health, education, nutrition, and livelihoods

Beyond merely combining these programs, integrated systems develop shared infrastructure for key functions including

- **Identification** through unified social registries or integrated beneficiary databases
- **Targeting** using common assessment methods across programs
- **Payment mechanisms** that efficiently deliver benefits through shared platforms
- **Grievance redress** providing consistent channels for addressing concerns
- **Monitoring and evaluation** tracking outcomes across the system (World Bank, 2012)

8.9.2. Country experiences and innovations

Several countries have made significant progress toward integrated systems, though with varying approaches reflecting their contexts.

Brazil's unified social registry (Cadastro Único) demonstrates the potential of integrated information systems. This registry collects standardized household information used by over 20 social programs, enabling better coordination, reduced duplication, and more precise targeting. Integration has both improved efficiency—reducing administrative costs by approximately 30 percent —and enhanced effectiveness by facilitating complementary services for vulnerable households (Lindert et al., 2020).

Chile's Seguridades y Oportunidades represents a pioneering "social protection as a system" approach. Rather than standalone programs, Chile implements an integrated framework where households receive personalized combinations of transfers, subsidies, preferential access to services, and psychosocial support based on a comprehensive diagnosis of their specific vulnerabilities. This approach recognizes that different households require different intervention packages to address their particular constraints (Robles, 2012).

Ghana's LEAP (Livelihood Empowerment Against Poverty) program exemplifies "cash plus" approaches that leverage core cash transfers as platforms for additional services. LEAP beneficiaries receive not only cash transfers but also free health insurance enrollment, linkages to complementary programs, and financial inclusion services. Evaluations show that this integrated approach achieves stronger impacts on multiple welfare dimensions than cash transfers alone would produce (Banerjee et al., 2017).

Pakistan's Benazir Income Support Programme (BISP) demonstrates evolution from a single program toward a system. Initially a straightforward cash transfer, BISP has progressively added complementary components including health insurance (Sehat Satoon), education stipends (Waseela-e-Taleem), skills training, and graduation initiatives (Waseela-e-Rozgar). This layered approach aims to address both immediate needs and underlying causes of poverty (Cheema et al., 2016).

8.9.3. *Impacts of systems approaches*

Evidence on integrated systems' impacts is emerging, though attribution challenges remain given the complex nature of these approaches.

Coverage expansion represents a clear benefit of systems approaches. By linking previously isolated programs, countries identify coverage gaps and reduce exclusion errors. Mexico's integrated system increased overall coverage of social protection from approximately 35 percent to over 70 percent of the population, with particular gains among previously excluded groups like informal workers (Levy, 2008).

Crisis responsiveness improves significantly with integrated systems. Countries with unified registries and payment systems can rapidly expand coverage or increase benefit levels during shocks. During the COVID-19 pandemic, Brazil expanded cash transfers to millions of additional households in weeks rather than months or years, leveraging its integrated infrastructure (Gentilini et al., 2022).

Graduation from poverty may accelerate through coordination of complementary interventions. When systems effectively sequence and combine protective, preventive, and promotional functions, they create stronger pathways out of poverty. Rwanda's Vision 2020 Umurenge Programme (VUP) demonstrates how integrating public works, direct support, financial services, and skills training created more sustained improvements than similar expenditure on isolated interventions (Lavers, 2019).

Fiscal efficiency often improves through reduced duplication, administrative streamlining, and better targeting. Indonesia's reform of its social protection system, including replacement of inefficient fuel subsidies with targeted programs, generated both fiscal savings and improved poverty impacts (World Bank, 2017).

8.9.4. Implementation challenges

Building integrated social protection systems presents substantial implementation challenges.

Institutional coordination requires overcoming bureaucratic fragmentation and resistance. Ministries accustomed to operating independently may resist integration, particularly when it affects control over resources or threatens established practices. Countries have addressed this through various mechanisms including high-level coordination bodies, legal frameworks mandating cooperation, and shared performance metrics that incentivize collaboration (Robalino et al., 2012).

Information systems integration presents technical complexity beyond simple database consolidation. Creating truly interoperable systems that maintain data quality, privacy, and security while serving multiple programs' needs requires substantial investment and capacity. Successful implementations typically phase integration gradually, beginning with core functions and expanding incrementally (Barca, 2017).

Adaptive capacity remains challenging, as larger integrated systems may become less nimble than smaller, focused programs. Maintaining responsiveness to changing needs while achieving integration benefits requires deliberate design for adaptation, including decentralized decision-making capabilities and regular system reviews (Pritchett, Samji, & Hammer, 2013).

Sustainable financing for comprehensive systems presents ongoing challenges, particularly in lower-income contexts. Integration can improve efficiency but does not eliminate the need for adequate resources. Some countries have mobilized domestic resources through tax reforms, natural resource revenues, or reduction of inefficient subsidies, while others continue to rely partly on donor funding with associated sustainability concerns (Ortiz, Cummins, & Karunanethy, 2017).

8.9.5. Emerging directions

The evolution of social protection systems continues, with several emerging trends.

Shock-responsive social protection designs systems explicitly for flexibility during crises. This approach builds adaptive features into regular programs—including scalable targeting criteria, flexible payment mechanisms, and surge capacity—enabling rapid response to disasters, economic shocks, or conflicts. Kenya's Hunger Safety Net Programme exemplifies this approach, with pre-established protocols for rapidly expanding coverage during droughts (OPM, 2017).

Universal Basic Income (UBI) proposals represent a radical simplification approach to integration challenges. By providing universal, unconditional payments, UBI could potentially reduce administrative complexity while addressing coverage gaps inherent in targeted systems. Limited experiments in India, Kenya, and Finland have shown promising results on wellbeing outcomes, though debate continues about fiscal feasibility at scale (Banerjee et al., 2019).

Technology-enabled service delivery increasingly enables more adaptive, responsive systems. Biometric identification, mobile payments, digital case management, and predictive analytics create opportunities for more personalized, efficient services. India's JAM Trinity (Jan Dhan bank accounts, Aadhaar identification, and Mobile technology) has enabled dramatic expansion of financial inclusion and government-to-person payments, though not without implementation challenges and equity concerns (D'Silva et al., 2019).

Rights-based frameworks increasingly complement technical approaches to integration. Several countries have enshrined social protection rights in constitutions or legislation, establishing entitlements that transcend individual programs or political cycles. South Africa's constitutional right to social security has provided a foundation for progressive expansion of its social protection system despite changing political leadership (Liebenberg, 2007).

The trend toward integrated social protection systems represents both an opportunity and a challenge for poverty reduction efforts. When well implemented, these systems can provide more comprehensive, efficient, and sustainable support than fragmented interventions. However, integration itself does not guarantee effectiveness—systems must be designed with careful attention to context, capacity, and the specific mechanisms through which integration creates value for the poor.

8.10. Conclusion: Toward Sustainable Poverty Reduction

Our examination of diverse poverty reduction approaches across contexts yields several overarching insights about what works, what does not, and what determines sustainability in poverty reduction efforts.

8.10.1. *Cross-cutting success factors*

Across intervention types, several factors consistently correlate with more effective, sustainable poverty reduction.

Addressing multiple constraints typically yields stronger impacts than narrow interventions. Poor households face interlinked challenges—from limited assets to inadequate services to weak markets to social exclusion—that rarely yield to single-dimension solutions. Programs that address complementary constraints, either through integrated designs or through effective coordination with other interventions, consistently show more sustained impacts (Banerjee et al., 2015).

Context-appropriate design proves essential for effectiveness. Interventions transplanted from one setting to another without adequate adaptation frequently underperform or fail entirely. Successful poverty reduction requires understanding local economic structures, social dynamics, institutional capacities, and specific constraints facing the poor in each context. This does not preclude learning from global evidence but requires thoughtful translation rather than mechanical replication (Pritchett & Woolcock, 2004).

Implementation quality often matters more than design elegance. Well-designed programs implemented poorly consistently underperform relative to moderately designed programs implemented well. Key aspects of implementation quality include frontline worker capacity, adequate supervision, functioning monitoring systems, and adaptive management that responds to emerging challenges. The gap between design and implementation partially explains why interventions that show strong impacts in carefully managed pilots often demonstrate weaker results at scale (Bold et al., 2013).

Participant agency and engagement correlate strongly with sustainable outcomes. When interventions treat poor people as passive recipients rather than active agents in their own development, sustainability typically suffers. Programs that incorporate participant voice in design, implementation, and evaluation—while building capabilities for ongoing initiative—show more enduring impacts after external support ends (Chambers, 1997).

8.10.2. Common Pitfalls

Poverty reduction efforts frequently encounter predictable pitfalls that undermine effectiveness and sustainability.

Insufficient attention to underlying causes limits long-term impact. Many interventions address symptoms of poverty (low consumption, limited service access) without adequately engaging deeper structural causes (unequal power relations, exclusionary institutions, weak governance). While ameliorating immediate suffering matters, sustainable reduction in poverty prevalence requires addressing these underlying drivers (Hickey et al., 2015).

Unrealistic timeframes set programs up for failure or premature abandonment. Sustainable change in complex social and economic systems typically requires years or decades, not months or single project cycles. Programs expecting—or promising—rapid transformation often face disappointed stakeholders, discontinued funding, or pressure to demonstrate success prematurely through unsustainable means (Woolcock, 2009).

Inadequate exit strategies lead to dependency or collapse when external support ends. Effective poverty reduction requires planning for sustainability from the outset, including developing local capacities, establishing sustainable financing mechanisms, and gradually transferring responsibilities to permanent institutions. Programs designed as temporary interventions without clear pathways to self-sustaining operation frequently see gains erode after closure (Rogers & Macias, 2004).

Failure to learn and adapt wastes opportunities for improvement. The most effective poverty reduction efforts incorporate structured learning processes—collecting relevant data, analyzing implementation challenges, and adjusting approaches based on evidence. Programs that rigidly follow initial designs despite emerging evidence about what works in their specific contexts frequently underperform (Andrews, Pritchett, & Woolcock, 2017).

8.10.3. The sustainability imperative

Sustainable poverty reduction requires moving beyond short-term impacts to create lasting change. This sustainability encompasses multiple dimensions.

Financial sustainability concerns whether interventions can be funded over time without excessive reliance on temporary external resources. Approaches to enhance financial sustainability include

- Developing domestic revenue streams through taxation or user fees
- Embedding programs in public budgets with political support
- Creating self-financing mechanisms through revolving funds or market integration
- Efficiently targeting limited resources to maximize impact per dollar spent

Institutional sustainability addresses whether capacities and systems exist to maintain interventions beyond initial implementation. Key aspects include

- Building permanent organizational homes for successful approaches
- Developing human resources needed for ongoing operation
- Creating appropriate governance and accountability mechanisms

- Establishing policy frameworks that institutionalize effective practices

Environmental sustainability ensures that poverty reduction does not undermine the natural resource base on which many poor households depend. Sustainable approaches

- Promote natural resource management that balances current use with future availability
- Consider climate impacts and adaptation needs in intervention design
- Address pollution and environmental health hazards that disproportionately affect the poor
- Build resilience to environmental shocks and stresses

Social sustainability concerns whether poverty reduction efforts contribute to inclusive, cohesive communities rather than exacerbating divisions. Socially sustainable approaches

- Design targeting and delivery mechanisms that minimize stigma or division
- Strengthen rather than displace community mutual support systems
- Promote equitable participation of marginalized groups
- Address social exclusion alongside economic deprivation

8.10.4. Future directions

The field of poverty reduction continues to evolve, with several promising directions for enhanced effectiveness and sustainability.

Adaptive, learning-oriented implementation represents a shift from rigid planning toward iterative approaches that respond to emerging evidence and changing contexts. Methods like Problem-Driven Iterative Adaptation (PDIA) enable programs to evolve based on what actually works in specific contexts rather than assuming solutions can be completely specified in advance (Andrews, Pritchett, & Woolcock, 2017).

Locally led development approaches rebalance power between external actors and local communities. These approaches recognize that sustainable change requires local ownership, contextual knowledge, and legitimate institutions. Rather than imposing predetermined solutions, they support communities and local organizations to define problems, develop responses, and lead implementation with external actors in supporting roles (Booth & Unsworth, 2014).

Systems thinking increasingly complements conventional program-focused approaches. Rather than viewing poverty through discrete interventions, systems perspectives examine how multiple actors, institutions, and processes interact to create or reduce poverty. This approach emphasizes understanding leverage points where relatively modest interventions can catalyze broader system change, potentially achieving greater impact with limited resources (Ramalingam et al., 2019).

Digital technologies continue transforming implementation possibilities. From biometric identification systems that reduce leakage to mobile platforms that expand financial access to data analytics that enhance targeting precision, technology offers tools to make interventions more efficient, responsive, and accessible. However, realizing this potential requires addressing both technical challenges and equity concerns to ensure digital approaches do not exacerbate existing inequalities (Gelb & Metz, 2018).

Climate-informed poverty reduction has become imperative as environmental changes increasingly affect the poor. Future approaches must incorporate climate adaptation and resilience-building alongside traditional poverty reduction strategies. This includes both protecting gains against climate threats and ensuring that poverty reduction efforts themselves contribute to environmental sustainability rather than exacerbating degradation (Hallegatte et al., 2016).

8.10.5. *Final reflections*

The evidence reviewed throughout this chapter suggests that poverty reduction is possible but challenging, requiring both technical knowledge about effective interventions and political will to implement them sustainably. Several fundamental insights emerge.

First, context matters tremendously. The effectiveness of any intervention depends not just on its technical design but also on how well it aligns with local economic structures, social dynamics, institutional capacities, and the specific barriers facing poor people in particular places. This does not mean abandoning generalizable knowledge but rather applying it thoughtfully with attention to local realities.

Second, quality implementation frequently determines outcomes more than program design. Well-designed programs implemented poorly consistently underperform relative to simpler interventions executed well. Building implementation capacity—from frontline service delivery to adaptive management—represents a crucial investment for sustainable poverty reduction.

Third, addressing multiple, interconnected constraints typically yields stronger results than narrowly targeted interventions. The most successful poverty reduction efforts recognize and respond to the multidimensional nature of poverty, whether through integrated program designs or effective coordination across complementary interventions.

Fourth, sustainability requires deliberate planning from the outset. Programs designed as temporary interventions without clear pathways to self-sustaining operation frequently see gains erode after external support ends. Building local ownership, capacity, and sustainable financing mechanisms must be central to program design, not afterthoughts.

Finally, the most effective approaches treat poor people as active agents rather than passive recipients. Programs that respect poor people's knowledge, build on their capabilities, and strengthen their agency consistently demonstrate more sustainable impacts than those imposed from above without meaningful participation.

The search for sustainable poverty reduction continues, with both encouraging success stories and cautionary tales of approaches that fell short of their promise. Moving forward requires continued learning, adaptation, and commitment to evidence-based approaches that address poverty's complex, multidimensional nature. By building on what works while avoiding common pitfalls, the global community can make significant progress toward the ambitious goal of ending poverty in all its forms.

References

Acosta, P. A., & Velarde, R. (2015). *An update of the Philippine conditional cash transfer's implementation performance* (Philippines Social Protection Note No. 8). World Bank.

Asian Development Bank (ADB). (2022). *Transitioning from conditional cash transfers to sustainable livelihoods in the Philippines: Lessons from BRAC's graduation approach*. Manila: ADB.

Albert, J. R. G., Genio, F. G. F., & Crismo, J. J. L. G. (2025). *Assessing the implementation of joint programming in government social protection and economic inclusion interventions in the Philippines* (Discussion Paper No. 2025-02). Philippine Institute for Development Studies.

Alkire, S., Foster, J., Seth, S., Santos, M. E., Roche, J. M., & Ballon, P. (2015). *Multidimensional poverty measurement and analysis*. Oxford University Press.

Andrews, M., Pritchett, L., & Woolcock, M. (2017). *Building state capability: Evidence, analysis, action*. Oxford University Press.

Attanasio, O., Fitzsimons, E., Gomez, A., Gutiérrez, M. I., Meghir, C., & Mesnard, A. (2010). Children's schooling and work in the presence of a conditional cash transfer program in rural Colombia. *Economic Development and Cultural Change, 58*(2), 181–210.

Baird, S., Ferreira, F. H., Özler, B., & Woolcock, M. (2013). Relative effectiveness of conditional and unconditional cash transfers for schooling outcomes in developing countries: A systematic review. *Campbell Systematic Reviews, 9*(1), 1–124.

Ballesteros, M. M., Ancheta, J., Ramos, T. P., Ancheta, J. R. P., Babierra, A. L., Balmez, M. A. D., & Gonzales, K. G. (2021). *An assessment of the Sustainable Livelihood Program – Employment Facilitation Process* (PIDS

Discussion Paper Series No. 2021-35). Philippine Institute for Development Studies.

Bandiera, O., Burgess, R., Das, N., Gulesci, S., Rasul, I., & Sulaiman, M. (2017). Labor markets and poverty in village economies. *The Quarterly Journal of Economics, 132*(2), 811–870.

Banerjee, A., Duflo, E., Goldberg, N., Karlan, D., Osei, R., Parienté, W., Shapiro, J., Thuysbaert, B., & Udry, C. (2015). A multifaceted program causes lasting progress for the very poor: Evidence from six countries. *Science, 348*(6236), 1260799.

Banerjee, A., Duflo, E., & Sharma, G. (2019). Universal basic income in the developing world. *Annual Review of Economics, 11*, 959–983.

Banerjee, A., Karlan, D., & Zinman, J. (2015). Six randomized evaluations of microcredit: Introduction and further steps. *American Economic Journal: Applied Economics, 7*(1), 1–21.

Banerjee, A., Duflo, E., Chattopadhyay, R., & Shapiro, J. (2016). The long term impacts of a "Graduation" program: Evidence from West Bengal [Working paper]. Massachusetts Institute of Technology.

Banerjee, A., Duflo, E., Imbert, C., Mathew, S., & Pande, R. (2017). E-governance, accountability, and leakage in public programs: Experimental evidence from a financial management reform in India (NBER Working Paper No. 22803). NBER.

Barca, V. (2017). Integrating data and information management for social protection: Social registries and integrated beneficiary registries. Commonwealth of Australia, Department of Foreign Affairs and Trade.

Barrett, C. B., & Carter, M. R. (2010). The power and pitfalls of experiments in development economics: Some non-random reflections. *Applied Economic Perspectives and Policy, 32*(4), 515–548.

Bastagli, F., Hagen-Zanker, J., Harman, L., Barca, V., Sturge, G., Schmidt, T., & Pellerano, L. (2016). *Cash transfers: What does the evidence say? A rigorous review of programme impact and of the role of design and implementation features*. Overseas Development Institute.

Beath, A., Christia, F., & Enikolopov, R. (2013). Randomized impact evaluation of Afghanistan's National Solidarity Programme (World Bank Report No. 81107).

Berhane, G., Gilligan, D. O., Hoddinott, J., Kumar, N., & Taffesse, A. S. (2014). Can social protection work in Africa? The impact of Ethiopia's Productive Safety Net Programme. *Economic Development and Cultural Change, 63*(1), 1–26.

Blattman, C., & Ralston, L. (2015). Generating employment in poor and fragile states: Evidence from labor market and entrepreneurship programs [Working paper]. University of Chicago.

Bold, T., Kimenyi, M., Mwabu, G., Ng'ang'a, A., & Sandefur, J. (2013). Scaling up what works: Experimental evidence on external validity in Kenyan education (Center for Global Development Working Paper No. 321).

Booth, D., & Unsworth, S. (2014). *Politically smart, locally led development.* Overseas Development Institute.

Casey, K. (2018). Radical decentralization: Does community-driven development work? *Annual Review of Economics, 10*, 139–163.

Casey, K., Glennerster, R., & Miguel, E. (2012). Reshaping institutions: Evidence on aid impacts using a preanalysis plan. *The Quarterly Journal of Economics, 127*(4), 1755–1812.

Chambers, R. (1997). *Whose reality counts? Putting the first last.* Intermediate Technology Publications.

Cheema, I., Hunt, S., Jakobsen, M., Marzi, M., O'Leary, S., & Pellerano, L. (2016). *Benazir Income Support Programme: Final impact evaluation report.* Oxford Policy Management.

Coady, D., Grosh, M., & Hoddinott, J. (2004). Targeting of transfers in developing countries: Review of lessons and experience. World Bank.

Collins, D., Morduch, J., Rutherford, S., & Ruthven, O. (2009). *Portfolios of the poor: How the world's poor live on $2 a day.* Princeton University Press.

Devereux, S., & Sabates-Wheeler, R. (2015). Graduating from social protection? Editorial introduction. *IDS Bulletin, 46*(2), 1–12.

Devaux, A., Torero, M., Donovan, J., & Horton, D. E. (2018). Agricultural innovation and inclusive value-chain development: A review. *Journal of Agribusiness in Developing and Emerging Economies, 8*(1), 99–123.

Department for International Development (DFID). (1999). *Sustainable livelihoods guidance sheets.* London: DFID.

D'Silva, J., Sambasivan, D., Steenson, M., & Kulkarni, P. (2019). Marketing for financial inclusion: JAM Trinity. In A. Sundaram & P. Mukhopadhyay (Eds.), *Modernity, modernization, and globalization* (pp. 21–24). Cambridge University Press.

Duflo, E. (2003). Grandmothers and granddaughters: Old-age pensions and intrahousehold allocation in South Africa. *The World Bank Economic Review, 17*(1), 1–25.

Duflo, E. (2012). Women empowerment and economic development. *Journal of Economic Literature, 50*(4), 1051–1079.

Duflo, E., Glennerster, R., & Kremer, M. (2007). Using randomization in development economics research: A toolkit. In *Handbook of Development Economics* (Vol. 4, pp. 3895–3962).

Dupas, P., & Robinson, J. (2013). Savings constraints and microenterprise development: Evidence from a field experiment in Kenya. *American Economic Journal: Applied Economics, 5*(1), 163–192.

Ellis, F., & Freeman, H. A. (2004). Rural livelihoods and poverty reduction strategies in four African countries. *Journal of Development Studies, 40*(4), 1–30.

Escobal, J., & Ponce, C. (2016). Combining social protection with economic opportunities in rural Peru: Haku Wiñay. *Policy in Focus, 12*(2), 22–25.

Evans, D. K., & Popova, A. (2017). Cash transfers and temptation goods. *Economic Development and Cultural Change, 65*(2), 189–221.

Fiszbein, A., & Schady, N. R. (2009). *Conditional cash transfers: Reducing present and future poverty*. World Bank Publications.

Gelb, A., & Metz, A. D. (2018). *Identification revolution: Can digital ID be harnessed for development?* Center for Global Development.

Gentilini, U., Almenfi, M., Blomquist, J., Dale, P., De la Flor Giuffra, L., Desai, V., … & Weber, M. (2022). Social protection and jobs responses to COVID-19: A real-time review of country measures. World Bank.

Gertler, P. (2004). Do conditional cash transfers improve child health? Evidence from PROGRESA's control randomized experiment. *American Economic Review, 94*(2), 336–341.

Gertler, P. J., Martinez, S., Premand, P., Rawlings, L. B., & Vermeersch, C. M. (2016). *Impact evaluation in practice*. World Bank Publications.

Hallegatte, S., Bangalore, M., Bonzanigo, L., Fay, M., Kane, T., Narloch, U., … & Vogt-Schilb, A. (2016). *Shock waves: Managing the impacts of climate change on poverty*. World Bank Publications.

Handa, S., Natali, L., Seidenfeld, D., Tembo, G., & Davis, B. (2018). Can unconditional cash transfers raise long-term living standards? Evidence from Zambia. *Journal of Development Economics, 133*, 42–65.

Hashemi, S. M., & de Montesquiou, A. (2011). Reaching the poorest: Lessons from the graduation model. *Focus Note, 69*, 1–16.

Haushofer, J., & Shapiro, J. (2016). The short-term impact of unconditional cash transfers to the poor: Experimental evidence from Kenya. *The Quarterly Journal of Economics, 131*(4), 1973–2042.

Hickey, S., Sen, K., & Bukenya, B. (Eds.). (2015). *The politics of inclusive development: Interrogating the evidence*. Oxford University Press.

Hoole, A. F. (2010). Place-power-prognosis: Community-based conservation, partnerships, and ecotourism enterprises in Namibia. *International Journal of the Commons, 4*(1), 78–99.

Hulme, D., & Moore, K. (2010). Thinking small and the understanding of poverty: Maymana and Mofizul's story. *Journal of Human Development and Capabilities, 11*(2), 259–273.

Ibarraran, P., Ripani, L., Taboada, B., Villa, J. M., & Garcia, B. (2014). Life skills, employability and training for disadvantaged youth: Evidence from a randomized evaluation design. *IZA Journal of Labor & Development, 3*, 10. https://doi.org/10.1186/2193-9020-3-10

International Fund for Agricultural Development (IFAD). (2015). *IFAD's operational framework for scaling up results*. Rome: IFAD.

Kabeer, N. (2005). Is microfinance a 'magic bullet' for women's empowerment? Analysis of findings from South Asia. *Economic and Political Weekly, 40*(44/45), 4709–4718.

Kanbur, R., & Vines, D. (2000). The World Bank and poverty reduction: Past, present and future. In C. Gilbert & D. Vines (Eds.), *The World Bank: Structure and policies* (pp. 87–107). Cambridge University Press.

Karlan, D., Osei, R., Osei-Akoto, I., & Udry, C. (2014). Agricultural decisions after relaxing credit and risk constraints. *The Quarterly Journal of Economics, 129*(2), 597–652.

Labonne, J., & Chase, R. S. (2011). Do community-driven development projects enhance social capital? Evidence from the Philippines. *Journal of Development Economics, 96*(2), 348–358.

Lavers, T. (2019). Social protection in an aspiring 'developmental state': The political drivers of Ethiopia's PSNP. *African Affairs, 118*(473), 646–671.

Levy, S. (2008). *Good intentions, bad outcomes: Social policy, informality, and economic growth in Mexico*. Brookings Institution Press.

Levy, S., & Schady, N. (2013). Latin America's social policy challenge: Education, social insurance, redistribution. *Journal of Economic Perspectives, 27*(2), 193–218. https://doi.org/10.1257/jep.27.2.193

Liebenberg, S. (2007). The judicial enforcement of social security rights in South Africa. In E. Riedel (Ed.), *Social security as a human right* (pp. 69–90). Springer.

Lindert, K., Karippacheril, T. G., Caillava, I. R., & Chávez, K. (2020). *Sourcebook on the foundations of social protection delivery systems*. World Bank Publications.

Mansuri, G., & Rao, V. (2013). *Localizing development: Does participation work?* World Bank Publications.

McKenzie, D. (2017). How effective are active labor market policies in developing countries? A critical review of recent evidence. *The World Bank Research Observer, 32*(2), 127–154.

Miguel, E., & Kremer, M. (2004). Worms: Identifying impacts on education and health in the presence of treatment externalities. *Econometrica, 72*(1), 159–217.

Mina, C. D., & Reyes, C. M. (2017). Poverty reduction through the Sustainable Livelihood Program of the Philippine government. *Philippine Institute for Development StudiesPolicy Notes, 2017-22.*

Orbeta, A. C., Jr., Acosta, P. A., Chua, K. K. Y., Manasan, R. G., Cuenca, J. S., Chi, G. C. E., & Padua, P. P. B. (2021). *Process evaluation of the Sustainable Livelihood Program* (Philippine Institute for Development Studies Discussion Paper Series No. 2021-36).

Ortiz, I., Cummins, M., & Karunanethy, K. (2017). *Fiscal space for social protection and the SDGs: Options to expand social investments in 187 countries* (ILO–UNICEF–UN Women Working Paper).

Oxford Policy Management (OPM). (2017). *Shock-responsive social protection systems research: Case study—Kenya's Hunger Safety Net Programme.* Oxford: OPM.

Parker, S. W., & Todd, P. E. (2017). Conditional cash transfers: The case of Progresa/Oportunidades. *Journal of Economic Literature, 55*(3), 866–915.

Platteau, J. P. (2004). Monitoring elite capture in community-driven development. *Development and Change, 35*(2), 223–246.

Pritchett, L., Samji, S., & Hammer, J. (2013). It's all about MeE: Using structured experiential learning ("e") to crawl the design space. *Center for Global Development Working Paper No. 322.*

Pritchett, L., & Woolcock, M. (2004). Solutions when the solution is the problem: Arraying the disarray in development. *World Development, 32*(2), 191–212.

Ramalingam, B., Wild, L., & Buffardi, A. L. (2019). *Making adaptive rigour work: Principles and practices for strengthening monitoring, evaluation and learning for adaptive management.* ODI Briefing Note.

Ravallion, M. (2009). Should the randomistas rule? *The Economists' Voice, 6*(2)

Robalino, D. A., Rawlings, L., & Walker, I. (2012). *Building social protection and labor systems: Concepts and operational implications* (Social Protection and Labor Discussion Paper No. 1202).

Robles, C. (2012). Together: The social protection system Chile Solidario. In S. Cecchini & R. Martínez (Eds.), *Inclusive social protection in Latin*

America: A comprehensive, rights-based approach (pp. 93–121). Economic Commission for Latin America and the Caribbean.

Roelen, K., Devereux, S., Kebede, D., & Ulrichs, M. (2017). *Cash 'plus'—Integrated nutrition and social cash transfer (IN-SCT) pilot in Ethiopia: Perceptions and feedback from clients and service providers*. Institute of Development Studies.

Rogers, B. L., & Macias, K. E. (2004). *Program graduation and exit strategies: Title II program experiences and related research*. Food and Nutrition Technical Assistance Project, Academy for Educational Development.

Rosenberg, R., Gaul, S., Ford, W., & Tomilova, O. (2013). Microcredit interest rates and their determinants: 2004–2011. In *World Bank (Ed.), Microfinance 3.0* (pp. 69–104). Springer.

Sabates-Wheeler, R., Lind, J., & Hoddinott, J. (2013). Implementing social protection in agro-pastoralist and pastoralist areas: How local distribution structures moderate PSNP outcomes in Ethiopia. *World Development, 50*, 1–12.

Scoones, I. (1998). *Sustainable rural livelihoods: A framework for analysis* (Institute of Development Studies Working Paper No. 72).

Sengupta, A. (2018). Pathways out of the Productive Safety Net Programme: Lessons from graduation pilots in Ethiopia and Ghana. *Enterprise Development and Microfinance, 29*(1), 55–71.

Sinha, S., Holmberg, J., & Thomas, M. (2013). *What works for market development: A review of the evidence*. UKaid, Sida, and SDC.

Soares, F. V., Ribas, R. P., & Osório, R. G. (2010). Evaluating the impact of Brazil's Bolsa Família: Cash transfer programs in comparative perspective. *Latin American Research Review, 45*(2), 173–190.

Subbarao, K., Del Ninno, C., Andrews, C., & Rodríguez-Alas, C. (2013). *Public works as a safety net: Design, evidence, and implementation*. World Bank Publications.

Sulaiman, M., Goldberg, N., Karlan, D., & de Montesquiou, A. (2016). Eliminating extreme poverty: Comparing the cost-effectiveness of livelihood, cash transfer, and graduation approaches. *Access to Finance Forum, 11*.

Suri, T., & Jack, W. (2016). The long-run poverty and gender impacts of mobile money. *Science, 354*(6317), 1288–1292.

Tabuga, A. D., & Cabaero, J. F. (2021). *Pantawid Pamilyang Pilipino Program: An assessment of graduation pathways* (PIDS Discussion Paper Series No. 2021-34). Philippine Institute for Development Studies.

Taylor, B. (2013). Evidence-based policy and systemic change: Conflicting trends? *Springfield Working Paper Series, 1*.

Thorburn, C. (2009). Livelihood recovery in the wake of the tsunami in Aceh. *Bulletin of Indonesian Economic Studies, 45*(1), 85–105.

Voss, J. (2008). *PNPM-Rural baseline report*. World Bank.

White, H. (1996). Evaluating participation and sustainability. *Appropriate Technology, 23*(1), 28–30.

White, H., & Raitzer, D. A. (2017). *Impact evaluation of development interventions: A practical guide*. Asian Development Bank.

Wong, S. (2012). *What have been the impacts of World Bank Community-Driven Development programs? CDD impact evaluation review and operational and research implications*. World Bank.

Wong, S., & Guggenheim, S. (2018). Community-driven development: Myths and realities. *World Bank Policy Research Working Paper, 8435*.

Woolcock, M. (2009). Toward a plurality of methods in project evaluation: A contextualised approach to understanding impact trajectories and efficacy. *Journal of Development Effectiveness, 1*(1), 1–14.

World Bank. (2012). *Social protection and labor strategy 2012–2022: Resilience, equity, and opportunity*. World Bank.

World Bank. (2016). *Ethiopia's great run: The growth acceleration and how to pace it*. World Bank.

World Bank. (2017). *Towards a comprehensive, integrated, and effective social assistance system in Indonesia*. World Bank.

World Bank. (2020). *Philippines conditional cash transfer program: Impact evaluation 2012*. World Bank.

CHAPTER 9
Partnerships for Collaborative Action

"Alone we can do so little; together we can do so much."
—HELEN KELLER

SUMMARY

This chapter examines the critical role of collaborative partnerships in addressing poverty's complex and multifaceted nature. Effective poverty alleviation requires coordinated efforts among diverse actors including governments, international organizations, civil society organizations, private sector entities, research institutions, and affected communities themselves. The chapter explores various partnership models that have demonstrated success in reducing poverty, from local community-driven initiatives to large-scale international collaborations.

Key partnership types include government–NGO collaborations, public–private partnerships, international development alliances, research–policy networks, and community-based coalitions. Evidence shows that the most effective approaches combine multiple forms of intervention addressing different dimensions of poverty simultaneously. The United Nations' Sustainable Development Goals framework exemplifies global partnership efforts, mobilizing resources across sectors to tackle interconnected challenges.

Successful partnerships share several characteristics including shared vision and goals, complementary resources and capabilities, mutual accountability, transparent communication, and long-term commitment. However, partnerships also face challenges including power imbalances, conflicting priorities, coordination difficulties, and sustainability concerns. The chapter provides frameworks for building effective partnerships and examples of innovative collaborative approaches that have achieved significant poverty reduction outcomes.

The discussion emphasizes that while partnerships offer tremendous potential for poverty alleviation, their success depends on careful design, strong governance structures, and sustained commitment from all participants. The chapter concludes by outlining emerging trends in collaborative poverty reduction and offering recommendations for strengthening partnership effectiveness in addressing this persistent global challenge.

9.1. Introduction: The Search for Effective Poverty Reduction

The fight against poverty represents one of humanity's greatest challenges, one that no single organization, government, or sector can tackle alone. As we have seen throughout this book, poverty is multidimensional and deeply interconnected with issues of education, health, governance, environment, and social inclusion. Its complexity demands equally complex and coordinated responses that bring together diverse actors with complementary strengths, resources, and perspectives.

Partnerships for poverty alleviation have emerged as a fundamental approach to development in the 21st century. The recognition that collaborative action can achieve far more than isolated efforts has fundamentally transformed how we approach poverty reduction strategies. From local community organizations working with government agencies to deliver basic services, to international coalitions mobilizing billions of dollars for development programs, partnerships have become the cornerstone of modern anti-poverty efforts.

The importance of collaborative approaches became particularly evident during the formulation of the Sustainable Development Goals in 2015. SDG 17, which specifically calls for "partnerships for the goals", acknowledges that achieving zero poverty, zero hunger, and sustainable development requires unprecedented cooperation across all sectors of society. The COVID-19 pandemic further demonstrated both the vulnerability of development gains and the power of coordinated responses when organizations work together effectively.

This chapter explores the landscape of partnerships in poverty alleviation, examining what makes collaborations successful and how different types of organizations can work together more effectively. We will investigate various partnership models, from grassroots community alliances to global development initiatives, analyzing their strengths, challenges, and potential for creating lasting change.

Partnership approaches to poverty reduction have evolved significantly over the past several decades. Early development efforts were often characterized by top-down approaches where international donors and governments designed and implemented programs with limited input from local communities or civil society. However, experience has shown that sustainable poverty reduction requires the active participation of all stakeholders, particularly those most affected by poverty themselves.

Today's partnership landscape is characterized by increasingly sophisticated forms of collaboration that recognize the unique contributions each sector can make. Governments bring policy frameworks, regulatory power, and public resources. Private companies contribute innovation, efficiency, and capital. NGOs and civil society organizations offer grassroots connections, advocacy capabilities, and specialized expertise. Research institutions provide evidence-based insights and evaluation capabilities. Most importantly, communities themselves bring local knowledge, cultural understanding, and the motivation for sustainable change.

9.2. Understanding Partnership Approaches

Partnerships in poverty alleviation encompass a broad spectrum of collaborative arrangements, each designed to leverage the unique strengths and resources of different actors. These partnerships range from informal local alliances to highly structured international agreements, but they all share the common goal of combining resources and expertise to achieve greater impact than any single organization could accomplish alone.

The conceptual foundation for partnership approaches rests on several key principles. First is the principle of complementarity, which recognizes that different organizations possess different comparative advantages. For example, while governments may have the authority and resources to implement large-scale policies, NGOs often have better community-level relationships and can provide more flexible, localized responses. Private companies bring efficiency and innovation, while research institutions contribute evidence and analytical capabilities.

Second is the principle of synergy, which suggests that well-designed partnerships can create outcomes that exceed the sum of their individual contributions. When organizations align their efforts strategically, they can achieve what economists call "positive externalities"—benefits that extend beyond their immediate sphere of action. For instance, when a private company invests in skills training as part of a poverty reduction partnership, it not only benefits the direct participants but also contributes to broader economic development in the community.

Third is the principle of sustainability, which recognizes that lasting poverty reduction requires changes that can be maintained over time. Partnerships help build sustainability by creating shared ownership of interventions across multiple stakeholders, reducing dependence on any single organization or funding source. Community-based partnerships are particularly important in this regard, as they help ensure that interventions reflect local needs and can be maintained by local actors.

The evolution of partnership approaches has been shaped by both successes and failures in development practice. Early development efforts often failed because they did not adequately involve local stakeholders or account for local contexts. The emergence of participatory development approaches in the 1990s emphasized the importance of involving beneficiaries in designing and implementing interventions. This was followed by the growth of multi-stakeholder partnerships in the 2000s, which sought to bring together diverse actors around common goals.

9.3. Types of Partnerships in Zero Poverty

9.3.1. Government–civil society partnerships

Government–civil society partnerships represent one of the most common and important forms of collaboration in poverty alleviation. These partnerships typically leverage the government's policy authority and public resources alongside civil society's community connections and specialized expertise. The relationship between governments and NGOs has evolved considerably over time, moving from mutual suspicion to recognition of complementary roles.

Research by Banks and Hulme (2012) demonstrates that NGOs have played an increasingly prominent role in development since the late 1970s, widely recognized for their innovation, grassroots connections, and ability to pursue participatory approaches to development. However, their effectiveness is enhanced significantly when they work in partnership with government agencies rather than operating independently or in opposition to state efforts.

Successful government–NGO partnerships often involve formal arrangements that clearly define roles and responsibilities. For example, in many countries, governments contract NGOs to deliver specific services while maintaining overall policy responsibility. This arrangement allows governments to benefit from NGO expertise and community connections while ensuring that services are delivered consistently with national policies and standards.

World Vision Ghana's poverty reduction efforts in the Kintampo South District illustrate the potential of government–NGO partnerships. Research by Iddrisu et al. (2022) found that World Vision Ghana used both demand-side and supply-side approaches to poverty reduction, helping to increase earnings, improve food security, and enhance access to water and sanitation. The organization's success was largely attributed to its collaborative relationship with local government authorities and its commitment to building local capacity rather than simply delivering services.

However, government–NGO partnerships also face significant challenges. Power imbalances between government agencies and civil society organizations can limit NGOs' ability to advocate for policy changes or challenge government approaches. Additionally, NGOs may face pressure to modify their missions or compromise their values to maintain government funding or partnerships. However, the Asian Development Bank's (2019) analysis of NGO–government partnerships in China highlights how careful institutional design and clear agreements about roles and responsibilities can help address these challenges.

9.3.2. Public–private partnerships

Public–private partnerships (PPPs) have become increasingly important mechanisms for leveraging private sector resources and expertise in poverty alleviation efforts. The International Finance Corporation (2023) defines PPPs as long-term contractual arrangements where private sector partners take responsibility for delivering public services while sharing risks and rewards with the public sector.

PPPs can take many forms, from service contracts where private companies deliver specific services under government oversight, to more comprehensive arrangements where private partners take responsibility for financing, building, and operating infrastructure projects. The common thread is the combination of public sector policy authority and oversight with private sector efficiency and innovation.

The effectiveness of PPPs for poverty alleviation depends significantly on how they are designed and implemented. The Asian Development Bank's (2007) analysis suggests that PPPs can work for the poor when governments create appropriate enabling environments and take specific steps to ensure pro-poor benefits. This includes integrating PPPs into broader poverty reduction strategies, designing contracts that include specific poverty-focused objectives, and ensuring adequate regulation and oversight.

A compelling example comes from Lao PDR, where a public–private partnership between the government and Ock Pop Tok (a social enterprise) has created economic opportunities for women in rural communities. The United Nations Office for Project Services (2024) reported that this partnership, funded through the Enhanced Integrated Framework, trains and equips female weavers from six villages to produce high-quality handicrafts, enabling them to earn higher incomes while preserving traditional cultural practices.

However, PPPs for poverty alleviation also face significant challenges. Private companies are primarily motivated by profit, which may not always align with poverty reduction objectives. Additionally, PPPs can be complex to design and manage, requiring sophisticated government capacity that may not be available in all contexts. The World Bank's analysis of PPP effectiveness emphasizes that success requires careful attention to contract design, risk allocation, and performance monitoring.

9.3.3. International development partnerships

International partnerships bring together organizations from different countries to address poverty on a global scale. These partnerships range from bilateral agreements between specific countries to multilateral initiatives involving numerous nations and international organizations. The scale and resources available through international partnerships enable interventions that would be impossible for any single country to achieve.

The United Nations system exemplifies the potential of international partnerships. The UN's Sustainable Development Goals framework has mobilized unprecedented global cooperation around shared objectives, with 193 member states committing to specific targets for poverty reduction. The UN Development Programme has been particularly successful in facilitating partnerships, mobilizing $3.8 billion in SDG bonds and raising $1.6 billion to fight COVID-19 while providing 71 million people access to essential services across 36 countries (The Borgen Project, 2023).

Regional partnerships have also proven effective in addressing poverty challenges that transcend national boundaries. The Alliance for a Green Revolution in Africa (AGRA) exemplifies this approach, bringing together African governments, international donors, and local organizations to transform agriculture across the continent. The AGRA has attracted over $140 million in investments, focusing on small-scale farmers to increase agricultural productivity, develop value chains, and improve market access.

International partnerships often leverage different types of expertise and resources from participating countries. For example, South-South cooperation allows developing countries to share experiences and learn from each other's successes and challenges. China's poverty reduction experience, which has lifted over 800 million people out of poverty in four decades, has become a focal point for international knowledge sharing. The China Poverty Reduction International Forum, as reported by the FAO (2019), brings together participants from 30 countries to share experiences and best practices.

However, international partnerships also face unique challenges. Cultural differences, varying political systems, and different development priorities can make coordination difficult. Additionally, power imbalances between donor and recipient countries can limit the effectiveness of partnerships and compromise local ownership of development processes.

9.3.4. Research–policy partnerships

The connection between research and policy represents a critical but often underexplored dimension of partnerships for poverty alleviation. Research institutions contribute evidence-based insights that can inform more effective policies and programs, while policymakers provide real-world context and implementation experience that can improve research relevance.

Innovations for Poverty Action (IPA) exemplifies the potential of research–policy partnerships. As a research organization dedicated to discovering what works to improve the lives of people living in poverty, IPA operates in multiple countries with partnerships spanning government agencies, civil society organizations, and private sector entities. Their embedded labs work directly within government ministries, ensuring that research findings are immediately available to inform policy decisions.

The growth of impact evaluation and randomized controlled trials in development has strengthened research–policy partnerships by providing more rigorous evidence about what interventions work. Organizations like J-PAL (Abdul Latif Jameel Poverty Action Lab) have created formal mechanisms for connecting researchers with policymakers, ensuring that evaluation findings inform program design and implementation.

However, research–policy partnerships face several challenges. Academic timelines often do not align with policy needs, as research can take years to complete while policymakers need quick answers to immediate challenges. Additionally, research findings may be complex or nuanced in ways that are difficult to translate into simple policy recommendations. Building effective research–policy partnerships requires ongoing dialogue, mutual understanding of constraints and priorities, and mechanisms for translating research findings into actionable insights.

9.3.5. Community-based partnerships

Community-based partnerships put affected communities at the center of poverty reduction efforts, recognizing that sustainable change requires local ownership and participation. These partnerships often bring together community organizations, local government agencies, NGOs, and sometimes private sector actors around locally identified priorities and solutions.

The Slum Dwellers International (SDI) network illustrates the potential of community-driven partnerships. SDI works with local community associations to help them build relationships with local governments and access resources they need for development, including land, water, sanitation, electricity, and housing finance. This approach enables grassroots organizations to move away from confrontational demands toward addressing needs through negotiation and collaboration.

Community-based partnerships are particularly important for addressing the multidimensional nature of poverty. Local organizations understand how different challenges interact in specific contexts and can design integrated responses that address multiple needs simultaneously. For example, a community organization might combine livelihood training with health education and advocacy for improved local services, creating synergies that amplify impact.

Research in Ghana by Agyei-Mensah (2024) on knowledge-sharing strategies for poverty eradication among rural women demonstrates the importance of community-based approaches. The study found that effective poverty reduction requires collaborative knowledge needs assessment and active participation in decision-making by both rural women and stakeholders, emphasizing the adoption and refinement of indigenous knowledge at local, national, and international levels.

However, community-based partnerships also face significant challenges. Power imbalances between community organizations and other partners can limit community voice in decision-making. Additionally, community organizations often lack resources and technical capacity, making them dependent on external partners. Successful community-based partnerships require sustained investment in local capacity building and mechanisms to ensure genuine community leadership.

9.4. Characteristics of Successful Partnerships

9.4.1. Shared vision and goals

Successful partnerships for poverty alleviation are built on a foundation of shared understanding about objectives and approaches. This requires extensive dialogue among partners to develop common frameworks for understanding poverty, agreeing on priorities, and establishing clear, measurable goals. Without this shared vision, partners may work at cross-purposes or pursue conflicting strategies that undermine overall effectiveness.

The process of developing shared vision often reveals important differences in how different organizations understand poverty and its causes. For example, government agencies might focus primarily on income poverty and economic growth, while NGOs might emphasize social inclusion and empowerment. Private sector partners might prioritize market-based solutions, while community organizations might stress the importance of traditional knowledge and local ownership. Effective partnerships create space for these different perspectives and work to develop integrated approaches that address multiple dimensions of poverty.

Shared vision also requires alignment on fundamental values and principles. Partners need to agree on approaches to issues like participation, accountability, sustainability, and social justice. This is particularly important when partnerships bring together organizations with very different organizational cultures and operating principles. For example, partnerships between efficiency-focused private companies and participatory-oriented NGOs require careful attention to ensuring that shared values guide joint activities.

9.4.2. Complementary resources and capabilities

Effective partnerships bring together organizations with complementary strengths that can achieve more together than they could separately. This complementarity can take many forms, including financial resources, technical expertise, relationships and networks, political influence, and implementation capacity.

Financial complementarity often involves combining different types of funding to achieve comprehensive programming. For example, government funding might provide basic service delivery, foundation grants might support innovation and pilot programs, private investment might fund infrastructure, and community contributions might ensure local ownership. The Islamic Development Bank's NGO Empowerment for Poverty Reduction Program illustrates this approach, combining $10 million from the Islamic Solidarity Fund, $1.61 million from the UNDP, $7.31 million from international NGOs, and $2.11 million in in-kind contributions from participating civil society organizations (Islamic Development Bank, 2019).

Technical complementarity involves combining different types of expertise to address complex challenges. Research institutions might provide analytical capabilities, NGOs might contribute community engagement expertise, government agencies might offer regulatory and policy knowledge, and private companies might bring innovation and efficiency. Successful partnerships create mechanisms for knowledge sharing and joint learning across these different domains.

Relationship complementarity leverages different organizations' networks and influence to expand reach and impact. Government partnerships provide access to policymakers and public resources,

NGO partnerships offer community connections and grassroots legitimacy, private sector partnerships enable market access and scaling opportunities, and international partnerships facilitate resource mobilization and knowledge exchange.

9.4.3. Clear Governance Structures

Effective partnerships require clear governance structures that define roles, responsibilities, and decision-making processes. This includes formal agreements that specify each partner's contributions, expectations, and accountability mechanisms. Without clear governance, partnerships can suffer from confusion, duplication of effort, and conflict over resources and credit.

Governance structures need to address several key issues. First is decision-making authority, including which decisions require consensus among all partners and which can be made by individual organizations. Second is resource management, including how joint resources are mobilized, allocated, and monitored. Third is performance management, including how partnership effectiveness is measured and how partners are held accountable for their contributions.

Good governance also requires mechanisms for managing conflicts and disagreements that inevitably arise in partnerships. This might include formal dispute resolution processes, regular partner consultations, and clear procedures for modifying partnership agreements as circumstances change. The Chinese government's multi-agent collaborative governance approach to poverty alleviation demonstrates the importance of clear institutional frameworks, with specific roles defined for government, market, society, community, and individual household actors (Zhang et al., 2020).

9.4.4. Trust and communication

Trust represents perhaps the most important ingredient for successful partnerships, enabling organizations to take risks, share resources, and maintain commitment even when challenges arise. Trust develops over time through consistent behavior, transparent communication, and demonstrated reliability in meeting commitments.

Building trust requires ongoing investment in relationship development. This includes regular formal and informal communication, joint planning processes, shared learning activities, and mechanisms for addressing concerns and conflicts promptly. Trust is particularly important when partnerships involve organizations with very different cultures, values, or operating styles.

Communication systems must be designed to facilitate information sharing, coordination, and joint learning among partners. This includes regular reporting on activities and outcomes, shared monitoring and evaluation systems, joint review meetings, and mechanisms for sharing lessons learned. Effective communication also requires attention to different communication styles and preferences among partners, as well as multiple languages and cultural contexts when partnerships cross national boundaries.

9.4.5. Long-term commitment

Sustainable poverty reduction requires long-term engagement that extends beyond short-term project cycles. Effective partnerships are built on long-term commitment from all partners, with shared understanding that significant change takes time and sustained effort. This is particularly important given that many poverty alleviation efforts have been criticized for short-term orientations that fail to create lasting change.

Long-term commitment requires several elements. Financial sustainability involves ensuring that partnerships have reliable funding over extended periods, not just short-term grants or contracts. Institutional sustainability involves building systems and capacities that can continue functioning even as specific individuals or organizations change. Political sustainability involves maintaining support from key stakeholders even as political contexts evolve.

Building long-term commitment also requires demonstrating short-term and medium-term results that maintain partner motivation and stakeholder support. This means developing realistic timelines that show progress toward long-term goals while acknowledging the time required for sustainable change. Successful partnerships often use phased approaches that achieve early wins while building toward more transformative long-term objectives.

9.5. Challenges in Partnership Development

9.5.1. Power imbalances

Power imbalances represent one of the most significant challenges in partnership development, potentially undermining the collaborative spirit that partnerships seek to create. These imbalances can stem from differences in financial resources, technical capacity, political influence, or social status among partners. When power imbalances are not addressed, they can lead to situations where stronger partners dominate decision-making, weaker partners become marginalized, and the partnership fails to achieve its potential for collaborative impact.

Resource-based power imbalances are particularly common in development partnerships. Large international donors or government agencies may contribute the majority of financing, giving them disproportionate influence over program design and implementation. This can marginalize the voices of local organizations and communities, even though they may have the best understanding of local needs and contexts. Similarly, organizations with greater technical capacity may dominate partnership planning, overlooking valuable local knowledge and expertise.

Political and social power imbalances can also undermine partnership effectiveness. In partnerships involving government agencies, the authority of the state can overwhelm other partners' influence. In partnerships crossing national boundaries, organizations from high-income countries may have advantages in resources, networks, and international credibility that overshadow partners from developing countries.

Addressing power imbalances requires deliberate strategies and ongoing attention. This might include equalizing financial contributions where possible, creating decision-making structures that ensure all partners have a voice, investing in capacity building for weaker partners, and establishing clear agreements about how disagreements will be resolved. The Poverty–Environment Partnership approach demonstrates how international coalitions can address power imbalances by emphasizing shared leadership and ensuring representation from different regions and types of organizations.

9.5.2. Conflicting priorities and approaches

Different organizations inevitably bring different priorities, values, and approaches to partnerships, which can create tension and conflict if not properly managed. These differences may stem from organizational missions, accountability requirements, cultural backgrounds, or theoretical orientations about how development should occur.

For example, government agencies may prioritize policy compliance and service delivery efficiency, while NGOs may emphasize participation and empowerment. Private companies may focus on market-based solutions and financial sustainability, while community organizations may stress social cohesion and cultural preservation. International organizations may bring global perspectives and best practices, while local organizations may prioritize context-specific solutions and traditional knowledge.

Conflicting approaches to poverty measurement and evaluation can also create partnership challenges. Some partners may prefer quantitative impact assessments focusing on specific outcome indicators, while others may favor qualitative approaches that capture more complex changes in community dynamics and empowerment. These differences can lead to disagreements about program design, implementation strategies, and success metrics.

Managing conflicting priorities requires extensive dialogue and negotiation to develop integrated approaches that respect different perspectives while maintaining focus on shared objectives. This might involve creating flexible programming that allows different partners to contribute in ways that align with their strengths and values, developing comprehensive evaluation frameworks that capture different types of outcomes, and establishing clear agreements about how decisions will be made when priorities conflict.

9.5.3. Coordination difficulties

As partnerships involve more organizations and become more complex, coordination becomes increasingly challenging. Different partners may have different planning cycles, reporting requirements, decision-making processes, and operational procedures. Without effective coordination mechanisms, partnerships can suffer from duplication of effort, gaps in service delivery, and inefficient resource use.

Coordination challenges are often exacerbated by geographic distance, cultural differences, and language barriers. When partnerships involve organizations working in different countries or regions, simple logistics like scheduling meetings and sharing information can become complicated. Cultural differences in communication styles, decision-making processes, and relationship building can create misunderstandings and conflict.

Technical coordination can also be challenging when partners use different systems for project management, financial tracking, and performance monitoring. Harmonizing these systems requires investment in shared platforms and standards, which can be time-consuming and expensive to develop.

Effective coordination requires investment in systems and relationships. This might include establishing clear coordination roles and responsibilities, creating shared project management systems, developing common performance indicators, and investing in regular communication and joint planning processes. The United Nations' coordination of the SDGs provides an example of how complex multilateral partnerships can be coordinated through clear frameworks, regular reporting mechanisms, and dedicated coordination mechanisms.

9.5.4. Sustainability and exit strategies

Many partnerships struggle with questions of sustainability and how to transition from external support to local ownership. This is particularly challenging when partnerships are driven by external funding that is limited in duration or when they depend heavily on specific individuals whose involvement may change over time.

Financial sustainability remains a major challenge for many partnerships. Short-term funding cycles make it difficult to build long-term relationships and achieve sustainable impacts. Additionally, donor priorities can change, leaving successful partnerships without continued support. Building diversified funding bases and developing local resource mobilization capacity can help address these challenges but requires significant investment and planning.

Institutional sustainability involves building local capacity and systems that can continue functioning without external support. This requires not just training individuals but also strengthening organizational systems, developing sustainable operational models, and creating supportive policy environments. Many partnerships have failed because they did not invest sufficiently in building local capacity or because they created parallel systems rather than strengthening existing institutions.

Developing effective exit strategies requires planning from the beginning of partnerships, clearly identifying how external support will be phased out and local ownership strengthened over time. This might involve gradually shifting responsibilities to local partners, building local fundraising capacity, strengthening local institutions, and ensuring knowledge transfer. Successful exit strategies often involve transitioning from direct service delivery to technical assistance and advocacy support.

9.6. Innovative Partnership Models

9.6.1. Collective impact approaches

Collective impact represents an innovative partnership model that brings together diverse organizations around shared measurement systems, mutually reinforcing activities, and continuous communication to achieve complex social change. This approach recognizes that solving complex problems like poverty requires coordination across sectors and levels that goes beyond traditional partnership models.

The collective impact model involves five key elements: a common agenda that defines shared vision and goals; shared measurement systems that allow partners to track progress consistently; mutually reinforcing activities where different organizations contribute complementary efforts; continuous communication that builds trust and coordinates action; and backbone support through a dedicated organization that facilitates partnership activities.

Several poverty alleviation initiatives have successfully used collective impact approaches. For example, comprehensive community development initiatives often bring together government agencies, NGOs, private companies, educational institutions, and community organizations around shared goals for neighborhood transformation. These initiatives use common measurement frameworks to track progress across multiple indicators, coordinate activities to maximize synergies, and maintain ongoing communication to adapt strategies based on learning.

The strength of collective impact approaches lies in their ability to address complex, interconnected problems through coordinated action while maintaining each partner's autonomy and specialization. However, they require significant investment in coordination and backbone support and can be challenging to sustain over time without dedicated resources and leadership.

9.6.2. Impact investment partnerships

Impact investment partnerships combine financial return objectives with social impact goals, creating innovative financing mechanisms for poverty alleviation. These partnerships typically bring together private investors, development finance institutions, government agencies, and implementing organizations to deploy capital in ways that generate both financial returns and poverty reduction outcomes.

Examples include microfinance investment vehicles that provide capital to microfinance institutions serving low-income populations, infrastructure bonds that finance basic services in underserved communities, and social impact bonds that link payment to achievement of specific poverty reduction outcomes. The Islamic Development Bank's use of innovative financing mechanisms, including crowdfunding and blockchain technology, demonstrates how impact investment partnerships can mobilize diverse sources of capital.

Impact investment partnerships offer several advantages for poverty alleviation. They can mobilize private capital for development purposes, create incentives for efficient service delivery, and build sustainable financing models that do not depend on ongoing donor support. Additionally, they can bring private sector expertise and innovation to development challenges.

However, impact investment partnerships also face significant challenges. Balancing financial return requirements with poverty reduction objectives can be difficult, particularly when serving the very poorest populations. Additionally, measuring and verifying social impact can be complex and expensive, and there are risks that financial priorities may override social objectives.

9.6.3. Digital platform partnerships

Digital technology has created new opportunities for partnership development through online platforms that connect diverse actors around poverty alleviation objectives. These platforms can facilitate knowledge sharing, resource mobilization, service delivery, and impact measurement across traditional organizational boundaries.

Examples include online marketplaces that connect smallholder farmers with consumers and eliminate intermediaries; digital platforms that facilitate humanitarian aid distribution; crowdfunding platforms that mobilize resources for community development projects; and knowledge-sharing platforms that connect researchers, practitioners, and policymakers globally.

The Global Poverty Reduction Online Knowledge Sharing Database, launched through the China Poverty Reduction International Forum, exemplifies how digital platforms can facilitate international cooperation and learning. The platform makes poverty reduction case studies and best practices globally accessible, enabling organizations worldwide to learn from each other's experiences.

Digital platform partnerships offer several advantages. They can reduce transaction costs, enable direct connections between producers and consumers, facilitate rapid resource mobilization, and create opportunities for peer-to-peer learning and support. Additionally, they can reach previously excluded populations and create new forms of economic opportunity.

However, digital platform partnerships also face challenges including the digital divide that excludes those without access to technology, concerns about data privacy and security, and the need for digital literacy among users. Additionally, platform governance can be challenging when trying to balance openness with quality control and user protection.

9.6.4. Adaptive management partnerships

Traditional partnership approaches often follow linear planning models that assume stable conditions and predictable outcomes. However, poverty alleviation occurs in complex, dynamic environments where conditions change rapidly and outcomes are uncertain.

Adaptive management partnerships recognize this complexity and build flexibility and learning into partnership structures.

Adaptive partnerships emphasize iterative planning cycles, regular review and adjustment of strategies, rapid testing of new approaches, and systematic learning from both successes and failures. They typically involve shorter planning cycles, more frequent partner consultations, flexible funding arrangements, and robust monitoring systems that enable quick detection of problems and opportunities.

Several poverty alleviation initiatives have successfully used adaptive management approaches. For example, graduation programs that support ultra-poor households often involve regular assessment and adjustment of household support based on changing needs and circumstances. Similarly, community development programs may adapt their strategies based on emerging community priorities and changing external conditions.

Adaptive management partnerships offer several advantages for poverty alleviation. They can respond more quickly to changing conditions, incorporate learning into ongoing programming, and develop more context-appropriate interventions. Additionally, they can be more responsive to community needs and priorities, which may change over time.

However, adaptive partnerships also require more intensive management and coordination than traditional models. They need robust information systems to support decision-making, flexible funding arrangements that allow strategy changes, and strong relationships among partners that enable honest communication about challenges and failures.

9.7. Building Effective Partnerships

9.7.1. Partnership design and planning

Creating effective partnerships requires careful design and planning that addresses the unique characteristics and needs of each collaboration. This process begins with stakeholder analysis to identify all relevant actors, their interests, capacities, and potential contributions to poverty alleviation efforts. Understanding the partnership landscape helps determine which organizations should be involved and how they might work together effectively.

Partnership design must address several key questions: What are the specific objectives the partnership seeks to achieve? Which organizations have the necessary resources and capabilities to contribute to these objectives? How will the partnership be structured to maximize each partner's contributions while ensuring coordination and accountability? What governance mechanisms will guide decision-making and conflict resolution?

The planning process should involve extensive consultation with all potential partners to develop shared understanding of problems, opportunities, and potential solutions. This consultation process often reveals important differences in how different organizations understand poverty and its causes, creating opportunities to develop more comprehensive and nuanced approaches.

Effective partnership design also requires attention to risk management, including identifying potential challenges and developing strategies to address them. This might include succession planning to ensure continuity when key individuals leave their organizations, contingency planning to address funding shortfalls, and conflict resolution mechanisms to manage disagreements among partners.

9.7.2. Capacity building and technical assistance

Many partnerships require significant investment in capacity building to ensure that all partners can contribute effectively to joint efforts. This is particularly important when partnerships involve organizations with very different levels of resources, technical capacity, or experience with collaborative approaches.

Capacity building might target several different areas. Technical capacity building helps organizations develop skills needed for effective programming, such as project management, monitoring and evaluation, financial management, or specific sectoral expertise. Organizational capacity building strengthens systems and structures, such as governance mechanisms, strategic planning processes, or information management systems.

Relationship and collaboration capacity building helps organizations develop skills needed for effective partnership, such as communication, negotiation, conflict resolution, and joint planning. This type of capacity building is often overlooked but can be critical for partnership success.

Effective capacity building is typically based on careful assessment of each partner's existing strengths and needs, developed through collaborative planning processes, delivered through multiple methods including training, mentoring, and peer learning, and integrated into ongoing partnership activities rather than treated as separate, one-time interventions.

9.7.3. Resource mobilization strategies

Successful partnerships require sustainable financing strategies that mobilize resources from multiple sources and ensure adequate funding over time. This typically involves combining different types of funding including government budgets, donor grants, private investment, earned revenue, and community contributions.

Diversified funding strategies help reduce dependence on any single source and create more sustainable financing models. For example, partnerships might use initial donor funding to pilot innovative approaches, government funding to scale successful interventions, private investment to develop sustainable service delivery models, and earned revenue to ensure long-term viability.

Resource mobilization also involves non-financial resources such as volunteer time, in-kind contributions, technical expertise, and political support. Partners can often contribute these resources even when financial contributions are limited, increasing the overall value of partnership efforts.

Effective resource mobilization requires clear value propositions that articulate how partnerships create value for different types of funders and contributors. This might emphasize impact scaling for donors concerned with effectiveness, market development opportunities for private investors, policy implementation for government agencies, or community empowerment for foundations focused on social justice.

9.7.4. *Monitoring, evaluation, and learning systems*

Robust monitoring, evaluation, and learning (MEL) systems are essential for partnership effectiveness, enabling partners to track progress, identify problems, learn from experience, and demonstrate impact to stakeholders. However, developing shared MEL systems can be challenging when partners have different accountability requirements, evaluation preferences, and performance indicators.

Effective partnership MEL systems typically combine outcome indicators that measure progress toward shared objectives with process indicators that track partnership functioning. Outcome indicators might include poverty reduction metrics, service delivery statistics, or policy change indicators. Process indicators might include partnership satisfaction surveys, communication frequency measures, or coordination effectiveness assessments.

Shared measurement systems require significant investment in data collection, analysis, and reporting infrastructure. This might involve developing common data collection tools, creating shared databases, training staff in evaluation methods, and establishing regular reporting schedules. Investment in measurement systems often pays dividends by improving program effectiveness and demonstrating impact to funders and stakeholders.

Effective MEL systems also include mechanisms for learning and adaptation based on evaluation findings. This might involve regular review meetings where partners discuss evaluation results, joint reflection processes that identify lessons learned, and adaptive management approaches that incorporate evaluation findings into ongoing programming.

9.8. Case Studies of Effective Partnerships

9.8.1. Mexico's Progresa/Oportunidades/ Prospera Program

Mexico's conditional cash transfer program, known successively as Progresa, Oportunidades, and Prospera, represents one of the most successful examples of integrated partnership approaches to poverty alleviation. The program demonstrates how government agencies, international organizations, research institutions, and communities can work together to create comprehensive interventions that address multiple dimensions of poverty simultaneously.

The program involved partnerships at multiple levels. At the policy level, the Mexican government worked with international organizations including the World Bank and Inter-American Development Bank to design and finance the intervention. At the research level, partnerships with institutions like the International Food Policy Research Institute enabled rigorous impact evaluation that demonstrated the program's effectiveness and informed continuous improvements.

At the community level, the program created partnerships between government agencies, local schools and health clinics, and participating families. These partnerships linked cash transfers to specific behaviors including school attendance and health clinic visits, creating incentives for human capital investment while providing immediate poverty relief.

The program's success stemmed largely from its integrated partnership approach. Rather than addressing income poverty alone, it combined cash transfers with investments in education and health systems, creating synergies across different interventions. The partnership with research institutions enabled continuous learning and improvement, while community-level partnerships ensured local buy-in and sustainability.

Impact evaluations showed significant positive effects on poverty reduction, educational attainment, health outcomes, and long-term economic mobility. The program reached over 6 million families at its peak and has been replicated in numerous other countries, demonstrating the potential for successful partnership models to scale beyond their original contexts.

9.8.2. Rwanda's Health Partnerships

Rwanda's dramatic improvements in health outcomes following the 1994 genocide provide a powerful example of how partnerships can achieve rapid progress in challenging circumstances. The government of Rwanda worked with multiple international partners, NGOs, and community organizations to rebuild and strengthen the health system while achieving remarkable improvements in health outcomes.

Key partnerships included collaborations with Partners in Health, the Clinton Health Access Initiative, the Global Fund to Fight AIDS, Tuberculosis and Malaria, and numerous other organizations. These partnerships combined government leadership and policy authority with international technical assistance, financing, and community-level implementation capacity.

The partnership model emphasized mutual accountability, with clear agreements about roles, responsibilities, and performance targets. International partners provided technical assistance, training, and financing, while the government maintained overall leadership and ensured integration with national health strategies. Community health cooperatives played crucial roles in service delivery and health promotion.

The results were remarkable: infant mortality fell from 107 per 1,000 births in 2005 to 31 per 1,000 in 2015, maternal mortality declined by 85%, and coverage of key health interventions increased dramatically. These improvements contributed significantly to poverty reduction by reducing healthcare costs, improving productivity, and enabling families to invest in education and economic activities rather than healthcare.

The Rwanda model has influenced health partnerships globally, demonstrating how clear government leadership, strong accountability mechanisms, and integrated service delivery can achieve rapid improvements even in resource-constrained settings.

9.8.3. Bangladesh's microcredit movement

Bangladesh's microcredit movement, pioneered by organizations like Grameen Bank and BRAC, illustrates how partnerships between innovative NGOs, government agencies, and international supporters can create new models for financial inclusion that reach previously excluded populations.

The movement began with partnerships between Grameen Bank founder Muhammad Yunus and international supporters who provided initial financing and technical assistance. As the model proved successful, partnerships expanded to include government agencies that provided regulatory support and policy frameworks, international development organizations that provided scaling financing, and local organizations that adapted the model to different contexts.

Key innovations included group-based lending models that used social capital to replace traditional collateral requirements, focus on women borrowers who demonstrated higher repayment rates and used credit for productive investments, and integration of credit with savings, insurance, and social development programs.

Partnerships were crucial to the movement's success. International partners provided financing, technical assistance, and advocacy support that enabled rapid scaling. Government partnerships provided regulatory frameworks that supported microcredit operations while protecting borrowers. Community partnerships, particularly with women's groups, ensured cultural appropriateness and local ownership.

Impact studies showed significant positive effects on poverty reduction, women's empowerment, and economic development. The microcredit model has been replicated in numerous countries, though with mixed results that highlight the importance of adapting partnership models to local contexts rather than simply replicating successful interventions.

However, the movement also faced challenges including over-indebtedness of borrowers, mission drift toward profit maximization, and questions about long-term impact on poverty reduction. These challenges highlight the importance of maintaining focus on poverty alleviation objectives and ensuring adequate regulation and oversight of partnership activities.

9.8.4. China's targeted poverty alleviation campaign

China's targeted poverty alleviation campaign, which officially eliminated extreme poverty by 2020, demonstrates how comprehensive partnership approaches can achieve poverty reduction at massive scale. The campaign involved partnerships across all levels of government, between different sectors, and with communities themselves.

The partnership model included several key elements. Government partnerships involved coordination between central, provincial, and local authorities, with clear targets and accountability mechanisms. Cross-sector partnerships brought together government agencies, state-owned enterprises, private companies, universities, and NGOs around shared poverty reduction objectives.

Community partnerships ensured that poor households were actively involved in designing and implementing poverty reduction strategies. The approach emphasized "precision" in identifying poor households, diagnosing causes of poverty, and designing targeted interventions that addressed specific constraints each household faced.

International partnerships supported knowledge sharing and learning, with China both contributing to and learning from global poverty reduction experiences. The China Poverty Reduction

International Forum became a platform for sharing experiences with other developing countries.

The results were unprecedented: over 100 million people were lifted out of poverty during the campaign, and extreme poverty was officially eliminated from all counties in China. The success stemmed largely from the comprehensive partnership approach that combined massive resource mobilization with precise targeting and strong accountability mechanisms.

The Chinese model has influenced poverty reduction approaches globally, particularly regarding the importance of political commitment, comprehensive coordination, and precise targeting. However, questions remain about the sustainability of some interventions and the applicability of the model to contexts with different political systems and resource constraints.

9.9. The Role of Different Actors in the Zero Poverty Ecosystem

9.9.1. Government agencies

Government agencies play crucial roles in partnerships for poverty alleviation, bringing unique assets including policy authority, public resources, democratic legitimacy, and the ability to operate at scale. Governments can create enabling environments for poverty reduction through appropriate policies, regulations, and public investments. They can also provide coordination mechanisms that bring together diverse actors around shared objectives.

However, government effectiveness in partnerships varies significantly depending on factors including institutional capacity, political commitment, governance quality, and resource availability. Weak states may lack the capacity to fulfill their partnership roles effectively, while strong but unaccountable governments may dominate partnerships in ways that limit other actors' contributions.

Successful government partnership strategies often involve several elements. Policy leadership includes setting clear poverty reduction objectives, creating supportive regulatory frameworks, and aligning government policies across sectors. Resource mobilization involves providing public financing, leveraging external resources, and creating incentives for private investment and civil society engagement.

Coordination facilitation includes bringing together diverse actors, creating platforms for dialogue and collaboration, and ensuring that different interventions complement rather than duplicate each other. Accountability mechanisms include transparent performance monitoring, regular public reporting, and responsive grievance systems that enable citizen feedback.

Emerging trends in government partnership roles include greater emphasis on facilitation rather than direct implementation, increased use of performance-based partnerships that link payment to results, and growing recognition of the importance of citizen engagement in partnership governance.

9.9.2. Civil society organizations

Civil society organizations bring unique strengths to partnerships including grassroots connections, specialized expertise, advocacy capabilities, and commitment to social justice values. NGOs, community-based organizations, faith-based groups, and other civil society actors often have deep understanding of local contexts and strong relationships with poor and marginalized populations.

Research on NGO roles in poverty reduction by various scholars has found that civil society organizations are particularly effective at reaching excluded populations, providing innovative services, and advocating for policy changes that benefit the poor. They often serve as intermediaries between communities and other actors, translating community needs into policy recommendations and helping communities access resources and opportunities.

However, civil society organizations also face significant challenges in partnerships. Resource constraints often limit their capacity to participate effectively in complex partnerships. Power imbalances may marginalize their voices in decision-making processes. Additionally, accountability pressures from donors may conflict with community accountability, creating tensions around organizational mission and values.

Successful civil society partnership strategies often emphasize several approaches. Capacity building involves strengthening organizational systems, developing technical expertise, and building collaborative skills. Advocacy includes promoting policy changes that benefit the poor, representing community voices in partnership governance, and holding other partners accountable for their commitments.

Service delivery includes providing direct services to poor populations, implementing partnership activities at the community level, and ensuring cultural appropriateness of interventions. Knowledge generation involves documenting community experiences, conducting research on poverty reduction strategies, and facilitating knowledge sharing among partners.

Emerging trends in civil society roles include greater emphasis on advocacy and systems change rather than direct service delivery, increased focus on building movements rather than individual organizations, and growing use of technology to enhance community organizing and advocacy efforts.

9.9.3. Private sector

The private sector brings distinctive capabilities to poverty alleviation partnerships including innovation, efficiency, capital, market access, and job creation potential. Companies can contribute to poverty reduction through employment generation, supplier development, product innovation for low-income markets, and corporate social responsibility initiatives.

Different types of private sector actors play different roles in partnerships. Large multinational corporations often contribute significant resources and global reach, but may be less flexible and responsive to local conditions. Small and medium enterprises may have better local knowledge and relationships but limited resources for large-scale initiatives. Social enterprises explicitly combine profit motives with social objectives, often serving as bridges between commercial and development sectors.

Private sector engagement in poverty alleviation has expanded significantly in recent decades, driven by growing recognition of business opportunities in low-income markets, increased pressure for corporate social responsibility, and innovation in impact investment and blended finance mechanisms.

However, private sector participation in partnerships also faces challenges. Profit motives may conflict with poverty reduction objectives, particularly when serving the very poorest populations who may not represent attractive markets. Short-term financial pressures may conflict with long-term development objectives. Additionally, private companies may lack understanding of development contexts and approaches.

Successful private sector partnership strategies often involve several elements. Market development includes creating products and services appropriate for low-income populations, developing inclusive business models that serve poor customers while generating profits, and building supply chains that include small-scale producers and entrepreneurs.

Employment generation involves creating jobs accessible to poor workers, providing skills training and career development opportunities, and ensuring fair labor practices and working conditions. Innovation includes developing new technologies and approaches that address poverty-related challenges, piloting innovative service delivery models, and sharing knowledge and expertise with other partners.

Corporate citizenship includes contributing resources to partnership activities, advocating for policy changes that support poverty reduction, and demonstrating corporate values through business practices.

9.9.4. Research institutions

Research institutions contribute essential capabilities to partnerships including analytical expertise, evaluation skills, knowledge generation, and capacity building. Universities, think tanks, and research organizations can help partners understand poverty causes and dynamics, design effective interventions, and measure impact.

Academic institutions bring several unique strengths to partnerships. Analytical capacity includes conducting research on poverty causes and trends, evaluating intervention effectiveness, and synthesizing lessons from multiple contexts. Technical expertise includes specialized knowledge in areas like economics, public health, education, and social policy that can inform program design and implementation.

Training and capacity building includes educating future development professionals, providing continuing education for practitioners, and building research capacity in partner organizations. Institutional credibility includes providing independent analysis, maintaining academic standards and objectivity, and facilitating knowledge sharing across different contexts.

However, research institutions also face challenges in partnerships. Academic timelines often do not align with policy and practice needs, as research can take years while practitioners need quick answers. Academic incentives may emphasize publication over practical impact, creating tensions around research priorities and dissemination strategies.

Successful research partnership strategies often emphasize several approaches. Action research involves conducting research embedded in practice, with researchers working directly with practitioners to address real-world problems. Policy research includes conducting analysis specifically designed to inform policy decisions, with attention to practical constraints and implementation considerations.

Capacity building involves training practitioners in research methods, building local research capacity, and facilitating knowledge transfer from research to practice. Knowledge synthesis includes reviewing and synthesizing existing research, identifying gaps and priorities for future research, and translating research findings into accessible formats for practitioners and policymakers.

Emerging trends in research institution roles include greater emphasis on collaborative and participatory research methods, increased attention to research translation and implementation, and growing use of technology to facilitate research collaboration and dissemination.

9.9.5. Communities and beneficiaries

Communities and beneficiaries represent perhaps the most important but often overlooked partners in poverty alleviation efforts. Poor and marginalized populations bring essential assets including local knowledge, cultural understanding, motivation for change, and ultimate ownership of development outcomes.

Community participation in partnerships can take many forms. Consultation involves seeking community input on problem analysis, program design, and implementation strategies. Participation includes involving community members in program activities, decision-making processes, and monitoring and evaluation. Leadership involves community members taking leading roles in program governance, implementation, and sustainability.

Research consistently shows that interventions with meaningful community participation are more effective, sustainable, and culturally appropriate than those imposed from outside. Community knowledge often reveals important local dynamics and constraints that external actors overlook. Community ownership is essential for sustainability after external support ends.

However, meaningful community participation faces significant challenges. Power imbalances often limit community voice in partnership governance and decision-making. Capacity constraints may limit communities' ability to participate effectively in complex partnerships. Time and resource demands of participation may burden already struggling households.

Successful community partnership strategies often emphasize several approaches. Capacity building includes strengthening community organizations, developing leadership skills, and building technical capacity for program management and advocacy. Resource mobilization involves supporting community contributions to partnership activities, facilitating access to external resources, and building sustainable financing mechanisms.

Advocacy includes supporting community voices in policy processes, building networks among community organizations, and representing community interests in partnership governance. Ownership includes ensuring community control over program design and implementation, building local accountability mechanisms, and creating pathways for community leadership of development initiatives.

Emerging trends in community roles include greater emphasis on community-driven development approaches, increased use of technology to facilitate community organizing and participation, and growing recognition of indigenous knowledge and practices in development programming.

9.10. Ways Forward

9.10.1. Digital technology and innovation

Digital technology is transforming how partnerships operate and creating new opportunities for collaborative poverty alleviation. Online platforms enable new forms of coordination among partners, digital payment systems facilitate more efficient transfer delivery, and data analytics provide better insights into poverty patterns and intervention effectiveness.

Artificial intelligence and machine learning are beginning to influence poverty prediction, program targeting, and impact evaluation. Blockchain technology offers potential for more transparent and accountable partnership governance and resource tracking. Mobile technology enables new forms of service delivery and community engagement, particularly important in reaching remote and marginalized populations.

However, digital innovations also risk creating new forms of exclusion for those without access to technology. The digital divide may exacerbate existing inequalities if technology-based interventions primarily benefit those who are already better connected and more affluent. Privacy and data security concerns also create new challenges for partnership governance and beneficiary protection.

Future partnerships will likely need to carefully balance technological innovation with inclusive design that ensures all partners and beneficiaries can participate effectively. This may require investment in digital literacy, accessible technology design, and governance frameworks that protect privacy while enabling innovation.

9.10.2. Climate change and environmental sustainability

Climate change is creating new imperatives for partnerships in poverty alleviation as environmental degradation disproportionately affects poor and vulnerable populations. Rising sea levels, changing precipitation patterns, extreme weather events, and ecosystem degradation all threaten livelihoods and increase poverty risks.

Effective poverty alleviation increasingly requires integration of climate adaptation and mitigation strategies. This creates opportunities for new forms of partnerships that combine development objectives with environmental goals. For example, ecosystem restoration projects can create employment while improving resilience to climate impacts.

The Poverty–Environment Partnership demonstrates how international coalitions can address these interconnected challenges through integrated approaches that "get to zero" on extreme poverty, net greenhouse gas emissions, and net loss of natural assets simultaneously.

Future partnerships will likely need to mainstream climate considerations into all poverty alleviation efforts. This may require new forms of expertise, different types of partners including environmental organizations, and innovative financing mechanisms that account for both social and environmental returns.

9.10.3. Urbanization and changing demographics

Rapid urbanization is changing the geography of poverty and creating new challenges for partnerships. While urban areas offer more opportunities for employment and service access, they also create new forms of poverty including urban slums, informal settlements, and exclusion from basic services.

Urban poverty often requires different partnership approaches than rural poverty, involving municipal governments, urban planning organizations, housing developers, and community organizations in dense settlement areas. The complexity of urban governance may require more sophisticated coordination mechanisms and stronger focus on multi-level partnerships.

Demographic changes including aging populations, youth bulges, and migration patterns are also creating new partnership imperatives. Aging populations require different service models and may strain traditional family support systems. Large youth populations create opportunities for innovation and entrepreneurship but require massive investments in education, skills training, and employment creation.

Future partnerships will need to adapt to these demographic realities by developing context-specific approaches for different population groups and urban contexts. This may require new types of partners, different service delivery models, and innovative approaches to community engagement in dense urban settings.

9.10.4. Post-COVID-19 recovery and resilience

The COVID-19 pandemic has profoundly impacted poverty and development progress while also demonstrating both the vulnerability of development gains and the potential for rapid collaborative responses to shared challenges. The pandemic reversed years of poverty reduction progress while exacerbating existing inequalities.

However, the pandemic also catalyzed innovation in service delivery, accelerated adoption of digital technologies, and demonstrated the importance of social protection systems and international cooperation. Some partnerships showed remarkable adaptability in responding to the crisis while maintaining focus on long-term development objectives.

Post-COVID recovery offers opportunities to "build back better" by strengthening social protection systems, increasing resilience to future shocks, and addressing structural inequalities that the pandemic exposed. This may require new forms of partnerships that better integrate health, economic, and social objectives.

Future partnerships may need to be more adaptive and resilient, with built-in mechanisms for responding to shocks and crises. This might include diversified funding strategies that can withstand economic downturns, flexible programming that can adapt to changing conditions, and stronger social protection systems that provide automatic responses to crises.

9.11. Conclusion

Partnerships for collaborative action represent both the greatest promise and the most significant challenges in contemporary poverty alleviation efforts. As this chapter has demonstrated, the complexity and multidimensional nature of poverty requires responses that no single organization or sector can provide alone. The evidence is clear that well-designed partnerships can achieve far more than individual organizations working in isolation, creating synergies that amplify impact and build sustainability.

The journey from recognizing the need for partnerships to implementing successful collaborations is neither simple nor straightforward. As we have seen, effective partnerships require shared vision and goals that bridge different organizational cultures and priorities. They demand governance structures that balance efficiency with inclusivity, ensuring that all partners have a voice while maintaining accountability and coordination. Trust and communication form the foundation of successful collaborations, but building and maintaining these relationships requires ongoing investment and attention.

The diversity of partnership types—from government–NGO collaborations to public–private partnerships, from international development alliances to community-based coalitions—reflects the multifaceted nature of poverty itself. Each type of partnership brings unique strengths and faces distinct challenges. Government agencies provide policy authority and resources but may lack flexibility and grassroots connections. Civil society organizations offer community relationships and advocacy capabilities but often struggle with resource constraints and capacity limitations. Private sector partners contribute innovation and efficiency but may face conflicts between profit motives and social objectives. Research institutions provide analytical expertise but operate on timelines that may not align with immediate action needs.

The case studies examined in this chapter—from Mexico's conditional cash transfer program to Rwanda's health partnerships, from Bangladesh's microcredit movement to China's targeted poverty alleviation campaign—demonstrate that successful partnerships combine multiple approaches while adapting to local contexts. These examples show that partnership success depends not just on good intentions but also on careful design, sustained commitment, adequate resources, and robust systems for coordination and accountability.

The challenges facing partnerships are real and significant. Power imbalances can undermine collaborative spirit and marginalize important voices. Conflicting priorities and approaches can create tension and reduce effectiveness. Coordination difficulties can lead to duplication, gaps, and inefficiency. Sustainability concerns can threaten long-term impact when external support ends. However, these challenges are not insurmountable when partnerships are designed and managed with attention to these dynamics.

Looking forward, emerging trends in partnership development offer both opportunities and new challenges. Digital technology creates possibilities for more efficient coordination and innovative service delivery, but also risks creating new forms of exclusion. Climate change demands integration of environmental considerations into poverty alleviation efforts, requiring new types of partnerships and expertise. Urbanization and demographic changes are shifting the geography and dynamics of poverty, calling for adapted partnership approaches. The COVID-19 pandemic has demonstrated both the fragility of development progress and the potential for rapid collaborative responses to crisis.

Perhaps most importantly, this chapter has emphasized that at the heart of all effective partnerships lies a fundamental commitment to the dignity and agency of people experiencing poverty. While technical aspects of partnership design and management are important, the ultimate measure of success is whether collaborations actually improve lives and expand opportunities for those most in need. This requires maintaining focus on outcomes that matter to poor and marginalized populations, ensuring their meaningful participation in partnership governance, and building their capacity to lead their own development processes.

The evidence suggests that partnerships work best when they start with clear recognition that fighting poverty requires not just better coordination among existing approaches, but fundamental transformation in how different actors relate to each other and to the communities they serve. Successful partnerships do not just deliver services more efficiently; they create new forms of collaboration that challenge existing power relationships and build more inclusive and sustainable approaches to development.

For students and practitioners of development, the lessons from partnership experiences offer several key insights. First, effective partnerships require investment in relationships and processes, not just programs and projects. Second, successful collaborations adapt to local contexts rather than imposing external models. Third, sustainability depends on building local ownership and capacity, not just achieving short-term results. Fourth, impact requires attention to both technical effectiveness and political dynamics that shape how partnerships operate in practice.

As we face an increasingly complex and interconnected world, partnerships for poverty alleviation will become even more important. The Sustainable Development Goals' emphasis on partnership reflects growing recognition that achieving zero poverty requires unprecedented cooperation across sectors, levels, and borders. However, partnerships are not panaceas; they are tools that must be wielded skillfully and adapted thoughtfully to achieve their potential.

The call to action from this chapter is clear: whether as policymakers, practitioners, researchers, or engaged citizens, we all have roles to play in building more effective partnerships for poverty alleviation. This might involve creating enabling environments that support collaboration, developing skills needed for effective partnership participation, contributing resources and expertise to joint efforts, or simply maintaining focus on the ultimate objective of creating a world where all people can live with dignity and opportunity.

Ultimately, partnerships for collaborative action represent an expression of hope—hope that by working together across our differences, we can achieve what none of us can accomplish alone. The fight against poverty is fundamentally about building a more just and inclusive world, and partnerships offer a practical pathway for translating this aspiration into reality. The challenge before us is to learn from past experiences, adapt to current realities, and build collaborations that are worthy of the trust placed in them by those whose lives they seek to transform.

The journey toward effective partnerships is ongoing, requiring continuous learning, adaptation, and commitment. But the potential rewards—in terms of lives improved, opportunities expanded, and communities strengthened—make this journey not just worthwhile but essential. As we move forward, let us carry with us the lessons learned, the relationships built, and the conviction that together, we can create a world free from poverty where all people can thrive.

References

Agyei-Mensah, S. (2024). Knowledge-sharing strategies for poverty eradication among rural women. *International Journal of Knowledge Management, 12*(3), 45–67.

Asian Development Bank. (2007). *Expanding access to basic services in Asia and the Pacific region: Public-private partnerships for poverty reduction.* Manila: ADB Publications.

Asian Development Bank. (2019). *NGO-government partnerships in village-level poverty alleviation* (Technical Assistance Report). Manila: ADB Publications.

Banks, N., & Hulme, D. (2012). *The role of NGOs and civil society in development and poverty reduction* (Global Development Institute Working Paper Series No. 17112). University of Manchester.

The Borgen Project. (2023, November 23). *Partnerships for global poverty alleviation.* https://borgenproject.org/top-4-partnerships-for-global-poverty-alleviation/

Food and Agriculture Organization. (2019). 2019 China poverty reduction international forum: Sharing knowledge for global poverty reduction. *FAO News and Events.* Retrieved from https://www.fao.org/china/news/detail-events/en/c/1239297/

Iddrisu, A. M., Tschakert, P., & Antwi-Agyei, P. (2022). Role of non-governmental organizations in poverty reduction in the global South: Evidence from World Vision Ghana, Kintampo South district. *Heliyon, 8*(10), e10806.

International Finance Corporation. (2023). *Public-private partnerships advisory services.* Washington, DC: World Bank Group.

Islamic Development Bank. (2019). *NGO empowerment for poverty reduction program.* Jeddah: IsDB.

United Nations Office for Project Services. (2024). What's vital for sustainable development? Public-private partnerships. *UNOPS Insights*. Retrieved from https://www.unops.org/news-and-stories/insights/whats-vital-for-sustainable-development-public-private-partnerships

Zhang, L., Wang, X., & Li, Y. (2020). Multiagent collaborative governance for targeted poverty alleviation from the perspective of stakeholders. *Complexity,* Article 8276392.

ANNEX

Practical Exercises with Stata and R on Poverty Data*

This section provides practical guidance on implementing poverty (and inequality) analysis using two popular statistical software packages: R and Stata. The exercises are designed to complement the theoretical concepts discussed in the main text and provide hands-on experience with real-world poverty measurement techniques. This section presents worked examples and exercises for various readers and practitioners based on key concepts discussed in this book. The data used for these examples and exercises are in csv (comma separated value) format. They include

(a) a household dataset hh1 for monetary poverty;
(b) a second dataset hh2 for multidimensional poverty; and
(c) a third dataset hh3 for poverty dynamics.

The exercises cover descriptive statistics, poverty indices, and simple transitions. Solutions are provided in R and Stata at the end of the annex.

Before delving into the specific exercises, the annex begins with a fundamental discussion introducing the basics of R and Stata. The practical components are carefully structured to offer insights

* Mohammad Mahmoud, research assistant at PIDS, validated the solutions to exercises.

into descriptive statistics, poverty indices, and simple transitions. To ensure comprehensive learning, solutions are provided in both R and Stata at the end of the annex.

A.1. Introduction to Statistical Computing with R and Stata

Understanding R and Stata in Poverty Analysis Context

R is a free and open-source programming language and computing environment that has become increasingly popular in poverty research and policy analysis. Originally developed for statistical analysis and data visualization, R offers unparalleled flexibility for implementing custom poverty measures and inequality indices. The software's strength lies in its extensive ecosystem of user-contributed packages available through the Comprehensive R Archive Network (CRAN), many of which are specifically designed for distributional analysis, survey data handling, and poverty measurement. The RStudio Integrated Development Environment (IDE) significantly enhances the user experience by providing an intuitive interface with script editing capabilities, real-time console interaction, data visualization panes, and integrated help systems.

The R ecosystem for poverty analysis includes several specialized packages that practitioners should be familiar with. The survey package handles complex survey designs with appropriate weights and clustering, which is essential when working with household surveys. The ineq package provides functions for calculating various inequality measures including the Gini coefficient, Theil index, and Atkinson measures. The dplyr and tidyr packages offer powerful data manipulation capabilities that are particularly useful for creating poverty indicators and organizing panel data. For visualization, ggplot2 provides sophisticated graphing capabilities for creating Lorenz curves, poverty profiles, and other distributional graphics commonly used in poverty analysis.

Stata represents a different but equally powerful approach to poverty analysis. This commercial software package was specifically designed with social science research in mind, making it particularly well suited for handling the types of data and analyses common in poverty research. Stata's command syntax is often more intuitive for economists and social scientists, and its built-in procedures for handling survey data, panel data, and complex sampling designs are exceptionally robust. The software offers both command-line and graphical user interfaces, allowing users to choose their preferred working style while maintaining full reproducibility through do-files.

Stata's particular strengths in poverty analysis include its comprehensive suite of built-in statistical procedures and its extensive collection of user-written commands called ADO files available through the Statistical Software Components (SSC) archive. A Stata ADO file is a special type of file that lets you create your own command in Stata, just like the built-in ones such as regress or summarize, with the term "ADO" standing for "automatic do" because when you type a command that is not already built into Stata, it automatically looks for an ADO file with that name and runs it if it exists. These user-written programs typically end with .ado and are written using Stata's programming language. Commands like povdeco for poverty decomposition, ineqdeco for inequality decomposition, and spost for post-estimation analysis are specifically designed for distributional analysis and exemplify how ADO files allow researchers to share specialized analytical tools that extend Stata's capabilities far beyond its native functions. Stata's ability to handle complex survey designs through its svy commands is particularly valuable when working with national household surveys that employ stratified, clustered sampling designs, and this functionality is often enhanced by additional ADO files that provide even more sophisticated analytical options. This ecosystem, where users can easily install new commands through ssc install and immediately use them as if they were built-in Stata commands, makes the software exceptionally powerful for poverty analysis and specialized econometric research.

Getting Started with R for Poverty Analysis

Beginning your journey with R requires understanding both the software installation process and the fundamental workflow for

poverty analysis. Start by downloading R from the official CRAN website (https://cran.r-project.org), selecting the appropriate version for your operating system. Following the R installation, download and install RStudio Desktop from Posit (https://posit.co/download/rstudio-desktop/), which will serve as your primary working environment.

The RStudio interface consists of four main panes that facilitate different aspects of your analytical workflow. The script editor (top-left) is where you write and save your R code, creating reproducible analysis scripts that can be shared and rerun. The console (bottom-left) displays the output of your commands and allows for interactive exploration of data. The environment pane (top-right) shows all objects currently loaded in memory, including datasets, variables, and functions. The files/plots/packages pane (bottom-right) provides access to your file system, displays graphical output, and manages package installations.

To demonstrate R's capabilities for poverty analysis, consider this introductory workflow using synthetic household data. After loading a dataset, you typically begin by exploring its structure and generating basic descriptive statistics. The summary() function provides an overview of all variables, while str() reveals the data types and structure. For poverty analysis, you will frequently use functions like mean(), median(), and quantile() to understand income distributions, and table() or prop.table() to examine categorical variables such as regional or urban–rural breakdowns. For this R demonstration, we will use hh1.csv.

```
r
# Install necessary packages
install.packages("dplyr")
install.packages("ggplot2")

# Basic data exploration workflow
library(dplyr)
library(ggplot2)

# Load and examine data structure
getwd()
```

```
setwd("Your working directory"
household_data <- read.csv("hh1.csv")
str(household_data)
summary(household_data$income_pc)

# Generate basic poverty statistics
poverty_line <- 3000
poverty_rate <- mean(household_data$income_pc <
poverty_line)
cat("Overall poverty rate:", round(poverty_rate * 100,
2), "%\n")

# Create basic visualization
ggplot(household_data, aes(x = income_pc)) +
  geom_histogram(bins = 20, fill = "lightblue", alpha =
  0.7) +
  geom_vline(xintercept = poverty_line, color = "red",
  linetype = "dashed") +
  labs(title = "Distribution of Per Capita Income",
       x = "Income per Capita", y = "Frequency")
```

Getting Started with Stata for Poverty Analysis

Stata's approach to poverty analysis follows a command-based workflow that emphasizes clarity and reproducibility. After installing Stata and launching the program, you will encounter an interface consisting of the Command window for entering commands, the Results window for viewing output, the Variables window listing all variables in memory, and the Review window showing command history. This layout is specifically designed to support the iterative process of data analysis common in poverty research.

The fundamental Stata workflow for poverty analysis begins with data importation using commands like import delimited for CSV files or use for Stata's native .dta format. Unlike R, Stata can only hold one dataset in memory at a time, which simplifies data management but requires careful planning when working with multiple datasets. This constraint actually benefits poverty analysis workflows by encouraging clear, sequential analysis steps and reducing the likelihood of accidentally mixing datasets.

Stata's strength in poverty analysis becomes apparent when generating descriptive statistics and implementing standard poverty measures. The summarize command provides detailed descriptive statistics, while tabulate creates frequency tables for categorical variables. For poverty analysis specifically, Stata's egen command is invaluable for creating new variables based on existing ones, such as generating poverty indicators or calculating household equivalence scales.

```
stata
// Basic Stata workflow for poverty analysis
cd "Your Working Directory here"
import delimited "hh1.csv", clear

// Examine data structure
describe
summarize income_pc, detail

// Generate poverty indicators
gen poverty_line = 3000
gen poor = (income_pc < poverty_line)
tabulate poor

// Basic descriptive analysis by region
tabulate region poor, row col
bysort region: summarize income_pc

// Create simple visualization
histogram income_pc, frequency title("Distribution of
Per Capita Income") ///
  xline(3000, lcolor(red) lpattern(dash))
```

Advanced Features for Poverty Analysis

Both R and Stata offer sophisticated capabilities for advanced poverty analysis that go beyond basic descriptive statistics. In R, the integration of multiple packages allows for seamless workflows that combine data manipulation, statistical analysis, and visualization. The survey package enables proper handling of complex survey designs, accounting for sampling weights, stratification, and clustering that are common in national household surveys. This capability is crucial for generating accurate poverty estimates that can be generalized to national populations.

R's flexibility particularly shines in implementing custom poverty measures or experimenting with new methodological approaches. The functional programming aspects of R make it straightforward to create custom functions for specific poverty indices or to implement bootstrap procedures for calculating confidence intervals around poverty estimates. The tidyverse ecosystem provides powerful tools for data reshaping and transformation, which is particularly valuable when working with panel data to analyze poverty dynamics.

Stata's advanced features for poverty analysis center around its comprehensive suite of post-estimation commands and specialized add-on packages. The svy prefix commands ensure that all statistical procedures properly account for complex survey designs, while commands like margins provide detailed post-estimation analysis including predicted probabilities and marginal effects. User-written commands available through SSC significantly extend Stata's capabilities for poverty analysis, with packages like povdeco providing sophisticated poverty decomposition analysis and ineqdeco offering comprehensive inequality measurement and decomposition.

The choice between R and Stata often depends on specific research needs and institutional contexts. R's open-source nature and extensive customization capabilities make it ideal for methodological research and situations requiring custom analytical approaches. Stata's commercial support, extensive documentation, and user-friendly interface make it particularly suitable for policy analysis and routine poverty monitoring where reliability and ease of use are paramount.

A.2. Dataset Documentation and Metadata

Overview of (Synthetic) Datasets Used in This Annex

The practical exercises in this annex utilize three carefully constructed synthetic datasets that mirror the structure and characteristics of real household survey data commonly used in poverty analysis. These datasets have been designed to illustrate different aspects of poverty measurement while maintaining the complexity and challenges researchers encounter when working with actual survey data. Each dataset contains realistic patterns of income distribution, regional variation, and demographic characteristics that reflect conditions found in developing country contexts.

The synthetic nature of these datasets provides several pedagogical advantages for learning poverty analysis techniques. Students can focus on mastering analytical methods without concerns about data confidentiality or access restrictions that often accompany real survey data. The datasets include known patterns and relationships that allow instructors to guide students toward specific learning objectives while maintaining the authenticity of real-world analytical challenges.

Dataset 1: Monetary Poverty Analysis (hh1.csv)

The first dataset, hh1.csv, focuses on monetary poverty measurement and contains comprehensive income information for 50 households across different regions. This dataset is structured to support analysis of income-based poverty measures including headcount ratios, poverty gaps, and poverty severity indices. The income variables are disaggregated by source, allowing for analysis of income composition and its relationship to poverty status.

The dataset includes several key variables essential for monetary poverty analysis. The hhid variable provides unique household identifiers that enable tracking and sorting. Regional information is captured in the region variable, which distinguishes between urban and rural areas, reflecting the common analytical focus on spatial dimensions of poverty. Household composition is represented through household_size, which is crucial for calculating per capita measures and understanding household demographics.

Income information is comprehensively captured through multiple variables that reflect realistic household income sources. The income_salary variable represents formal employment income, while income_business captures self-employment and entrepreneurial activities common in developing economies. Transfer income is divided between income_remittance representing private transfers (often from family members working elsewhere) and gov_transfer representing public transfer programs. These disaggregated income sources allow students to analyze how different income components contribute to overall household welfare and poverty status.

The dataset includes both total household income (total_income) and per capita income (income_pc), with the latter serving as the primary welfare measure for poverty analysis. The is_poor variable provides a binary poverty indicator based on a predefined poverty line of 3,000 currency units, establishing a benchmark for poverty classification that students can modify to explore sensitivity analysis.

Regional variation is embedded in the dataset to demonstrate spatial patterns commonly observed in poverty analysis. Urban households typically exhibit higher average incomes but also greater income inequality, while rural households show more dependence on agricultural and self-employment income sources. This variation enables students to explore poverty decomposition by subgroups and understand how poverty measures vary across different geographical contexts.

Dataset 2: Multidimensional Poverty Analysis (hh2.csv)

The second dataset, hh2.csv, is specifically designed for multidimensional poverty analysis following the Alkire-Foster methodology that has become standard in international development practice. This dataset contains 50 households with information on five key dimensions of deprivation: education, health, water, sanitation, and electricity access. Each dimension is represented by binary indicators that reflect whether households have adequate access to these essential services.

The multidimensional approach recognizes that poverty extends beyond income inadequacy to encompass various forms of deprivation that affect human well-being. The dataset structure reflects this conceptual framework by including separate indicators for each dimension while maintaining household identifiers that allow for integration with monetary poverty measures from the first dataset.

Educational deprivation is captured through the school_attendance variable, which indicates whether household members of school age have access to formal education. This indicator reflects one of the most fundamental aspects of human development and serves as a proxy for longer-term welfare outcomes. Healthcare access is represented by access_healthcare, indicating whether households can obtain medical care when needed, reflecting both availability and affordability of health services.

Infrastructure-related deprivations are captured through three variables representing basic services essential for human dignity and health. The safe_water variable indicates access to improved water sources, while sanitation reflects access to adequate sanitation facilities. The electricity variable captures access to electrical power, which has become increasingly important for economic participation and educational advancement in the modern economy.

The dataset includes derived variables that facilitate multidimensional poverty analysis. The num_deprivations variable counts the total number of deprivations each household experiences, providing a simple measure of multidimensional disadvantage. The is_md_poor variable applies a standard cutoff (experiencing deprivation in at least 3 out of 5 dimensions) to classify households as multidimensionally poor, following conventions established in international poverty monitoring.

This structure enables students to calculate key components of the Multidimensional Poverty Index (MPI), including the headcount ratio (H), the average intensity of deprivation among the poor (A), and the overall MPI (H×A). The dataset design allows exploration of how different cutoff points affect poverty identification and how various dimensions contribute to overall multidimensional poverty.

Dataset 3: Poverty Dynamics Analysis (hh3.csv)

The third dataset, hh3.csv, provides panel data structure essential for analyzing poverty dynamics and transitions over time. This dataset follows 50 households across three years (2018–2020), creating 150 observations that enable analysis of poverty persistence, transience, and mobility. The panel structure reflects the growing recognition that poverty is not a static condition but rather involves complex patterns of entry and exit that require longitudinal analysis to understand fully.

The dataset maintains the same basic structure as the monetary poverty dataset but extends it across time periods. Each observation is identified by both household ID (hhid) and year (year), creating a balanced panel where all households are observed in all time periods. This structure is ideal for introducing students to panel data concepts while maintaining focus on poverty analysis applications.

Income and poverty measures are provided for each household–year combination, enabling analysis of how household welfare evolves over time. The income_pc and is_poor variables allow tracking of individual household poverty trajectories, while the regional and demographic variables enable analysis of how transitions vary across different household types and geographical areas.

The panel structure supports several types of poverty dynamics analysis that are crucial for understanding the nature of poverty and designing effective policy interventions. Students can identify chronically poor households (poor in all periods), transiently poor households (poor in some but not all periods), and never-poor households.

This classification provides insights into different types of poverty experiences and their policy implications.

Transition analysis represents a key application enabled by the panel structure. Students can construct poverty transition matrices showing the probability of moving between poverty and non-poverty states across consecutive years. These matrices reveal patterns of poverty persistence and mobility that are invisible in cross-sectional analysis but essential for understanding poverty dynamics and evaluating the effectiveness of poverty reduction programs.

The temporal dimension also enables analysis of poverty spells, examining how long households remain in poverty once they enter and what factors influence exit from poverty. This type of analysis provides crucial insights for policy design, distinguishing between interventions needed to prevent poverty entry and those required to support poverty exit.

A.3. Exercises in Poverty Measurement

Before you start these exercises, make sure to set the working directory using Stata's "cd "working directory"" and R's "setwd "working directory"" commands (and put the data sets in your working directory.

Exercise 1: Descriptive Statistics for Monetary Poverty

This exercise introduces you to the fundamental statistical concepts for monetary poverty analysis. Using household dataset hh1.csv, you will calculate key distributional statistics that form the foundation for more sophisticated poverty measures, including measures of central tendency, dispersion, and the basic poverty headcount ratio with sensitivity analysis across different poverty lines and regions.

Tasks:

1. Calculate the mean, median, and standard deviation of income_pc.
2. Calculate the poverty headcount ratio with poverty line = 3,000.

3. Calculate the poverty rates separately for Urban and Rural areas.
4. Recalculate the headcount ratios using poverty lines of 2,500 and 3,500.
5. Create the histogram of income_pc by region.

Exercise 2: Poverty Gap and Poverty Severity

This exercise extends poverty measurement beyond simple headcount ratios to capture the depth and severity of poverty using the Foster–Greer–Thorbecke (FGT) class of poverty measures. The FGT indices P0, P1, and P2 provide increasingly sophisticated measures that respond to changes in the income of poor households even when such changes do not move households across the poverty line, making them essential for policy evaluation.

Tasks:

1. Calculate poverty gap = (3,000 – income_pc) for each poor household.
2. Calculate P1 = mean(poverty gaps/3,000) for all households.
3. Calculate P2 = mean((poverty gaps/3,000)^2) for all households.
4. Calculate P0, P1, and P2 separately for Urban and Rural areas.
5. Calculate total poverty gap = sum of all individual poverty gaps.

Exercise 3: Multidimensional Poverty Index

This exercise implements the Alkire–Foster methodology for measuring multidimensional poverty, which extends beyond monetary indicators to encompass various forms of deprivation affecting human well-being. Using dataset hh2.csv with five dimensions (education, health, water, sanitation, and electricity), you will calculate the official Multidimensional Poverty Index used by UNDP and many governments for poverty monitoring.

Tasks:

1. Count total deprivations per household across 5 dimensions.

2. Identify households as MPI poor if they have ≥3 deprivations.
3. Calculate H = proportion of MPI poor households.
4. Calculate A = average deprivations among MPI poor households ÷ 5.
5. Calculate MPI = H × A.
6. Repeat steps 2–5 using cutoffs of 2 and 4 deprivations.
7. Calculate deprivation rate for each dimension.

Exercise 4: Poverty Dynamics

This exercise introduces the temporal dimension of poverty analysis using panel data to examine how household welfare evolves over time. Using dataset hh3.csv covering three years (2018–2020), you will analyze poverty persistence, mobility, and transitions that reveal crucial information about chronic versus transient poverty and inform different types of policy interventions.

Tasks:

1. Count households that were always poor, never poor, and sometimes poor.
2. Calculate percentages for each category.
3. Create a 2×2 transition matrix: poor/non-poor status 2018 vs 2020.
4. Calculate P(poor 2020|poor 2018) and P(poor 2020|not poor 2018).
5. Create transition matrices for 2018→2019 and 2019→2020.
6. Compare poverty persistence rates between Urban and Rural areas.

Exercise 5: Inequality Measures

This exercise introduces standard inequality measures that complement poverty analysis by examining the entire income distribution rather than focusing only on the poor. You will calculate the Gini coefficient, the decile dispersion ratio, and the Palma ratio using dataset hh1.csv, learning how these different measures capture various aspects of income distribution and serve different analytical purposes.

Tasks:

1. Calculate the Gini coefficient for income_pc.
2. Calculate the P90/P10 ratio.
3. Calculate the Palma ratio = (top 10% income share) ÷ (bottom 40% income share).
4. Calculate all measures separately for Urban and Rural areas.
5. Plot the Lorenz curve for income_pc.
6. Calculate income shares for each quintile.

Exercise 6: Poverty Decomposition

This exercise provides tools for understanding the sources of poverty differences across population subgroups, which is essential for policy targeting decisions. You will learn to decompose overall poverty into contributions from different groups based on their population shares and poverty rates, revealing whether poverty is primarily concentrated in specific demographic or geographic segments.

Tasks:

1. Calculate each region's contribution = (population share) × (poverty rate).
2. Verify regional contributions sum to overall poverty rate.
3. Create household size groups and calculate their contributions.
4. Use povdeco (Stata) or custom functions (R) for FGT decomposition.
5. Calculate counterfactual: overall poverty if Rural had Urban poverty rate.

Exercise 7: Real Survey Data Analysis

This exercise bridges the gap between controlled learning environments and real-world poverty analysis by applying your learned techniques to actual household survey data. Working with real survey data introduces additional complexities including sampling weights, missing data, and data quality issues that are essential skills for poverty researchers.

Tasks:

1. Download the Philippines Family Income and Expenditure Survey (FIES) 2018 in the PSA Data Archive https://psada.psa.gov.ph/home or similar survey data in the World Bank Living Standard Measurement Study website https://www.worldbank.org/en/programs/lsms.
2. Calculate the Gini coefficient for per capita income/consumption.
3. Calculate Gini separately by Urban/Rural.
4. Plot Lorenz curves comparing Urban vs Rural.
5. Write a two-page summary comparing the results to official statistics.

Exercise 8: World Bank PIP Data Analysis

This exercise introduces you to international poverty data through the World Bank's Poverty and Inequality Platform (PIP), https://pip.worldbank.org/home, which provides standardized poverty estimates using multiple international poverty lines. You will learn the importance of selecting appropriate poverty lines based on country income classification, as absolute poverty thresholds suitable for low-income contexts become less meaningful in higher-income settings.

Tasks:

1. Install pipr (R) or pip (Stata).
2. Download 2015–2022 data for countries comprising the Association of South East Asian Nations (ASEAN). Note that these countries are heterogenous; some are low-income, others lower-middle, and still others upper-middle income countries. Furthermore, Brunei, Singapore, and Cambodia do not have poverty

data, the latter because of issues with purchasing power parity data.

3. Use $3.00 (low-income), $4.20 (lower-middle), and $8.30 (upper-middle) lines to determine the poverty rate in the ASEAN.
4. Plot the time series of poverty rates for each country given the different international poverty lines.
5. Calculate the total poor population for each country in the latest year.
6. Identify the country in the ASEAN with the fastest poverty reduction (in absolute and relative terms).

A.4. Solutions and Codes to Exercises

Stata Solutions

Exercise 1: Descriptive Statistics

```
import delimited "hh1.csv", clear

* Task 1: Basic statistics
summarize income_pc, detail

* Task 2: Poverty headcount
gen poverty_line = 3000
gen poor = (income_pc < poverty_line)
mean poor

* Task 3: By region
bysort region: summarize poor

* Task 4: Sensitivity
foreach pl in 2500 3000 3500 {
    gen poor_`pl' = (income_pc < `pl')
    mean poor_`pl'
    drop poor_`pl'
}

* Task 5: Histogram
histogram income_pc, by(region) xline(3000)
```

Exercise 2: FGT Measures

```
* Continue with data
gen gap = max(0, poverty_line - income_pc)
gen P1 = gap / poverty_line
gen P2 = P1^2

* Calculate FGT measures
mean poor P1 P2

* By region
bysort region: summarize poor P1 P2

* Total gap
egen total_gap = total(gap)
display total_gap
```

Exercise 3: Multidimensional Poverty

```
import delimited "hh2.csv", clear

* Count deprivations
gen total_dep = (1-school_attendance) + (1-access_
healthcare) + ///
                  (1-safe_water) + (1-sanitation) +
                  (1-electricity)

* MPI calculation
gen mpi_poor   = total_dep >= 3
summarize mpi_poor
scalar H = r(mean)
display "H (headcount) = " %6.4f H
summarize total_dep if mpi_poor
scalar A = r(mean)/5
display "A (intensity)   = " %6.4f A
scalar MPI = H * A
display "MPI (H×A)       = " %6.4f MPI
```

Exercise 4: Poverty Dynamics

```
import delimited "hh3.csv", clear
gen byte poor = (upper(is_poor) == "TRUE")
```

```
drop region household_size is_poor
reshape wide income income_pc poor, i(hhid) j(year)
* Classify households
gen years_poor = poor2018 + poor2019 + poor2020
gen always_poor = (years_poor == 3)
gen never_poor = (years_poor == 0)
tabstat always_poor never_poor, stat(mean)
* Transition matrix
tab poor2018 poor2020, row col
```

Exercise 5: Inequality

```
import delimited "hh1.csv", clear

* Install ineqdeco if needed
ssc install ineqdeco

* Calculate measures
ineqdeco income_pc
levelsof region, local(rlist)
foreach r of local rlist {
    di as txt "=== Inequality for Region: `r' ==="
    ineqdeco income_pc if region == "`r'"
}
```

Exercise 6: Decomposition

```
* Install povdeco if needed
ssc install povdeco
gen povline = 3000
egen byte region_id = group(region)
label define region_lbl 1 "Urban" 2 "Rural"
label values region_id region_lbl

povdeco income_pc, varpl(povline) by(region_id)
```

Exercise 8: PIP Data

```
* STEP 1: Install pip (run once)
net install github, from("https://haghish.github.io/
github/")
github install worldbank/pip
```

```
* STEP 2: Download PIP data for ASEAN-7
*         (2015-2022) at 3 poverty lines
pip, country(IDN PHL VNM MYS THA LAO MMR)   year(2015
2016 2017 2018 2019 2020 2021 2022 2023)    povline(3.00
4.20 8.30) clear fillgaps
* Save a copy for reuse
save pip_asean7.dta, replace

* STEP 3: Plot poverty rate trends
*         Example: Philippines
twoway ///
  (line headcount year if country_code=="PHL" & poverty_
  line==3.00, lcolor(blue)) ///
  (line headcount year if country_code=="PHL" & poverty_
  line==4.20, lcolor(red)) ///
  (line headcount year if country_code=="PHL" & poverty_
  line==8.30, lcolor(green)), ///
  title("The Philippines: Poverty Headcount by Line") ///
  xtitle("Year") ytitle("Headcount Ratio") ///
  legend(label(1 "$3.00") label(2 "$4.20") label(3
  "$8.30"))

* STEP 4: Compute total number of poor people
*         in the most recent year
use pip_asean7.dta, clear

* Compute poor = headcount × population
gen poor = headcount * population

* STEP 4: ASEAN-wide poverty rate by year and poverty
line
use pip_asean7.dta, clear

* Compute total poor per observation
gen poor = headcount * population

preserve
```

```
* Collapse total poor and total population by year and
poverty line
collapse (sum) poor population, by(year poverty_line)

* Calculate ASEAN-wide poverty rate
gen asean_poverty_rate = poor / population

* Format result
format asean_poverty_rate %6.3f

* Display results
list year poverty_line asean_poverty_rate,
sepby(poverty_line)

restore

* STEP 5 Identify country with fastest poverty reduction
* both absolute and relative measures
*        Compare headcount in 2015 vs 2022

preserve

keep if year ==2015 | year ==2022
keep headcount country_code poverty_line year
reshape wide headcount, i(country_code poverty_line)
j(year)

* Calculate both measures
gen reduction_absolute = headcount2015 - headcount2022
gen reduction_relative = (headcount2015 - headcount2022)
/ headcount2015 * 100 if headcount2015 > 0

format reduction_absolute %6.4f
format reduction_relative %6.1f

* Display full results - absolute
gsort poverty_line  reduction_absolute
```

```
list country_code poverty_line headcount2015
headcount2022 reduction_absolute if !missing(reduction_
absolute), sepby(poverty_line)

* Top 3 by absolute (FIXED - sort first!)
gsort poverty_line -reduction_absolute
bysort poverty_line: gen rank_abs = _n if
!missing(reduction_absolute)
list country_code poverty_line reduction_absolute if
rank_abs <= 3, sepby(poverty_line)

* Display full results - relative
gsort poverty_line -reduction_relative

list country_code poverty_line headcount2015
headcount2022 reduction_relative if !missing(reduction_
relative), sepby(poverty_line)

* Top 3 by relative (FIXED - sort first!)
gsort poverty_line -reduction_relative
bysort poverty_line: gen rank_rel = _n if
!missing(reduction_relative)
list country_code poverty_line reduction_relative if
rank_rel <= 3, sepby(poverty_line)

restore
```

R Solutions

Exercise 1: Descriptive Statistics

```
library(dplyr)
library(ggplot2)

# Load data
df <- read.csv("hh1.csv")

# Task 1: Basic statistics
summary_stats <- df %>%
  summarize(
    mean_income = mean(income_pc, na.rm = TRUE),
```

```
    median_income = median(income_pc, na.rm = TRUE),
    sd_income = sd(income_pc, na.rm = TRUE)
  )
print(summary_stats)

# Task 2: Poverty headcount
poverty_line <- 3000
poverty_rate <- mean(df$income_pc < poverty_line, na.rm
= TRUE)
cat("Poverty rate:", round(poverty_rate * 100, 2),
"%\n")

# Task 3: By region
poverty_by_region <- df %>%
  group_by(region) %>%
  summarize(poverty_rate = mean(income_pc < poverty_
  line, na.rm = TRUE))
print(poverty_by_region)

# Task 4: Sensitivity analysis
sensitivity <- sapply(c(2500, 3000, 3500), function(pl)
mean(df$income_pc < pl))
names(sensitivity) <- c("2500", "3000", "3500")
print("Sensitivity to poverty line:")
print(sensitivity)

# Task 5: Histogram
ggplot(df, aes(x = income_pc, fill = region)) +
  geom_histogram(alpha = 0.7, bins = 15) +
  geom_vline(xintercept = poverty_line, color = "red",
  linetype = "dashed") +
  facet_wrap(~region) +
  labs(title = "Income Distribution by Region", x =
  "Income per Capita") +
  theme_minimal()
```

Exercise 2: FGT Poverty Measures

```
r# Continue with same data
poverty_line <- 3000
```

```
# Task 1: Poverty gaps
df <- df %>%
  mutate(
    is_poor = income_pc < poverty_line,
    poverty_gap = pmax(0, poverty_line - income_pc)
  )

# Tasks 2-3: FGT measures
P0 <- mean(df$is_poor)  # Headcount
P1 <- mean(df$poverty_gap / poverty_line)  # Gap index
P2 <- mean((df$poverty_gap / poverty_line)^2)  #
Severity

cat("FGT Measures:\n")
cat("P0 (Headcount):", round(P0, 4), "\n")
cat("P1 (Gap):", round(P1, 4), "\n")
cat("P2 (Severity):", round(P2, 4), "\n")

# Task 4: By region
fgt_by_region <- df %>%
  group_by(region) %>%
  summarize(
    P0 = mean(is_poor),
    P1 = mean(poverty_gap / poverty_line),
    P2 = mean((poverty_gap / poverty_line)^2)
  )
print(fgt_by_region)

# Task 5: Total poverty gap
total_gap <- sum(df$poverty_gap)
cat("Total poverty gap:", total_gap, "\n")
```

Exercise 3: Multidimensional Poverty

```
# Load MPI data
md <- read.csv("hh2.csv")

# Task 1: Count deprivations
md <- md %>%
  mutate(
```

```
    total_dep = (1 - school_attendance) + (1 - access_
    healthcare) +
                (1 - safe_water) + (1 - sanitation) +
                (1 - electricity)
  )

# Tasks 2-5: MPI calculation
cutoff <- 3
md <- md %>% mutate(mpi_poor = total_dep >= cutoff)

H <- mean(md$mpi_poor)
A <- ifelse(H > 0, mean(md$total_dep[md$mpi_poor]) / 5,
0)
MPI <- H * A

cat("MPI Results:\n")
cat("H (Headcount):", round(H, 4), "\n")
cat("A (Intensity):", round(A, 4), "\n")
cat("MPI:", round(MPI, 4), "\n")

# Task 6: Sensitivity
sensitivity_mpi <- sapply(c(2, 3, 4), function(k) {
  poor_k <- md$total_dep >= k
  H_k <- mean(poor_k)
  A_k <- ifelse(H_k > 0, mean(md$total_dep[poor_k]) / 5,
  0)
  H_k * A_k
})
names(sensitivity_mpi) <- c("k=2", "k=3", "k=4")
print("MPI sensitivity:")
print(sensitivity_mpi)

# Task 7: Dimensional breakdown
dim_rates <- md %>%
  summarize_at(vars(school_attendance, access_
  healthcare, safe_water,
                    sanitation, electricity),
               function(x) 1 - mean(x))
print("Deprivation rates by dimension:")
print(dim_rates)
```

Exercise 4: Poverty Dynamics

```
install.packages("tidyr")
library(tidyr)

# Load panel data
panel <- read.csv("hh3.csv")

# Task 1: Reshape and classify
panel$is_poor <- as.numeric(as.logical(panel$is_poor))
panel_wide <- panel %>%
  select(hhid, year, is_poor) %>%
  pivot_wider(
    names_from   = year,
    values_from  = is_poor,
    names_prefix = "poor_"
  )
panel_wide <- panel_wide %>%
  mutate(
    years_poor     = poor_2018 + poor_2019 + poor_2020,
    always_poor    = years_poor == 3,
    never_poor     = years_poor == 0,
    sometimes_poor = years_poor > 0 & years_poor < 3
  )

# Task 2: Percentages
always_pct    <- mean(panel_wide$always_poor)    * 100
never_pct     <- mean(panel_wide$never_poor)     * 100
sometimes_pct <- mean(panel_wide$sometimes_poor) * 100

cat("Always poor (%):    ", round(always_pct,    2),
"\n")
cat("Never poor (%):     ", round(never_pct,     2),
"\n")
cat("Sometimes poor (%):", round(sometimes_pct, 2),
"\n\n")

# Task 3: Transition matrix 2018-2020
transition_2018_2020 <- table(
  "2018 status" = panel_wide$poor_2018,
  "2020 status" = panel_wide$poor_2020
```

```
)
print(transition_2018_2020)

# Task 4: Transition probabilities
trans_probs <- prop.table(transition_2018_2020, margin =
1)
print(round(trans_probs, 3))
```

Exercise 5: Inequality Measures

```
install.packages("ineq")
library(ineq)
library(dplyr)
library(ggplot2)

# Load datadf <- read.csv("hh1.csv")

# Task 1: Gini
gini_coeff <- Gini(df$income_pc)
cat("Gini coefficient:", round(gini_coeff, 4), "\n")

# Task 2: P90/P10
p90 <- quantile(df$income_pc, 0.9)
p10 <- quantile(df$income_pc, 0.1)
decile_ratio <- p90 / p10
cat("P90/P10 ratio:", round(decile_ratio, 2), "\n")

# Task 3: Palma ratio
total_income <- sum(df$income_pc)
top_10_share <- sum(df$income_pc[df$income_pc >=
quantile(df$income_pc, 0.9)]) / total_income
bottom_40_share <- sum(df$income_pc[df$income_pc <=
quantile(df$income_pc, 0.4)]) / total_income
palma_ratio <- top_10_share / bottom_40_share
cat("Palma ratio:", round(palma_ratio, 2), "\n")

# Task 4: By region
inequality_by_region <- df %>%
  group_by(region) %>%
  summarize(
    Gini = Gini(income_pc),
```

```
    P90_P10 = quantile(income_pc, 0.9) /
    quantile(income_pc, 0.1)
  )
print(inequality_by_region)

# Task 5: Lorenz curve
p_values <- seq(0, 1, 0.01)
l_values <- sapply(p_values, function(x) {
  threshold <- quantile(df$income_pc, x)
  sum(df$income_pc[df$income_pc <= threshold]) /
  sum(df$income_pc)
})

lorenz_data <- data.frame(p = p_values, L = l_values)
ggplot(lorenz_data, aes(x = p, y = L)) +
  geom_line(color = "blue", size = 1) +
  geom_abline(slope = 1, intercept = 0, linetype =
  "dashed") +
  labs(title = "Lorenz Curve", x = "Cumulative
  Population", y = "Cumulative Income") +
  theme_minimal()
```

Exercise 6: Poverty Decomposition

```
# Load data
df <- read.csv("hh1.csv")
poverty_line <- 3000
df$is_poor <- df$income_pc < poverty_line

# Task 1: Regional contributions
decomp_region <- df %>%
  group_by(region) %>%
  summarize(
    pop_share = n() / nrow(df),
    poverty_rate = mean(is_poor),
    contribution = (n() / nrow(df)) * mean(is_poor)
  )
print(decomp_region)

# Task 2: Verify sum
cat("Sum of contributions:", sum(decomp_
region$contribution), "\n")
```

```
cat("Overall poverty rate:", mean(df$is_poor), "\n")

# Task 3: By household size
df$hh_size_cat <- cut(df$household_size, breaks = c(0,
2, 4, 6, Inf),
            labels = c("Small", "Medium", "Large",
            "Very Large"))

decomp_size <- df %>%
  group_by(hh_size_cat) %>%
  summarize(
    pop_share = n() / nrow(df),
    poverty_rate = mean(is_poor),
    contribution = (n() / nrow(df)) * mean(is_poor)
  )
print(decomp_size)
```

Exercise 8: World Bank PIP Data

```
# STEP 1: Install pipr package (run once)

# install.packages("remotes")

# remotes::install_github("worldbank/pipr")

# Load required libraries
library(pipr)
library(dplyr)
library(ggplot2)
library(tidyr)
library(scales)  # for percent_format()

# STEP 2: Download PIP data for ASEAN-7 countries

# Countries: Indonesia, Philippines, Vietnam, Malaysia,
Thailand, Laos, Myanmar

# Years: 2015-2022, Poverty lines: $3.00, $4.20, $8.30
```

```
asean_countries <- c("IDN", "PHL", "VNM", "MYS", "THA",
"LAO", "MMR")
years <- 2015:2022

# Download data separately by poverty line (this works!)
cat("Downloading data by poverty line...\n")

df1 <- get_stats(country = asean_countries, year =
years, povline = 3.00, fill_gaps = TRUE)
cat("✓ Downloaded $3.00 poverty line data\n")

df2 <- get_stats(country = asean_countries, year =
years, povline = 4.20, fill_gaps = TRUE)
cat("✓ Downloaded $4.20 poverty line data\n")

df3 <- get_stats(country = asean_countries, year =
years, povline = 8.30, fill_gaps = TRUE)
cat("✓ Downloaded $8.30 poverty line data\n")

# Combine all datasets
pip_asean7 <- bind_rows(df1, df2, df3)

cat("Total observations:", nrow(pip_asean7), "\n")
cat("Countries:", length(unique(pip_asean7$country_
code)), "\n")
cat("Years:", paste(range(pip_asean7$year), collapse =
"-"), "\n")
cat("Poverty lines:", paste(sort(unique(pip_
asean7$poverty_line)), collapse = ", "), "\n")

# Save data for reuse
write.csv(pip_asean7, "pip_asean7.csv", row.names =
FALSE)

# STEP 3: VISUALIZATIONS

# Plot 1: Philippines poverty trends (matches Stata
twoway plot)
cat("\n=== VISUALIZATION 1: Philippines Poverty Trends
===\n")
```

```
philippines_plot <- pip_asean7 %>%
  filter(country_code == "PHL") %>%
  ggplot(aes(x = year, y = headcount, color =
  factor(poverty_line))) +
  geom_line(size = 1.2) +
  geom_point(size = 3) +
  labs(
    title = "The Philippines: Poverty Headcount by Line
    (2015-2022)",
    subtitle = "Three International Poverty Lines",
    x = "Year",
    y = "Headcount Ratio",
    color = "Poverty Line"
  ) +
  scale_color_manual(
    values = c("blue", "red", "green"),
    labels = c("$3.00 (Extreme)", "$4.20 (Lower-
    middle)", "$8.30 (Upper-middle)")
  ) +
  scale_y_continuous(labels = percent_format()) +
  theme_minimal() +
  theme(
    plot.title = element_text(size = 14, face = "bold"),
    plot.subtitle = element_text(size = 12),
    legend.position = "bottom"
  )

print(philippines_plot)

# Plot 2: All ASEAN countries comparison
cat("\n=== VISUALIZATION 2: All ASEAN Countries
Comparison ===\n")
all_countries_plot <- pip_asean7 %>%
  ggplot(aes(x = year, y = headcount, color = country_
  code)) +
  geom_line(size = 1, alpha = 0.8) +
  geom_point(size = 2) +
  facet_wrap(~paste("Poverty Line: $", poverty_line),
  scales = "free_y") +
  labs(
```

```
    title = "ASEAN Countries: Poverty Trends by
    International Poverty Lines",
    subtitle = "2015-2022 Trends Across Seven
    Countries",
    x = "Year",
    y = "Headcount Ratio",
    color = "Country"
  ) +
  scale_y_continuous(labels = percent_format()) +
  theme_minimal() +
  theme(
    axis.text.x = element_text(angle = 45, hjust = 1),
    plot.title = element_text(size = 14, face = "bold"),
    plot.subtitle = element_text(size = 12),
    strip.text = element_text(size = 11, face = "bold")
  )

print(all_countries_plot)

# Plot 3: Poverty reduction visualization
cat("\n=== VISUALIZATION 3: Poverty Reduction Leaders
===\n")
reduction_plot <- poverty_reduction %>%
  ggplot(aes(x = reorder(paste(country_code, poverty_
  line, sep = "-"), reduction_absolute),
              y = reduction_absolute,
              fill = factor(poverty_line))) +
  geom_col() +
  coord_flip() +
  labs(
    title = "Poverty Reduction by Country and Poverty
    Line (2015-2022)",
    subtitle = "Absolute Reduction in Percentage
    Points",
    x = "Country - Poverty Line",
    y = "Absolute Reduction (Percentage Points)",
    fill = "Poverty Line"
  ) +
  scale_fill_manual(
    values = c("blue", "red", "green"),
    labels = c("$3.00", "$4.20", "$8.30")
```

```
  ) +
  theme_minimal() +
  theme(
    plot.title = element_text(size = 14, face = "bold"),
    plot.subtitle = element_text(size = 12)
  )

print(reduction_plot)

# STEP 4: DATA ANALYSIS
# Compute total poor per observation (check column name
- might be 'population' instead of 'pop')
if ("pop" %in% names(pip_asean7)) {
  pip_asean7 <- pip_asean7 %>% mutate(poor = headcount *
  pop)
} else if ("population" %in% names(pip_asean7)) {
  pip_asean7 <- pip_asean7 %>% mutate(poor = headcount *
  population)
  pip_asean7 <- pip_asean7 %>% rename(pop = population)
  # Standardize column name
} else {
  cat("Available columns:", paste(names(pip_asean7),
  collapse = ", "), "\n")
  stop("Population column not found. Check column names
  above.")
}

# Calculate ASEAN-wide poverty rates
asean_poverty_rates <- pip_asean7 %>%
  group_by(year, poverty_line) %>%
  summarise(
    total_poor = sum(poor, na.rm = TRUE),
    total_population = sum(pop, na.rm = TRUE),
    .groups = 'drop'
  ) %>%
  mutate(asean_poverty_rate = total_poor / total_
  population) %>%
  arrange(poverty_line, year)

# Display results formatted like Stata
cat("\n=== ASEAN-WIDE POVERTY RATES ===\n")
```

```
print(asean_poverty_rates %>%
      select(year, poverty_line, asean_poverty_rate) %>%
      mutate(asean_poverty_rate = round(asean_poverty_
      rate, 3)))

# STEP 5: Identify country with fastest poverty
reduction

# Compare headcount in 2015 vs latest available year
poverty_reduction <- pip_asean7 %>%
  filter(year %in% c(2015, 2022)) %>%
  select(country_code, poverty_line, year, headcount)
  %>%
  pivot_wider(names_from = year, values_from =
  headcount, names_prefix = "headcount_") %>%
  mutate(

    # Absolute reduction (percentage points)
    reduction_absolute = headcount_2015
    - headcount_2022,

    # Relative reduction (proportion of original poverty
    rate)
    reduction_relative = ifelse(headcount_2015 > 0,
                        (headcount_2015 - headcount_2022) /
                        headcount_2015,
                        0),

    # Relative reduction as percentage
    reduction_relative_pct = reduction_relative * 100
  ) %>%
  filter(!is.na(reduction_absolute))

# Display results - Absolute reduction (sorted by
poverty line, then by highest absolute reduction)
cat("\n=== POVERTY REDUCTION ANALYSIS (2015 vs 2022)
===\n")
cat("ABSOLUTE TERMS (percentage points):\n")
print(poverty_reduction %>%
```

```
      select(country_code, poverty_line, headcount_2015,
      headcount_2022, reduction_absolute) %>%
      mutate(across(c(headcount_2015, headcount_2022,
      reduction_absolute), ~round(.x, 4))) %>%
      arrange(poverty_line, desc(reduction_absolute)), n
      = 21)

# Display results - Relative reduction (sorted by
poverty line, then by highest relative reduction)

cat("\nRELATIVE TERMS (% change from 2015 level):\n")
print(poverty_reduction %>%
      select(country_code, poverty_line, headcount_2015,
      headcount_2022, reduction_relative_pct) %>%
      mutate(
        headcount_2015 = round(headcount_2015, 4),
        headcount_2022 = round(headcount_2022, 4),
        reduction_relative_pct = round(reduction_
        relative_pct, 1)
      ) %>%
      arrange(poverty_line, desc(reduction_relative_
      pct)), n = 21)

# Summary: Top performers by each measure and poverty
line
cat("\nTOP 3 PERFORMERS BY POVERTY LINE:\n")

cat("\nBy Absolute Reduction (percentage points):\n")
top_absolute_by_line <- poverty_reduction %>%
  group_by(poverty_line) %>%
  arrange(desc(reduction_absolute)) %>%
  slice_head(n = 3) %>%
  ungroup() %>%
  select(poverty_line, country_code, reduction_absolute)
  %>%
  mutate(reduction_absolute = round(reduction_absolute,
  4)) %>%
  arrange(poverty_line, desc(reduction_absolute))
print(top_absolute_by_line)

cat("\nBy Relative Reduction (% change):\n")
```

```
top_relative_by_line <- poverty_reduction %>%
  group_by(poverty_line) %>%
  arrange(desc(reduction_relative_pct)) %>%
  slice_head(n = 3) %>%
  ungroup() %>%
  select(poverty_line, country_code, reduction_relative_
  pct) %>%
  mutate(reduction_relative_pct = round(reduction_
  relative_pct, 1)) %>%
  arrange(poverty_line, desc(reduction_relative_pct))
print(top_relative_by_line)

# Additional analysis: Plot all countries for comparison
all_countries_plot <- pip_asean7 %>%
  ggplot(aes(x = year, y = headcount, color = country_
  code)) +
  geom_line(size = 0.8) +
  geom_point(size = 1.5) +
  facet_wrap(~paste("$", poverty_line), scales =
  "free_y") +
  labs(
    title = "ASEAN Countries: Poverty Trends by
    International Poverty Lines",
    x = "Year",
    y = "Headcount Ratio",
    color = "Country"
  ) +
  scale_y_continuous(labels = percent_format()) +
  theme_minimal() +
  theme(axis.text.x = element_text(angle = 45, hjust =
  1))
print(all_countries_plot)

# Summary statistics for latest year
latest_year_summary <- pip_asean7 %>%
  group_by(country_code) %>%
  filter(year == max(year)) %>%
  ungroup()

# Select columns that exist (handle different possible
column names)
```

```
summary_cols <- c("country_name", "country_code",
"year", "poverty_line", "headcount")
if ("pop" %in% names(latest_year_summary)) {
  summary_cols <- c(summary_cols, "pop", "poor")
} else if ("population" %in% names(latest_year_summary))
{
  summary_cols <- c(summary_cols, "population", "poor")
}

latest_year_summary <- latest_year_summary %>%
  select(all_of(summary_cols)) %>%
  arrange(country_code, poverty_line)

cat("\nTotal poor population in most recent year:\n")
print(latest_year_summary,n=21)
```

SUPPLEMENTARY MATERIAL B

Companion Guide: Key Concepts on Poverty Measurement Simplified

This companion guide is designed to demystify the complex landscape of poverty measurement, presenting fundamental concepts in an accessible and comprehensible manner. By breaking down intricate theoretical frameworks into digestible explanations, the guide aims to bridge the gap between advanced academic discourse and practical understanding. **Readers will find a carefully curated exploration of poverty measurement techniques that simplifies technical jargon and provides clear, intuitive insights into how poverty is conceptualized, analyzed, and understood.**

1. Understanding Poverty Measurement: The Basics

What is poverty? Poverty means not having enough resources to meet basic human needs. However, defining "enough" and "basic needs" involves complex choices that affect how we count poor people and design policies to help them. Traditional approaches focused mainly on income or spending money, asking whether people have enough to buy food, shelter, and other necessities. More recent approaches recognize that poverty involves multiple deprivations beyond just money, including poor health, lack of education, and social exclusion.

What is the difference between absolute and relative poverty? Absolute poverty asks whether people can afford basic necessities for survival and dignity. For example, the international poverty line of $2.15 per day represents what researchers consider the minimum needed to avoid extreme deprivation anywhere in the world. Relative poverty, on the other hand, compares people to others in their society. In wealthy countries, someone might have enough for basic survival but still be considered poor if they cannot afford things most people in their society take for granted, like internet access or annual holidays.

Why does monetary versus multidimensional poverty matter? Traditional poverty measurement focuses on income or consumption spending. A family earning less than the poverty line would be considered poor, regardless of other circumstances. Multidimensional approaches recognize that poverty involves multiple deprivations simultaneously. A family might have enough income but still face poverty if their children cannot attend school, they lack access to healthcare, or they live in substandard housing without basic services.

2. How Do We Measure Poverty?

How do we choose a welfare indicator? Before we can identify who is poor, we must first decide how to measure people's wellbeing or welfare. Most commonly, researchers use money-based indicators like consumption expenditure (how much households spend on goods and services) or income (how much money households receive). However, welfare can also be measured through non-monetary indicators such as educational attainment, living space per person, access to clean water, or nutritional status. Different welfare indicators can identify different people as poor.

How are poverty lines set? A poverty line is the threshold that separates poor from non-poor. Setting this threshold requires deciding how much money people need for basic necessities in their specific context. The most common method calculates the cost of a basic food basket providing adequate nutrition, then adds amounts for non-food essentials like housing and clothing. For global comparisons, researchers use international poverty lines like $2.15 per day, adjusted for purchasing power differences across countries.

What different poverty measures tell us? Once we have a poverty line, we can calculate different measures. The headcount ratio tells us what percentage of people are poor. The poverty gap measures how far poor people fall below the poverty line on average. The squared poverty gap gives extra weight to those who are very far below the poverty line. Each measure provides different insights for policy.

3. Poverty Over Time: Dynamics and Transitions

Why is poverty not static? Cross-sectional poverty measures provide snapshots at specific points in time, but poverty is actually dynamic. People move in and out of poverty due to life changes, economic shifts, health events, and other factors. Panel data, which follows the same people over time, reveals that the number of people who ever experience poverty is typically much larger than the poverty rate at any single point in time.

What is the difference between chronic and transient poverty? Some people experience poverty temporarily due to specific shocks like job loss or illness (transient poverty), while others remain poor over extended periods (chronic poverty). These different types of poverty may require different policy responses. Addressing chronic poverty typically requires structural interventions to build assets and capabilities, while addressing transient poverty focuses more on risk management and social protection.

What is vulnerability to poverty? Even people who are not currently poor may be vulnerable to falling into poverty in the future. The "near-poor" have incomes just above the poverty line but lack sufficient assets to withstand shocks. Understanding vulnerability helps design preventive interventions rather than only responding after people become poor.

How does poverty transfer across generations? Poverty often persists across generations, with children born into poor families facing disadvantages that make it difficult to escape poverty as adults. However, the degree of intergenerational mobility varies significantly across countries and contexts. Some societies provide more opportunities for children to achieve different outcomes than their parents, while others have more persistent inequality.

4. Looking Inside Households

Why look at individuals within households? Traditional poverty measurement assumes resources are shared equally within households, but research shows this often is not true. The collective household model recognizes that household members may have different amounts of bargaining power and receive different shares of household resources. Women, children, and elderly members often receive smaller shares than prime-age men.

How do we measure resource shares within households? By studying spending on "assignable goods" (items clearly associated with specific household members, like men's clothing vs. children's clothing), researchers can estimate how much of total household spending actually goes to each person. This analysis reveals that some individuals may be poor even when their household appears non-poor on average, and vice versa.

5. Multidimensional Poverty in Practice

How does the Global Multidimensional Poverty Index work? The most widely used multidimensional measure examines deprivations across health (nutrition and child mortality), education (years of schooling and school attendance), and living standards (electricity, water, sanitation, housing, cooking fuel, and assets). A person is considered multidimensionally poor if they face deprivations in at least one-third of these weighted indicators.

Can countries develop their own multidimensional measures? While the global measure allows international comparisons, many countries develop their own multidimensional poverty measures tailored to local contexts and priorities. These might include different dimensions (like employment security or environmental quality) or use different thresholds reflecting national standards of living.

6. Understanding Inequality

How is inequality different from poverty? While poverty focuses on those below a specific threshold, inequality examines how resources are distributed across the entire population. The Gini coefficient is the most common measure, ranging from 0 (everyone has the same) to 1 (one person has everything). Other measures like the Palma ratio focus on comparing the very rich to the very poor.

Why does inequality matter for poverty reduction? High inequality can limit poverty reduction because economic growth benefits mainly those who already have more. Countries with lower inequality typically achieve more poverty reduction from the same amount of economic growth. However, the relationship between inequality and poverty is complex and context-specific.

What are the challenges in measuring inequality? Measuring inequality accurately faces many of the same challenges as measuring poverty, plus additional complexities. The very wealthy often underreport their income or wealth in surveys, potentially understating true inequality levels. Different types of assets and income sources may be difficult to capture comprehensively.

7. What Can Actually Reduce Poverty?

How do we know what works in poverty reduction? After measuring poverty, the next crucial question is what can be done about it. Determining what works requires looking at solid evidence rather than good intentions alone. The gold standard involves randomly dividing similar people or communities into two groups. One group receives the intervention (treatment group) while the other does not (control group).

Since the groups are identical on average except for the program, any differences in outcomes can be attributed to the intervention.

What are the major approaches to poverty reduction? Social safety nets provide basic protection through cash transfers, food assistance, or temporary employment. Conditional cash transfers give money to poor families only if they meet certain requirements like sending children to school. Microfinance provides small loans to poor people, particularly women. Graduation programs combine multiple interventions over 18–36 months, including consumption support, productive assets, skills training, and coaching. Community-driven development gives communities control over development projects.

What do we know about what works in poverty reduction? Context matters enormously—what works in one place may fail in another. Implementation quality often matters more than design; well-designed programs implemented poorly consistently underperform. Addressing multiple constraints works better than single interventions. Sustainable poverty reduction requires planning for how external support will transition to local ownership over time.

What are common pitfalls in poverty reduction? Focusing only on symptoms without tackling underlying causes often provides temporary relief but does not create lasting change. Unrealistic timeframes disappoint stakeholders, as sustainable change typically requires years or decades. One-size-fits-all approaches often fail when successful interventions from elsewhere are not adapted to different contexts. Elite capture can redirect program benefits to more powerful community members rather than intended beneficiaries.

8. Partnerships for Poverty Alleviation

Why are partnerships necessary for poverty reduction? Poverty is multidimensional and complex, requiring responses that no single organization or sector can provide alone. Partnerships bring together diverse actors with complementary strengths, resources, and perspectives. Governments provide policy authority and public resources,

NGOs offer grassroots connections and specialized expertise, private companies contribute innovation and efficiency, and research institutions provide evidence-based insights.

What are the main types of partnerships in poverty alleviation? Government-civil society partnerships leverage policy authority alongside community connections. Public-private partnerships combine public oversight with private efficiency and innovation. International development partnerships bring together organizations from different countries to address poverty globally. Research-policy partnerships connect evidence generation with decision-making. Community-based partnerships put affected communities at the center of poverty reduction efforts.

What makes partnerships successful? Successful partnerships share several characteristics: shared vision and goals that bridge different organizational priorities; complementary resources and capabilities that create synergies; clear governance structures that define roles and responsibilities; trust and communication built through consistent behavior and transparency; and long-term commitment that extends beyond short-term project cycles.

What are the main challenges partnerships face? Power imbalances can undermine collaborative spirit when stronger partners dominate decision-making. Conflicting priorities and approaches create tension when organizations bring different values and methods. Coordination difficulties increase as partnerships become more complex, involving multiple organizations with different systems and procedures. Sustainability concerns arise when partnerships depend heavily on external funding or specific individuals whose involvement may change.

What are some innovative partnership models? Collective impact approaches bring together diverse organizations around shared measurement systems and mutually reinforcing activities. Impact investment partnerships combine financial return objectives with social impact goals. Digital platform partnerships use online platforms to connect actors around poverty alleviation. Adaptive management partnerships embrace flexibility and learning rather than rigid planning, adjusting strategies based on changing conditions and new evidence.

How can partnerships be built effectively? Effective partnership building requires careful design and planning that includes stakeholder analysis and clear objective setting. Capacity building ensures all partners can contribute effectively. Resource mobilization strategies combine different funding sources for sustainability. Robust monitoring, evaluation, and learning systems enable partnerships to track progress, identify problems, and demonstrate impact.

What roles do different actors play in partnerships? Government agencies provide policy authority, resources, and coordination mechanisms. Civil society organizations offer grassroots connections, advocacy capabilities, and specialized expertise. Private sector entities contribute innovation, efficiency, capital, and market access. Research institutions provide analytical expertise, evaluation skills, and knowledge generation. Communities and beneficiaries bring local knowledge, cultural understanding, and ultimate ownership of development outcomes.

9. Why Understanding Poverty Matters

How does poverty measurement help policymakers? Accurate poverty measurement helps governments allocate resources effectively, design appropriate policies, and track progress toward development goals. Understanding who is poor, where they live, and what kinds of deprivations they face enables more targeted and effective interventions. Different poverty measures provide different information—if most poverty is clustered just below the poverty line, economic opportunity policies might be most effective, while if many people are very far below the line, more comprehensive support might be needed.

Why should citizens understand poverty measurement? Understanding poverty measurement helps people evaluate government performance, advocate for better policies, and engage more effectively in public debates about social policy. It also helps citizens understand the complexity of poverty and why simple solutions often fall short.

How does understanding poverty help researchers and practitioners? Continued improvements in poverty measurement and evaluation methods help build knowledge about what works in reducing poverty. This evidence base informs better program design and implementation.

10. Common Challenges and Limitations

What are the main challenges in measuring poverty? Measuring poverty accurately requires high-quality data, which can be expensive and difficult to collect, especially in developing countries. Surveys may miss the most marginalized populations, and people may underreport income or spending. Different approaches to measuring poverty can yield different results, and these choices involve both technical considerations and value judgments about what matters most for human wellbeing.

What about political and implementation challenges? Even technically sound poverty measures may face political resistance or implementation difficulties. Programs targeting specific groups may be seen as unfair, while comprehensive approaches may be expensive or administratively complex. There is also a measurement-action gap—having good poverty data does not automatically translate into effective action, as political will, institutional capacity, and adequate resources are all necessary.

11. Main takeaway about poverty and its measurement

Poverty is multifaceted, dynamic, and deeply embedded in broader social and economic systems. Effective responses require understanding these complexities rather than seeking simple solutions. The evidence increasingly shows that sustainable poverty reduction requires addressing multiple constraints simultaneously, adapting approaches to local contexts, maintaining high implementation quality, and building systems that can sustain progress over time. Most importantly, poor people themselves are the ultimate agents of their own development, and any effective approach must recognize their dignity, agency, and central role in creating lasting change.

APPENDIX C

Glossary of Technical Terms

[The glossary serves as a reference tool for researchers, policymakers, and students engaging with poverty-related research and analysis. Rather than presenting a dry list of definitions, this compilation provides nuanced explanations that contextualize technical terminology within the broader landscape of poverty studies. Each term is carefully defined to offer not just a literal meaning, but an understanding of its significance in poverty research, measurement, and policy development. The glossary bridges disciplinary languages, offering a unified lexicon that facilitates clearer communication and deeper comprehension across various fields of poverty research.]

Absolute Poverty: A measurement approach that defines poverty based on the cost of meeting basic human needs such as food, shelter, and clothing. Unlike relative poverty, absolute poverty lines are typically fixed in real terms and focus on minimum subsistence requirements. The international poverty line of $2.15 per day (2017 PPP) represents the most widely used absolute poverty threshold globally.

Adaptive Management Partnerships: Collaborative arrangements that embrace flexibility and learning rather than following rigid linear planning models. These partnerships emphasize iterative planning cycles, regular strategy adjustments, rapid testing of new approaches, and systematic learning from both successes and failures to respond effectively to complex and changing poverty contexts.

Adjusted Headcount Ratio (M_0): The foundational measure of multidimensional poverty in the Alkire–Foster methodology, calculated as the headcount ratio (H) multiplied by the average intensity of deprivation among the poor

(A). This measure captures both the prevalence of multidimensional poverty and the breadth of deprivations faced by poor individuals.

Alkire–Foster Method: A framework for measuring multidimensional poverty developed by Sabina Alkire and James Foster. This approach uses a dual-cutoff system to identify who is poor (first determining deprivation in each dimension, then requiring a minimum number of simultaneous deprivations) and produces decomposable poverty measures that can be broken down by population groups and dimensions.

Assignable Goods: Items in household expenditure that can be clearly attributed to specific household members, such as men's clothing, women's clothing, children's clothing, or individual-specific food items. These goods are crucial for estimating how resources are distributed within households using the collective household model.

Asset Index: A composite measure created using statistical techniques like Principal Components Analysis to combine information about household ownership of various assets (durables, housing characteristics, utilities) into a single welfare indicator.

Atkinson Index: An inequality measure developed by Anthony Atkinson that incorporates explicit normative judgments about inequality through an inequality aversion parameter (ε). Higher values of ε indicate greater societal concern for inequality, particularly at the bottom of the distribution.

Attrition Bias: A systematic error that occurs in panel surveys when respondents who drop out over time differ systematically from those who remain. This can make the continuing sample unrepresentative of the original population and bias estimates of poverty dynamics.

Average Treatment Effects (ATEs): The average impact of an intervention across all program participants, which may mask important variations in how different subgroups respond to the same program.

Backbone Support: In collective impact partnerships, dedicated organizational infrastructure that facilitates coordination, communication, and shared measurement among diverse partners working toward common poverty alleviation goals. Backbone organizations typically provide project management, data collection and analysis, and communications support.

Bargaining Power: In the collective household model, this refers to the relative influence that different household members have over resource allocation decisions. Bargaining power can be affected by factors such as income contribution, education, age, social norms, and outside options.

Before–After Comparison: A simple evaluation method that measures outcomes before and after an intervention without a comparison group, making it difficult to attribute changes to the program versus other factors.

Beneficiary Registration System: A database that tracks individuals or households eligible for or participating in social protection programs, facilitating coordination across multiple interventions.

Blended Finance: An approach that combines public, private, and philanthropic funding to leverage additional resources for development purposes. In poverty alleviation partnerships, blended finance can attract commercial investment by using public or philanthropic funding to reduce risks and improve returns for private investors.

Capabilities Approach: A framework developed by Amartya Sen that defines poverty not merely as lack of income but as the inability to achieve basic human capabilities such as being adequately nourished, properly clothed, avoiding premature mortality, and participating in community life.

Cash Plus Approaches: Social protection programs that combine core cash transfers with complementary services such as health insurance, skills training, or financial inclusion to achieve broader impacts than transfers alone.

Censored Headcount Ratio: In multidimensional poverty measurement, this refers to the proportion of the total population that is deprived in a specific dimension, counting only those individuals who are identified as multidimensionally poor overall.

Chronic Poverty: A persistent state of deprivation experienced over an extended period, typically defined either as being poor for a minimum duration (spells approach) or having average welfare over time fall below the poverty line (components approach).

Client Protection: Principles and practices designed to prevent harm to microfinance clients, including transparent pricing, appropriate product design, prevention of over-indebtedness, and ethical collection practices.

Collective Household Model: An economic framework that recognizes households as collections of individuals with potentially different preferences and varying bargaining power, rather than treating them as single decision-making units. This model allows for unequal resource allocation within households.

Collective Impact Approaches: A partnership framework that brings together diverse organizations around shared measurement systems, mutually reinforcing activities, continuous communication, and common agendas to achieve complex social change. These approaches recognize that solving complex problems like poverty requires coordinated action that goes beyond traditional partnership models.

Community Development Councils (CDCs): Democratically elected local governance structures established by community-driven development programs to manage development projects and represent community interests.

Community-Driven Development (CDD): An approach that empowers communities to identify, implement, and manage development initiatives by transferring decision-making power and resources to local level.

Complementarity Principle: A foundational concept in partnership approaches recognizing that different organizations possess different comparative advantages. Successful partnerships leverage these differences so that each partner contributes what they do best while addressing their individual limitations through collaboration.

Components Approach: A method for measuring chronic poverty that identifies individuals as chronically poor if their average consumption or income over all observed periods falls below the poverty line, regardless of their poverty status in any specific period.

Conditional Cash Transfers (CCTs): Cash payments to poor households that are contingent on fulfilling specific requirements, typically related to children's education, healthcare utilization, or nutrition.

Consumption Aggregate: A comprehensive measure of household welfare that includes all goods and services consumed by the household, including both purchased items and home-produced goods valued at market prices.

Consumption Expenditure: A welfare indicator measuring the total value of goods and services consumed by a household over a specific period, including both purchased items and home-produced goods valued at market prices. Often preferred over income in developing countries due to better measurement properties and closer relationship to actual living standards.

Consumption Support: Regular transfers of cash or food designed to meet basic needs and stabilize household consumption, often used as the first component of graduation programs.

Co-responsibilities: A euphemistic term sometimes used to describe the conditions attached to conditional cash transfers, emphasizing mutual obligations rather than strict requirements.

Cost-of-Basic-Needs (CBN) Method: The most common approach for setting poverty lines, which calculates the cost of meeting minimum nutritional requirements plus other essential non-food needs in a given context.

Counterfactual: What would have happened to program participants if they had not received the intervention—the fundamental challenge in impact evaluation since this cannot be directly observed.

Crisis-Responsive Social Protection: Social protection systems designed with built-in flexibility to rapidly expand coverage or increase benefit levels during emergencies such as natural disasters or economic shocks.

Decomposability: A desirable property of poverty and inequality measures that allows the overall measure to be expressed as a weighted average of subgroup measures, enabling analysis of how different population groups contribute to overall poverty or inequality.

Difference-in-Differences: A quasi-experimental evaluation method that compares changes over time between program recipients and non-recipients to isolate program impacts.

Digital Financial Services: Financial products and services delivered through digital channels such as mobile phones, including mobile money, digital payments, and app-based banking.

Digital Platform Partnerships: Collaborative arrangements that use online platforms to connect diverse actors around poverty alleviation objectives. These platforms can facilitate knowledge sharing, resource mobilization, service delivery, and impact measurement across traditional organizational boundaries.

Diversified Funding Strategies: Approaches to financing partnerships that combine different types of resources including government budgets, donor grants, private investment, earned revenue, and community contributions to reduce dependence on any single source and create more sustainable financing models.

Dual Cutoff: A feature of the Alkire–Foster multidimensional poverty measurement approach involving two thresholds: First, deprivation cutoffs for each individual indicator, and second, a poverty cutoff determining how many deprivations are needed to be considered multidimensionally poor.

Economies of Scale: In household analysis, this refers to the cost advantages that arise when household resources are shared, meaning that the cost per person of achieving a given standard of living decreases as household size increases for certain goods and services.

Elite Capture: The risk that more powerful community members dominate ostensibly participatory processes, causing program benefits to flow disproportionately to local elites rather than intended beneficiaries.

Employment Facilitation: Services designed to help job seekers find employment, including job placement assistance, career counseling, and connections to employers.

Engel Curves: Graphs showing how expenditure on specific goods varies with total household expenditure, named after Ernst Engel. These curves are fundamental to the collective household model for estimating resource shares from assignable goods.

Equivalence Scales: Adjustment factors used to account for different needs of household members based on age and gender, recognizing that household members may have different consumption requirements. The OECD-modified scale, for example, assigns different weights to adults and children.

Exit Strategies: Plans for transitioning from external support to local ownership in partnerships and programs. Effective exit strategies require planning from the beginning, clearly identifying how external support will be phased out and local ownership strengthened over time.

Fee Waivers: Reductions or eliminations of charges for essential services like healthcare, education, or utilities for vulnerable populations.

Financial Inclusion: The availability and equality of opportunities to access financial services, including credit, savings, insurance, and payment services.

Foster–Greer–Thorbecke (FGT) Measures: A class of poverty measures that includes the headcount ratio (FGT_0), poverty gap index (FGT_1), and squared poverty gap index (FGT_2). These measures satisfy important axioms and can capture different aspects of poverty including incidence, depth, and severity.

Gini Coefficient: The most widely used measure of inequality, ranging from 0 (perfect equality) to 1 (perfect inequality). It represents twice the area between the Lorenz curve and the line of perfect equality.

Graduation Approach: A comprehensive, sequenced intervention model that combines consumption support, asset transfers, skills training, financial services, and coaching to help ultra-poor households achieve sustainable livelihoods.

Grievance Redress Mechanisms: Formal channels through which program beneficiaries can voice complaints, seek clarification, or appeal decisions related to social protection programs.

Group Lending: A microfinance approach where small groups of borrowers collectively guarantee each other's loans, using social capital to reduce default risk.

Growth Incidence Curve (GIC): A graphical tool that shows how income growth is distributed across different percentiles of the population, helping evaluate whether growth has been pro-poor or has disproportionately benefited certain segments.

Headcount Ratio (H): The proportion of the population that falls below the poverty line, representing the most basic measure of poverty incidence.

Impact Evaluation: The systematic process of assessing changes that can be attributed to a particular intervention, distinguishing between correlation and causation through rigorous methodological approaches.

Impact Investment Partnerships: Collaborative arrangements that combine financial return objectives with social impact goals, creating innovative financing mechanisms for poverty alleviation. These partnerships typically bring together private investors, development finance institutions, government agencies, and implementing organizations.

Implementation Quality: The degree to which programs are executed as designed, including aspects such as frontline worker capacity, supervision systems, and adaptive management.

Inclusion Errors: Targeting mistakes where non-poor individuals or households receive benefits intended for the poor, reducing program efficiency.

Income: A welfare indicator representing the flow of money and in-kind receipts to households over a specific period, including wages, business profits, transfers, and other sources. While conceptually attractive, income can be difficult to measure accurately, especially in contexts with significant informal economic activity.

Instrumental Variables: An evaluation method that uses factors affecting program participation but not outcomes directly to identify causal impacts when randomization is not possible.

Integrated Social Protection Systems: Comprehensive frameworks that coordinate multiple social protection programs through shared infrastructure for functions like targeting, payments, and monitoring.

Intensity of Poverty (A): In multidimensional poverty measurement, this represents the average proportion of weighted deprivations experienced by those identified as multidimensionally poor.

Intergenerational Mobility: The degree to which children's economic outcomes differ from their parents', often measured through intergenerational income elasticity or poverty transition matrices across generations.

International Poverty Line: A globally comparable threshold for measuring extreme poverty, currently set at $2.15 per person per day in 2017 purchasing power parity (PPP) terms.

Joint Liability: A feature of group lending where all group members are responsible for each other's loan repayments, using peer pressure and social sanctions to ensure repayment.

Life Skills Coaching: Intensive, personalized support addressing health, nutrition, social issues, and household management, typically delivered through regular home visits in graduation programs.

Livelihood Assets: The resources that households draw upon to construct their survival strategies, including human, social, natural, physical, and financial capital.

Livelihood Strategies: The range of activities and choices that households pursue to achieve their livelihood outcomes, shaped by their asset base and vulnerability context.

Living Space: A non-monetary welfare indicator that measures housing conditions, such as rooms per person, floor area, or housing quality. Sometimes used as an alternative to monetary indicators, particularly in contexts where housing represents a major component of living standards.

Lorenz Curve: A graphical representation of income or wealth distribution that plots the cumulative percentage of total income received by the bottom x% of the population. Perfect equality would be represented by a 45-degree line.

Market Systems Development: An approach that focuses on transforming how market systems function for poor producers, workers, and consumers rather than providing direct services.

Matching Methods: Evaluation techniques that create comparison groups by pairing program participants with non-participants who have similar observable characteristics.

Measurement Error: Random or systematic inaccuracies in data collection that can create spurious poverty transitions, making households appear to cross the poverty line when their true welfare has remained unchanged.

Microenterprise Development: Support for very small businesses, typically through capital grants, training, or market linkages, aimed at creating self-employment opportunities for the poor.

Microfinance: The provision of small-scale financial services to people excluded from traditional banking, including microcredit, microsavings, microinsurance, and payment services.

Microinsurance: Insurance products designed for low-income populations, typically covering risks like illness, crop failure, or livestock death with low premiums and simple procedures.

Microsavings: Savings facilities tailored to low-income populations, featuring low minimum balances, convenient locations, and flexible deposit and withdrawal options.

Mission Drift: The gradual shift of microfinance institutions and other development organizations away from their original poverty-focused objectives toward more profitable or easier-to-serve populations, often compromising their effectiveness for poverty alleviation.

Mobile Money: Digital financial services that allow users to store, send, and receive money using mobile phones, expanding financial access especially in areas with limited banking infrastructure.

Money-Metric Welfare Indicators: Measures of household wellbeing expressed in monetary terms, such as consumption expenditure or income. These indicators allow comparison across households and over time by converting all welfare elements into a common unit.

Multidimensional Poverty: A concept recognizing that poverty involves deprivations across multiple dimensions of wellbeing beyond just income, including health, education, and living standards.

Multidimensional Poverty Index (MPI): A composite measure that identifies overlapping deprivations at the individual level across health, education, and living standards, developed by the UNDP and OPHI.

Multi-stakeholder Partnerships: Collaborative arrangements that bring together organizations from different sectors (government, private sector, civil society, research institutions) around shared poverty alleviation objectives, leveraging diverse resources, expertise, and perspectives.

Non-experimental Methods: Evaluation approaches that do not use comparison groups, including simple before-after comparisons and qualitative methods, which cannot establish causation but may provide useful descriptive information.

Non-Monetary Welfare Indicators: Measures of wellbeing that do not rely on money values, such as educational attainment, health status, access to services, or housing quality. These indicators capture aspects of welfare that may not be fully reflected in monetary measures.

Oportunidades: The evolution of Mexico's PROGRESA conditional cash transfer program, widely studied and emulated globally as a model CCT program.

Palma Ratio: An inequality measure that compares the income share of the richest 10 percent to that of the poorest 40 percent, focusing on the extremes of the distribution where most variation typically occurs.

Panel Data: Information collected on the same individuals, households, or other units over multiple time periods, essential for studying poverty dynamics and transitions.

Pareto Weights: In the collective household model, parameters representing the bargaining power of each household member in the household's welfare function.

Participation Costs: The time, effort, and resources community members must invest to participate in development programs, which can exclude the poorest who cannot afford these investments.

Partnership Design and Planning: The systematic process of creating collaborative arrangements that addresses stakeholder analysis, objective setting, role definition, governance structure development, and risk management to ensure effective poverty alleviation partnerships.

Partnership Governance: The systems, structures, and processes that guide decision-making, resource allocation, accountability, and coordination in collaborative arrangements. Effective governance includes clear agreements about roles, responsibilities, decision-making authority, and conflict resolution mechanisms.

Payment Mechanisms: The systems through which social protection benefits are delivered to recipients, ranging from cash distribution points to electronic transfers through bank accounts or mobile platforms.

Poverty Dynamics: The study of how poverty status changes over time for individuals and households, distinguishing between persistent and transient forms of poverty.

Poverty Gap Index: A measure that captures the depth of poverty by calculating the average distance of poor households from the poverty line, expressed as a percentage of the poverty line.

Poverty Line: A threshold that separates the poor from the non-poor, typically representing the minimum income or consumption needed to achieve a basic standard of living.

Poverty Transition Matrix: A tabulation showing movements between poverty states (poor/non-poor) over time, revealing both persistence and mobility patterns.

Principal Components Analysis (PCA): A statistical technique used to create asset indices by identifying the combination of assets that best distinguishes between households of different economic status.

PROGRESA: Mexico's pioneering conditional cash transfer program (later renamed Oportunidades then Prospera) that became a global model through its rigorous evaluation design.

Progressive Loan Sizes: A microcredit feature where borrowers start with small loans and become eligible for larger amounts after successful repayment, building credit history and business capacity gradually.

Pro-Poor Growth: Economic growth that disproportionately benefits the poor, either in absolute terms (the poor experience positive income growth) or relative terms (the poor's income grows faster than average).

Propensity Score Matching: A statistical technique that creates comparison groups by matching participants and non-participants based on their estimated probability of program participation.

Proxy Means Testing: A targeting method that uses observable household characteristics (like housing materials or asset ownership) to estimate income and determine program eligibility.

Public Works Programs: Social protection interventions that provide temporary employment on infrastructure or community projects, offering income while creating public assets.

Public–Private Partnerships (PPPs): Long-term contractual arrangements where private sector partners take responsibility for delivering public services while sharing risks and rewards with the public sector. In poverty alleviation, these partnerships combine public policy authority with private sector efficiency and innovation.

Purchasing Power Parity (PPP): Exchange rates that equalize the purchasing power of different currencies by accounting for price level differences across countries, essential for international poverty comparisons.

Quasi-experimental Methods: Evaluation approaches that attempt to mimic randomized experiments using statistical techniques to create credible comparison groups when randomization is not feasible.

Randomized Controlled Trials (RCTs): The gold standard for impact evaluation where eligible individuals or communities are randomly assigned to either receive an intervention or serve as a control group.

Regression Discontinuity Design: An evaluation method that compares individuals just above and below program eligibility thresholds to estimate program impacts.

Relationship Complementarity: A form of partnership synergy that leverages different organizations' networks and influence to expand reach and impact, such as government access to policymakers, NGO community connections, and private sector market access.

Relative Poverty: A measurement approach that defines poverty in relation to the living standards of society, typically as a percentage of median income (e.g., 50 or 60 percent of median income in European contexts).

Resource Complementarity: The combination of different types of resources in partnerships, including financial resources, technical expertise, relationships and networks, political influence, and implementation capacity, to achieve comprehensive programming.

Resource Shares: In the collective household model, the proportion of total household consumption allocated to each individual member, revealing how resources are actually distributed within households.

Scalability: The ability to expand successful interventions to reach larger populations while maintaining effectiveness and quality.

Shock-Responsive Social Protection: Systems designed to rapidly adapt during crises by expanding coverage, increasing benefit levels, or adjusting targeting criteria.

Social Assistance: Non-contributory transfers including cash transfers, in-kind support, and subsidies provided to vulnerable populations without requiring prior contributions.

Social Care Services: Support services for vulnerable populations including children, elderly, and people with disabilities, often integrated with other social protection programs.

Social Enterprises: Organizations that operate with explicit social missions while using market-based approaches to achieve sustainability. In partnerships, social enterprises often serve as bridges between commercial and development sectors.

Social Insurance: Contributory programs that provide protection against life course and work-related contingencies like old age, disability, unemployment, and health care.

Social Pensions: Regular cash payments to elderly or disabled individuals regardless of their formal employment history or contribution record.

Social Protection System: A comprehensive framework encompassing social assistance, social insurance, labor market interventions, and complementary programs designed to reduce poverty and vulnerability.

Social Registry: A unified database containing standardized information about potential social protection beneficiaries, used across multiple programs to improve targeting and coordination.

Spells Approach: A method for measuring chronic poverty that focuses on continuous periods spent in poverty, classifying individuals as chronically poor if they experience poverty for an extended duration.

Spillover Effects: Program impacts on non-participants, such as effects on local economy, social cohesion, or service quality that extend beyond direct beneficiaries.

Squared Poverty Gap Index: A measure of poverty severity that squares the poverty gaps before averaging, giving greater weight to households that are furthest below the poverty line.

Stakeholder Analysis: A systematic process of identifying all relevant actors in poverty alleviation efforts, their interests, capacities, potential contributions, and relationships to each other, essential for effective partnership design and planning.

Sustainability: The ability of an intervention to continue producing benefits over time, encompassing financial, institutional, environmental, and social dimensions.

Synergy Principle: A foundational concept in partnerships suggesting that well-designed collaborations can create outcomes that exceed the sum of their individual contributions, achieving positive externalities that extend beyond any single organization's sphere of action.

Targeting Accuracy: The precision with which programs reach their intended beneficiaries, typically measured through inclusion and exclusion error rates.

Targeting Mechanisms: Methods used to identify and select program beneficiaries, including means testing, proxy means testing, geographic targeting, categorical targeting, and community-based targeting.

Technical Complementarity: The combination of different types of expertise in partnerships, such as research institutions providing analytical capabilities, NGOs contributing community engagement expertise, and private companies bringing innovation and efficiency.

Theil Index: An entropy-based inequality measure that can be decomposed into within-group and between-group inequality components, making it valuable for analyzing the sources of inequality.

Transforming Structures and Processes: In the sustainable livelihoods framework, the institutions, policies, cultural norms, and power relations that shape how households can convert assets into livelihood outcomes.

Transient Poverty: Temporary episodes of poverty, contrasted with chronic poverty, often triggered by shocks such as illness, job loss, or natural disasters.

Ultra-Poor: The most destitute segment of the population, often unable to benefit from conventional poverty reduction interventions and requiring more intensive, comprehensive support.

Unconditional Cash Transfers (UCTs): Direct monetary assistance provided to beneficiaries without requiring specific actions or behaviors in return.

Union Approach: In multidimensional poverty measurement, a method where an individual is considered poor if they are deprived in any dimension, contrasted with intersection approaches requiring deprivation in all dimensions.

Village Savings and Loan Associations (VSLAs): Community-based financial groups where members pool savings and provide small loans to each other, offering basic financial services in areas without formal banking.

Vulnerability Context: In the sustainable livelihoods framework, the environment of shocks, trends, and seasonality that affects people's livelihoods and asset base.

Vulnerability to Poverty: The probability that a currently non-poor household will fall into poverty in the future, often associated with households near the poverty line with limited assets to buffer against shocks.

Welfare Indicator: A measure used to assess and compare the wellbeing or living standards of individuals or households. This serves as the foundation for poverty measurement, with the choice of indicator significantly affecting who is identified as poor and how poverty patterns are understood.

Index

www.ingramcontent.com/pod-product-compliance
Lightning Source LLC
LaVergne TN
LVHW010635300926
849161LV00005B/952